AESTHETICS AS PHENOMENOLOGY

STUDIES IN CONTINENTAL THOUGHT

John Sallis, *editor*

Consulting Editors

Robert Bernasconi	William L. McBride
Rudolph Bernet	J. N. Mohanty
John D. Caputo	Mary Rawlinson
David Carr	Tom Rockmore
Edward S. Casey	Calvin O. Schrag
Hubert Dreyfus	†Reiner Schürmann
Don Ihde	Charles E. Scott
David Farrell Krell	Thomas Sheehan
Lenore Langsdorf	Robert Sokolowski
Alphonso Lingis	Bruce W. Wilshire
	David Wood

AESTHETICS AS PHENOMENOLOGY

THE APPEARANCE OF THINGS

GÜNTER FIGAL

Translated by
JEROME VEITH

INDIANA UNIVERSITY PRESS
Bloomington & Indianapolis

This book is a publication of

Indiana University Press
Office of Scholarly Publishing
Herman B Wells Library 350
1320 East 10th Street
Bloomington, Indiana 47405 USA

iupress.indiana.edu

Published in German as Günter Figal, *Erscheinungsdinge*
© 2010 Mohr Siebeck GmbH & Co. KG Tübingen
English translation © 2015 by Indiana University Press
All rights reserved

No part of this book may be reproduced or utilized in any form or by any means, electronic or mechanical, including photocopying and recording, or by any information storage and retrieval system, without permission in writing from the publisher. The Association of American University Presses' Resolution on Permissions constitutes the only exception to this prohibition.

⊖ The paper used in this publication meets the minimum requirements of the American National Standard for Information Sciences—Permanence of Paper for Printed Library Materials, ANSI Z39.48–1992.

Manufactured in the United States of America

Cataloging information is available from the Library of Congress.

ISBN 978-0-253-01551-8 (cloth)
ISBN 978-0-253-01558-7 (paperback)
ISBN 978-0-253-01565-5 (ebook)

1 2 3 4 5   20 19 18 17 16 15

For A. M. E. S. with love

Enough now of preposterous theories. No conceivable theory can mislead us with respect to the *principle of all principles:* that *every originally giving intuition is a legitimating source of cognition,* that everything that *offers* itself to us *originarily in "intuition"* (in its corporeal actuality, so to speak) *is to be accepted simply as what it is presented as being,* but also *only within the limits in which it is presented there.*
—Edmund Husserl, *Ideas I*

CONTENTS

Preface	ix
Translator's Foreword	xi
Introduction	1
1. Art, Philosophically	7
2. Beauty	42
3. Art Forms	97
4. Nature	140
5. Space	183
Notes	223
Bibliography	247
Index of Names	263
Index of Subjects	267
Index of Terms	273

PREFACE

Upon completing my book *Gegenständlichkeit*, which appeared in 2006 [the English translation appeared as *Objectivity* in 2010], I decided to undertake a new, intensive engagement with art. I wanted to know in more detail how the objective itself is constituted, and I wanted to clarify this by means of artworks, the objects par excellence. The present work also became a demonstration of gratitude to all the artists and artworks that have enriched my life. I am also grateful to all who have assisted in the creation of the volume.

First in this regard is my wife Antonia Egel, without whom the book could not have begun and without whom it could not have been completed. There is not a single important idea we have not put to the test conversationally, no aspect we have not scrutinized together in its correctness and consistency. Even the experiences of art that nurture the book were made together.

My thanks also go to my friends Damir Barbarić, Rudolf Bernet, Gottfried Boehm, Donatella Di Cesare, Lore Hühn, Toshitaka Mochizuki, Dennis J. Schmidt, Manfred Trojahn, Bernhard Zimmermann, and special thanks this time to John and Jerry Sallis, who made my visit to Fallingwater possible.

An invitation from the Freiburg Institute for Advanced Studies (FRIAS) to spend my winter semester 2009–2010 as a Fellow of the School for Language and Literature made it possible to complete the present work calmly. I would like to thank the other fellows in the program, especially Richard Eldridge, Rolf-Peter Janz, and Marisa Siguan, for their stimulating conversations. I extend my heartfelt thanks to the literature director of the School for Language and Literature, Werner Frick.

Finally, I would like to thank David Espinet, Tobias Keiling, and Nikola Mirković for their thorough reading and helpful responses, and Anna Hirsch and Ole Meinefeld for their careful editing of the text.

Günter Figal
Freiburg im Breisgau
May 2010

TRANSLATOR'S FOREWORD

This is a book about the experience of art. As the title *Aesthetics as Phenomenology* suggests, Günter Figal takes a phenomenological approach to aesthetic experience, rendering an account of what unifies it and distinguishes it from other experiences. In taking this approach, he aims to avoid the many pitfalls and dead ends of prior aesthetic theories, which in his view have either failed to delineate the proper object of aesthetics or to engage with it on adequate terms. The book's title also indicates, conversely, the significance that aesthetic experience holds for phenomenological philosophy itself. It is by way of an artwork's thing-like appearance, according to Figal, that we first encounter spatiality as such, thereby experiencing the very conditions of our embodied access to the world and unselfconsciously performing a Husserlian ἐποχή. (The German title, *Erscheinungsdinge*, rendered here as the subtitle *The Appearance of Things*, captures this prominence of phenomenality.)

The book is thus instructive in two directions at once. On the one hand, it shows that philosophy can still—and is perhaps now especially prepared to—contribute to the understanding of art and its enriching effect. Accordingly, Figal considers a wide range of artworks, noting every aspect of how they appear, and deftly engaging the history of thought in his analyses. On the other hand, we see that art provides a corrective to philosophy itself, directing our attention to a relational, lived space of which artworks are exemplary appearances. In this regard, the works considered in the present volume are more than mere illustrations of a theory; they instead shift our gaze precisely to the appearance of things.

Both of these directions circulate in the text's overall sensibility. It is clear not only that Figal has experienced firsthand the artworks of which he speaks, but that he has thought deeply about them. What pervades the book is a sense of astonishment concerning our very ability to have such experiences and converse about them. Readers will thus likely encounter familiar artworks in fresh ways, and glean inspiration to discover and discuss new ones. For those readers interested in the broader conceptual underpinnings of the present volume, I highly recommend Figal's presentation of relational ontology in his prior systematic work, *Gegenständlichkeit* (translated by Theodore D. George as *Objectivity: The Hermeneutical and Philosophy* and published by the State University of New York Press in 2010).

I have tried throughout the volume to retain the author's tone and style and to maintain his clarity at all costs. This meant, in many instances, formulating terms and phrases that are perhaps not standard English usage but whose meaning is nevertheless immediately apparent. Thus, readers will encounter adjectival locutions like "decentered" and "imagistic," as well as substantivizations such as "closedness" and "producibility." These are often novel constructions even in the original, but they are built from everyday language and are intended precisely to avoid conceptual rigidity.

Much of the book's terminology, moreover, is guided by its dialogical engagement with ideas spanning the history of philosophy. One of Figal's great strengths is to develop his argumentation by way of these ideas, and in the process glean helpful phrasings from his interlocutors. Where these prove crucial or interesting to the argument, I have kept the original term in square brackets. As the primary sources serve mainly to advance the present book's systematic intentions, however, I have chosen not to meticulously align Figal's citations with their counterparts in existing English translations. Thus, unless otherwise specified, all translations of French or German sources are my own. Page numbers in parentheses refer to the source in the note that precedes them.

It has been a pleasure to translate this text and to work with Professor Figal directly in its preparation. I have learned a great deal in the process, and I trust that anyone who reads the book will have a similarly enriching experience.

Jerome Veith
Seattle, Washington
July 2013

AESTHETICS AS PHENOMENOLOGY

Introduction

The question of the essence of art no longer stands at the center of philosophy. This may have to do with art itself—with the fact that it barely still makes religious or life-reforming claims, or dissolves traditional structures and thus compels reflection. Even the effective but short-lived totalizing of aesthetic relativity under the name of postmodernism, which was also to envelop philosophy, has meanwhile become historical. As concerns art, a state of normalcy has come to dominate. The entrenchments, provocations, and absolutizations of emphatic modernism have passed; the postmodern attempt to replace emphatic modernism with a hodgepodge of styles reminiscent of the *Gründerzeit* has remained devoid of consequences and appears in retrospect as no more than a curiosity. By now, the modern artistic problematics developed in the nineteenth and especially in the twentieth century, as well as their corresponding modes of composition, are considered valid without question. One has entered the state of a placid modernism, which need no longer assert itself over against tradition and thus combines casually with it. Unlike emphatic modernism with its challenges, placid modernism appears to be less compelling of philosophical reflection.

There is another reason that art no longer counts as an overriding theme for philosophy. Philosophical reflection on art has been replaced more and more by research in media studies and semiotic or symbolic theories. This has gone hand in hand with a relativization of the art-character of art; one inquires less about this character than about the medial or symbolic form of text and image—aspects not limited to art alone.

Inquiries of this kind are no doubt justified; they can even be immensely fruitful. Yet they do not put to rest the question concerning the essence of art. In an image that is a work of art, its image-character is more distinct and clear; a poetic text is more able to be experienced as a text than an arbitrary piece of writing, and the experience of hearing a musical work of art could not be replaced even by the most successful of popular music pieces. Yet the question of what makes an image, a text, or a piece of music into an artwork cannot be answered through image, text, or music theory, for the art-character is common to visual, poetic, and musical artworks. Insofar as the question of the art-character of artworks demands a general answer, it is a distinct question for philosophy.

The transition from emphatic to placid modernism should be favorable to the discussion of this question. Philosophical clarifications need distance from their subject matter; every partisan for or against something loses the clarity of vision necessary for philosophy. Only when one no longer associates the philosophical discussion of art with partisan intentions can art as such be seen. Only then is a circumspect answer possible to the question of what experience art induces.

Such an answer must be especially prudent, because in modernism it was associated with either too high or too low of a demand. The conviction that art reveals truth, however this is conceived, stood over against the conviction that art is nothing other than an occasion to try out one's own possibilities of experience in especially intense, perhaps even liberated and thus inspiring ways. The quarrel between these convictions is that between philosophy of art and philosophical aesthetics.

Philosophy of art and philosophical aesthetics have their strengths and their weaknesses. While the philosophy of art, in its various forms from Hegel and Schelling to Nietzsche to Heidegger, Gadamer, and Adorno, has developed impressive analyses of the structure of artworks, it was at the same time in danger of overloading or instrumentalizing this structure historically or anthropologically. One thereby lost track of the fact that art, despite all its interwovenness into life-contexts, is only identifiable as art if it is experienced in a way that comparable life-moments and cultural objects are not. Furthermore, one neglected that the experience of art is not unique; the experience of use-objects and of nature can be similar, in some cases even the same as the experience of artworks. This is precisely what the proponents of philosophical aesthetics—that is, Kant and Kantians of various sorts—realized and converted into the conception of a unified experience that can be called "aesthetic." Of course, this conception had its price as well. If many things or almost all things can become occasions of aesthetic experience, it appears arbitrary. It is especially no longer clear, then, why aesthetic experience prefers to deal with artworks at all. This difficulty is already decisive for Kant's *Critique of Judgment,* the foundational work of philosophical aesthetics. Although Kant ranks the aesthetic experience of nature much higher than that of artworks, an essential determination of aesthetic experience, namely its sociability that finds expression in communicability and critical conversation, applies above all to the experience of artworks.

The intention of the present investigation is to combine the strengths of the philosophy of art and philosophical aesthetics, and to avoid their respective weaknesses. The point will be to describe the essential constitution of artworks as precisely as possible and to keep in mind that artworks as such are identifiable because they themselves demand a specific attitude, namely the aesthetic attitude. Anything that does not demand this attitude is not an artwork. Yet if that is the case, then the aesthetic attitude cannot be arbitrary or gratuitous. If there is something that requires the attitude, then everything that can adequately be experienced in the aesthetic attitude must bear an essential relation to this. In that case, artworks are of such a kind as to be essentially made for the aesthetic attitude. They need not be exhausted by this attitude, but can also have their place in social-political or religious contexts—generally in contexts that are important for cultural or historical understanding and self-understanding. Yet the fact that they are artworks is demonstrated, above all, in the possibility of the aesthetic attitude.

In order to grasp the essence of art more precisely, and with it the essence of the aesthetic attitude, one need merely reflect on the fundamental conception of philosophical aesthetics. This conception, using Kant's formulation, was to be an "analytic of the beautiful." Correspondingly, that which one now matter-of-factly calls "art"—as if there were no such thing as the art of healing or the art of speaking—is to be grasped as fine art [*schöne Kunst*]. The term may sound dated, like the eighteenth century from which it stems. But it should become evident that it still denotes the subject matter of art as appropriately as ever. In order to see this, one need merely relinquish the sedimented prejudices about the beautiful that Kant already partially refuted. The beautiful is neither the pleasant nor what is harmonious in feeling; it is also not the sterile perfection that one associates with the products of classicism. Even modern artworks are beautiful as such—indeed, especially so; their beauty needs to be conceptually elucidated, because it is only in this way that their essence can be revealed.

To be sure, such an elucidation belongs within the context of philosophical aesthetics as it has been determined by the tradition. The elucidation, however, also immediately leads beyond this context. After all, insofar as philosophical reflection on aesthetic experience is concerned with the subject matter of this experience, and thereby especially with artworks, it is phenomenological. It only begins as a reflection upon experience in order to recognize experience's correlate; it wishes to clarify how experience is determined by this correlate. In this regard, art is no arbitrary theme of phenomenological description; it is not that an artwork can, like all other things, be observed as a phenomenon instead of in its factual being. Rather, an artwork is essentially phenomenal; it is an appearance that is not to be taken as the appearance of something, but instead purely as appearance. Accordingly, aesthetics essentially is phenomenology; it must be phenomenology if it wishes to grasp that which can be aesthetically experienced, and grasp it by way of art in its clearest and most distinct shape.

Aesthetics, thus understood, does not merely possess a phenomenological character to the extent that it is one possible form of phenomenology. Aesthetics also at the same time alters phenomenology, insofar as phenomena capable of being experienced aesthetically are not pure correlates of consciousness, but rather things. Artworks are thing-like; it is only for this reason that perception is essentially connected to the experience of them. Yet artworks are things of a special sort—not things that can also be viewed as phenomena, but rather essentially phenomenal things, or conversely, phenomena that are essentially thing-like. Artworks are, in a word, appearing things [*Erscheinungsdinge*]—thing-like appearances, things that are essentially made in order to appear. As appearing things, artworks are beautiful.

The present investigation intends to develop precisely what this means. At issue is the phenomenal essence of artworks, that is, that which makes the experience of art as such possible and irreplaceable. Thus, everything that the experience of art bears in common with other possibilities of experience can remain unconsidered without thereby narrowing the meaning of this essence. The experience of art, for instance, could not be described completely if one neglected its hermeneutic character. Artworks are essentially interpretable and in need of interpretation; they are inherently to be understood. Yet intelligibility and the demand of interpretation are not traits restricted to artworks. They are just as valid for juridical, religious, and philosophical texts, for historical events and for complex life-relationships in general. Conversely, the intelligibility of artworks is less idiosyncratic than their perceivability. Whereas, in the process of understanding philosophical texts, perception is nothing more than a necessary condition, it is constitutive for the understanding of artworks. Artworks are only understandable as perceived. Thus, the perceivability of artworks carries more weight for their essential determination than their intelligibility.

To grasp artworks as things of appearance means to make their thing-like appearance comprehensible as an interplay of various essential moments. This will occur—after an opening chapter that is dedicated to the possibilities of a philosophical discussion of art—in four steps, each taken with a chapter.

The second chapter will connect with Kant in clarifying the concept of beauty, initially merely from the aesthetic standpoint, then from an aesthetic-phenomenological one. It will thereby become evident that the beautiful as such is a *decentered order* that stands for itself as an *appearance*. A decentered order does not permit of being assigned to any conceptually identifiable object and thus being made comprehensible through this object. The order only exists by appearing. In artworks, this appearance is *deictic*. *Something* appears in its decentered order—for instance that which a picture shows, or that which a novel narrates. This something is *shown*, but only in such a way that an artwork itself shows itself. Artworks do not point to something that exists beyond them and that would be intended by the works themselves. What they show is rather only in them and with them, in the way that they show it.

It belongs to the self-showing of artworks that they are recognizable as artworks. One generally sees a picture that is a work of art *as* a picture; one does not take a novel to be a report of an actual course of events; an aria is not the expression of actually perceived joy or actually perceived pain. This recognizability of artworks has to do with their forms. Artworks show themselves and show in *forms of art* that are, as such, forms of appearance. The third chapter of the investigation is dedicated to these forms of art. At issue here is also the question of how the various art forms—image, poetic text, music—relate to one another. This question is already significant because there are combinations, intersections, and mixtures of the forms of art. It is only because the forms of art are not strictly separated from one another that one can speak *of art*. Yet the connection of art forms extends even further. We will see that every artwork as such is a mixture of various art forms; the work, as work, consists in just this mixture.

Artworks, however, do not merely show themselves and indicate through their forms, but essentially through the fact that they are perceivable. Unlike the mixture of forms, the perceptible aspect of artworks is simply there of its own accord; it stands before one's eyes or is audible. This perceptible aspect of artworks involves their naturalness, their belonging to *nature*, which the fourth chapter discusses. Just as the forms of appearance are especially recognizable as forms of art, so nature too stands out particularly clearly in the artwork. In the artwork, nature evinces itself as a *primordial appearance*.

The way in which the self-showing of artworks stands out is only possible because something else recedes in artworks' favor. Something must let the works show themselves; it must give the works to appearance so that these can exist as appearances. The fifth and final chapter elucidates this as *space*. Artworks as such are spatial. It is only from out of this spatiality that the demanding and binding aspects of artworks arises, and with these the possibility of an adequate experience of art. In their spatiality, artworks are the *objects* of aesthetic experience.

One concept pervades the present investigation as a basic theme: the concept of possibility. Decentered orders are never binding, always merely possible; insofar as they do not allow themselves to be grounded, they are apparent in their possibility. Even as appearances, artworks are possibilities. The appearance understood phenomenologically, that is, the phenomenon, is possibility and, in art, is set into the work as such. What the artworks show are, like Aristotle already knew, possibilities; that which they show becomes apparent in the ways it can be. The forms in which this showing occurs are forms of possibility—and as forms of appearance they are those possibilities of appearing that come forth in the self-showing of artworks as such. The perceptible aspect of artworks, too, the nature in them, is possibility. The comprehensible aspect of artworks arises out of the perceptible, and its own possibilities remain tied back to the latter. Yet the basic possibility of artworks is space. It is that which gives and enables, without therefore being the ground of artworks. Insofar as space gives artworks to appearance, they can simply be there and stand forth—as pure possibilities that have become things, and as things that have become pure possibilities.

ONE

Art, Philosophically

Why Art?

The question that stands at the outset here is sometimes also a reply. In that case, "Why art?" means: Are there not more important themes for philosophy, themes that are more urgent with respect to the understanding of life or for one's orientation in action? When posed in such a way, the question need not be answered; one need not contradict the reply that it already embodies. It suffices to clarify the presupposition that informs it and to see that this presupposition is not at all evident. Philosophy, so the question insinuates, gleans its sense from some utility for life, however this utility is conceived. Philosophy is taken to be subject to the question, as Nietzsche puts it, of "the advantage and disadvantage for life."[1] Yet there are philosophical clarifications that are not calculated toward effects and advantages—indeed, according to the traditional conviction that goes back to Plato and Aristotle, namely that philosophy is primarily theoretical, these clarifications are the most important.[2] Θεωρεῖν means observing, and observing means looking and describing, without further intentions. Observation would be superfluous if what it disclosed were also accessible in something other than observation, as for instance in action.

Even everyday experience attests to the fact that observation is irreplaceable: In our daily life replete with action, there are insights that cannot be won through acting, but instead only in pausing and reflecting, which can only lead to results if they are not subsumed under a purpose. Contrary to acting, observation is not oriented toward aims. The more it corresponds to its essence, the less it is concerned with a result posited beforehand. Observation could only be goal-oriented if one knew ahead of time what one wanted to experience. Yet precisely that remains open; that is why one observes thoroughly and is absorbed in something. Observation is not concerned with an aim but with a matter. The sole aim of observation is that the observed matter come forward as clearly and distinctly as possible. Insofar as action is embedded in states of affairs, this is also true for its realm; the conditions of action—the knowledge of which is required for any adequate action—only have a bearing if one steps back from the situation of action and its demands. One usually only sees this objective side of action, or sees it more clearly, when one relinquishes the pursuit of a goal and attempts to clarify the situation in which one finds oneself—without partiality to one's own interests.

For an observational philosophy concerned with objectively oriented clarification, the question of art is no simple issue among others. It concerns philosophy itself. Art approaches the observational attitude, and thus philosophy, in a peculiar way. Art awakens observation; it even opens up the attitude essential to philosophy in prephilosophical life. If one has any sense for art at all, observation—even in the extended sense that includes listening and reading—arises as if on its own.

An indication of this might be that one tends to dedicate oneself to art outside of one's working hours. One can spend free time in worse ways than with music, painting, and literature. That the occupation with art is typically only possible in one's free time, but is nourished precisely in this time, speaks against the action and purpose-orientation of life as a whole. In dealing with art, one senses another side of life, a side that has meaning for itself and not in relation to action or purposes. The occupation with art is no mere distraction, for it demands concentration. It does not serve the purpose of recreation, insofar as the latter is determined by the aim of recuperating one's capacity for work. The occupation with art is not directed toward the care of one's own abilities, but instead toward artworks; it is not "relaxation," but an activity that is effortlessly intent and thus particularly animated. When one feels vivified by the occupation with an artwork, this results on its own accord, not from the aim of recreation. One has been elsewhere than in the quotidian, and this, it seems, is a complement—as if now life were more complete. One has experienced something that was lacking in the everyday, and now once again feels entirely and encompassingly alive. That which complements is that which allows something to be whole. Art cannot replace action or goal-directed research. But it has a power that, as it seems, reaches and leads beyond these.

If this is the case, then art is part of human life. The history of art supplies further evidence for this. Art exists in all cultures; cave paintings such as those of Altamira and Lascaux demonstrate it in the earliest cultures. Further, the fact that art is part of life is something immediately evident; one senses it as soon as one turns to artworks. How else are we to explain, for instance, the attractive pull that exhibitions of significant paintings exert? Exhibitions that prompt true pilgrimages are rarely experienced as mere sensations. Whoever travels there simply because it is a "must-see" is able to anticipate their disappointment: One just sees pictures. Yet whoever understands what it means to observe will return enriched. It is comparable to literature and the joy of reading, which cannot be forced by anything. It is comparable to music; the excitement for great interpreters—singers as well as instrumentalists and conductors—is an indication of this.

It differs quite obviously from the fascination for athletic achievements, as the interpreters of artworks are not admired for their performance, but for the fact that they bring the works to fruition adequately and in particularly astonishing ways.

What speaks for art, therefore, is more than pleasure. One should rather speak of delight. Even the most serious of artworks, in all that they demand of their viewers, can exhilarate in such a deep way that dealing with them affects one's entire life-attunement. The experience of these works can even provide energy; one carries one's burdens more lightly, one feels newly adequate to the demands of life, if anything because one has experienced that there is something beyond these demands.

But there must be more involved. The interest in art is, in its essence, an interest in the variety of artworks. Each work is different and new; no work is simply an example of something general that could be called "art." One only looks or listens attentively, extensively, precisely, and repeatedly if there is something to be experienced that is only shown in this one work. Despite being bound to actual perception, artworks are not reducible to it. They have residual effects, engaging our reflection, and demanding a conceptually articulated account. Thus, the interest in art reveals a desire to understand, and it must be eminently important what artworks give us to understand. Why else would we turn, ever again, to a poem, a musical piece, or a painting?

That which is there to be understood in art is the work itself, and yet at the same time not just the work. In understanding an artwork, one understands something with it, in it, or through it. The understanding of artworks is not simply geared toward these alone, but discovers in them the possibility of also understanding other things. With respect to these other things, however, artworks are no mere means of understanding with the help of which one arrives somewhere and which, as soon as one arrives, one can relinquish. It seems that artworks mediate something that, through them, becomes accessible in a special and irreplaceable way. Every artwork mediates that which it alone can mediate. Otherwise, a novel like Tolstoy's *War and Peace* could be replaced with any other historical novel, or even by an arbitrary historical representation of Napoleon's campaign in Russia; a sociology of French bourgeois life would be as illuminating as Flaubert's *Madame Bovary*.

Yet this comparison and the competition it insinuates are alienating. Artworks can indeed be researched with a clarifying intention from a historical, sociological, psychological, or other angle, but they are not essentially historical or sociological sources, nor symptoms of social or psychological states. It is not to be denied that one can glean information from images, buildings, novels, poems, or musical pieces, but this has nothing to do with their character as artworks. To become involved with artworks is not to be informed of something, but to be touched in an originary way and displaced into a state of elemental openness: art provokes *wonder*—in all forms that wonder can take—from joy to irritation. If it is so, then art displaces one into that attitude that Aristotle described as the origin of philosophical observation.[3] Art, like all astonishing things, is wondrous in its lack of self-evidence. With artworks, something is revealed that was not known without them. They displace one into wonder because they allow an ignorance to appear.[4]

In the experience of art, this is an ignorance of a special sort. It has nothing to do with ignorance about states of affairs that one could learn about in a myriad of ways. With every work, one experiences something that one did not know before and that one could not anticipate in the way that it is experienceable in this work. An artwork cannot be "expected," and this not only in one's initial experience of it, but anew in every instance. One can think one knows an image; one has read a text several times or heard a musical piece countless times, and yet it will always again seem as if one encounters what is to be seen, read, or heard for the first time. Every experience that one has already had with the artwork thereby enters anew into the context of the present experience. It is as if, despite everything one already knows, one did not know the most important aspect about the work and needed to explore the work in an entirely new manner. But this ignorance—the suspension of all supposedly secure prior knowledge—is in turn rescinded by the work itself; it reveals, and does so anew each time. *Art is insight*. It is a relation to the states of affairs and things of the world, and aims to make these accessible in a way that is different from the manner that we are accustomed to: it makes them accessible in the work alone.

From the beginning, philosophy has viewed art, more specifically poetry, under the guise of insight. Philosophy's claim to knowledge was formulated in competition with poetry, and that only makes sense if poetry is either knowledge or at least counts as knowledge. Only then can poetry be shown to be insufficient in comparison to philosophy; only then can one argue whether poetry is truly knowledge, such that philosophy gains in profile through comparison with it. It is with this intention that Heraclitus speaks of "knowing-much" (πολυμαθίν) that does not teach one to have reason. He names Hesiod, Pythagoras, Xenophanes, and Hekataios as those who know much; they are not knowers in the sense of knowing those structures and orders that Heraclitus articulates around the term λόγος.[5] Heraclitus claims that Homer deserves to be thrown out of the competitions and thrashed, presumably for the same reason.[6]

What remains overbearing contempt in Heraclitus is developed much more soberly in Plato—though not without an ironic polemicism. Among other things, Plato criticizes the inability of poets to give accounts concerning that which they write about. They merely tell myths, stories,[7] and in this way even the early natural philosophers were still poets who treat their readers or listeners as if they were children.⁸ To be sure, as the *Apology* attests, the poets bring forth much that is beautiful. Yet this does not occur through established knowledge (σοφία), but by virtue of nature (φύσει) and in enthusiasm (ἐνθυσιασμός); poems are like the statements of soothsayers and oracle singers. Thus, almost all others speak better than poets themselves about that which they have brought forth.⁹

There are relevant elaborations in the second, third, and tenth books of the *Republic* that remain similar in tendency but are more extensive and oriented more by poetry itself. There, works of poetry are determined as "illusions"—not because they are fundamentally false, but because they present something in such a way that one cannot inquire as to its true nature and composition.¹⁰ Works of poetry do not owe their existence to clear, generally identifiable knowledge. That is also why they cannot be matter-of-factly evident, but rather only suggestive;¹¹ if one does not scrutinize their problematic character, one takes them at face value and does not ask questions. The question concerning the λόγος of a matter, of its true determination, remains foreign to the poets. This question can therefore only be brought to bear on their works as if from the outside.

The Platonic determination of the poet and of poetry continues to have an effect. When Kant, in the *Critique of Judgment*, determines "fine art" as the "art of genius" and says of this genius that it is "the inborn disposition (*ingenium*) through which nature [gives] the rule to art," this is not far removed from the Socratic-Platonic characterization of the poet by means of ἐνθυσιασμός. With Kant, the divine power that works through the poet has simply been replaced with nature, yet not in the sense of a world that obeys laws and is therefore knowable by science. Rather, nature is here meant in the sense of the inaccessible, that which occurs on its own, and that which allows a talent to be present or not. Since the talent, "as an artist's inborn, productive capacity, belongs to nature,"¹² it is not a form of knowledge that could be clearly articulated and passed on. The material that a scientist like Newton compiled is, as Kant articulates, clearly structured according to rules and can be learned accordingly. Yet no poet, according to Kant, could "show how his ideas, rich in fancy and yet also in thought, arise and meet in his mind"; he does not know it himself, and thus "cannot teach it to anyone else."¹³

The inaccessibility and unteachability of art, however, only count as a disadvantage if one takes an identifiable and thus teachable knowledge to be possible. Accordingly, any doubt concerning the possibility of such knowledge ushers in an appreciation of the poet and, finally, an identification of knowledge and poetry. If all knowledge arises from sources that remain opaque, then it has the character of poetry even if it is not "inspired." In this sense, Nietzsche took his task "to see science from the perspective of the artist, but to see art from the perspective of life"—for art is a reality of self-sustaining and increasing vitality.[14] Within the philosopher, the "theoretical human" (116) whose archetype is Socrates, Nietzsche discovers the inhibited, indeed the corrupted artist. Whereas "in all productive humans the instinct [is] precisely the creative-affirmative power," in Socrates "the instinct [becomes] the critic, consciousness becomes the creator—a true monstrosity *per defectum*." Socrates' "logical drive" (90) in its "uninhibited sweep" evinces "a force of nature, the likes of which we only meet, to our shuddering surprise, in the greatest of instinctive powers" (91). In Socrates, there is a logical and therefore no longer recognizable *ingenium;* even the knowledge of philosophical and later of scientific theory, seemingly so clear and controlled, is a force of nature, inaccessible as an "instinct" and not transparent.

With his critique of Socrates, Nietzsche reverses the valuation established by Plato. If the author of the *Republic* wanted to demonstrate the superiority of philosophy and situate his philosophical hero in Homer's place,[15] so Nietzsche replaces the central figure of philosophy with that of the artist. And just as Plato redetermined myth (and poetry as such) under the sign of philosophy, so Nietzsche understands philosophy as a special case of poetry, such that there are no longer any boundaries between philosophy or science and art. If purported knowledge is, in truth, art, then every knower proves to be an artist. The knower, especially the philosopher, misjudges himself if he conceives of himself as an observer, that is, if he understands himself theoretically. What he takes to be observation is actually a bringing-forth, such that the philosopher merely thinks he is "placed as an observer and listener before the great play of sights and sounds that is life." As Nietzsche, describing this "delusion," continues, the knower calls "his nature a *contemplative* one and overlooks the fact that he himself is also the actual poet and poetizer of life": "We, the thinking-feeling ones, are those that really and evermore *make* something that is not yet there: the entire ever-growing world of estimations, colors, weights, perspectives, stepladders, affirmations and negations."[16]

Both the ancient critique of poets and the modern apology for them are based on an unquestioned presupposition: It is alleged that the question concerning insight can be answered with reference to the relation of poetry and philosophy, by comparing poetic and philosophical knowledge. This, in turn, is grounded in the assumption that insight and knowledge are, in any case, to be understood as human properties that arise in the actions of a knower.[17]

For Plato, knowledge entails the possibility of recognizing the known for what it is under various conditions. That which is recognizable under various conditions must be determined as itself. Accordingly, one must be able to say what is the case independent of the various circumstances of its givenness. In this conception, the knowledge of the poets is, in fact, insufficient; they can neither justify nor elucidate that which they present and make known in their poetry. As they do not possess a situationally independent view of the matter itself, they cannot say *in other terms* what they know. They lack the insight into the matter's structure; to put it Platonically, they lack the insight into the εἶδος. It is only with a view to the εἶδος that different accounts can complement each other in their variation such that they result in a meaningful whole. Only when a matter is present independently of its respective circumstantial accounts can the presentation of the matter be transparent.

Nietzsche doubts the possibility of such an eidetic grasp of a matter. In his understanding, whoever varies his statements does not elucidate something grasped previously, but rather creates something new. No statement is sustained by the matter revealed in observation; instead every statement, according to its particular possibilities, brings something to appearance that is never given purely as itself. Even the philosopher who believes he is describing something that is grasped in observation is not a knower, but a *poet of life*.[18]

The results of Plato's and Nietzsche's determinations of the relation of poetry and philosophy are considerably different. Yet as concerns art, they agree; both neglect the same thing, namely the artwork. The artwork is neither a variable pronouncement of knowledge nor the expression of a view that changes from moment to moment. It stands for itself and is even withdrawn from its creator as soon as it is there. Assuming the poet Socrates interrogated in the *Apology* had had the opportunity to respond and had refuted the Socratic judgment concerning the poets' incapacity to elaborate on their work, he could nevertheless not have supplemented his work by means of an additional justifying or clarifying statement. He would have merely shown himself to be someone who can say illuminating things about an artwork, independently of the fact that he is the author. Yet as before, his work would stand simply for itself—unchangeable, not variable in any way.

This work nevertheless exists for Plato, and it is seen as a work about which there is something to say. What is more, Plato knew very well that his own writings are not artless treatises oriented solely by the factual, but are in fact poetry. These writings challenge one to inquire about the essence of a philosophy that articulates itself poetically and thus appropriates characteristics of poetry, but that is not exhausted by this. An answer to this question clearly presupposes a clarified understanding of the essence of poetry and its artistic character. Since it must begin with the artwork, the question concerning a free relation of poetry and philosophy can only be worked out in a philosophically elucidated determination of art. The free relation lies in this determination inasmuch as the latter lets art be as it is instead of using it for philosophical purposes. In contrast to this, Nietzsche, with his notion of a "poetry of life," makes art into an occasion for philosophical generalizations. This notion envelops *any* creation of something "that is not yet there,"[19] without the result being something one can relate to as to an artwork. Such a totalization of art dissolves art; it takes away that which makes art what it is—namely the artwork. Any discovery and joining of words would then appear as art, regardless of how tentative, processual, and ungraspable it may be.

Yet it is with respect to philosophy itself, and not only to art, that the competitively construed comparison between the artist and the philosopher yields so little. Unlike in early and classical antiquity, philosophy is no longer in its beginnings; it is established. It need no longer be distinguished from other forms of world-disclosure in order to show its peculiar profile. Even if the form of philosophy that goes back to Plato and Aristotle and is carried all the way over into modernity does not possess a matter-of-fact validity, there is no clear reason, following Nietzsche's suggestion, to dissolve it into literature.[20] Instead, the putting-in-question of philosophy belongs to its essence; its challenging of modernity is thus nothing special. As thoroughly as philosophical reflection turns against the handed-down form of philosophy that has, since Nietzsche, become questionable as "metaphysics," its own possibilities are so unmistakable that even the attempt to take them back into poetry cannot level them down.

Art can remind philosophy precisely of these possibilities. Because art invites one to observe, it gives philosophy an opportunity to reflect upon its own observational character, its theoretical essence, and to actualize this essence without inhibitions. Thus, through art, philosophy gains independence from all that has befallen the concept of theory in modernity and modernism. Instead of relinquishing its theoretical character to art,[21] philosophy can discover it anew. After all, the term is rarely still used in its classical meaning, but stands instead for a system of statements, determined by certain basic suppositions and concepts that describe a more or less limited realm of objects and explain circumstances specific to this realm. In this sense, theory is above all a matter for the sciences, yet this theory has little or nothing to do with θεωρία in the classical sense. If there are moments of classical θεωρία within modern science, these are not constitutive; thus, an orientation according to the modern sciences is not helpful in clarifying the observational essence of philosophy.

Viewed more closely, the relationship between philosophy and science never was any different. Even if the two belonged closer together in the tradition—so closely that, since Aristotle, philosophy can be called a science[22]—the peculiar aspect of philosophical observation, its origin in wonder and its enactment in impartial and purposeless looking, can never be explained from its character as a science. Philosophy exists independently of science. As, for example, the sayings of Heraclitus, the Platonic dialogues, the works of Nietzsche and the later Heidegger and Wittgenstein attest, philosophy remains independent of scientific procedures such as explanation or foundation. It does not fundamentally exclude these procedures, but it also does not need them. Because of its independence from science, philosophy is also not threatened by the fact that sciences make claims to clarify matters that have traditionally belonged solely to philosophy. Philosophy need not be a science in order to maintain its justification in the face of science. But for this, it does need to reflect upon its theoretical essence. Theory in the philosophical sense does not compete with science; it therefore need not capitulate before a successful science. Philosophy need not explain or provide a foundation. As the observation that it essentially is, it can be enacted in the description of what is there, as long as this description is conceptual and presuppositionless, which means if it is undertaken through a radical reflection about its concepts.

The fundamental condition for such a reflection is the orientation by that which is to be described. *Reflexio* means "bending back" or "turning." Concepts that one reflects upon are no longer directed straight at something they intend to grasp in its determinacy; rather, they are themselves contemplated. But this does not mean that attention is shifted from the matter to be comprehended and directed only at the process of comprehension. Aside from the question of whether comprehension can even be directed at the comprehensive process as if at the matter to be grasped,[23] a reflection that solely pursued the process of cognition would be unmotivated. Why should comprehension be reflected upon if not with respect to its meaning, that is, the comprehension of a matter? This matter first sets reflection in motion; it is only through the matter that reflection gains a point of reference.

Reflection is only ever possible if what is to be grasped does not simply acquiesce to the concepts that are directed toward it. This is already the case when something is difficult to grasp, and especially when it appears inconceivable. In these cases, the concepts do not simply turn out to be useless, but are played back into the process of comprehension. They can be checked, compared to others, and ultimately even replaced.

In these kinds of reflection-relations, the process of comprehension only enters one's attention to a certain degree; the concepts are reflected in relation with other concepts with respect to their adequacy, and possibly even with a view to the formation of new concepts. But the comprehension itself remains unquestioned as long as that toward which the concepts are directed appears according to the possibility of comprehension—that is, by way of comprehension. This only changes when comprehension and the will to comprehend encounter something that is revealed in its independence over against comprehension—something that, in its complex order and coherence, appears meaningful and laden with significance. Before it can be viewed according to its comprehensibility, it is already productive of insight—but in a way that is difficult to grasp. To be sure, the determinacy of its complex order must be discovered and accounted for, so that this order can be grasped in its particularity. Yet comprehension here no longer approaches a matter self-assuredly or matter-of-factly, but rather *responds*. It confirms or highlights something instead of determining by way of itself.

This is the case in hermeneutic experience, that experience of interpreting and understanding that is concerned with the conceptually guided characterization of a text. Here, the text that is to be characterized and determined according to its significance and meaning precedes insight; it provides in advance the context of comprehensibility and its possibilities. Accordingly, any determination related to the text is placed in the context of the text. The reflection of hermeneutical concepts does not arise from the activity of the one who interprets. The concepts are initially reflected by the text and turned toward the interpreter. It is only in this way that the latter can ponder them.

The experience of artworks is hermeneutical; they must be interpreted, and in this way they can be conceptually determined according to what they are. But the experience of art exceeds normal hermeneutical experience in that the significance and meaning essentially lead to astonishment. Because of this, an artwork as such cannot be experienced by simply viewing it in light of its significance and meaningfulness. In its emphatic existence that is never a matter of course, the experience of art always also belongs to the artwork as such. The work is consciously present to any adequate experience *as* an artwork; the significance and meaningfulness that are disclosed through the work are always those of an artwork that is transparent in its art-character. They belong to the experience of art that thereby also distinguishes itself from all other hermeneutic experience.

This does not mean, however, that the experience of art necessarily includes the expressly posed question of what art is. But this question does arise from the experience of art. It is not added onto this experience externally and after the fact. For this reason, the question also cannot be separated from the experience without losing its objective validity. The philosophical observation of art begins in the experience of art, and even when it leads to general determinations, it cannot sever its binding to the experience of art. Even the clarification of the observational essence of philosophy, which flows together with the philosophical elucidation of art, does not lead away from art. The clarification cannot become a mere self-understanding of philosophy for which art is simply an impetus, for as a clarification of observation, it remains bound to that which is observed. To be sure, the clarification of the observational essence of philosophy is not, in a strict sense, a forgetting of the self.²⁴ Yet it can only be a clarification of observation if it orients itself according to what is observed. When this occurs, philosophy has become what Goethe called "objective thinking" [*gegenständliches Denken*]. It appropriates Goethe's skepticism over against the demand "know thyself," which can "confuse people and lead them away from external activity toward a false inner clarity." It remains true even for the philosopher that he only knows himself "insofar as he knows the world."²⁵ Yet the knowledge of the world that rests upon objective thought is revealed like no other through the experience of art. This experience, in turn, leads to the foundation of philosophical thought.

Which Art?

Whoever begins to think philosophically about art has already found access to it. Prior to any reflection, there were experiences with artworks; the earliest and least pondered of them may even have been the most powerful. They aroused enthusiasm and interest and thereby paved the way for further discoveries; later experiences follow upon earlier ones and even by turning away from the latter remain bound to them. Talents supervened from the outset and determined one's inclinations; those gifted at hearing or seeing turn to the works that are respectively more accessible to them. This can be strengthened by artistic activity, even if it remains amateurish. Later, once reflection has set in, the inclination toward certain art forms, epochs, or works is also shaped by prejudices as they are articulated in scientific or philosophical schools of thought or writings. Thus conditions arise for the reflection upon art, conditions that tend to only rarely and gradually become completely transparent.

Yet even if influences of this type and the preferences they engender are unavoidable, they cannot simply remain valid in the philosophical reflection upon art. Despite being bound to the individual experience of artworks, the philosophical elucidation of art is answerable to the demand for universality; according to this demand, a philosophical consideration of art is a philosophy *of art as such*. One should therefore just as much avoid the one-sided orientation according to one form of art as the limitation to one epoch or one culture. Limitations of this sort not only leave the philosophical claim to universality unfulfilled, but also fall behind the reality of art and the actuality of its experience.

It is obvious for many artworks that they do not fall under one type. All forms of theater combine poetry with the imagistic character [*Bildcharakter*] of the stage; in opera, this occurs under the dominance of music. Word and image come together in titles and in writing, especially when the latter is a moment of the image itself, as in Paul Klee, Cy Twombly, or Anselm Kiefer. Lyric poetry is word art and sound art at the same time; in general, the sound of language belongs to poetry even when it is spoken and not sung.

If one were to limit the philosophical consideration of art to one epoch, one would abstract from the epoch-transcending mutual relation of artworks to each other, as well as from the complexity of the art experience itself. Habits of hearing and seeing cannot at all be limited to artworks from one epoch. Old music can never be heard as it was in its own time; performances on historical instruments and in older tunings will, in later times, always be heard in comparison to modern instruments. Conversely, the new and contemporary always stands before the background of older art. When new works cite the old ones—as for example Alban Berg in his violin concert cites a choral work of Bach's—then the continuity of art's tradition is overly evident. At this point it is also clear that one does not adequately understand the newer and contemporary works without their tradition.

It is similar with respect to the art of diverse cultures. Western art of modernity, especially, cannot be considered in isolation. Examples for this are Goethe's *West-Eastern Divan*, which takes up and transforms Persian lyric poetry, the cubist paintings of Picasso's that would be unthinkable without African and Polynesian influences, the Japanese-influenced architecture of Frank Lloyd Wright and Richard Neutra, even the music of Olivier Messiaen, which works with Indian and Asian sounds. Apart from this, in the meantime African and Asian art has engaged with the Western tradition and been shaped by it. Accordingly, no culture's art can be experienced independently from that of the West.

These states of affairs sketched here correspond to the essence of art; even if artworks come to exist in a specific tradition, at a specific time, and within a specific cultural context, they are not limited to this tradition, this time, and this cultural context. Art is art of the world. Every artwork is fundamentally open to anyone. It may help one group of listeners or viewers that prior knowledge and certain habits of hearing or seeing are conducive to the adequate experience of an artwork. But prior knowledge can be acquired, habits of hearing and seeing can be appropriated. Besides, it is often the case that the unprepared gaze grasps more, that the untrained ear hears more intensively. If artworks are initially foreign, the impartiality that they demand might come about more adequately.

Even if philosophical observation of art is thus directed at *all art*, it will not be able to consider all artworks equally. Yet art-philosophically developed concepts should also not exclude anything. They should be selected and developed in such a way that they can prove applicable to all artworks, to all—that means even to those that are not usually taken into consideration. It may be rare to find philosophical reflections on architecture or gardening that aim at universality, but these are not erroneous; generally, a tea bowl (*chawan*) that is used in Japanese tea ceremonies is hardly worth an art-philosophical glance. There is something like an art-philosophical canon; the philosophy of art has readily limited itself to the poetry, imagistic art, or sound art of the Western tradition. To be sure, its concepts as such are rooted in the philosophy that goes back to ancient Greek thought. But this does not mean that these concepts are only applicable to artworks that belong to this tradition. If an image like Paul Klee's *Black Signs* (1938) can be placed, as an artwork, over against a Japanese tea bowl in an illuminating way,[26] then this bowl must be an artwork related to Klee's image in some way. It is inessential whether the concepts that help determine its art-character stem from the same culture to which the bowl belongs. The philosophical discussion of art must strive for a universal, coherent concept of art. Thus, the task is to work out such a concept and argue for its rigor and plausibility in the context of the art-philosophical tradition and discourse.

The working out of a philosophical concept of art stands before a fundamental difficulty common to all formations of concepts. The formation of concepts aims at universality, and yet it must begin with the particular. The concept may not contain anything that only pertains to a particular instance, such that its universality would be compromised. Thus with a particular, it is essential to distinguish its particularity from that which is specifically universal about it.

This sketched difficulty is intensified in a peculiar way with respect to art. An experience of art is always an experience of the particular, indeed of the radically individual; it is the experience of the singular work that cannot be replaced by any other. That which makes the works into works of art can therefore not be clarified in turning away from the individual and particular. The path to the concept of art is neither an "empirical" variation that surveys different factually given cases, nor a "free" variation that places the given into a "horizon of openly infinite manifold free possibilities of always new variations."[27] Such a procedure can certainly extrapolate the forms of art that are brought about in individual works in a universally identifiable way. Yet that which makes an artwork an artwork can only be experienced in the individual work; the work is not an artwork because it fulfills universally formulable conditions, but solely because it is what it is in all singularity. One can certainly describe in detail what this means by attempting to uncover the inner structure of artworks. But this can only ever occur *critically*, that is, with a view toward works in which this structure fulfills itself in the sense of an actual artwork. Kant succinctly observed with respect to art that there can be no science of it, "but rather only critique."[28]

That is why the decision concerning the artworks around which a philosophical observation is to orient itself cannot be arbitrary. The observed artworks must be unquestionable *as artworks* in order that the determinations developed regarding them can be universally illuminating. From this vantage point, the question "Which art?" poses itself anew. It can be understood as the question about those artworks that deserve *exemplary priority*.

The prevailing answers to this question follow a pattern that can be seen as a variation of the *querelle des anciens et des modernes*.²⁹ This schema preassigns philosophical observation of art to the alternative of taking either the classical or the decisively modern as binding; whereby the decisively modern is not simply the contemporary or novel, the work of today, but is that which is emphatically present—the new that essentially breaks with retrospective historical connections. The contrast is still quite effective. It is ingrained in the most important art-philosophical conceptions of modernism and thus continues to determine the philosophical discussion of art. It is also the reason why the critical discussion of the ancient-modern dichotomy is a step toward presuppositionlessness in the philosophy of art.

Hegel's *Lectures on Aesthetics* represent an especially consistent orientation of the philosophy of art around the classical. According to Hegel's conviction, Greek art, more specifically Greek sculpture, is art par excellence in comparison with which no later art, particularly that of modernity, fulfills the concept of art. In modernity art as such is "something past for us, according to the aspect of its highest determination." It has "lost the real truth and liveliness" and is "more displaced into our *imagination*" than being able to "assert in reality its erstwhile necessity and take its highest place."³⁰ "Thought and reflection" have "surpassed fine art" (24), and therefore "the *science* of art" has now become "far more of a need than at the time when art, for itself, was already fully satisfying as art." Art nowadays invites "thoughtful observation, not for the sake of bringing forth more art, but for the sake of scientifically recognizing what art is" (25–26).

Hegel's classicism is historical; he dwells in the certainty that "the beautiful days of Greek art, just as the golden age of the late Middle Ages," are over. (24) And in his own way, he repeats the competition between art and philosophy that dominates the beginning of Greek philosophy, only that now philosophy need not constitute itself any longer as another possibility of knowledge and presentation over against art (more specifically poetry); instead, philosophy can take art up into scientific observation and treat it as one of its own prior stages in the development of spirit. Hegel's philosophy of spirit explains his historicism: *past* art is decisive for him because it is the only object of possible "truth and liveliness" in an age of science and reflection. In modernity spirit retreats from art, and that is why new art has become inessential. Taken in itself, it is not even worthy of scientific observation. It only deserves attention in order to make evident the superiority of science and philosophy.

Yet Hegel's orientation by way of the classical does not absorb completely into its historical fitting. Even if Greek art is past and is therefore the art of another epoch, its exemplarity must have a supertemporal character. Greek art can only be classical because one can at all times experience the essence of art in it.

Hans-Georg Gadamer has underlined the supertemporality of the classical. He emphasizes this temporality partly to counteract what he takes to be a problematic historicizing of the classical, by which the latter is reduced to "a unique past greatness." To be sure, this militates against the retrospective stance of the epigones, which is characterized by "a consciousness of decline and distance."[31] Nevertheless, one cannot fail to hear the tacit critique of Hegel. The classical, for Gadamer, is not what was once uniquely actualized, but that which "stands firm over against historical critique" (292). It is "lifted out of the difference between changing time and its altering tastes," and for this reason is always "accessible in an immediate way." The classical is connected to "a consciousness of a remaining, [. . .] the inalienable meaning that is independent of all temporal circumstances [. . .] that [means] simultaneity with every present" (293). The supertemporality of the classical, as Gadamer understands it, thus does not lie in a classical work's sheer timelessness. Rather, the classical is temporal in a special way, in that it is present at every time; it is *simultaneous* in the way that Jesus of Nazareth is *simultaneous* as Christ for the believing Christian.[32] Thus, as Kierkegaard (to whom the concept of simultaneity can be traced) emphasizes, the apostles who lived with Jesus did not have any advantage over later believers. It is not contemporaneity that matters, but alone the belief that this human being is Jesus of Nazareth, God made human.[33] Accordingly, contemporaneity does not guarantee understanding; it might make a work appear to be more accessible, but it is no guarantee that the work is truly illuminating. Following Gadamer, this is revealed by the fact that a work is illuminating unconditionally, free from determinate temporal circumstances.

Yet the classical, as Gadamer conceives it, is not determined strictly by the immediacy of its illumination. It would not be distinguishable, in its illumination, from a contemporary work and its "electric touch, as it were."[34] It is far more decisive that a work illuminate in the present without being bound to the conditions of the present, and this in turn finds support in the indication that the work, in shifting times, was previously experienced as illuminating. The classical in Gadamer's understanding is certainly not historically fixed; it does not belong to a determinate age as a unique formation of art. It is not historical [*historisch*], but it is also not entirely timeless; rather, it is "historical" [*geschichtlich*]. The timelessness of the classical proves to be, as Gadamer puts it, "a mode of historical being" (295); it consists in a validity that is ongoing and always proving itself anew, that cannot be historically dated, and can only be grasped as valid in retrospect. The classical, Gadamer continues, is "a truly historical category precisely by virtue of the fact that it is more than an epochal concept or a concept of historical style, and yet is nevertheless not a trans-historical notion of value." The concept of the classical indicates "the historical preference of preservation that—in continually new testing—[lets] something true exist" (292). The classical is the supertemporal that only proves to be such temporally, namely in having-been, as not being bound to time.

The counterposition to this orientation along the classical seems to be free from such an interlocking of the temporal with the timeless. Whoever takes themselves to be a partisan of decisively modern art has seemingly adjusted solely to time, namely to the radical presence of art, and wishes to raise this to the measure of its persuasiveness. In this sense Theodor W. Adorno, the leading representative of an emphatic modern philosophy of art, has called those artworks "authentic [. . .] that unreservedly give themselves over to the historical content of their time." Artworks are experienced as "more true [. . .] the more their historical substance is that of the experiencer."[35] For Adorno, exemplary art is thus emphatically today's art. This art is able to illuminate because it deeply corresponds to the situation of those who experience it.

Of course, Adorno's conception of radically modern art also bears, as Gadamer states, "a normative and a historical side."[36] Not every art of the present whose "historical substance is that of the experiencer" will be justified in claiming authenticity for itself. For that, one needs an increase in artistic possibilities and their experience, resisting what is usual and completely understandable for a certain present. Modernity, in Adorno's sense of authentic art, is not to be grasped "as a vague *Zeitgeist* or adept being-up-to-date." Instead, it will "oppose the respectively dominating *Zeitgeist*" and thus appear "antiquatedly serious and thus also crazy to decided culture-consumers."[37] Modernity alone can be an "art of progressive consciousness [. . .] in which the most advanced and differentiated methods interpenetrate with the most advanced and differentiated experiences" (57).

Just like classical art, then, radically modern art thus does not dissolve into its own time. But its supertemporality does not show up retrospectively; it shows up in the temporal look forward. To employ a term that Adorno uses pervasively but does not clarify himself, it is "avant-garde."

Initially, "avant-garde" is a military concept; it indicates the vanguard, that part of the army that proceeds ahead of the main army and is therefore the first to face the dangers of a campaign. Avant-garde art is ahead of its time. In a term of Richard Wagner's most likely inspired by Ludwig Feuerbach, it is "the artwork of the future."[38] This does not indicate the work that is still to come, but instead the work whose formative possibilities have become free from those of the respective present. The artwork of the future does not belong to the present, but instead comes toward it, and thus, measured by the standards of its respective present, it is irritating or disturbing; it violates the established forms of creation and the reigning taste.

Its "authenticity" certainly does not stem from its unconventionality, but solely from a promise: the promise of being the actual, real artwork whose possibilities cannot be reached by the respective present, let alone be exhausted. Its modernity permits it to be foreign in the present. It is an intervention in this present, something that does not belong to the present, a haunting occurrence. There is a reason Adorno always emphasizes the sudden, discontinuous aspect of authentic art. Every artwork, he claims, is "a moment [*Augenblick*]";[39] it is an "explosion, [. . .] the catastrophe of the moment that ruptures temporal continuity" (41), in which a sense lights up that is inaccessible to the present. Like Gadamer, then, Adorno proves to be Kierkegaardian. The concept of simultaneity that Gadamer picks up corresponds to the Kierkegaardian concept of the moment in Adorno; the moment signifies an "atom of eternity," a temporally experienced irruption into time that nevertheless does not dissolve in time.[40]

The inexhaustibility that Adorno portrays in modern art is also an aspect of classical art, if one follows Gadamer. The word "classical" means "that the persistence of a work's immediate saying-power [is] fundamentally unlimited."[41] That which has always again been illuminating will hardly exhaust its "saying-power" in the present. It contains possibilities of understanding that cannot even be intimated in the present. As Friedrich Schlegel, whom Gadamer cites as support for his thought, states: "A classical text need never be able to be completely understood. But those who are educated and who cultivate themselves must always wish to learn more from it."[42]

Classicism and avant-garde approximate each other in the notion of inexhaustibility, but they remain infinitely separated. Whereas an orientation along the classical takes the inexhaustibility of the artwork as a confirmation of its always already effective "saying-power," the avant-garde position sees its inexhaustibility in the present incommensurability of the artwork. Classical art is exemplary because it is timelessly in constant temporal effect; avant-garde art is exemplary in the timelessness of the moment that juts into time. With its "saying-power," the classically oriented stance underscores what is illuminating and accessible about artworks; the avant-garde position brings forth the inaccessible, hermetic aspect of artworks (measured by respective conditions of the present). Yet both the evidence and the incommensurability of artworks are solely presented in temporal respects in the classical and the avant-garde. It remains open how evidence and incommensurability are themselves to be understood. The concept of the classical, just as the concept of the avant-garde, remain external to the essence of art. They project concepts onto history and historical experience that purport to determine the essence of art without clarifying these concepts.

It is only through this projection that the concepts of the classical and the radically modern acquire their meaning. Accordingly, as antitheses they belong together in their involvement with history. The classical is the nonmodern; it is that which is not merely of the present. The modern is the unabiding; it is the new that has not always already been valid. Accordingly, just as in the *querelle des anciens et des modernes,* the concepts have a *positional* sense; one takes a stance with them by standing over against another position. Whoever calls something "classical" raises its value over against that which is present without a past, and which might therefore be ephemeral; this is evident enough in Gadamer's indication of the "electrical touch, as it were, that occasionally characterizes a contemporary creation."[43] Conversely, whoever calls something "modern" underscores its worth in distinction from that which is proven and purportedly valid in a timeless way. One can illustrate this position with a comment of Adorno's on Anton Bruckner. (One could supplement it with countless other passages from Adorno's works.) Bruckner's symphonies, according to Adorno, are led by the question of whether "something old can indeed still be possible, namely as something new." The question bears witness to "the irresistibility of modernity, the 'indeed still' already being an untruth that the conservatives of Bruckner's days could derisively point to as an inconsistency."[44] This is how it appears when, following the principle of Adorno's *Ästhetische Theorie,* it became a matter of self-evidence that nothing concerning art was self-evident anymore" (9). The only "authentic" thing for the proponent of radical modernity is the continuing state of exception. Over against this, the exponent of the classical holds up the sustaining power of the normal case. Yet each needs the other if what they say is to be delimited.

This does not mean that the concepts of the classical and the radically modern are useless in all respects. Yet with regard to the valuation of art, they can be understood, at most, as pragmatic approximations. They only answer preliminarily, in the sense of an initial and unproven orientation, the question of which artworks one should take into art-philosophical consideration. The concept of the classical keeps one from relating philosophical thoughts about art to marginal works or to those works whose art-character is still in question. In contrast to these, those works that have proven themselves and that continually demonstrate their convincing power anew are the better choice. The concept of radical modernity might prevent one's falling prey to blatantly conventional works or to those that adhere far too strongly to the taste of the times. The doubtworthy and contested against which the classical position takes its stand is just as unfitting as an object of art-philosophical observation as the routinized, pleasing, and popular that avant-gardism despises.

As mentioned, the concepts of the classical and the emphatically modern do not serve anything other than an initial orientation. If one raised them to the rank of fundamental concepts, one would not only restrict art-philosophical observation in a problematic way to historical-philosophical premises, but one would also relegate this observation to the limits of positional thinking. Above all, its relation to the matter at hand would be curtailed in a most disadvantageous way, for the rigid alternative of "classical" or "modern" does not do justice to the plenitude and variety of artworks.

Not every work that lends itself or even offers itself to art-philosophical observation is univocally graspable as classical or emphatically modern. There are newer works that are not emphatically modern in Adorno's sense but that are illuminating as artworks. Moreover, in order to demonstrate their quality these works need not have proven themselves over against "historical critique" in the flux of ages, and are thus not classical in Gadamer's sense. One might consider, for example, Gerhard Richter's paintings, Peter Handke or Botho Strauss' texts, Manfred Trojahn or Wolfgang Rihm's music.

In addition, there are works—such as the so-called "New Vienna School's" music, Franz Kafka's texts, Gottfried Benn's poetry, or the paintings of Mark Rothko or Barnett Newman—that were considered radically modern and in the meantime have stood the test of historical critique such that one speaks of them—not without paradox—as embodying a "classical modernity." Apparently works that were once considered radically modern join the tradition. This brings to attention the fact that these works already stood in manifold relations to tradition, and this in turn rehabilitates works that resisted the demands of forced modernity without becoming epigonal or anachronistic. There is "modern" art that does not close itself off against a time's taste, that is even pleasing without its artistic rank being seriously called into question—one might think of Matisse's painting, Richard Strauss' music, Thomas Mann's narrative art. And there are the developed individualists who combine classical awareness of form with obvious modernity—the middle Stravinsky, Picasso in the early 1920s, Ernst Jünger in his literary diaries and essays.

Art's freedom from historical positioning can take place in a way that is at once both more demure and more decisive. There are artworks that are neither classical nor modern; they easily deflect any attempt to categorize them. A Japanese tea bowl in the Raku style never had to stand the test of historical critique since it was never suspected of merely being a product that electrifies contemporary taste. At the same time, however, the bowl is also not a momentary interruption of continuous time that resists current taste. It is simply there in its delicate and strict simplicity. It stands sturdy on its narrow base and nevertheless strives upward in the quiet waves of its irregular walls whose thin black glaze has a matte sheen and lets the porous shaping of the clay shine through. When one holds the bowl in one's hands, feels its lightness and its soft surface—when one drinks tea from it and thereby admires it—it is illuminating in its existence without any historical situation.

If the historical concepts are unsuitable for the philosophy of art beyond an initial pragmatic orientation, then there remains a simple answer to the question "Which art?" The philosophical observation of art can take its orientation unproblematically from any work whose art-character is evident. The answer is liberating; one can leave the historical determinations of tradition and emphatic modernity behind—not to mention the fixity of their dogmatic variants, the apology for tradition and forced modernism. But the answer also puts one in a quandary. It seems to place the philosophical observation of art in a circle; philosophical observation apparently needs to assume the art-character of the works that it considers, yet it is precisely tasked with first clarifying this character. If there are no historical criteria for the philosophical observation of art, in the sense of the classical or the radically modern, then there remains only the possibility of a universal, *formal* determination of the art-character of art that is free from historical presuppositions. Yet that which this determination is to contain needs to always already be effective in the experience of artworks.

The circle, of course, is unproblematic; just as the hermeneutic circle is not a *circulus vitiosus*.[45] The understanding of art does not first enter the world through the philosophical clarification of it essence. Rather—and we already had occasion to indicate this—the art-philosophical clarification of the essence of art has the character of reflection. It belongs into the experience of art; the clarification develops its concepts within this experience, beginning from it and always returning to it. Putting it in Aristotle's terms, the philosophy of art begins with what is known and familiar.[46] It is only in this respect that it has the character of elucidation; but it can only clarify what is already known and familiar.

That which is known and familiar here, the art-character of artworks, is always already present in the understanding relation to an artwork. In experiencing an artwork, one knows that it is an artwork. One knows it when one really experiences the artwork instead of keeping it at a distance through prejudices, superficiality, apathy, or refusal. In experience, the art-character of an artwork reveals itself as if on its own.

The recognition of the artwork in its art-character with which we are concerned here does not have the character of an identifying determination. In Platonic or Aristotelian terms, one is not referring to an εἶδος, such that one could glean from this reference *what* this thing there is. To be sure, this possibility exists with regard to artworks, but it is not decisive for the experience of the art-character. It is usually not difficult to say what this artwork here is: it is a house, an image, a poem, a piece of music, perhaps even a standing stone that hardly bears any signs of modification. But not every house, image, poem, or sound is an artwork, and certainly not every standing stone. The determination that this thing here is an artwork joins with the answer to the question of what it is. The determination demonstrates that this thing here is not just something, not even just something made (and thus a work), but a work of art, and this in turn means, in an initial and very preliminary answer: it is "artful" or "artistically" made.

By calling something an artwork, one accordingly does not say what something is, but instead *how* it is. This *how* of the artistic is not a quality like materiality, color, or even durability. It is encompassing and therefore difficult to grasp; it relates to every aspect of the work that is considered an artwork: to that which it is, as well as to its qualities. Thus, the art-character of a painting allows one to experience it in a special way as a painting. Yet it is not simply a different image than an advertisement or a photo from the family album. Everything about it is different because it is an artwork; everything about it is a moment of that which one could call its "art-character." Everything about it is influenced by this art-character.

If one begins from this term, it may seem obvious to develop the art-character in a determination of "art." Yet the word "art" does not designate what is sought here; it designates a peculiar type of knowing and being-able-to-do, which is not at all limited to the *how* that we are looking for. In earlier uses of language, such as the Latin *artes* and the Greek τέχναι, it refers to all forms of knowledge and capability that find their fulfillment in the production of something; in today's usage it is usually reserved for the "fine arts" [schönen Künste].

This term, which broke through in the eighteenth century and gradually narrowed upon art in the emphatic sense,[47] hints at how the supposed art-character of artworks is to be grasped: as *beauty* [Schönheit]. If one follows the earlier language usage, then it is the beauty of artworks in the emphatic sense that differentiates them from other things—from other houses, sculptures, poems, and pieces of music. Beauty is that wherein the aforementioned formal determinations of the "art-character" find their fulfillment.

This, then, answers the question of "Which art?" It is *fine* art that sets the standard for the philosophical observation. The art-philosophical reflection must grow out of the experience of this fine art, and be bound back into it. Because artworks are primarily experienced sensibly, and as their beauty is thus revealed in sensory perception, it can be called *aesthetic*. In its reference to fine art, art-philosophical observation has the character of aesthetic reflection.

Philosophy of Art and Aesthetics

The conclusion of our foregoing considerations might appear not to be very original. By presenting philosophical observation as aesthetic reflection, one identifies it as belonging to that philosophical mode of questioning that, since its establishment in the middle of the eighteenth century, was understood as being responsible for the elucidation of the beautiful. It sounds like a matter of course to deem philosophical thoughts concerning art and the beautiful "aesthetic," and indeed in many pertinent discussions the expression "aesthetic" is no more than a manner of speaking. Trivializations, such as the terms "aesthete" or "aestheticism" to designate sophisticated lovers of beautiful things, have done the rest. As we will soon see, there are reasons for this development. But it is only the habitual use of "aesthetic" that is disagreeable, partly because the meaning of philosophical concepts should never be presupposed without reflection. It is far more important, in the case of the aesthetic, that the concept is not in any way neutral; it does not align with every philosophical elucidation of art. The concept of the aesthetic is not trivial. It should therefore be a conscious decision to label a discussion of art "aesthetic." The decision requires reasons; it should be justified. To do this, one should deal with the establishment of philosophical aesthetics in modernity.

Alexander Baumgarten's *Aesthetica*, to which philosophical aesthetics owes its name, was intended as an elucidation of αἰσθητικὴ ἐπιστήμη, of perceptual knowledge. In this light, its topic is art as knowledge. As such it is, as Baumgarten states, *gnoseologia inferior*, epistemology concerned not with higher, purely conceptual knowledge, but with sensible knowing (*cognitio sensitiva*).[48] Even though that sounds like a devaluation of sensible knowing, Baumgarten's is the first systematic attempt in modern philosophy to dignify sensible or sensibly dominated knowledge in its peculiarity and to demonstrate its possibilities. In a certain way, Baumgarten's discovery is also a rediscovery. Above all in *De Anima*, but also in *De Sensu* and other shorter writings, Aristotle had developed a conception of sensible knowing in which perception is not understood as a mere limiting condition to human knowledge; we will return to this later.[49]

The aesthetic approach founded the modern philosophical elucidation of art. Yet Kant's *Critique of Judgment* was more influential in this regard than Baumgarten's *Aesthetica*. Although Kant avoids using the term "aesthetics" for his endeavor,[50] philosophical aesthetics really begins with him; Baumgarten is the prehistory to this, no more than an object of historical research. Kant, on the other hand, not only took up previous discussions of the beautiful and the experience thereof, placing them together in a systematic design of exemplary integrational skill, he also gave philosophical aesthetics a significance pertaining to philosophy as such. One should recall emphatically that Kant did not found a philosophical discipline with his *Critique of Judgment*, but instead placed the aesthetic mode of questioning into the center of philosophy's self-clarification. The question of aesthetic experience pertains to the "transition" between concepts of nature and freedom, and thus to the inner cohesion of theoretical and practical philosophy within a whole. To be sure, for Kant there is an "immense gulf" between "the domain of the concept of nature" that encompasses everything falling under natural laws, and the "domain of the concept of freedom" that is determined by its own legislation. But the recognition of this gulf could not be the final word, if it is not to remain a paradox that beings determined by freedom are also natural beings and can only operate under natural conditions. As Kant puts it, the concept of freedom is to be able to actualize in the sensible world the ends posited by its laws, and nature must "therefore also be thought in such a way that its lawfulness can at least harmonize with the possibility of actualizing ends of freedom."[51] Kant sees this harmony actualized in the peculiar abeyance [*Schwebe*] of aesthetic experience. In looking at beautiful things, one recognizes that one is "related" to something "that is not nature, also not freedom," but is "connected [. . .] with the ground" of freedom, namely with "the supersensible." Thus, the supersensible is given in the sensible and natural aspect of aesthetic experience in such a way that it does not oppose the sensible; supersensible freedom arrives in intuition with the sensible of aesthetic experience, without being able to unify with the latter. Nature and freedom are not identical, but they harmonize in aesthetic experience because the latter pertains at once both to the "inner possibility in the subject" as well as to the "external possibility of a corresponding nature."[52] Kant formulates this state of affairs tersely and powerfully in a bequested note: "Beautiful things show that humans belong in the world."[53]

The question regarding the unity of philosophy and thus of nature and freedom kept the generations after Kant in suspense; whoever wishes to understand the philosophy of German Idealism is directed back to Kant's systematic endeavor, such that one could designate German Idealism, riffing on Whitehead,[54] as a series of footnotes to the *Critique of Judgment*. But post-Kantian philosophy failed to follow Kant in a decisive respect. Instead of conceiving nature and freedom as harmonizing or being congruent, the attempt took hold of showing their inner unity by retreating to a principle that grounds it; the "I," "the absolute," and *"Geist"* are just a few designations for this principle. This development coincided with a turn away from Kant's conception of the aesthetic. His conception certainly always continued to find advocates and apologists, but this aesthetics stands in a peculiar orthogonal relation to the development of the philosophical discussion of the beautiful after Kant. This also means that designating a philosophical reflection concerning art as "aesthetic" lacks self-evidence. Aesthetics, in Kant's plentiful sense, is not the subject matter of post-Kantian philosophy.

This thesis can be elucidated in the following way: While Kant's philosophical endeavor is directed at clarifying the *judgment of taste* and, with this, at the experience of the beautiful, the philosophical discussion of the beautiful turns toward the question of how the beautiful arises and thereby increasingly loses interest in understanding what the beautiful actually is. The shift of emphasis is synonymous with a limitation of the area of study: While the experience of the beautiful, for Kant, envelops the beautiful in art and in nature, philosophy after Kant deals mainly or exclusively with a topic that, in Kant's determination of the genius in the *Critique of Judgment*, was no more than a tangential theme: artistic production and its inner possibility. In this topic, one sees freedom mediated with nature; it is considered a particularly evident manifestation of the one reality that unites freedom and nature.

Hegel expressly takes this turn. He retains the term "aesthetics" but distances himself from that which it designates. "Aesthetics" thus signifies the "science of sense, of *sensation*"; it considers artworks "with respect to the sensations [. . .] that they are to bring forth."[55] Yet because, according to Hegel's conviction, artworks are not understood in their effects but only as a human activity that "has sprung forth from spirit" and thus also belongs "to the ground of spirit" (48), it is the sensible manifestation of spirit, accomplishing itself in human action, that centrally holds Hegel's interest. The term "aesthetics" is irrelevant to Hegel's undertaking; it is "immaterial to us as a mere name," but "has entered general language" in such a way "that it can [. . .] be retained as a name." The "actual expression" for the science that bears developing is "philosophy of art," more precisely "philosophy of fine arts" (13).

This decision coincides with a marginalization of the naturally beautiful. Nothing that can be found in "immediate actuality" does justice to the actuality of spirit as such, and thus it is the task of art "to externally present the appearance of liveliness and especially of spiritual animation in its freedom, and to make the external accord with its concept" (202). The task of art is an idealization that may not lead to "banality, lifelessness, and characterless superficiality," but should instead correspond to the determinacy of individuality presented in it; as Hegel states, the ideal includes "at the same time individuality of content and also of form" (227). In any case, an aesthetics that has become a philosophy of art in Hegel's sense has forgotten "the broad realm of the beautiful" that it still invokes in its opening line. (13) Its measure is the spiritual activity that is actual for itself.

The art-philosophical program formulated here, along with its philosophical grounding in a principle, remains binding. This does not mean that Hegel's conception of the principle as spirit remains authoritative, the understanding of art as the objectivization of something subjective that rediscovers itself in the objectivization and is thereby rejoined with itself in the free individuality that is actualized in the artwork. (133) Even before Hegel, Schelling found a related but significantly different solution by conceiving art as a reflection of the absolute identity of subject and object, or conscious and unconscious activity, and deduced these from the absolute as the absolute unity of the conscious and consciousness-less.[56]

Schopenhauer, Nietzsche, Heidegger, Gadamer, and even Adorno—despite his insistent consideration of natural beauty—have followed Hegel's and Schelling's example, each in his own way. As distinct as their approaches may be, they are all concerned with clarifying how art *occurs*. This interest centers around the peculiar occurrences of spirit, will, life, truth, or rationality that are manifest in the artwork but that can only be adequately understood as occurrences. Despite all their Kantian influence, this is also true of Conrad Fiedler's thoughts on the "expressive movement"[57] of art and of John Dewey's pragmatic thoughts on the "act of expression."[58]

Idealist and postidealist philosophy of art thus proceeds beyond Kant by going back behind him. Even Baumgarten's *Aesthetica* was already interested less in the experience of the beautiful than in an activity that could be called "beautiful," which he conceived as knowing, as *cognitio*. The "beauty of sensible knowing" does not refer to its object, but instead to its own beautiful consistency. It is conceived as an agreement of thoughts (*consensus cogitationum*) that articulates itself as the beauty of order and arrangement (*consensus ordinis et dispositionis*) in order to then appear as the beauty of designation (*pulchritudo significationis*).[59] Sensible knowing is at work in art; this knowing, or some comparable activity, is the beautiful with which aesthetics, but especially the philosophy of art, deals.

If one assumes that the systematic intentions of aesthetics in Kant's sense only find their fulfillment in the philosophy of art, then the latter contains an accusation against Kant that Hegel first clearly formulated and that Heidegger and Gadamer repeated. According to Hegel, Kant only regards "beautiful objects of nature and art [. . .] from the side of the reflection that subjectively judges them."[60] Thus, one might add, he does not do justice to the actuality of "beautiful objects."

Heidegger and Gadamer take up this critique by bringing the concept of experience [*Erlebnisses*] to bear on the subjectivity of aesthetic experience that they view as problematic.[61] In experiencing [*Erleben*], so Heidegger puts it in the *Contributions to Philosophy*, something is taken "as being presented *toward itself* as the relational center," and is thus integrated "into 'life.'"[62] The aesthetic experience is not thereby taken as one form of life among others, but as the most intensive form of experiencing as such. As Heidegger states in a lecture course held during the time of the *Beiträge*, "'the experience' as such" becomes decisive in aesthetically understood art, such that the artworks become "mere exciters of experience" [*Erlebniserreger*].⁶³

Like Heidegger, Gadamer underscores the self-relatedness of the experience by designating "everything experienced" as something "self-experienced." It plays into the meaning of the experience that it belongs "to the unity of this self [. . .] and thus [contains] an unmistakable and irreplaceable relation to the totality of this one life."⁶⁴ And, like Heidegger, Gadamer takes experiencing to come into its own in aesthetic experience. The "aesthetic experience" is "not just one kind of experience next to others," but instead represents "the essential form of experience as such" (75).

One can elucidate Heidegger's and Gadamer's characterizations of experience by turning to the meaning of the word. The word *"Erlebnis"* can signify both the occurrence of the experience as well as that which is experienced. Accordingly, one can say that everything experienced is determined primarily or exclusively by experience. Dilthey already recognized that in experience, "awareness and the content of which I am aware are one."⁶⁵ Something is an experienced thing when the independence of its subject matter is inessential and it dissolves completely in experience.

The inessentiality of the subject matter in experience can derive from the power of experience; in that case, the experience is so strong that what is experienced is overlooked in its independence. But experience also offers the possibility of being indifferent to this independence, or to ignore it by means of a special attitude. According to Gadamer, the latter is the case in aesthetic experience. For him, aesthetic experience is characterized by an "abstraction"⁶⁶ that he calls "aesthetic differentiation." With respect to artworks, this consists in disregarding "that wherein a work is rooted as its original life-context." One also ignores "all conditions of access through which the work shows itself," and finally "all those moments of its content that determine our substantial, moral, or religious stance toward it." What thus counts is solely the aesthetic quality, or that which is aesthetic about the artworks. "In terms of reproductive arts," this can be distinguished from the quality of the work as the quality of the performance. The aesthetic differentiation effects a peculiar "simultaneity" (93); in characterizing it, Gadamer refers to André Malraux's notion of the *musée imaginaire*. (93)⁶⁷ Under the category of the aesthetic, one can conjoin that which is unrelated in terms of subject matter or content. In this sense, it would be a result of aesthetic differentiation, a manifestation of "aesthetic consciousness,"⁶⁸ to have a museum in which one encounters Babylonian reliefs, Gothic altarpieces, courtly portraits, art nouveau vases, a felt-and-fat arrangement by Joseph Beuys, and finally a shoddy steel sofa by Franz West with a colorful cloth thrown over it. The museum shows that there are no limits for the aesthetic consciousness and for the aesthetic differentiation in which it constitutes itself. Its bounds are not even delimited by the walls of the museum. The aesthetic consciousness in Gadamer's sense is sovereign. Its sovereignty consists in "accomplishing such aesthetic differentiation everywhere and in being able to look at everything 'aesthetically'" (90).

If one thinks of what Rüdiger Bubner called the "aestheticization of the life-world,"[69] Gadamer's considerations are not implausible. When there is barely anything left that cannot be viewed as an *event*, one has indeed reached what Gadamer describes as the ubiquity of experiencing. Heidegger conceived this ubiquity, in the context of a comprehensive diagnosis of modernity, as complimentary to "machination," the "interpretation of beings in which their ability to be produced comes to the forefront."[70] Where everything loses its bindingness because everything is producible, everything also becomes aesthetically experienceable.

Yet even if this is more or less the case, it is doubtful whether aesthetic differentiation can be equated with that leveling of the bindingness of the life-world that Bubner designates with the term "aestheticization"; it is not convincing to say that aesthetic consciousness as such merges completely with an indifferent and hedonistic attitude to things and events in the "life-world." It is more plausible to surmise that the "aestheticization of the life-world" is a derivation and trivialization that cannot be blamed on aesthetic consciousness as such; the attempt at such blaming is just as unconvincing as the attempt to pass off fanaticism or bigotry as essential moments of religion.[71]

Even if one limits aesthetic consciousness to a narrower scope, it poses difficulties for its critics; Gadamer's critique of "aesthetic differentiation" is not even convincing with regard to art understood in the emphatic sense. The thesis according to which aesthetic differentiation derives from an abstraction is itself a work of abstraction; it ignores the complexity of the experience of art in several ways.

To begin with, what is supposedly abstracting about distinguishing a work from its performances? By considering and assessing the quality of a performance, one does not disregard the work but, conversely, inquires whether and in what respect the performance was adequate to the work. If one could not ask this question, then one would not have understood something essential about artworks, namely their need of being interpreted. The fact would remain hidden that the richness of a great work is not simply there, but must be actualized in various performances. Thus, aesthetic differentiation makes it possible to speak of artworks' "effective history" and thereby also of hermeneutic experience in Gadamer's sense. The effective history of an artwork is essentially that of its interpretations.

It is problematic, further, for Gadamer to assert that the aesthetic understanding of art rests upon a gathering of heterogeneous things that ignores their "belonging to the world." The image of the imaginary museum is certainly accurate in that aesthetically experienceable art can encompass extremely different works; if one assesses the collected presentation according to the type and origin of the works, it can appear arbitrary. But if the gathered works are illuminating as works of *fine* art, then it is a merely alleged arbitrariness. If beauty is capable of being experienced, and is even determinable in conceptual reflection upon that experience, then there is no reason to claim that "aesthetic consciousness" is "the experiencing center from which everything that counts as art" is measured.[72] If the beautiful can be experienced, it cannot be the result of a subjective impression. Then it is also not an "ideal" that is opposed to the reality of life, no "illusory masking, veiling, or transfiguration," as it appears to be in Gadamer's interpretation of Schiller's letters on aesthetic education (88). Gadamer can only appeal to Schiller's letters on aesthetic education because he ignores the experiential quality that the beautiful has for Schiller.[73]

If one takes into account that Gadamer describes aesthetic experience in opposition to a belonging to the world, then it is not Schiller but Hegel who is the first theorist of aesthetic consciousness in Gadamer's sense. It was Hegel who described the experience of art solely as art and diagnosed the loss of the subject matter's bindingness that goes along with this experience. Of course, this loss was not an abstractive accomplishment in Hegel's view, but instead the result of the fact that "spirit has the need to satisfy itself strictly in its own interior as the true form for truth" and not in the sensible exteriority of art. For spirit there is such a thing as *"after* art," and this is reached when spirit no longer finds its actuality in pictorial works. The "art can rise more and more and complete itself, but its form has ceased to be spirit's highest need." "However splendid we find the images of Greek gods, however dignified and fulfilled we see God, Christ, and Mary presented to us—it has no use, we do not bend our knee anymore."[74]

Hegel's thoughts undeniably lie behind Gadamer's notion that art only fulfills its meaning when it is experienced in its "original life context" and thus in its "religious or profane function" (142). Yet by following this notion that stems from Hegel, Gadamer becomes embroiled in precisely that historicism he had criticized in Hegel's understanding of the classical.[75] If one took this notion seriously, then an adequate understanding of Greek tragedies would have to be impossible after the downfall of the Greek polis. The same would be the case for that work that no longer has a "religious or profane function" in one's life-world.

Put in Heidegger's terms, the artwork belongs "only in the realm that the work itself opens up."⁷⁶

Unlike Gadamer's talk of religious and profane functions, of course, Heidegger's formulation is ambiguous. On the one hand, Heidegger too sees artworks as assigned to their respective worlds, and in this way he shares with Gadamer a Hegelian historicism with respect to art. As soon as the world, as the context of signification and meaning for the artwork, is withdrawn or crumbles, then the works are, as Heidegger says, "no longer those that they were." They are "those that have been," and as such they only encounter us "in the realm of tradition and preservation" (26–27). Yet on the other hand, if the works "open up" the world to which they belong, they cannot have a "function"; then they are not determined within the world context, but are effective upon it. That, in turn, is only possible if the works are lifted out of the world that they open up. Then the artworks belong to the world because they do not belong in the world.

Heidegger's notion of the opening up of a world, however, is very specific. When he speaks of an opening or even of a "setting up" (30) of a world, he is thinking of the opening of a historical Dasein in its totality, one that is essentially oriented to the divine. The world is "that which is always non-object-like, to which we are subordinate as long as the courses of birth and death, blessing and curse [keep us] carried away into Being": "Where the essential decisions of our history fall, are taken over or abandoned by us, are misjudged or newly questioned, that is where the world worlds" (30–31). This can be demonstrated well with the example that Heidegger selects, the Greek temple; the temple opens the "view" of a historical life, provided that "in the work-like setting-up, the holy is opened up as holy and the god is called into the openness of its presence" (30). Heidegger certainly takes other artworks to be capable of opening up a world; for instance, Van Gogh's still life representing a pair of shoes, which Heidegger—not without controversy—interpreted as the representation of a farmer's shoes.⁷⁷ Yet Heidegger does not say with respect to Van Gogh's still life what it would mean that, in the opening up of a world, "all things [glean] their whiling and haste, distance and nearness, their expanse and density."⁷⁸ Van Gogh's painting is certainly opening—in a still rather imprecise sense; it lets something appear, not by referring to something but instead by itself being there. But what is opened up is certainly no historical world. Above all, the painting is not allocated to such a world. It has an emphatic worldlessness, just as Cézanne's still lifes and landscapes, Matisse's *Intérieurs,* Newman or Rothko's glowing color surfaces, one of Bach's violin sonatas, or Goethe's *Über allen Gipfeln ist Ruh'*. If these artworks show something, then it is not in their "belonging to a world," but as artworks: in their beauty. But this is a matter of aesthetic consciousness. What is opened in beauty is only revealed as such in aesthetic experience.

Aesthetic experience should not here be pitted against "belonging to a world" in Gadamer's sense. The two do not exclude each other, but they also do not join together. The experience of the beautiful does not dissolve into world-belonging, but it also does not contradict it. Why should a devout Christian be denied the beauty of Bach's mass in B minor, or why should a pious Buddhist be denied the beauty of the statue of the Miroku Boddhisattva in the Chuguji temple of Nara? By being artworks in the emphatic sense, Bach's mass and the anonymously carved statue are distinguished from any random liturgy and any random figure set up in a temple. Nevertheless, both works can be grasped in the context of religious life; most likely, they even reveal religious life more deeply than works that lack beauty.

With respect to art, Heidegger and Gadamer speak less of beauty and all the more about truth. As concerns beauty, Heidegger limits himself to the laconic observation that beauty is "a way in which truth [holds sway] as unconcealment" (43). Truth is "the openness of the open" (48) that is "set into" the work by art. (49) But one does not find out the way this occurs, nor how this differs from other ways of truth. In his lecture course on Nietzsche that Heidegger held in 1936–37, and which was thus most likely written at the same time as the later version of "The Origin of the Work of Art," Heidegger elaborates a little more on the concept of beauty. His thoughts, which are developed in connection to Plato,[79] aim at the notion that the beautiful lets "Being shine" in such a way that it moves humans "through themselves and beyond themselves to Being itself."[80] What Hegel, in his history of spirit, developed as a path over the stages of art and religion to philosophy, is here summarized in one sentence and brought into a determination of the beautiful. The beautiful is a crossing; it is a way station. Even if, with Heidegger and very loosely with Plato, it is "that which attracts" (242), it does not itself take one in, but points to Being in its truth.

Gadamer's considerations on the concept of beauty are more extensive and more precise. Yet, tellingly, they are not to be found in the first part of *Truth and Method* that deals with art, but the in the third part, the theme of which is "Language as Horizon of a Hermeneutic Ontology."[81] Gadamer, too, allies himself with Plato. Yet, in distinction from Heidegger, the beautiful for Gadamer is not that which attracts and refers beyond itself, but that which illuminates. Beautiful things are those "whose value is self-illuminating," "that which can let itself be seen"[82] is beautiful; it is that which "in its Being, immediately makes itself illuminating." The latter formulation clearly resonates with Heidegger. Yet Gadamer's conception of Being differs from Heidegger's in that Gadamer does not take it to mean the open [*das Offene*], but instead linguistic revealability [*sprachliche Offenbarkeit*] and thus the truth of something. That which is "immediately illuminating" in its linguistic revealability is beautiful. It is "the evidence of the matter" (485), the subject matter insofar as it is simply understandable. Accordingly, Gadamer could conceive of art as "transformation into truth," as the "sublation" of something real "into truth" in which one recognizes: "so it is" (118).

It is obvious what is problematic about this determination of the beautiful. The beautiful only avoids being a way station to "Being" because it is simply equated with Being understood as revealability. To be consistent, then, everything illuminating would have to be beautiful, and this leads to the concept of the beautiful becoming dissolved in a general hermeneutical determination. Gadamer does not take into consideration the possibility that artworks, in their beauty, have their own evidence that differs from the undisguised and thus true presence of a thing.

Gadamer's work *The Relevance of the Beautiful*, written in 1974, repeats this identification of the beautiful and the true; the beautiful is that which "compels us to the agreement: 'That is the true!'"[83] To be sure, aesthetics is here no longer discussed in terms of a reduction to "experience," as it was in *Truth and Method*, but it is still criticized. The aesthetic approach, so Gadamer now claims, does not do justice to the "problem of unity between the classical tradition of art and modern art." In light of the "experimental art-practices of our day," the "means of classical aesthetics" are insufficient; instead, one needs a "retreat to more fundamental human experiences" than those elaborated in classical aesthetics. In this sense, Gadamer inquires into the "anthropological basis of our experience of art," and intends to answer this question in the elucidation of "play," "symbol," and "festival" (113). He thereby takes up considerations that he had already developed in *Truth and Method*. Here, as there, the guiding idea is that art does not stand over against us in the work, but is instead an occurrence that draws in the one who experiences by delegating to him or her the task[84] of building up the work. The "identity of the work" is "not guaranteed by some classical or formalistic determinations," but is instead "cashed out in the manner in which we shoulder the building-up of the work as a task."[85] This is especially the case in modern art, which "aims to break through the distance over against the work of art in which viewerships, groups of consumers, and audiences [maintain] themselves" (115). The experience of art is always "a constant being-active along-with" (117); as Gadamer states in a later work, art exists "in enactment."[86] By relating the art-philosophical determination of occurrence—which since Schelling and Hegel had usually applied to artistic production—Gadamer comes dangerously close to the indifference he criticized about aesthetic experience; one experiences art in "being-active along-with" it, even if the experiencing is not subjective but is the living embeddedness in the truth-occurrence of art. Here, too, content and occurrence are one. Yet one thereby loses the tarrying with "that which individually appears," which Gadamer himself takes to be the fundamental trait of the experience of the beautiful.⁸⁷ It is thus no wonder that, in Gadamer's considerations of play and festival in *the Relevance of the Beautiful*, there is hardly any mention of the beautiful.

Of course, this alleged omission could be rooted in the nature of the subject matter. After all, modern art—whose challenge Gadamer explicitly wishes to take up—has the reputation of refusing the category of the beautiful. There is proverbial talk of the "no-longer fine arts"⁸⁸ and, as always, it is common to attribute to modern art a "loss of the center,"⁸⁹ a "muteness,"⁹⁰ and the dissolution of traditional forms. Even Adorno, as a decided partisan of modernity, stressed that in modernity, the "materials [had lost] their self-evidence,"⁹¹ and modern art was determined by a "process of disillusionment without reservation" (32). If modern art is recognized in its own right, this does not align with a demonstration of its beauty. Instead, as in Gadamer, beauty is marginalized or replaced by the category of the sublime, through the indication that modern art is not to be viewed from a distance but intends to carry one away and overwhelm.⁹² Besides, beauty is considered outmoded. Adorno already takes the "reconciliation" that occurs in beauty to be an "act of force" and considers it as treason against "unreconciled life."⁹³

These reservations over against the beautiful do not hold up to closer scrutiny. It must be an idyllic understanding of beauty that views the latter as incompatible with an assumedly awful total state of the world;⁹⁴ one can already correct this understanding with reference to a verse by Rilke, according to which the beautiful is "the beginning of terror [. . .] that serenely disdains to destroy us."⁹⁵ Furthermore, if art was ever beautiful, its beauty never prevented it from presenting the evil and bad, the failed and stranded. Art is not "beautiful" in that it simulates a "reconciled life"; it is beautiful in its works that need not shy away from any topic.

The reservation against beauty proves to be unconvincing even with respect to peculiarities of modern artworks. The "muteness" or "speechlessness" that Arnold Gehlen emphasizes in modern works does not militate against these works' beauty; the muteness just consists in the fact that modern works do not, on their own, join into a self-evident context of meaning. In a room with paintings by Rothko or Newman, one does not see any saints or mythological figures, just as in the small-scale works of Paul Klee, there are no familiar landscapes or vedutas, and no genre-scene of middle-class life confirms the certainty that one knows one's way around. The images do not speak, which means they lack the confirmation through the familiar. Because of this, their "special restraint and stillness" allows the modern works to appear more present and perhaps even more beautiful. By no longer being "conversational,"⁹⁶ they stand over against us and thus for themselves. Yet this is no hermetic refusal, but it is a challenge to look, listen, and read—again and again. The less an artwork offers its own assistance in understanding, the more decisively it binds hermeneutic reflection into perception. In this way, modern art just makes especially clear what every artwork demands. Thus modern art is no special case, and most certainly no threshold of disappearance. Instead, it offers the possibility of a shift in experience, through which one might even see traditional works more aptly.

Just as the concept of the beautiful is not threatened by the alleged hermetic character of modern art, it is also not at risk from the concept of the sublime. For the latter concept either designates a mere modification of the beautiful and not an alternative, such that it refers to the possibility of the soul's enthusiastic ascension to the divine and thus to the beautiful.[97] Or it is a concept that relates not to artworks but to natural appearances[98] or human moods,[99] retaining of course some of the essential traits of the experience of beauty; in this sense, Kant viewed the experience of the sublime as an observing one, and thus tied it to the condition of distance; looking at threatening cliffs or a thunderstorm is only aesthetic "when we find ourselves in safety."[100] If one takes into account that "power," attributed by Kant here to nature under the guise of the sublime, was an essential trait of the beautiful according to classical conceptions, then the claim that modern artworks cannot be beautiful turns out to be the result of a constrained concept of beauty—oriented perhaps more by what is pleasing; or it is a consequence of the insinuation that modern art is polemically directed against traditional art, art typically understood as beautiful. As soon as one lifts this insinuation and modern artworks are experienced without its bias, one can also discover their beauty. The opposition of modern and traditional art—an inheritance of the aforementioned excess in the philosophy of history that the *querelle des anciens et des modernes* underwent in advanced modernity—loses its effect. Commonalities and connections that remained unrecognizable under the sign of forced modernity move into the foreground. Now there is a path that runs from Giotto to Rothko, from Bach to Alban Berg, from Dante to Rilke, from the masterpieces of classical Japanese architecture to Tadao Ando's buildings. One grasps that the art of this century and the previous one was less concerned with dissolution, destruction of forms, or the presentation of crude material; it was rather about reduction, expansion of form, and not least about the rediscovery of the sensibly perceivable. One looks or listens, one reads more closely and discovers works in their beauty.

Yet it remains to be developed what this means more precisely. Characterizing the beautiful as the *"how"* of an artwork that encompasses all of its moments[101] only gives a preliminary indication of how the question of artworks' beauty is to be phrased and developed. Determinations like autonomy, incipience, originariness, and sensibility can only be shown to be aesthetic by way of the concept of the beautiful.

Posed in the context of philosophical aesthetics, the question of the artistically beautiful does not stand on its own but instead belongs to the question of the beautiful in general. The beauty of artworks connects them with all beautiful things, regardless of whether these are produced or natural. Aesthetics really has to do with the "broad realm of the beautiful."

But this does not mean that a statement regarding something's beauty applies to all beautiful things in the same way. In general, beautiful objects of use are primarily seen as objects of use. It is similar with nature's beauty—with layerings of stone, with landscapes in changing light, with the beautiful shape of life forms and the constellations. Their beauty is a basic trait that retreats in everyday life, that is not always perceived in itself, and that is thus less clear in showing "that human fit into the world." Artworks are different. Their beauty determines and pervades them entirely; it is part of their essence to be primarily or even exclusively perceived and experienced as beautiful. Because artworks are *essentially* beautiful, they bear a primacy for aesthetic reflection. In their essential beauty, they also reveal the beauty of use-objects and of nature. A beautiful object of use does not dissolve in its usage. Because it is beautiful, it also invites observation and in this way is like an artwork. As soon as the use of a thing—such as a Japanese tea bowl—belongs together with its observation, its art-character is apparent. Stones and flowers are observed in their beauty as if they were artworks. The experience of artworks can awaken, foster, and complete the experience of the naturally beautiful.

One should not confuse the aesthetic primacy of artworks with their *art-philosophical* distinction. The latter may be more obvious because it is exclusive, but it does not really characterize art. The philosophy of art does not conceive of art within the "broad realm of the beautiful," but instead sorts it into a reality that is only manifested in art in a certain way. Understood as the reality of spirit, as the manifestation of will or of life, or as the occurrence of truth, art is always grasped by means of something else that does not exhaust itself in art nor dissolve into it. The beautiful, conversely, is absolutely and unreservedly present in art, without being given solely in art. With respect to the beautiful, art has a non-fundamental primacy. It reveals the beautiful, but does not explain it.

Even if the artwork bears this honor for aesthetic experience and thus for aesthetics in general, one should not begin with a determination of the artwork, but with aesthetic experience. The artwork, in its beauty, is only given in this experience; the aesthetic experience of art *is* the experience of its beauty. Conversely, an attempt at a direct determination of art risks determining the artwork from something other than itself. Art-philosophical derivations of art in Schelling's and Hegel's sense are only possible because they leap over aesthetic experience as something purportedly merely "subjective."

Thus, aesthetic reflection begins, to put it in Aristotelian terms, with what is "known to us," in order to proceed from this to what "known as such,"[102] to that which is experienced, to the beautiful work. If one begins with the subjective side of experience, the path to the experienced thing results on its own. After all, the thing is always present in experience. By reflecting upon and grasping experience, the subject matter that conditions it comes to the fore.

TWO

Beauty

Free Play

If one wishes to describe and grasp aesthetic experience, one should begin with Kant. He developed the prevailing determination of aesthetic experience, in part because he discovered its autonomy. Baumgarten's conception of a *cognitio sensitiva* may have lifted out the independent claim of a "beautiful knowledge," but this knowledge remains conditioned by sensibility and is thus a merely narrowed modification of actual knowledge that is conceived as purely conceptual. Kant, on the other hand, carefully delimits the experience of the beautiful from all other possibilities of affective relation, of perception and thinking, and presents it in its uniqueness.

Of course, Kant's leap beyond Baumgarten also has its irritating aspects. In the *Critique of Judgment*, he essentially takes aesthetic experience to be a process internal to consciousness. Thus one might doubt whether it really deals with experience and knowledge at all. Yet upon closer inspection, the process Kant describes is neither solipsistic nor autosuggestive. There is something toward which this process is directed, and accordingly one cannot rule out the possibility that Kant's conception of the aesthetic connects to experience and knowledge. It merely depends on what experience and knowledge are in this case. Perhaps Kant's inconsistent or maybe only alleged internalism of the aesthetic first offers the possibility of adequately grasping aesthetic experience and knowledge in their essence. Precisely this possibility could remain ruled out if one took one's bearings from a predetermined conception of experience and thus remained caught in a notion of the knowable or known object that is inadequate to aesthetics. As Kant does not exclude object-relations in the context of the aesthetic, one can speak of aesthetic experience—even if only in a sense that remains unclear. It is crucial, then, to understand aesthetic experience in its peculiar relation to objects.

Kant's endeavor rests upon an essential presupposition. He assumes that aesthetic experience is an experience of the beautiful, and is thus one of *taste*. Taste, in turn, is to be understood as a *capacity for judgment*. Taste is a sensible capacity for judgment that rests immediately upon perception, has a valuing character, and entails a demand for validity that reaches beyond momentary inclinations. In taste, then, individual preference unites with knowledge of what is distinguishable in its diversity and, on the basis of this joining, connects with bindingness. Possessing taste thereby becomes a social ideal; the person to whom one accords taste with regard to lifestyle—furnishings, clothing, manners—enjoys recognition and authority.[1] Kant takes up this ensemble of determinations in order to make something entirely different out of it: a determination of the possibility of judgments concerning the beautiful that accounts for their singularity.[2]

In this sense, Kant is the first to emphasize the *disinterestedness* of the aesthetic judgment. Whoever finds something beautiful is not interested in the increase of their own well-being and also does not see it under the guise of utility or general desirability. The beautiful is neither something pleasant nor something good. It deserves neither affinity nor respect, but only favor,[3] which means: The beautiful is viewed *benevolently;* one enjoys it without this enjoyment uniting with the notion of appropriation or the notion that the beautiful object should exist. One grants it its existence.

Since the aesthetic judgment is disinterested, it can also not be founded upon any sensation. It is "independent of stimulus and affect" (B 38, 223); one is neither stimulated nor induced into inner motion by the beautiful as such. That which is likeable about it is that it gives an occasion for *reflection*. The judgment that something is beautiful is cashed out in reflection, and accordingly the taste for the beautiful is a "reflective taste" (B 22, 214). It may be that something stimulates or induces inner motion, and at the same time gives occasion for reflection. If one follows Kant, however, only the latter is a confirmation of the thing's beauty. The other aspects merely go along with the experience of beauty and contribute to making it more opaque.

Reflection, as it is conceived here, is the attempt at grasping something in the context of or totality of its moments, without being able to determine this totality as such. As Kant says, a judgment is reflective when something particular is given to which the universal is to be found.[4] The judgment is essentially reflective when one can skirt around this universal, as it were, but not directly determine it. That which is somehow coherent or harmonious does not align with any one concept, nor to any "general notion [. . .] of what is common to multiple objects."[5] Beauty is not a property, such as size or color, that an object or living being has in common with something else that is equally called "beautiful." Instead, the expression "beautiful" demonstrates something's incomparability; the beautiful is only experienceable as something individual in each case, as something that one has to "subject to one's eyes."[6] "If one judges objects solely by concepts," Kant says, "then all notion of beauty is lost" (215). Nevertheless, that which is individual, insofar as it is beautiful, is an occasion thoughtful activity. If it were perceived by a thinking being solely as something individual and not as an individual in its beauty, its categorization under general concepts would be inevitable. That which is individual first comes into its own right by being thought in a way that corresponds to it, and that is the case in the reflection of the beautiful.

Despite this, the reflection that belongs to the experience of the beautiful has *universal validity*. This does not mean that someone else must recognize it and accept it as correct or binding. It is not absolute [*allgemeingültig*], but generally valid [*allgemein gültig*], which means one can advocate it without thereby limiting it to the communication of one's preference or sensation. One takes oneself "to have a general voice for oneself, and makes claims upon everyone's agreement" (216).

The aesthetic judgment that is cashed out through reflection bears a general validity that becomes evident in the judgment's relation to its subject matter. When one designates something as beautiful, one should say, "The thing is beautiful," for one expects "the same delight from others"; one does not judge "merely for oneself, but for everyone," and one thus speaks "of beauty as if it were a property of things" (B 20, 212).

Yet for Kant, beauty is not such a property, and accordingly the universality that one draws on with the aesthetic judgment can only ever be a "subjective universality" (B 18, 212). The universality comes to expression in a statement about an object, but it is not, in Kant's view, founded upon this objectivity. To be sure, one will always speak "as if beauty were a property of the object," but one thereby fails to recognize that an aesthetic judgment only contains "a relation of the presentation of the object to the subject" (B 18, 211).

If this is the case, then the aesthetic judgment is caught in a *structural self-deception*. Without being objective, it can only be formulated with reference to an "object." Kant does not even consider the possibility of adequately communicating the experience of the beautiful in sentences like "I find this beautiful." For then he would be forced to conceive of the experience of the beautiful as a "private feeling" that only has to do with one's own comfort. But regarding the beautiful, as Kant stresses, "no private conditions can be found as grounds for delight" (B 17, 211); one is not bound affectively to that which one judges as beautiful, as if it promises to satisfy some need that one feels. The beautiful is no balancing of deficiency, as the beverage that quenches thirst or the food that satisfies hunger. Thus the experience of the beautiful is not mixed with pleasure and nuisance, as is the case with all forms of pleasure that derive from a lack, according to Plato's *Philebus*.[7] One is, as Kant puts it, "completely free"[8] vis-à-vis the beautiful.

Kant elaborates a more precise grasp of this freedom with what is probably the most prominent notion in his conception of aesthetic experience. The notion is to explain, at the same time, how the subjective universality of aesthetic judgment arises. If the aesthetic judgment does not refer to an object in such a way as to conceptually determine it, and so must "be thought without a concept of the object," then the ground for the aesthetic judgment could be "nothing other than the mental state that we find in the relation between the presentational powers insofar as they refer a given presentation to *cognition in general*" (b 28, 217).[9] If one appeals to someone for agreement with an aesthetic judgment, this appeal has validity because one understands—however opaquely—that aesthetic judgments are a matter of cognition. To be sure, the aesthetic judgment is no cognitive judgment, but it pertains to knowing in general, to "cognition as such." This cognition is involved because the cognitive faculties—the imagination and understanding—"are set into free play" by a presentation. This play of the cognitive faculties is free "because no particular concept [limits] them to a certain rule of cognition," that is, to determining something in a particular way that would also be possible for other objects. Thus one is not only free with regard to the beautiful because it does not bind one affectively; one is especially free because it lets thinking be free. It need not be determined in a way that is valid and thus objective for others. It thus does not burden thought with the discipline necessary to determine objects with the aim of universal agreement.

Kant himself did not expand on the "free play of the cognitive faculties" (B 28, 217); he only states that it takes place in the experience of the beautiful, but he does not say how. From the character of the two cognitive faculties that he names, however, one can easily ascertain how their free activity—one that is not directed at the determination of an object of knowledge—is to be conceived. The imagination, as the intermediary between the manifold of intuitions and the faculty that mediates concepts,[10] provides understanding with a manifold of intuitions, somehow structured, that understanding ought to bring into the unity of a concept. But such a unified determination of a structured manifold does not occur. Concepts are certainly brought to bear on the structured manifold; otherwise the understanding would not be involved at all. But the concepts that are brought into play are not suited to envelop the structured manifold. They cannot even lift out single moments such that there might result a "general presentation [. . .] of that which is common to several objects."[11] The concepts can grasp and highlight something about the structured manifold, but what is grasped in this way belongs so inextricably to its context that it becomes featureless on its own. That is why understanding plays every formed concept back to the structured manifold and the imagination, which in their turn can set free new concept formations.

The free play of the cognitive faculties, elaborated in this way, is nothing other than the activity of reflective judgment, determined aesthetically—and that means by perception. Because of its determination through perception, this activity is bound to the singular and individual in the way that the imagination grasps it together into a respectively "given presentation." This presentation is "singular and without comparison to others." Yet it does not withdraw from conceptual grasping, but instead bears "an agreement with the conditions of universality"—the knowing of the understanding; this knowing can feel bolstered by the presentation without having to surmount it, and indeed without being able to.[12] So precisely by being bound to the incomparable, the capacity to grasp is free; it can unfold playfully, in the free interplay of the two faculties involved, because it is not obligated to a result given through cognitive judgment.

In this way, the activity of reflective judgment is indeed related to "cognition as such." Cognition as such comes to bear through the inconclusiveness of aesthetic reflection, which is not fulfilled in any particular cognition. As Kant states, the faculties of cognition are brought "into the proportioned harmony that we demand for all cognition" (B 31–32, 219). In this proportioned harmony, *the possibility of cognition itself* is at play. That is to be understood in a twofold manner: Because the activity of the cognitive faculties in aesthetic reflection is incomplete, it remains within the possibility of being continued; the aesthetic reflection does not fulfill or exhaust itself, but is always still possible. In addition, the free play of the cognitive faculties makes clear *how* cognition is possible—as an interplay of the two faculties. This can only become evident in an interplay that does not lead the cognitive faculties together to the result of a determinate knowing, but keeps them apart and at the same time allows them to be related to each other. Held apart, the two cognitive faculties are at play in their idiosyncrasy; insofar as they are related to each other by playing to each other, they allow for cognition's possibility.

If the free play of the cognitive faculties proceeds in this way or similarly, it must be a very intensive experience; clearly a heightened sense of living accompanies the free activity of the cognitive faculties. In this sense, Kant speaks of a "sensation" that consists "in the eased play of the mental powers that are enlivened through mutual harmony" (219), and a little later he mentions the "enlivening of the cognitive faculties" (B 37, 222). Kant had already stated in the opening paragraphs of the *Critique of Judgment* that in the judgment of taste, a presentation is related "entirely to the subject, namely to its sense of living" (B 4, 204). Yet Kant does not here go into the cognitive character of experience that is signified in the formulation of the free play of the cognitive faculties. Instead, he takes the reference toward the "enlivening of the cognitive faculties" to say everything decisive about aesthetic experience. Since, in aesthetic experience, the cognitive capacities are not directed cognitively toward an object, the latter is related to the subject solely "with regard to its delight"; the subject relates to the object strictly in such a way as to attribute the "predicate of beauty" to it. The "subjective unity" of understanding and imagination in aesthetic experience is not "intellectual"—that is, given in some kind of mental activity—but is rather identified solely "through sensation." The judgment of taste postulates nothing but the "universal communicability" of this enlivening of the cognitive faculties. In a relation of the cognitive faculties that is not determined by a concept, "no other consciousness of this [relation is possible] than a sensation of the effect that consists in the eased interplay of both mental powers enlivened through mutual harmony" (219).

According to these definitions, aesthetic reflection would have to do with a differentiated as well as intensified mental activity that is experienced strictly as sensation. But this activity, as interplay of the *cognitive faculties*, cannot be exhausted in the sensation of being-enlivened. The "sociability" (B 162, 296) that Kant couples with the experience of the beautiful ultimately only arises if a rational exchange is possible regarding the communication of judgments of taste. And if Kant formulates the maxims of this exchange to be "thinking for oneself," the capacity to "think in the place of another" and the possibility of thinking "anytime in harmony with oneself," then he is giving hermeneutical directions "as parts of the critique of taste" that are to be taken to heart in aesthetic discourse. (B 158, 294)[13] Accordingly, one has to imagine the articulation of the free play of the cognitive faculties as follows: in the free play, the faculties emerge by bringing the aesthetically experienced thing to language in as unprejudiced and consistent a way as possible, and in a way that adjoins to others' statements. The claim that this here, for instance this water lily painting by Claude Monet, is beautiful can be no more than an *announcement* of aesthetic reflection, one that designates the status of everything that is subsequently said about Monet's painting and that connects with the demand to join the aesthetic conversation. If one wishes to dispute this, one has to take the activity of judgment in the judgment of taste as tautologous, such that the judgment of taste always and only makes the same observation: one senses delight and expresses it by claiming—about something that is no more than an arbitrary occasion for sensation—that it is beautiful and beautiful and beautiful.[14]

Even if there are places to find support for this interpretation in the *Critique of Judgment*, the reduction of aesthetic experience to sensation cannot capture the sense of an approach that takes aesthetic experience to be primarily *reflection*. The primacy of reflection is unquestionable for Kant; it is only because Kant grounds aesthetic delight in the free play of the cognitive faculties that he can describe it as their "effect."[15] If this free play, in its "universal communicability," did not precede the "feeling of pleasure," then aesthetic pleasure would be impossible. It would, as Kant states, be nothing but "the mere pleasantness of sensory perception" and could thus "only possess private validity according to its nature" (B 27, 216–217). Nevertheless, Kant apparently shies away from conceiving aesthetic reflection as related to an object. Thus, he develops the notion of a mental activity that only arises in delight, and of a delight that has its ground in this mental activity that remains concealed.

Kant's reasoning for the dependence of aesthetic pleasure on the reflection of aesthetic judgment indirectly explains his proceeding in this way: in his view, neither aesthetic pleasure nor aesthetic reflection can relate to an object, because the objective relation is affectively and cognitively different: a pleasure that is evoked by an object must be pleasure concerned with the pleasant, and thus a private feeling; a cognitive act that relates to an object can only be thought as a conceptual determination. Under these premises, Kant's argumentation is comprehensible and consistent, but also plausible. The price paid for this argument is the assumption of [the additional] premise that aesthetic experience amounts to a structural self-deception. In this deception, aesthetic experience shrinks to a "feeling of oneself," which can be occasioned by anything and everything.[16] The value of this deception is that of "free psychogymnastic exercises of the cognitive faculties"[17] for the sake of their enlivening effect.

The solution to the Kantian problem, then, is apparent: one need only take seriously his determination of aesthetic reflection as a free play of the cognitive faculties. Yet how are cognitive faculties to be involved if nothing is cognized, in whatever sense? Aesthetic experience is certainly to be differentiated from conceptual cognition in its relation to objects. As an experience of "cognition as such," it is an experience of cognition itself, and for this reason alone it cannot be normal cognition.

To be sure, this relation of aesthetic experience to something is not graspable within the framework of Kant's conception of aesthetics; Kant simply has no terms for the relation. But the relation exists, and it cannot be reduced to a structural self-deception. We thereby get an uneven picture: Kant continually denies the fact that there is *something* to be experienced aesthetically, and at the same time this state of affairs is thoroughly present in the *Critique of Judgment*. This is due to the nature of the matter; the free play of the cognitive faculties can only exist if aesthetic experience is pervasively related to something. Besides, the basic motive of Kant's third *Critique* cannot be cashed out without paying heed to objective relations. One can only speak of a harmony or congruence of freedom and nature in aesthetic experience if something stands over against freedom with which it can harmonize. In this way, the Kantian analysis of the experiential side of aesthetic experience is always already geared toward an understanding of what is experienced. This is why one can repeat, with Adorno, that Kant's analysis of aesthetic judgment does not amount to a "subjectivism"; rather, this subjectivism carries "its specific weight [. . .] in its objective intention, in the attempt to rescue objectivity by means of the analysis of subjective moments."[18]

The side of the experienced is already in play when Kant calls the judgment of taste "contemplative";[19] observation is always the observation of something. As if he had not said earlier that an aesthetic judgment relates a presentation "entirely to the subject and to its sense of life" (B 4, 209). Kant now accepts as self-evident the relation of aesthetic contemplation to something, and even says what this relation entails. The aesthetic judgment is one that, "in looking at the existence of an object indifferently, only holds its complexion up to our feeling of pleasure and displeasure" (209). In contemplation, an object is not grasped under the guise of its appropriation or use, nor in any other mode of real givenness; it exists, but one is not interested in its real "existence." What is held together "with the feeling of pleasure and displeasure" is not the object as such, but its "complexion." But a complexion is, in some way, determinate. If, in its determinacy, it is the counterpart to aesthetic experience, then it cannot be a mere heightening of the "sense of life."

Accordingly, Kant does not always conceive of aesthetic reflection as an inner process that is to show itself in the liveliness of aesthetic delight. Thus, he states at one point that pleasure in the beautiful is pleasure "of mere reflection," and adds the clarification that this pleasure accompanies "the common grasp of an object," that is, that grasp accomplished in imagination and understanding. This does not keep Kant from proceeding to claim that aesthetic reflection is concerned solely with "sensing the presented object with pleasure" (B 155, 292) (But this cannot be the case if the delight in the beautiful must "depend on the reflection about an object that leads to some concept (not determined which)"; it is only by this dependence on concepts, Kant adds, that it distinguishes itself from the pleasurable, "which rests entirely on sensation" (B 11, 207). Aesthetic reflection is thus not objectless, and it engages its object in respectively determinate ways. But in the free play of the cognitive faculties, it treats its concepts playfully; it does not settle on any determinate concept with which to arrive at a definite judgment, and precisely in this way it does justice to that which it finds in its object.[20] Just prior, Kant had noted that beautiful things "do not depend on any determinate concept, and yet are delightful."[21]

In this consideration, Kant presupposes his determination of beauty, and to that extent his expectation is justified that the notion of an object-related aesthetic experience might find itself confirmed in this conception of beauty. Indeed, by developing his concept of beauty, Kant elaborates on beauty as a quality of objects to such an extent that the claim that the aesthetically experienced thing is just an occasion and thus undetermined cannot remain convincing. This does not mean that Kant does justice to all aspects of the object-relation of aesthetic experience. But by taking beauty to be a complexion, something about objects, he hits upon something decisive, as we shall see; aesthetic experience relates to something that is not exhausted by normal determinations of things and which therefore can only be approximately called a "quality" of things. In any case, this naming is not very specific; because it stems from a quandary, it lags behind the objective essence of the beautiful.

Kant determines beauty as the "form of purposiveness of an object [...] insofar as it is perceived in the object without a presentation of purpose" (B 61, 236). The formulation is paradoxical, but the paradox can be explained. Kant's determination of beauty is a liminal concept, comparable to the concept of the "end in itself" that Kant discovers as a person's dignity.[22] Whereas in the latter case the person is viewed from the purview of others' ends of action, in the context of which the person can be taken as a means, the talk of purposiveness without a purpose is oriented along the process of production. In both cases the orienting analogy only serves the goal of rejecting the notion being considered. Insofar as people do not possess "mere [...] relative worth, i.e. a price, but instead have an inner worth, i.e. dignity,"[23] it is in essence inappropriate to regard them as foreign ends and thus as valuable or useful to someone else. This produces that derivation of the categorical imperative according to which one should act in such a way as to treat "humanity," in one's own person as well as in everyone else's, simultaneously as an end, and never merely as a means. (429). Insofar as what is beautiful is purposive without a purpose, it cannot, in its reality, be traced back to a preceding notion of what or how it should be. Something is only ever a purpose in relation to a concept that is understood as the "cause" for that which is the purpose. Accordingly something is purposive when, in the "what" and the "how" of its existence, it can be understood by way of a purpose; purposiveness in Kant's sense is "the causality of a concept in view of its object"[24] and not, as one might think according to the usual usage, the suitability of an end as a means.

Insofar as there is no purpose with regard to beauty, one strictly cannot speak of its purposiveness. It must rather be such that beauty sets up the notion of a purposiveness that cannot be cashed out in the same way as with normal imputations of purposiveness: namely, by trying to find—or assuming as given—the concept that was the cause of that which is viewed as purposive. Kant places great value on the fact that no such imputation occurs with regard to beauty; beauty, for him, is not something purposive whose purpose one simply does not know how to indicate. The case of beauty, then, is different from an archaeological find, for instance, which one takes to be somehow purposive, even without being able to recognize a purpose. Beautiful things, by contrast, are taken to be beautiful "because one finds in the perception of them a certain purposiveness which, when we judge it, is not related to any purpose" (B 61, 236 n. 1).

That should explain the paradox of Kant's determination of beauty. But the explanation keeps the puzzle intact in its paradoxicality. The impertinence of

Kant's determination, after all, lies in the fact that the notion of purposiveness is not simply eschewed, but that it appears to be somehow adequate while actually being inadequate. The inadequacy, as we saw, can be immediately grasped; there is no such thing as purposiveness without purpose. Conversely, the adequacy of the determination is the problem, and so we need to clarify this adequacy.

One only gets so far in this clarification by pursuing the indication that the notion of purposiveness stems from the realm of production. To be sure, the beautiful comes to be either naturally or through art, and Kant says of nature that it is only beautiful when it "at the same time [looks] like art" (B 179, 306). But this formulation is directed less at natural beauty than at a teleology of nature, in which natural products are viewed as if they had come into being "not through mere coincidence, but intentionally as it were, according to lawful ordering" (B 170, 301). But the beautiful in nature is not purposive in this sense; whoever judges something natural as beautiful does not consider its "natural purpose," according to which some analogy could still be made to something produced. (B 49, 229) This having-been-produced is inessential even to artworks; the "purposiveness in the products of fine art" must, "even if it is intentional, not appear to be intentional" (B 180, 306–307). Something is not beautiful insofar as it is made, and thus beauty cannot be determined by taking production as one's orientation. The beauty of an artwork, therefore, also cannot be understood as the effect of a concept-driven intention. Instead, beauty involves the nonessentiality of intention. As soon as something appears "intended" in art and is a transparent effect, one no longer calls it beautiful.

Nevertheless, Kant calls beauty "purposive." Since the term undeniably comes from the context of production but Kant eschews the productive orientation, the term must mean something that belongs in the context of production but does not pertain to the process of production as such, something that is only evident if one takes the productive process as one's orientation but does not mean it as such.

A question of this type is how something is *possible* as that which it is and the way in which it exists. One automatically inquires about something's possibility if one asks what it came from and how. If something appears to be somehow coherent and convincing, the question of its possibility arises almost on its own. This is the only way to justify the analogy of nature and art with regard to the beautiful. If something natural is beautiful, then it strictly speaking does not appear "as art." But it can be understood within the conceptual frame of reference that is decisive for art. For then the question of the *basis* of its coherence is obvious. Something that coheres but is not self-evident arouses the question: How, on what basis, is it possible? The question of its possibility and the latter's basis is an expression of its lack of self-evidence. Kant calls the concept by which something is determined as a purpose "the real basis of its possibility" (220). Since the talk of purposiveness without purpose does not refer to something having been produced, it can only refer to the jointure of the possible with its basis.

If one inquires into something's possibility and, through this, into the grounds of possibility, one goes beyond the thing in order to comprehend it by virtue of something else. Viewed by way of this other thing, it stands as a possibility; it is something that *can* be and does not simply exist. It is not a self-evident existent that is only given as itself. Only something that has that character can be determined without further ado; it stands within the relational field of self-evident concepts. Its existence corresponds to the self-evidence of these concepts; both complement each other and create the world of all things that exist self-evidently. It is the world of self-evidently existing things and of self-evident, universally applicable concepts. Something can only exist in a self-evident way if it is determinable through unquestionably valid concepts; concepts can only remain unquestionably valid insofar as they grasp something that exists, something that, as determinable, is not questioned and is thus self-evident.

In the world of the self-evident, there is a fine and thus barely noticeable rift that opens as soon as that which exists no longer simply stands in the web of self-evident concepts, but instead, in order to be adequately understood, demands inquiry into a concept underlying it. In that case, it is no longer a matter of simple cognition that graspingly subsumes something under its concepts, but it is instead the case that cognition conceives "the object itself [. . .] as an effect that is possible only through a concept of that effect" (220)[25] In this case, the concepts do not simply lie on the side of determination; instead, they also show up on the side of what is to be determined. As Kant puts it, a concept precedes that which is to be determined as "the real ground of its possibility." It is purposive insofar as, having been led back to this basis, it can be understood by virtue of it. If it is recognized in its purposiveness, the cognizing concept coincides with the concept that underlies that which is to be cognized.

The rift that arose through the doubling of concepts can still remain open even when one no longer assumes a concept on the side of what is to be cognized. This is possible if one can continue thinking beyond what is to be cognized. Indeed, if this thinking-beyond does not lead to an underlying concept, the rift will be even more pronounced. In that case, one thinks beyond something, but without the presumption of a concept as a real basis, that which is to be cognized no longer allows itself to be cognized by reference to anything else. With respect to its cognizability, it is *groundless*. Yet it remains something possible within this groundlessness; it remains that which can be. It is no simple existence accessible to concepts.

Of course, one can only speak of what is to be cognized as being without basis if it continues to be conceived with regard to a basis. It is without ground in such a way that the ground is in play as that which is missing. To speak with Heidegger, the ground is not itself presented, but precisely therein lies a relation to the ground; the relation, according to Heidegger, can "persist precisely through its absence."[26] It is directed at *emptiness*, but one that is not an indeterminate, indifferent emptiness, but is instead, paradoxically put, the emptiness of something.

Upon closer inspection, however, the state of affairs is the opposite. The emptiness that has opened up is, as such, not to be conceived by reference to something specific that could fill it. Rather, one can only inquire about the specific thing, in this case the real ground, because the inquiry proceeds beyond the given into an openness in which a real ground might lie. The openness that one experiences when the question concerning something's possibility remains without ground is that empty space that can be occupied by determinate grounds. If the question about the ground remains without a definite answer, it leads into the "abyss" [*Ab-Grund*];[27] it leads to the empty space for a ground that is fundamentally conceivable, but not thinkable in the given case.

It is in this way that the "without purpose" of Kant's determination of beauty is to be thought. It is the possible thing the possibility of which cannot be determined by virtue of something else that is *without purpose*. As something possible, it nonetheless only comes under scrutiny insofar as one can inquire where it is from and through what it came to be. It must exist in such a way that the question is evident, yet still is not posed as the question of a specific ground. It is not that the question is posed and is then left unanswered; in this case something would not be without a purpose, but instead just without a known or recognizable purpose. The question about a specific ground is eschewed; it is crossed out. This leads to the indeterminate openness of any provenance, to the empty space for all reasons. Specific reasons cannot be conceived without this empty space; one could not even inquire about them. After all, the question to which the indication of a specific ground is the answer leads into emptiness, into the yet undetermined. It is from this alone that the possibility of an answer arises.

The question concerning something's purpose leads one to consider its purposiveness. Something is experienced as purposive when its complexion induces the question of where it is from, how it exists. As purposive, it exists according to the "measures of the purpose"—the purpose that it was for the concept through which it was brought about. What is purposive in this sense is *coherent;* it coheres with itself, it is *ordered*. As Plato formulates it in the *Gorgias*, everything about it is brought into order; what is different is compelled to join that which is different from it, in order to be adequate and to cohere with it, so that the whole stands in itself as an arranged and well-ordered matter.[28] Everything that is ordered in such a way shows its well-orderedness (κόσμος) as arrangement (τάξις).

But there can also be something coherent without arrangement. The most prominent example is the happy coincidence that is recognized as such; elements have found their way together in such a way that they form an order. That might initially remind one of an arrangement. But if the coincidental formation is recognized as such, it is immediately clear that it is not an arrangement. Something allows itself to be regarded according to the measure of a purpose, and yet one knows at the same time that such a purpose does not exist. Insofar as the notion of a purpose is in play, the order can be described as purposive. In that case it is purposive without a purpose, and that means more precisely: it is of such a kind that its coherence could be called "purposive" if one assumed a purpose. Because the assumption of a definite purpose is out of the question, one also crosses out this purposiveness. But the order indicates where the notion of purposiveness has its place. One only has this notion on the basis of an experience of coherence that is not accessible via the concept of purpose. On the contrary; through order and its possibility an empty space becomes accessible in which every question is inscribed that aims at a definite answer concerning the possibility of something, concerning its purpose and purposiveness. The experience of the coherent that, without ground, is something possible is the experience of beauty.

Kant tries to do justice to this essence of the beautiful—which is not comparable to anything—through his selection of examples: parrots, hummingbirds, birds of paradise, presumably attractive due to their colorful plumage, and "a number of crustaceans from the sea." He also mentions "drawings *à la grecque,* leafwork on trimming or wallpaper"[29] and later adds English gardens and baroque furniture.[30] The examples are unconventional, not least in their conglomeration; indeed, they are too unconventional to be traced back to a harmless preference for the ornamental and decorative. Kant evidently seeks something he could not find in the works of art that were familiar to him.

Gadamer saw with a critical eye what is going on here. For Kant, the only beautiful things are "things of nature into which no human has placed any meaning whatsoever," or "things of human shaping that consciously [withdraw] from any placement of meaning" and are "solely a play of shapes and colors"; in the Kantian sense, art would be less beautiful than design—the "trivial form of decorative handiwork."[31]

This accusation hits upon a decisive point and yet misses what is really decisive. To be sure, Kant's concept of the beautiful is not developed under the aspect of possible "placements of meaning"; what Kant tries to conceive is "beauty free from concepts and meaning."[32] But this does not mean that Kant's understanding of the beautiful is oriented by mundane plays of color and shape. If this were the case, the beautiful could hardly evoke a free play of the cognitive faculties. This play can only be provoked if something is present that can awaken cognition and yet withdraw from the synthesizing possibilities of cognition. It is there in the objects of cognition and yet does not belong to them as a normal property. That is how it is with the plumage of parrots, hummingbirds, and birds of paradise, which in their colorful splendor can induce certain observations and descriptions without these contributing to any further understanding of the birds. One need not even know what kinds of birds they are. "Aside from the botanist, hardly anyone" knows what a flower is, "and even [the botanist]," when he judges "about it through taste [. . .] pays no heed" to this knowledge. The ornament, too, reveals itself in a lightness and elegance without one needing to pay attention to the meaning of that which is decorated with it. The beauty of an English garden, for example the Ilm-park in Weimar, is not found in the inventory of its trees, bushes, and lawns; rather, it is in the fact that these [elements] configure themselves into new images with every point of view. What Kant tries to elucidate with his examples is the coherence within things and among things, which is radically different from their immanent, conceptually graspable order. One is dealing with beauties that are "beauties for themselves" and "belong to no object determined by concepts as to [their] purpose." Instead, these beauties are pleasing "freely and in themselves."[33] They are "free beauties" (B 48, 228). Beauty is an experience of freedom.

This result makes evident how the freedom in the play of cognitive faculties is to be conceived. It can only be prompted by the freedom of the beautiful, which for its part is experienced and brought to bear in the free play of the cognitive faculties. Accordingly, the freedom in the play of the cognitive faculties would have nothing to do with ethical freedom, which Kant conceives as autonomy. To be sure, Kant himself draws this parallel between aesthetic and ethical freedom; he says of aesthetic freedom that, "in looking at objects of such a pure delight," it gives "itself the law" and to that extent the beautiful is to be understood as "the symbol of the ethically good." But the parallel between aesthetic and moral freedom is especially coherent in their distinction: certainly, neither is "subject to [. . .] the heteronomy of laws of experience" (B 258, 353). And indeed, aesthetic and moral freedom are still freedom, since their essence is spontaneity.[34] But spontaneity is not autonomy, and the latter is not found in aesthetic reflection. Aesthetic reflection is a free play without law, and thus the only remaining possibility is to clarify this play's freedom on the basis of the free beauty that is experienced in it.

Kant elucidated free beauty as *pulchritudo vaga*;[35] in its literal sense, it is aimless, erratic, and independent. This distinguishes it from *pulchritudo adhaerens*

(229), which is more perfection than beauty. That is why only in this case can there be an attempt to regulate the judgment of taste by means of an orientation along an "ideal of the beautiful" which, as "archetype of taste," is presented by the imagination. (B 54, 232)[36] This serves as an aesthetic refutation of classicism, even before Hegel, in his alignment with Winckelmann, could raise the latter to the guiding notion of the philosophy of art. Beauty is not cognized by means of an ideal, but in its freedom; by virtue of the fact that something withdraws from regulation because it always only is what it is "for itself," incomparable to anything else.

Kant elaborated this unregulated coherence of the beautiful by means of a natural process he called "free formation" [*freie Bildung*]. What he means is something fluid that congeals in such a way that, "in becoming congealed, [it takes] on a definite shape or fabric (figure or texture)," just as "crystallization" and the formation of similar natural structures in general. (B 249, 348)[37] Of course, one can also designate as free formation what Kant calls an "aesthetic idea" and elucidates by means of poetry. Aesthetic ideas are presentations for which, "as inner intuitions, no concept can be fully adequate" (B 194, 314). An aesthetic idea is a "presentation of the imagination that is connected with such a multitude of partial presentations in their free use that no expression can be found for it which designates a specific concept" (B 197, 316). Kant elaborates this by way of notions like the "kingdom of the blessed," the "realm of hell," "eternity," or "creation" (B 194, 314). In poetic works like Dante's *Divine Comedy* or Milton's *Paradise Lost*, presentations have congealed in a coherent yet unpredictable and undeducible way. The individual presentations complement each other, derive from each other, or join together associatively; they are connected by allusions, similarities, and transfers in a way that is to be discovered and traced, but which can never be conclusively or exhaustively reconstructed. An aesthetic idea, and especially a web thereof, possesses an inner multiplicity that exceeds every notion of homogenous totality.

What Kant says about free formation and aesthetic ideas remains indicative and allusive. It is nevertheless the point at which he most succeeds in presenting the groundless coherence that, in his view, the beautiful is. Besides, Kant's remarks are specific enough to be grasped more exactly and developed in greater detail.

To this end, one should first take up Kant's indication of the fabric-like character of some free formations. A beautiful order never has the character of a shape [*Gestalt*]; it is indeed more like a fabric than a firmly jointed construction, more *horizontal* than vertical—more a mutual interiority and mutual proximity than something strictly and hierarchically ordered. Besides, a beautiful order is *irregular* in the strict sense that no rule underlies it. Kant notes at one point that "everything stiffly regular [has] something about it that is repugnant to taste."[38]

It does not stimulate aesthetic reflection; it may bear insight, but it does not delight. A beautiful order, in its irregularity, can indeed be copied, but it cannot be repeated—as, for example, a geometrical construction. The moments of the order are not derived constructively, but *arose;* it is as if they came about from out of each other or with each other. For this reason, the beautiful order is also never static in the sense that the status of its moments is determined once and for all. Despite all fixity, the order is *variable;* every moment can be assigned in a manifold way, and depending on what other moment one views it from, it can enter into a new coherent correspondence. On the basis of these characteristics, there can be no concept that organizes a beautiful order in a unifying way. The order is to be conceived by way of each of its moments and is therefore *decentered.*

With all of their moments, decentered orders are still *orders.* They can be very exact and specific; one should not confuse decenteredness with vagueness. It is simply a fact about decentered orders that they cannot be cognized at a glance, as it were. One only grasps them by getting involved with them and experiencing them—in a concentrated way and not without rigor—in the coherent multitude of their relations.

Kant grasped the essence of the beautiful as a decentered order with impressive intuition, and he attempted to determine this essence as thoroughly as the philosophical language in his possession allowed. The difficulty of the endeavor lay in the nature of the matter and, paradoxically, in the fact that Kant had a clear awareness of it. Beauty is no modification of truth; it is no exceptional state of things. Because it is *sui generis,* the concepts that apply to things, purposes, or sensations essentially do not apply to the beautiful. Kant showed that beauty can precisely not be attached to things insofar as they are identifiable things. It belongs, rather, on the periphery of things or in their interstices; it does not attach to *what* things are, to their firm, conceptually graspable determinacy. Instead it is located on the surface that is not determined by way of their identical center. This, and not some bizarre preference for the decorative, is the explanation for Kant's examples. It is precisely in these examples that Kant discovers that the world is not exhausted by that in it that is determinable and realizable or accessible with respect to purposes.

This inexhaustibility, this excess (from the point of view of determinate things), the peripheral and decentered aspect of the beautiful, is essential to Kant's systematic aims; it pertains directly to the guiding question of the *Critique of Judgment,* the inquiry into the alignment of human freedom and nature. If one follows Kant's determination of the beautiful, then the situation that "humans belong to the world"[39] is not indicated by beauty mirroring (in the world) human autonomy and the positing of purposes that occurs from freedom. If there were a clearly recognizable purposiveness and conceptual determination in nature that corresponded to human positing of aims and the conceptual access to things that is operative in it, then humans would merely encounter themselves in the foreign. This, in turn, would make superfluous the question regarding the agreement of humans and nature; the question would make as much sense as inquiring about the congruence of a mirror image with its original. There can only be agreement or congruence between what is different, and whose difference is not relativized and ultimately dissolved by retreating to a principle that grounds everything—as occurs after Kant in the absolute speculation of German Idealism. Thus, it is entirely in line with the situation Kant has in mind when he does not bind the agreement of freedom and nature to the notion that subjectively experienced purposiveness occurs by way of transposing real purposes into nature, that is, teleologically. Rather, nature "shows in all of its free formations a great mechanical tendency to produce forms that seem made, as it were, for the aesthetic employment of our power of judgment; and nature gives us no grounds whatever for supposing that [the production of such forms] requires anything more than nature's mechanism—considered as nothing but nature—since nature's mechanism can make these forms purposive for our judging of them even if they are not based on any idea."[40]

When, with regard to the notion of agreement between humans and the natural world, Kant sticks to a purposiveness that makes do without a purpose, this is no philosophical thrift or modesty. On the contrary, despite all speculative restraint, it is the more radical solution over against German Idealism, the solution that delves deeper.[41] The notion of a purposiveness without purpose, as a "purposive congruence that occurs on its own and in a coincidental way,"[42] leads, unlike the transfer of real purposes into the natural world, to just that *"possibility"* that was mentioned in the Introduction to the *Critique of Judgment*. (B xix–xx, 176) Beyond willfully posited purposes, it is not purposes that are "derived" (B 33, 220) and thus gleaned through alignment with the notion of a will, which ultimately render conceivable an agreement of the natural world with the conceptually guided positing of purposes. Instead, it is the decentered orders, as Kant elucidated them by means of "free formations," that do this. Decentered orders of such a type are distinctly different from purposive orders. Precisely for this reason, they explain how purposive orders are possible in the world; they offer a notion of that which makes purposive orders realizable without their being necessary. In other words, what renders the possibility of a "causality" through concepts conceivable is not the concept transferred into the world, but only the empty conceptual space that is indicated by the formula "without purpose"; it is the groundless possibility of decentered orders.

Kant himself does little with the demonstrated agreement between freedom and nature, and indeed he is not obliged to. Through the verification of the agreement, the systematic aim of the *Critique of Judgment* is already fulfilled; Kant does not plan for a further exploration of it. Thus the question remains open of what possibilities for exploration still exist for aesthetic reflection as such. Here, too, Kant was mostly interested in establishing reflection's significance; pursuing the experience of the beautiful in its individual cases no longer belongs within the task of critical philosophy.

Yet such an indication of the task and the thematic scope of the *Critique of Judgment* alone does not do everything to clarify Kant's lack of interest in a more exact determination of aesthetic reflection. It is also significant that, for Kant, aesthetic reflection is unregulated and, as he probably assumes, fundamentally uncontrollable in its enactment. This uncontrollability is all the more bearable when aesthetic reflection is not supposed to be autonomous. As Kant conceives it, reflection joins into social intercourse; he does not envision a systematically driven interpretation of artworks.

The autonomy lacking in aesthetic reflection belongs together with Kant's conception of the beautiful as a "quality" of things. The reflection that is dedicated to the beautiful is as peripheral as the beautiful itself. It is an addition, either of such a sort that it occurs independent of any determination of things and leaves this determination for others, or as a thinking that accompanies the normal conceptual cognition of things and thus remains independent of it. In terms of the former sense, Kant had assured that in order to find a flower beautiful, one need not know what a flower is. In the second sense, he characterizes the aesthetic idea as something that allows one to "add to a concept many unnamable things in thought" and thereby connect "spirit with language as mere letters" (B 197, 316). Thus, that which is thought in aesthetic reflection receives its determinacy solely through the conceptual cognition of its object, to which it only adds "unnamable things" or, as Kant also phrases it less strictly, by unfolding something to which no "determinate thought, that is, *concept*, can be adequate" and that "consequently no language fully reaches" (B 193, 314). The primordial possibility appropriate to aesthetic reflection lies in "spirit" as the "enlivening principle in the mind" (B 192, 313); it accounts for the liveliness of a development of thought.

By proceeding in this way, aesthetic reflection behaves in a way that entirely corresponds to its object, as Kant understands it. That is because an artwork, for Kant, is "a beautiful presentation of a thing" (B 188, 311), or, more precisely, the "beautiful presentation of an object, a presentation that is actually just the form of presentation of a concept through which this concept is universally communicated." An artist presents something conceptual, but in a way that is enriched by "accompanying notions" (B 190, 312) that are merely "associated" with "a given concept." One then grasps the guiding concept in the presentation and communication of this complex of ideas, and the "accompanying notions" (B 196, 316), the aesthetic ideas, give one "a lot to think about" (B 193, 314). This thinking happens in aesthetic reflection.

It should be easy to see that this conception of the matter is not adequate. According to it, one would already grasp what is decisive about a novel such as *War and Peace* through its title, and everything that the novel unfolds as a decentered order of people, relations, events, and reflections would have to be taken as a giant ensemble of "accompanying notions." But the opposite is the case; Tolstoy's novel only delivers to comprehension that which its title announces by being the decentered order that it is, realized as a narrative with people, relations, events, and reflections. The decentered order here is just as little an additional ingredient as in any other poetic work; it *is* the artwork. An artwork is not an ensemble of "accompanying notions" organized around one or several concepts, but instead an autonomous decentered order.

Kant has no term for this autonomy. It has to remain inconceivable to him, because as "quality," the beautiful can never be autonomous. Thus the next step in the discussion of the beautiful leads beyond Kant. Yet this only occurs in order to develop further the determination of the beautiful that we gleaned with Kant. It will turn out that the beautiful is not just a decentered order; it is also *appearance*. Only through a determination of its character of appearing can one also do justice to its ordered character. A decentered order exists by appearing.

Appearances and Things

It is clear to the point of self-evidence what appearances are. They are thus like anything else without which life in the world cannot be led or conceived. It is there, but one can really only say that it is there, while every description seems to slide off of it. It is incomparable. It is simply what it is; it is not derivable or explainable by way of anything else. But all this is a sign that something awaits philosophical reflection and description. These must attempt, by means of the words that surround the self-evident and barely articulable, to illuminate and grasp it in its inner structure. They must dissolve its opaque and dense self-evidence, spread it out and designate its moments. By attempting to grasp something in its structure and to structure it by means of language, one reveals it.

The word "appearance" reminds one of a highlighted presence; something is not simply there amidst other things or even there as belonging to other things, but instead bears the effect of having stepped forward. It stands out from its surroundings, lifts itself off from these, and thereby appears. A painting can be something that appears in this way when it so evidently does not belong to its surroundings that one attends to it and none of the things around it. It can also be the tone of a violin that, in the melody of a Bach sonata, detaches from the accompanying sounds and raises itself above them, also a poem that, as soon as one quietly speaks the first line to oneself, demands a different composure toward language and is thus never simply something said, but is instead language that appears.

To be sure, the appearance of artworks is occasionally dramatic or spectacular, but never overwhelming. It never has the character of "real presence"[43] or epiphany; the burning bush is not an artwork. An appearance can be quite unassuming without disappearing in reticence. Webern's musical miniatures do not appear any less than a lavishly arranged symphony; a quatrain can be more powerfully present than a work of language that arrives in majestic waves of prose. The presence of an approximately hand-sized drawing by Paul Klee outstrips many works of such a gigantic format that were already designed in the studio with the museum wall in mind. And appearances are never sensational; something that must achieve its appearance with effects is not in itself an appearance.

Something's appearance can certainly be the result of an occurrence; in that case, something has come forward and come to appearance. But the appearance itself is not an occurrence. Rather, it lends meaning to that which occurs—as the presence toward which something can occur. It is not in vain that one speaks of something coming to appearance. The possibility of appearance is already there, and then it is fulfilled by something. Appearances do not depend on events; quite often something appears when nothing happens. In rest and stillness, appearance is there undisturbed, and something's character of appearance, such as a sculpture's, can accordingly be all the more powerful without movement, in uniform light, in the expanse of a quiet room.

The fact that artworks are appearances is confirmed in the comportment toward them. The disinterested pleasure that is essential for this comportment can only be explained by its relation to something that is simply there, that thus does not induce any desires of appropriation and that is not available to be used or altered. This is precisely the case with appearances; they are not only present, they are nothing but present. For this reason they are ungraspable, only accessible in looking or listening or reading; they are unreachable because they only are what they are through distance. Besides, as appearance, an artwork is untouchable; anyone who tampers with an artwork does not merely alter it, but damages or destroys it. Even someone who comes too close to an appearance in the false hope of grasping it more precisely can lose it. That which, moments before, had been the facade of a cathedral in bright daylight is suddenly just a diffuse turbulence of oil streaks on a canvas. One cannot master an appearance; one can also not produce it, but at most induce it by creating the conditions of its arising. Things can be appropriated, appearances cannot.

Appearances, as they have been described here, exist. They are not phantasms or hallucinations, nor are they even just inner states. This is especially evident in the way that appearances are present for perception. For what is present in perception must impinge upon it in order to be in it. But perception cannot be equated with impingement. The astounding aspect of perception is that something that impinges upon it is not experienced as an impingement (or not solely as such), but has always already, from the first moment of perception, entered into appearance. A sound affects the sense of hearing and has thus already appeared as audible; something colorful that stands in the light affects the eye and has entered into appearance as visible. Thus what is perceived is no inner image and also no inner presentation; is it something that appears, and that means it exists *in* the appearance, which exists for perception but is not in it. Perception, too, stands in appearance. It is open for appearance and allows itself to be affected by what appears in it; it is only in appearance that that which appears affects perception. Thus, as Aristotle says, the reality of perception and the reality of what is perceived are one and the same, but their being is not the same.[44] They find their common reality in the appearance, which does not mean that appearance as such is a reality.

Thus, insofar as appearances are perceived, *something* is *there* by way of them, and one can refer more or less intelligibly to this. That which appears, then, is as such not independent from the fact that it is perceived. Whereas things, states of affairs, or events can exist without someone pointing them out, something that appears must be there *for someone;* that which appears requires the experience that relates to it, or else it remains an undeveloped possibility. Something might well be there, but it exists as if folded up. It is only when someone comes to it in an experiencing way that it unfolds into appearance.

This unfolding remains dependent upon the respective possibilities of perception and of imagination. Something only ever appears in the way that it can both appear for perception and be placed within the context of other imagined appearances. Yet this does not mean that an appearance would be reduced to its respective givenness. There is no reason to reduce appearances to one respective perception of them, nor even to a perception accomplished by one person. Appearances are not infinitesimal units. They are structured in complex and even rich ways. They can be investigated precisely in this structuring, and the path of inquiry can in turn be communicated and thereby shared with others—under normal circumstances, human cognitive faculties do not differ so vastly as to make this impossible.

Accordingly, the appearance is a complex state of affairs. It includes something that appears and likewise the experience for which it appears. Yet the appearance is, upon closer inspection, not the sum of these two. Each can in turn only be explained, as appearing or as an experience of appearance, by appearance itself. So the appearance is the encompassing dimension into which the two belong. The relatedness of experience (especially perception) to something is essentially an openness to appearance, and that which is experienced, especially the perceivable, only exists in the appearance. The appearance lies between both like an immaterial thread; it is the *third thing* that encompasses both and thus connects them.

The notion of such a third thing stems from Plato. In the *Republic*, vision stands above all other senses by virtue of the fact that there is no immediate connection between it and the visible. Instead, both are connected by something of another kind, by a third thing. This third thing is light, which binds together the sense of sight and the possibility of being seen as if under a yoke.[45] Yet light, as making vision possible, cannot be as strictly distinguished from visible and seen colors as is done here. Even if the eye only sees insofar as it is sensitive to light and thus by being related to the light-giving sun (508b); even if colors must stand in light to be visible—light only brings about the connection between vision and visibility by pervading the colors and, as their glowing, striking the eye in colorful reality as a "gleam."[46] As that which connects, light has always already appeared; it is only insofar as it is in appearance that it has its connecting power, and that means that the connecting power is the power of appearance.

It is difficult to grasp appearance as that which connects. Perhaps this explains the attempt that Socrates makes in the *Republic* of going behind the appearance and grasping its possibility on the basis of something else, namely of light. Insofar as experience stands within appearance, it only seems capable of sustaining itself in the span of individual perception and the certainty of having access to something in this perception. In this span, the appearance can gain varying accentuations—as something that is more an appearance *to me,* or more an appearance of *something*. Yet it only becomes distinct *as* appearance if the subjective appearance and that which appears can retreat and leave the possibility of attending, within the appearance, to the *appearance itself,* namely to the fact that it is an appearance, and along with this attending to its articulation, inner gradations, clarity, and opacity.

This possibility lies in the experience of the beautiful. The beautiful is not just mere appearance; if one follows its traditional determination, it is appearance in its greatest intensity. This is what Plato aims at in the *Phaedrus'* characterization of beauty as ἐκφανέστατον, that is, as something that appears in a manner that cannot be superseded. The term is the superlative of ἐκφανής, which means "brightly glowing" or "shining," and where the prefix ἐκ- denotes this glowing or shining as being complete or fulfilled.[47]

It is precisely this complete having-come-forth, essential to beauty, that Heidegger sought to understand as the way station to truth and that led Gadamer to equate beauty with truth as evidence.[48] Yet the beautiful is neither unconcealment in the sense of ἀλήθεια, nor is it the self-givenness of a thing. When it is said in the *Symposium* of "beauty itself"[49] that it cannot be attached to anything, neither to a countenance nor to anything else that takes part in the body, but also not to a statement (λόγος) nor to a cognition (ἐπιστήμη) (211a), it is clear that the experience of the beautiful lies neither in perception nor in the cognition *of something*, but rather—joining the determination as set forth in the *Phaedrus*—in an appearance that is nothing other than the appearing itself. The *Phaedrus*, too, underscores that beauty is not the sensibly experienceable manifestation of knowledge; beauty is seen, whereas knowing (φρόνησις) is invisible.[50]

The pure appearance with which beauty is equated is thus especially understood in Plato to be independent of what is sensibly or intellectually given. Because the beautiful does not dissolve neatly either into the perceivable or into the thinkable, one can only speak of it *with respect to itself*, and even then only in the appropriate eternal simplicity.[51] To be sure, the *Symposium* also offers a presentation of the path that leads to an experience of beauty itself. (210a–210e). Yet it remains open how beauty itself is to be experienced; there is no answer in Plato to the question of how differently the world appears through the experience of pure appearance, of beauty. Yet such an answer must exist if beauty's intensity of appearance is not just overpowering but also recognizable. It must be recognizable as something that makes cognition possible, thereby making itself known as that-which-makes-possible.

Schiller made a decisive step in this direction in his letters *On the Aesthetic Education of Man*. Moving beyond the essence of beauty, he programmatically developed the possibility of a conduct that is both made possible by the essence of beauty and which can take account of this essence. The aesthetic appearance [*Schein*], as Schiller understands it, is *sui generis*; it is different from "reality and truth," but also from the "logical [. . .] appearance" that can deludingly take the place of reality and truth and thus be "mistaken for them."[52] Yet the aesthetic appearance also no longer bears any relation to what Kant called "appearance." After all, in the appearance as Kant understood it, "the objects, and indeed even the properties that we ascribe to them, are always regarded as something actually given." Thus the object itself is taken "as appearance" and simultaneously distinguished "from the same object as object *in itself*."[53] Appearance is here the appearance *of something*; it is that thing's givenness as conditioned by particular respective possibilities of perception and cognition. Accordingly, the appearance can only ever be grasped as such by way of the object that appears in it. This is where Schiller sets in. As he attempts to show, the aesthetic appearance can free one from confinement in the things that one presumes to be real, and thus also lead to a liberated stance over against that which is normally experienced as reality. Whereas mere sensibility (the "highest stupidity") and conceptual knowledge (the "highest reason") both only sought the "real" [*das Reelle*], the "indifference to the real and the interest in appearance [is] a true expansion of humanity and a decisive step toward culture."[54]

Schiller's indications of how he envisions this culture are sparse yet revealing. Quite along Kant's lines, he understands the "world of appearance" as the "insubstantial realm of imagination." But he views the possibility opened in this realm differently than Kant did: it is not just a creation of secondary presentations that join with a conceptual determination. The imagination in Schiller's sense pertains to presentations in general. It evinces its power in the free variation of these presentations. With "unbound freedom," the human can "join together that which nature separated, as long as he can somehow think it together, [. . .] and separate what nature connected, as long as he can detach it in his reason" (658). Accordingly, the "world of appearance" would be the realm of *possibilities* in which the combination and division of presentations are not bound to the standards of reality.

Schiller leaves open the question of what is gained through this sketched enactment of the power of imagination. He understands its play in the "world of appearance" strictly as a confirmation of human freedom, more precisely as the exercise of "the human right of sovereignty" over against a nature understood as a "foreign power" (658). Accordingly, the "world of appearances" is the community of individuals that encounter each other as no longer being under the reign of natural forces, but instead as having become free through aesthetic education and recognizing each other in their freedom. (cf. 666–667) Yet Schiller does not consider that the aesthetic freedom he develops could have anything to do with a knowledge that adjusts to the varying experience of the possible. In this regard, Schiller remains a Kantian. As for Kant, there is no knowledge in the "realm of appearance" for Schiller; there is only knowledge with respect to reality.

Nevertheless, it is easy to see what is gained through the variation of possibilities: one experiences possibilities as such. One not only sees *that* something can be otherwise, but especially *how* this can be the case, by running through its possible variations in the imagination. This is, in fact, only possible in the "world of appearance." Something actually given is just what it is; one can only attempt to grasp it just as it is and to describe it as well as possible. As soon as one observes something given under the guise of its possibility of being otherwise, one ignores its real givenness. One only takes it as something that appears [*Erscheinendes*], the reality of which is not crucial. It stands as equal next to other variants of appearances, and thus enters the context of possibilities.

Appearances in this sense are *phenomena* in the classical sense of phenomenology as developed by Husserl. He develops what Schiller would never have dared to think: the program of a knowledge that moves entirely within appearances and is precisely thereby an exceptional form of knowledge, as it is superior to knowledge that refers to factually given things. Husserl is concerned with providing a new foundation for philosophical research, and for this reason his project cannot serve in every respect as a guide for the understanding of aesthetic appearances that is at stake here. Yet one can take one's bearings from Husserl's project, not only in order to better understand the cognitive function of appearances, but also for a delineating clarification of beauty in its character of appearing, and especially for a better grasp of the appearing character and cognitive character of art.

This orientation is momentous for the philosophical reflection on beauty and art. When aesthetic appearance [*Schein*], and with it the artwork as appearance [*Erscheinung*], opens up via the phenomenological concept of the phenomenon, aesthetics becomes phenomenology. That, in turn, is a transformation that also affects phenomenology. As we will see, art and aesthetic appearance are no mere cases of application for a universally determinable method of phenomenological observation that would be valid for all possible objects in the same way. Since the phenomenal character of aesthetic appearance, and especially of artworks, embodies and reveals the essence of phenomena in a unique way,[55] phenomenology itself changes through its reference to aesthetic appearance and art. Because aesthetics becomes phenomenology by way of an inner consistency, its objects become decisive for phenomenology. This, in turn, transforms phenomenology.

Husserl took the procedure of free variation—already mentioned above[56]—to be central for phenomenology, as it serves to clarify the "essential form" of intentionality, the fundamental relatedness of every act of consciousness to something. This notion is based on the insight that relating to something never occurs in isolation, but instead always belongs to a multiplicity of possible relations. This "multiplicity of possible perceptions, memories, indeed of any intentional experiences at all, which [is] 'univocally' relatable to one and the same thing," has an "*essential style* [Wesensstil] that is identical for every thing as such," a style that only differs "from individual to individual thing."[57] The essence of a matter, "that which is invariable," "the unbreakably same," only proves to be such in the "otherwise and always-again-otherwise" (254). What a matter essentially is cannot show itself through an isolated relation to it; if one sees something for the first time, one cannot distinguish what belongs to its essence and what is simply a moment of its particular givenness. Only through modification can it become clear what varies and what is not itself a modification. In this way, "essential research" [*Wesensforschung*] in Husserl's sense is always an investigation of possibilities that must clarify the possibilities of relation to a thing, as well as the possibilities of givenness of this thing itself. Every particular relation to something is only understandable within the context of the multiplicity of relations, which is in turn unified through an "essential style." Each relation is a variant that only bears its meaning within the variational whole of an "essential form of the manifold real and possible [. . .] intentionality." The essential form, in turn, corresponds to the "essential kind" (253) [*Wesensart*] of the given matter.[58]

Husserl later designated this sketched mutual dependence of relational possibilities and possibilities of givenness as the "a priori of correlation."[59] He means the originary mutual relation between the "world" and "its subjective modes of givenness" (168). Yet as Husserl already states in *Formal and Transcendental Logic*, the "ontical a priori," that is, something's "essential kind," is only ever possible "as the correlate of an a priori that is concretely united with it, that is concretely indivisible from it."[60] It is only within the complete frame of relational possibilities that something can "constitute" itself in its determinacy, that it can develop and reveal its structure. In the frame of these relational possibilities, then, something gains its validity by being what it is. Husserl does not take "constitution" to be a creative process by which a representation is produced in consciousness, and that would have nothing to do with that which is outside of consciousness. At one point, he even speaks of constitution as the "self-actualization of the object" that occurs "in my activity."[61] Since consciousness, in the a priori of correlation, is essentially related to the world, this world can be there in consciousness.

According to this line of thinking, the concept of phenomenology can be determined more precisely. Something is a phenomenon insofar as it is understood not in its factual givenness, but in its possibility of being given. This possibility, in turn, is always already folded into a multiplicity of possibilities of givenness; these latter possibilities come to bear on the consciousness' possibilities of relating to something. The concept of phenomenon encompasses both aspects: as a phenomenon, something is the intentional correlate of consciousness, and also that which, in the correlation, can appear to consciousness as what it is in the manifold of its possibilities, that is, as itself. Or, put in Husserl's terms: The constitutive and the ontical a priori find their way together in the phenomenon, that is, in the appearance.[62]

However, the phenomenon can only be seen as such by ignoring the factual givenness of both the subjective conditions of appearance and that which appears. Both certainly exist, but when one refers to their factual givenness, one accesses neither the substantiality of the experience nor the determinacy of what is recognized. These only come to bear in the "phenomenological reduction,"[63] namely by being viewed strictly in their phenomenal correlation with one another; neither is what it is without the other, and one must therefore view them in their belonging-together. Yet they belong together within the third thing called "phenomenon," in which both the appearance according to possibilities of consciousness, as well as the appearing thing that is there in consciousness, are always already connected.

Husserl is meticulous in his grasp of this mutuality in the correlation between intentionality and its object. Nevertheless, he always developed it by emphasizing intentionality, the subjective side, and this leads to phenomenology's sometimes appearing to be the internalistic conception of a philosophy of transcendental subjectivity. Yet the transition from a subjective to a correlative conception of phenomenology is fluid. At one point, phenomenology is described as a "science of cognitive phenomena in the double sense, of cognitions as appearances, presentations, acts of consciousness, in which such and such objectivities come to presentation, become raised to consciousness, passive or active, and on the other hand [a science] of these objectivities themselves in their presentation." While Husserl here still conceives of phenomenology's task under the guise of the correlation, in the immediately subsequent elucidation of the concept of phenomenology, he shifts the correlation toward subjectivity. The "word 'phenomenon,'" Husserl states, is "ambiguous due to the essential correlation between *appearing* and *that which appears.*" φαινόμενον "actually [means] 'that which appears'" and is "nevertheless the preferred term for the appearing itself, the subjective phenomenon," if, Husserl adds, "this crude, misunderstandably psychological term may be permitted."[64]

Of course, even if the appearance is not misunderstood to be "psychological," that is, with respect to the factually given acts of consciousness, it is "subjective" for Husserl; it is a process in consciousness, an instance that "has" and presents appearances. From the fact that appearances cannot be experienced without this instance, Husserl seems to conclude that appearances are dependent on consciousness, that there is an ontological primacy of consciousness. In this sense, he speaks in *Ideas I* of consciousness as a "context of being that is closed in itself,"[65] which needs no other matter in order to exist;[66] in *Formal and Transcendental Logic,* everything "outside" is taken to be what it is in the "inside" of consciousness and to have "its *true* being from the self-givings [*Selbstgebungen*] and trials within this interior";[67] in the *Crisis,* Husserl notes of the correlational a priori that the "inclusion of human subjectivity in the problematic of correlation would necessarily force a radical change in the significance of this whole problematic, and must ultimately lead to the phenomenological reduction to absolute transcendental subjectivity."[68]

The distinction of subjectivity that Husserl undertakes here is not obligatory. Indeed, it is even problematic, if one takes seriously the notion of the correlational a priori. The correlational a priori is *symmetrical;* it indicates a relation that allows both relata to be what they are. Accordingly, just as that which appears can be viewed from the angle of its appearing in consciousness, the appearing first proves to be what it is by way of that which appears. Yet this symmetry can only be kept open, if the appearing and that which appears are viewed in their belonging-together. The appearance or phenomenon is a definite presence, open with respect to its contexts, that first permits one to think either of the "subjective phenomenon" of appearing or of the appearing matter. The appearing is what it is through the presence of an appearance; that which appears is what it is in its presence as appearance.

Although Husserl's distinction of appearing and thus of consciousness violates the idea of the correlation, it is still understandable. It seems to be demanded by the essence of phenomena themselves. If phenomena are possibilities that can only be adequately experienced through free variation, there does not seem to be any other choice. Phenomena in this sense can apparently only be given in representation, that is, through the imagination, or as Husserl puts it, through phantasy.

Husserl elaborated this through the example of geometry and took this example to be analogous to phenomenology in such a way that everything that is shown in geometry is also valid for the phenomenological relation to phenomena. "In his researching thought, [the geometer operates] incomparably more on the figure or model in phantasy than in perception." Phantasy offers the geometer "incomparable freedom in the arbitrary transformation of simulated figures, in the running-through of continuously modified possible formations, i.e. in the generation of a myriad of new structures." This is a freedom that first gives the geometer "access to the vast reaches of essential possibilities with their infinite horizons of essential cognition." Compared to this givenness in the geometer's phantastical activity, the fixedly drawn figures generated through variation are secondary. The drawings "normally [follow] the phantasy-constructions and the eidetic pure thinking that occurs on their basis"; they serve "mainly to fixate stages of the previously accomplished procedure, and thereby to bring it to presence more easily."[69]

Yet the procedure of a free variation that forgoes fixation is associated with a danger that Husserl himself addresses indirectly. "In phantasy," the geometer must "aim at clear depictions, of which the drawing and the model" relieve him. (147) Appearances that are merely imagined are thus often unclear. The more complex they are, the more difficult they are to grasp. If one does not stabilize them, they alter and shift into other appearances. As long as they only exist in consciousness, they are also governed by the dynamics of the consciousness process and easily dissolve into the continuum of appearances that are part of this process. After all, insofar as the process of consciousness "stretches into a horizon of open endless manifold free possibilities of ever new variants,"[70] it has the tendency to lose itself in the boundlessness of variation and thus in the infinite. It is the unlimitedness of the consciousness process itself that, observed in itself, is a pure occurrence. The phenomena that were actually intended to be clarified through this process are carried along in it like flotsam and sink in its amorphous flowing.

Husserl must have seen this danger; otherwise one cannot explain the fact that he takes the clarity and distinctness of phantastical presentations to be special tasks. The key is to "prolifically train the phantasy in the complete clarification demanded here." Phantasy must work against its own unboundedness so that it can do justice to the phenomena that it seeks to investigate.

This consideration leads back to the discussion of aesthetic appearance and art. After all, as Husserl emphasizes, art gains a leading significance for the practice of phantasy. The latter can draw "an extraordinary amount of use" from the "offerings of history, to an even higher degree from those of art and especially poetry." To be sure, these are "figments," but "with respect to the originality of new formations, the plenitude of individual traits, the completeness of motivation, [they rise high] above the achievements of our own phantasy." They are also superior "on the basis of the suggestive power of artistic means of presentation," through which poetic creations, "when grasped comprehendingly, [become] completely clear phantasies with considerable ease." Husserl concludes this thought by virtually determining art as the role model for phenomenological research. If one loves "paradoxical speeches" and grasps "ambiguous meaning," one can say "in strict truth that 'fiction' is the living element of phenomenology and of all eidetic science"; it is the "source [. . .] from which knowledge of 'eternal truths' [draws] its sustenance."[71]

Husserl's declaration has all the more weight as it is one of the few statements on art he ever made. It is the only one found in a published work. Artworks are certainly present in many of his investigations, especially those on image consciousness and the experience of time. But unlike in the thoughts cited above, in these cases the concern is not with the art-character of art, and certainly not with relating this character to phenomenological research. Although Husserl's consideration remains quite general, its decisive idea is clear enough. Art, and especially poetry, is capable of mediating "clear phantasies," because it uses "suggestive means of presentation." The artistic and especially the poetic phantasies are thus clear *on the basis of their presentation,* that is, because they have been lifted out of consciousness' continuous process of variation and become determined. Only thus, through fixation in the artwork, can the "plenitude of individual traits" and the "completeness of motivation," that is, the coherent connection of phantasized possibilities, be recognized.

One can proceed one step further in the coherent train of his thought. It is only by being fixed in the artwork that Husserl's so-called "phantasies" are constituted as that which they actually are; it is strictly their fixation that unfolds them as appearances or phenomena in phenomenology's sense. It is not until they gain "self-realization" or independence in the artwork—a position that permits them to be distinguished from subjective appearing—that they can be observed as themselves. The appearances of an artwork are liberated and set apart from the subjective appearing. They no longer belong to an artist's stream of consciousness, in which they would be malleable first in this way and then in that; in the artwork, they have instead found a determinacy and designation in which they can clearly and distinctly be what they are: possibilities that can be recognized in the context of other possibilities.

Yet the appearances in the artwork are not separated solely from the subjective appearing. They equally allow one to ignore the factual givenness of what appears and thereby fulfill precisely that condition of being accessible as pure appearances that Husserl took to be fulfilled by the immanence in consciousness. Once, in a letter to Hugo von Hofmannsthal from January 12, 1907, Husserl goes into this phenomenological significance of artworks. He writes that artworks, on their part, induce an attitude that is very similar to the phenomenological attitude. The "intuition of a *pure* aesthetic artwork" occurs "by way of strict elimination of any existential reaction on the part of the intellect, and any reaction on the part of the emotions or the will that would [presuppose] such an existential reaction." Husserl sees this as grounded in the artworks themselves. In his view, the artwork "induces (virtually forces us into) the state of pure aesthetic intuition that rules out any taking of a position."[72] But Husserl does not pursue this thought any further. Instead of holding onto the way that artworks condition aesthetic intuition, he emphasizes the proximity of "phenomenological seeing" and "aesthetic seeing in 'pure' art," without attributing any status of knowledge to the latter. Aesthetic experience is far more of an enjoyment to him or, in the case of the artist, an intuitive appropriation of the "phenomenon of the world [. . .] in order to glean from this [the] abundance of formations, materials for creative composition."[73]

Husserl's indication of the phenomenological significance of the artwork is helpful and deserves to be worked out. It allows the pure appearances of the artwork to be grasped adequately, which means to be understood in their cognitive value. The fact that artworks are pure appearances does not mean that what appears in them does not exist for the experience of art. Art does not displace one into a world of appearances that has nothing to do with the real world. Artworks are not "fictional," if by this one understands not only a composition or formation, but an invention. The term "fiction," which Husserl himself uses, is misleading because it suggests that everything that belongs to an artwork must be invented and its reality merely feigned. But that is evidently not the case; Titian's equestrian portrait of Charles V does not invent the depicted king. But it also does not refer to him in such a way that the portrait would only be adequately understood through an engagement with the king as a historical figure. Rather, what is true of everything that is observed phenomenologically is also valid for that which appears in the artwork: it is "bracketed" in its real givenness, it is set in ἐποχή.[74] A city in a novel, for example—Paris in Proust's *In Search of Lost Time*, Vienna in Heimito von Doderer's *Strudlhof Steps*, Boston in Henry James' *Bostonians*—is nothing but appearance. One knows that Paris, Vienna, or Boston exist, but insofar as one reads the novel as an artwork and not as a cultural document, one will not refer its depictions to the real cities. These cities exist, but the supposition of this reality is abrogated in the novel. The reading of a novel, in other words, is not guided by the thesis that Husserl calls the "natural attitude." What is described in a novel when one reads it as a novel is not "conscious as 'reality' that exists"; it does not carry "the character of 'there,' of 'present-at-hand.'"[75] To be sure, Proust invented the rue du Faubourg St. Honoré just as little as Doderer invented the Alsergrund district of Vienna or James invented Charles Street;[76] none of these authors replaces the real world with an invented one. Yet the question concerning the reality of these locations is not important; it is not a condition for understanding the novel, and the same thing applies here that Husserl reserved for immanence in consciousness: it needs nothing besides itself to exist.[77]

This lack of importance for the novel of what is really given can be indicated in the novel itself. For instance, locations that occur in the novel can remain anonymous or, even if they could be clearly identified, can be named differently. Because the reality of the town of Illiers is not crucial, Proust's novel transforms it into "Combray."[78] Whatever is not tied back to a factual givenness can be varied. Art does not invent an artificial world, but it does also not stand under the compulsion of reality; derivations, embeddings, and new combinations are possible. It is not without irony that Dorothy Sayers, in her novel *Gaudy Night*, places Shrewsbury College on the cricket ground of Balliol College. One can reconstruct many real "role models" for a figure like the Marquis of Saint-Loup in Proust.[79] Picasso, in his images, takes the human form apart in painterly variation and puts it back together in a way that is adequate to the appearance of the image.

The fact that artworks are appearances in the sense elaborated here does not depend on the attitude of the observer. Contrary to phenomenological observation, in which one must switch from the "natural" to the "phenomenological" attitude, there is no aesthetic attitude that is decisive for artworks' character of appearance. As Husserl writes to von Hofmannsthal, the artwork "virtually forces" the attitude that one takes toward it. Yet when this attitude is phenomenological, the artworks are no random correlates for phenomenological observation. They are not things initially given in the natural attitude that then become phenomena through the phenomenologically enacted ἐποχή. Artworks *are* phenomena; they are pure appearances that neither belong within subjective appearance nor that derive what they are from that which appears. They do not belong within the enactment of eidetic thinking, and the natural attitude that takes them as real givens fails to grasp their essence. Artworks are appearances in themselves. This is also the reason why one does not need a trained phenomenological gaze to recognize them as such. Insofar as artworks can be experienced as artworks on their own, they open up a phenomenally oriented and simultaneously prephenomenological attitude that can then be developed phenomenologically in conceptual reflection.

Precisely because the phenomenal character of artworks do not first become evident through phenomenological observation, they are predestined for this type of observation; they are the only phenomena that the phenomenological observer comes across in such a way that he or she can rely on "originally giving intuition" in order to recognize them as phenomena.[80] Artworks are phenomena par excellence, because they are evidently phenomena for their own part. In this way, they evince the *possibility* of phenomenology; not least by virtue of their setting their own independent phenomenality over against phenomenological observation. Because the appearances of artworks are fixed, they cannot be freely varied without missing the mark of the works as such. A novel, for example, cannot be extended through variation, modification, or continuation of the story as told; one must take the novel as the work that it is. The observer is cut off from that which is realized in the artwork, the free variation of givens that have become appearances.

Despite their resistance to free variation, the art's appearances are possibilities in the full sense of Husserl's understanding of phenomena. The story, for instance, that is told in a novel *can be;* something could occur or could have occurred just as it is told. If the novel is understood as an artwork (in other words, in its character of appearance), one takes the story in precisely this sense; one takes it as a possibility of occurrence with respect to which the question of fact or actual occurrence does not even arise. It is not the reconstruction of occurrence that is revealing, the unpacking of the states of affairs, or the persons involved; rather, what is revealing is just the possibility that the novel presents as an appearance. As the reality of an occurrence is not what matters, the novel's appearance allows one to understand its structure through the sequence, the motivation, and the relation of characters to one another. The novel develops the *inner possibility* of the occurrence such that one understands *how* that which is told can exist in the interplay of events, people, and places. In a novel, as pure appearance of the possible, the recounted story becomes transparent as such.

It is in this sense that Aristotle determined the topic of poetry to be the possible (τὸ δυνατόν).[81] The task of the poet is not to bring to language that which has occurred, but instead those ways in which something may occur, in other words, the possible in its possibility or necessity, or, as one might add, in its plausibility and its inner stringency.[82] That is why poetry is more philosophical and more valuable than historiography; it deals more with the universal, whereas historiography brings to language the particular.[83] Poetry offers appearances, in other words possibilities of what can be. It does not detach itself from the factual by grasping this universally in concepts, but it also does not hold itself to the particulars of a factual givenness. It stands in the middle by being more general than the depiction of what has happened and yet more concrete than any general determination. Contrary to the concept's general determination, poetry aims at the particular without taking it as the factually given in each case; it presents it as a particular possibility that is certainly not exemplary, but is rather unfolded in itself, as an inner possibility of the particular. Poetry can make the particular's structure transparent in a way that is inaccessible both to the concept and to the description of the factually given.

Poetry's capacity of structural disclosure—and one can extend Aristotle's point to art as such—rests upon the fixity and immutability of the works. It is only through these that structures become accessible in a way that is not available to the free variation of consciousness. Since free variation continually proceeds, it can certainly transform possibilities and thereby discover new ones. Yet the simultaneous observation of possibilities in the process of consciousness is extremely difficult, if not downright impossible. Husserl himself indicates that earlier stages of variation are more easily brought to presence through fixation.[84] But over and above this, through their fixation these stages enter into a context that they do not and could not have in consciousness. In the artwork, fixed appearances become moments of an *appearance-framework* or, what amounts to the same, of a structured, complex appearance. Thus, the inner context of a story told in a novel is understandable in a manner that is barely matched by verbal reporting and which after a certain point of complexity can no longer be reached in this way. Because the story told in a novel, in its written fixation, is accessible at any time and in any of its moments, in theory all events, situations, motives, and people can be related to one another. The same is true of a musical score and especially for an image, whose complete presence allows one to see each of its moments in relation to every other.

Yet this relatedness is determined solely through the framework of moments. As long as the framework persists as a multitude of moments of appearance that are related to each other in various ways, the moments are not reducible to any unity that encompasses them. As possibilities, they are also always possibilities of relation, which are codetermined by the possibilities to which they relate. They are therefore determined differently according to each relation, yet without losing their identity. Thus a figure in a novel is understood differently according to which other figures, situations, things, or motives one sees it as relating to; a patch of color in a painting evinces itself as different, or at least differently accentuated, according to the other surfaces with which one sees it in relation. On the basis of the framework in which they stand, the possibilities in an artwork cannot be viewed with respect to some invariant essence that would surface through them. What can be experienced as a unified matter in a novel or a play, for example love and marriage in Goethe's *Elective Affinities,* or jealousy in Shakespeare's *Othello,* only exists in "repeated mirrorings"[85] and not as a conceptually determined unity of essence. For just therein lies the power of art over conceptual thinking. It can be said in a general manner what love and marriage or jealousy are. But that which makes up their inner possibility as such, how the latter can develop in certain situations and in constellations of individuals, how it can manifest itself as a possibility of life: this one only experiences through art. Because artworks, to use Aristotle's words, offer neither general concepts nor descriptions of the factually particular, there is no encompassing unity by which they are organized, but there is also nothing that factually appears to which their appearances would be related. Artworks are frameworks of appearance and, as such, *decentered orders.* Their peculiar evidence and beauty lies in the fact that they are decentered orders of appearances, and thus appearing decentered orders.

The decentered order of an appearance-framework only exists in some fixation. Conversely, the character of this order as a simultaneous inner relationality offers some clarity as to how the fixation is to be understood. The latter cannot be of the same kind as the geometrical drawings elaborated by Husserl; the fixation we are concerned with does not follow some consciousness process that would be divided into "clear intuitions"[86] and that would only be captured, externalized, and made accessible through symbols of some kind. The simultaneous inner relationality of artworks is rather first established through fixation. A work of poetry does not first exist in the author's imagination, only to be subsequently linguistically articulated for the sake of communication; rather, the work only exists in language, just as a painting does not exist in the mind of the painter, but solely on the canvas. It is only in language, in the image, and in music that the order of an artwork takes shape. The order thereby stands over against the process of consciousness that in many respects guides and coordinates the work's creation. The appearances that are artworks, as we have already mentioned, can only be instigated, not produced.[87] Thus the more determinately an artwork comes to presence, the more clearly it detaches itself from the consciousness of the artist. Accordingly, its linguistic, imagistic, or musical form cannot be taken as an instruction on how to repeat its "originary production" by "actively re-understanding" it.[88] Rather, for the person who understands, the artwork is what it also became for the artist in its coming-to-presence: it is an *object* [*Gegenstand*] in the precise sense that it stands over against [*entgegensteht*] one, and can only be adequately understood in its standing-over-against [*Entgegenstehen*].[89]

The fact that artworks are objects also means that they are not simply object-like [*gegenständlich*]. Anything can become object-like that, in its standing-over, possesses the possibility of pressing the understanding in such a way that one must do justice to the thing in its independence. Something is always object-like when it does not belong within a familiar context of significance and meaning and thereby manifests itself as what it is. Objects in this sense are essentially object-like; they cannot be otherwise than object-like. It belongs to the artwork to be an object.

The object character of artworks is given along with the determinations that we have already developed. It arises from the essential properties designated in these determinations. These together make up the eminent objectivity [*Gegenständlichkeit*] of artworks. Accordingly, artworks are objects as appearance-frameworks in decentered orders, which are fixed as such and can therefore be experienced in "originarily giving intuition." Artworks are seen or heard, more seldomly felt, but never tasted; their fixity is irreconcilable with consumption. Nevertheless, scent can belong to an artwork; Wolfgang Laib's wax rooms[90] and Josef Beuys' *Olive Stones*[91] are examples of this.

In their fixity, artworks are *thing-like;* they only have existence in the world through thing-like persistence. It is not only images, sculptures, or buildings that are thing-like; the same applies to poems and compositions that would not exist without written fixation.[92] Music is thing-like when it does not sound without instruments. Even if one might hesitate to call spoken poetry, sung music, or dance thing-like, these works have a thing-like presence in a further sense. Insofar as one takes them to be artworks, they are not taken to be expressions of individuals. To be sure, they are performed by individuals, but it belongs to the essence of the performance that the performers instigate a presence that is not their own. They de-individualize themselves, and in a fully conscious and recognizably enacted process of interpretation, they become "persons" through whom something "resounds" in an instrumental, thing-like way that is quite akin to things. This becomes audible in the trained "artistic" voice, and it becomes visible in costume—especially impressive in the masks of Greek tragedy and of Japanese No theater, in the figures of Oskar Schlemmer's *Triadic Ballet*.

If one expands the conception of things far enough, artworks can be understood as *appearing things* [*Erscheinungsdinge*]. They possess thing-like reality in their own ways, yet this reality dissolves in their appearance. As appearing things, artworks are bound in a thing-like fashion; they are appearances that are actualized in a thing-like way. In this way, artworks are unique; they are the only phenomena that are thing-like as such. Whereas appearances—as the third that connects subjective appearance and that which appears—are otherwise unthing-like, artworks stand amidst things as appearances.

Appearances are possibilities. While the possible is typically concealed in things, and only holds any sway through the anticipation of the reality that would fulfill it,[93] in artworks it is directly perceivable and immediately understandable. A literary narrative does not report events that actually occurred, but instead realizes the complex possibility of a framework of places, situations, occurrences, people, and their relations. A painting does not depict anything factually given, but rather realizes a possible arrangement of color and form that, as such, can be understood. Music does not make anything factual audible, but instead just a harmonious possibility of notes and sounds.

The possibilities, that is, the appearances in the artwork, are fixed as decentered orders. Beyond art, decentered orders only exist on the periphery of things, never in such a way that they make up these things' thinghood. To use Kant's account, they show up as "free formations," or are experienced as more or less coincidental arrangements of things that stand out in their form. Thus, if one follows Kant's distinction between free and dependent beauty, the former only ever exists *on* things, and is never the beauty *of* the things. Artworks, on the other hand, are thing-like formations that are decentered orders as such; they are formations of free beauty that stand over against one in their beauty as appearances.

As appearing things, artworks are simultaneously perceived and understood. That is because the appearances that can be understood exist within what is perceivable. What is to be understood in a story only exists in the language that is audible and visible as writing; the understandable aspect of an image is in color just as the understandable part of a piece of music is in the sound. Whoever wishes to understand artworks must look or listen very precisely; the understandability is always already at play in hearing and seeing, and it is strictly because of this that they both play toward each other in the "free play of the cognitive faculties." The mutual interpenetration of perceivability and understandability always confirms anew that the appearances of artworks are given in a thing-like manner, and conversely that everything thing-like about artworks is an appearance. Art's appearance is not detachable from its perceivability as a product of phantasy; as soon as such a phantastical object is formed, its appearance is strictly speaking no longer that of an artwork. The reflection that tries to rely solely on phantasy and memory quickly becomes groundless. Thus, if it is guided by an insight into the essence of artworks, it always pushes back to hearing, seeing, and reading. This lends the concept of appearance a characteristic ambiguity in relation to artworks: *An artwork is only ever an appearance if it itself is that which appears.* Artworks are the only appearances that, as such, are simultaneously that which appears.

The state of affairs is evident, but it is difficult to grasp it conceptually because typically the appearance, as possibility, is only possible through a "bracketing" of that which appears. This, in turn, easily leads to the problematic conclusion that the appearance, as understandable possibility, is detachable from the artwork that actually appears, and that the latter is a carrier of an imaginable or imagined appearance.

In pursuing this problem, Husserl distinguished between "image-thing" and "image-object" in one of his reflections on image perception.[94] Whereas the image-thing is the actually given object, for example the painting realized as oils on canvas, that image-object has the character of an "image-fiction"; it is "an appearance raised up [*aufgehoben*] into itself," where "appearance" is taken here in the sense of that which appears.[95] The image-object is not taken to be something real and is thus not "illusory." It is perceived, and yet is not a perception in the usual sense because it "cannot bear the positing of reality" (490). What is perceived is strictly only the image-thing. It functions, in Husserl's estimation, as a "substrate, an image-substrate for an image in the narrow sense"; it is the "designated actuator for a specific image-appearance that is precisely the appearance of this image" (492). Husserl in turn takes this function to be "a kind of sign-relation," "a kind of relation of indication and reference" (491); the image-thing has a "meaning," and it lies "in the image, namely in that image-object that [appears] in a certain orientation of the image-thing" (492).

Husserl's attempt to grasp this relation, the relation between the image in its real givenness and the "image-object," as a relation of signs or meaning, is not persuasive. The actually given image does not stand for a meaning as a straight white arrow on a blue background stands for the order to only drive straight. Furthermore, the actually given image does not refer to the "image-object," and it is certainly not the case that one would need to "nullify" the actually given image in its givenness in order to see that which Husserl calls the "image-object."⁹⁶ The "image-object" is instead directly there with the actually given image. It is there *as image* and is understood as image. Malevich's *Black Square on White Background*⁹⁷ does not refer to a black square, but instead *is* an imagistically given black square.⁹⁸ Similarly, Titian's painting in the Prado does not refer to a portrait of Charles V, but rather *is* this portrait. One would have to view the "image-thing" in quite a strange way—for example, as if its surface were mirrored—to not immediately take it to be an "image-object." Husserl himself indicates that the "image-thing" does not stand out in its thingness when viewed in a "normal position."⁹⁹ But this does not go for just one specific image; nearly everything can be viewed in such a way that one does not know what it is. Yet as soon as one recognizes an "image-thing" as such, one has simultaneously seen the "image-object."

The mutual belonging-together of "thing" and "object" does not exist solely in visual art. Even the sentences of a novel do not refer to a story, but are the story; the sounding of the orchestra in the second movement of Bruckner's Seventh Symphony does not refer to the tension between sustained rest and dramatic eruption; rather, this tension is there in the orchestra's sound.

It was Merleau-Ponty who saw the peculiar interpenetration of appearance and what appears in the artwork as a philosophical challenge. Even in his late fragmentary work *The Visible and the Invisible,* the question of the "bond" between the visible and the "inner machinery" that allows it to become manifest and conceals it counts as the most difficult question for a phenomenology of the perceivable, which is also to be a phenomenology of meaning.¹⁰⁰ The difficulty concerns the inseparability of invisible "ideas" from that which is perceivable. Merleau-Ponty had already made clear in his *Phenomenology of Perception* what he would take as an adequate description of the relation between "ideal" appearance and factual appearing to be: he sees it in analogy to the human body. In *Phenomenology of Perception,* Merleau-Ponty wants to clarify the body by way of the artwork, whereas his later reflections on the conception of the unity of "ideas" and perceivability are oriented by the phenomenon of the body. The body, according to the early Merleau-Ponty, is not a physical object, but rather, like the artwork, is a nodal point of living significations;¹⁰¹ like an artwork, it is an individual being, a being in which one cannot distinguish between expression and expressed, and whose meaning is only accessible in direct contact.¹⁰²

Merleau-Ponty later finds the indistinguishability of expression and expressed realized in the nature of the body, and to such a degree that it not only has to be declared an indistinguishability but can even be considered as "reversibility." This reversibility is, to begin with, a dual determination of perception which Merleau-Ponty elaborates by way of a state of affairs first described by Husserl: the hand that touches something is itself touchable.[103] Yet whereas Husserl only sees in this touchability the possibility of a localization of sensations, for Merleau-Ponty it becomes evidence of the relation to something as such. The relation to anything is only possible because the relating belongs to the same world as its correlate. The touch can only occur if my hand that touches something is also accessible from the outside, is itself touchable, for example by my other hand.[104] It is because the touching and the touchability "cross over"[105] in the hand that there is touch.

In dissent from Husserl,[106] this relation is transferred not only to vision, but to language as well. Just as seeing itself must be visible in order to be vision,[107] so, in Merleau-Ponty's view, the meaning of sounded speech must be transformable back into the sounded speech itself. The meaning radiates back to its means and appropriates speech to itself, and this is possible because speech has always already opened itself to the meaning that comes back to it. (202) Whoever wishes to understand a spoken utterance can stick to the sounding and audible speech; its meaning is revealed through that which one hears. This, for Merleau-Ponty, shows the intertwining of meaning and the sensibly perceivable. It is evinced in the reversibility between speaking as the articulation of meanings on the one hand, and being heard on the other; for Merleau-Ponty, this is structurally the same reversibility as that between touching and being touched, of seeing and being seen. Thus, reversibility is also the "ultimate truth"[108] with respect to the interpenetration of perceivability and understandability as well.

In one sense, Merleau-Ponty's description of speech is plausible. Perception and understanding do indeed belong together; one does not arbitrarily connect what one perceives, for instance hears, with a meaning; instead, it *has* meaning that is perceived in hearing.[109] On the other hand, however, the description is not specific enough. The meaning of an utterance is not guaranteed by way of its audibility; the audible, or the perceivable in general, must be of a certain makeup in order to be experienced as meaningful. This is not captured in the idea of reversibility. This idea only captures the notion that the "ideal" meaning and the perceivable articulation of meaning are intertwined. But it remains open how this intertwining is to be understood. To clarify this, one has to state *how* something perceivable must be such that it not only connects to a meaning, but such that one can perceive it as meaningful in itself.

This question remains unnoticed in Merleau-Ponty, as he attaches the issue of the intertwining of perceivability and meaning solely to the question of the essence of the relation to something and thus to the process of meaning articulation. Against Husserl's notion of a pure reflection that occurs in phantasy,

Merleau-Ponty wants to demonstrate the phenomenological unavoidability of embodied being.[110] What matters for him is the corporeality of the relation to something, the intentionality and the reflection, such that the question of a perceivable thing's constitution as meaningful in itself, something perceivable with meaning in itself, does not arise. The notion of reversibility shifts the free gaze toward something that is experienceable in it, because according to this, anything that is perceivable and simultaneously graspable in its meaning immediately reenters the process of perception and meaning articulation. If this idea is the "ultimate truth" about the perceivable and meaningful world, then the perceivable and meaningful must also always be perceiving and articulating meaning. Then the perceiving, meaning-articulating relation to something is a gaze into a mirror, in which one only ever encounters the relation as a relation. Merleau-Ponty indeed once compared perception to such a mirroring. It is like two mirrors facing each other, "in which two infinite rows of interlaced images face each other, which in truth belong to neither of the two surfaces, as each is only a reply to the other, and thus both together form a pair that is more real than either one of them separately."[111]

The corporeality of human life that guides Merleau-Ponty's work from the *Phenomenology of Perception* onwards cannot be adequately grasped with the notion of reversibility. This becomes especially evident with regard to expressive behavior. To be sure, another human being is as perceivable and understandable to oneself as one is to them; and indeed, another's expressive behavior is always such that one can always respond through one's own expressive acts. But there is an asymmetry at work in this mutuality that Merleau-Ponty does not consider: one does not perceive the perception and expression of another human being in the same way that one undertakes perception and expression oneself; perception and the perceived perception are as distinct as the expression on the one hand and the perceived and understood expression on the other. As concerns perception, the asymmetry determined by distance is apparent. One does not see the vision of another person; one instead sees someone who sees. One does not hear the hearing of another, but rather someone who hears. This is the case, for instance, when the other answers a call; in hearing their answer, one understands that the other has heard the call. Perception and the understanding of expression are just as asymmetrical. By seeing another's countenance or expressive posture, one has access to something that one does not see in oneself, and that one certainly does not have to understand. The corporeal expression is only perceivable and understandable as an *appearance of something that appears,* an appearance that is distinct from one's own perceiving and understanding. Accordingly, the interlacing of appearance and what appears cannot be grasped by way of corporeality and embodied expression. Rather, the discussion of corporeality and embodied expression refers one to the question concerning the interpenetration of appearance and what appears.

Showing and Self-Showing

The interpenetration of appearance and what appears can be understood *deictically*. In order to develop this notion, one can extend Merleau-Ponty's considerations. Even though they are lacking, they make evident that the relation of appearance and what appears is not to be understood along the lines of the relation between meaning and its carrier. Someone who expresses pain through a gesture, for example, is not a carrier of meaning who, by whatever means, communicates this meaning. Rather, this person *is* in the state of pain. The gesture is not the pain, but comes out of it and communicates it. Yet what it communicates is not an independent meaning that would be separable from this person, and which could be labeled with the word "pain"; what it communicates is the pain of this person. Nevertheless, that which is expressed through the gesture is something nameable that can be differentiated from the person who performs the gesture. The gesture has a meaning, but this meaning is bound to the person who performs it.

It is precisely in this respect that the described state of affairs is deictic. The expression is a showing that is internally differentiated; it only exists as a *deictic difference*. The expression *shows something*, but this occurs in such a way that *in the expression, someone shows themselves*. The showing and self-showing belong together in the expression, such that the one is not possible without the other. One can only show oneself in the expression if one expresses something; one can only show something expressively by showing oneself. Whoever shows themselves steps into appearance—not in an undifferentiated, simple fashion, but rather in a determinate appearance like that of the pain. The appearance of the pain, in turn, is that of someone that appears. Someone appears in an appearance that solely occurs through them, through a determinate gesture. The gesture shows something by giving it presence; it allows this determinate thing to be accessible. Yet the gesture's showing is not an indication; it is not directed at something that would be there independent of it and that would only rise to attention because of it. The gesture instead presents; it presents by means of itself. That which comes to expression in the gesture is in the gesture. And as the gesture is not separate from the person who performs it, that which the gesture shows is in this person who, by showing, shows themselves. It is in this sense of showing that the expression has its phenomenality. The expression is perceived and understood in this deictic phenomenality.

Even if the deictic essence of phenomenality can be demonstrated by means of the expression, the latter is not a universally binding model for the comprehension of phenomenality. On the contrary, it is the deictic determination of phenomenality that is universally valid, if one follows the determination of phenomenality Heidegger gives in *Being and Time*. Heidegger gleans this determination by way of the Greek term φαινόμενον, which he translates as "that which shows itself." The meaning of "phenomenon" is thus "to be captured as: that which shows itself by way of itself."[112] Thus phenomena are determined in their phenomenality by self-showing.

One may detect in Heidegger's delineation of the phenomenon a silent reference to Husserl's determination, in which the phenomenon was grasped through the appearance in consciousness. It is not the "subjective correlate" that makes something a phenomenon, but the fact that it is there "in itself." Yet Heidegger limits this "in-itself" by binding it to the necessity of exhibition [*Aufweisung*]. According to Heidegger, phenomena only have to become thematic for phenomenology because they require "explicit exhibition." This, in turn, only applies to that which "initially and for the most part precisely does *not* show itself, which is *concealed* over against that which initially and usually shows itself" (47). Something only reveals itself to be self-showing in itself, and thus a phenomenon, by being "explicitly" shown.

One reason for this more precise determination of the phenomenon is evident; if phenomena were automatically accessible, phenomenology would not be necessary. This does not overrule the basic determination of the phenomenon as that which shows itself in itself. The showing entailed in phenomenology is only possible by taking into account the self-showing of what is shown; phenomenology is fulfilled in the shown thing's self-showing in itself. It is only in this self-showing in itself that phenomenology has its meaning.

Yet Heidegger's more exact determination of the phenomenon stems from another motive as well. It is not just that he wishes to legitimize phenomenology by taking phenomena to be more than simple revealed entities. He also aims to clarify why a phenomenon can be experienced as such to begin with. This is motivated by a dissatisfaction with the arbitrariness by which Husserl conceived the transition from the natural to the phenomenological attitude. Ever since his first lecture after World War I, Heidegger takes Husserl's conception of phenomenology to stand under the "governance"[113] of the theoretical, and thus to miss the originary access to the phenomenon. If phenomena do not already reveal themselves through a change in attitude, as Husserl thought—such that anything would be a phenomenon that reveals itself through a bracketing of factual givenness—then the essence of phenomena, their phenomenality, must be discernible by other means. This is especially the case if phenomena are not conceived in the sense of the "vulgar concept of phenomenon," as something that is "accessible in Kant's sense of empirical intuition."[114] Heidegger takes the discernibility of non-"vulgar" phenomena to be ensured through their stepping forth out of concealment. A phenomenon is something that is not simply there, but that instead shows itself in an eminent way in this stepping-forth. Heidegger persisted with this thought over the decades of his thinking. He formulated it most distinctly in his understanding of truth as unconcealment (ἀλήθεια).

The notion that phenomena reveal themselves as such by stepping forth from concealment may be understandable. They are there in an eminent way because they show themselves in their stepping-forth. Yet at the same time, the determination is problematic; if phenomena were determined by their stepping-forth, having stepped forth they would no longer be phenomena. Phenomenology in Heidegger's sense would lose its correlates in the same moment in which it fulfilled its showing task. Heidegger's determination can only be saved if one takes phenomenality to be a state of exception, as a lighting up or flashing that delivers the shining of self-showing into the night of self-evidence, but that only illuminates this night for an instant.

This is the path that Heidegger, in fact, followed. Even the "authenticity" of Dasein that is developed in *Being and Time* and that captures the condition of possibility of phenomenology cannot be retained. Authentic understanding is "momentary" (447–448); the "resoluteness" that captures authenticity as a whole can immediately turn back into "unresoluteness" (396).[115] Even the concept of the "appropriative event" [*Ereignisses*] that was so central for Heidegger from the mid-1930s onward was coined partly to capture the inaccessible momentariness of phenomenality. The exceptional state of phenomenality is presented perhaps most clearly in the essay "On the Origin of the Work of Art." Here, what is "unusual" about the work is "this fact, that it *is* as such." This unusualness lies in the "event of its having been created." This event "does not merely [quiver] along with the work; instead the eventfulness that the work, as this work, [is . . . throws] the work out in front of itself [and has] constantly thrown this around itself."[116] Artworks are exceptional events; in them, the "original strife" of the truth of concealment and "unconcealment" is set into the work, such that "clearing and concealing," openness and closedness, step apart. (54) This is why, in Heidegger's view, artworks thrust up the "extraordinary" and topple what has "until now appeared safe"; they step "out of the conventional" and set free the possibility of "ceasing henceforth with all common acting and estimating, knowing and looking" (54).

Heidegger himself sensed that the experience of the artwork, despite all of its unusualness and lack of self-evidence, cannot be a state of exception. When he concludes the sentence just cited by stating that the point is "to tarry within the truth that occurs in the artwork" (54), this does not quite fit with the emphasis on the eventfulness and "extraordinary" character of artworks. The exceptional state of the event of truth cannot be set up permanently. The tarrying before the artwork does indeed require a quiet presence, just like the showing of phenomenological activity that is made possible by phenomena themselves. Yet this quiet presence cannot exclude the discernibility of phenomena that Heidegger takes to be secured with the stepping-forth from concealment. Even if phenomena are to be experienced in tarrying, in quiet observation their recognizability must be secured.

This recognizability is given with the deictic determination of phenomena that Heidegger initiated but did not develop. What shows itself in being shown is already brought through this showing to stand out from the obvious givenness of phenomena in the "vulgar" sense.[117] In everyday life, showing is already a special process; it is not possible without a special attention that is directed at something, and what is shown is there in an emphatic way. Certainly, what is shown can be taken as factually given; one can point to something or raise it to attention through a sentence, thereby underscoring that what is shown is in fact given there and that it in fact is what it was pointed out to be. But this underscoring of factual or matter-of-fact givenness does not lie in the essence of showing; even if it occurs in indicative showing, it adjoins the showing itself. What showing, taken by itself, induces is nothing other than something's appearance. Showing is not fulfilled through factual givenness but through this appearing.

There is a *correlation* between showing and self-showing. One points to something or indicates something, and it shows itself. Or something shows itself, steps forth on its own, and this stepping-forth can be verified by pointing to it or indicating it. Showing is geared toward the appearance into which something steps by showing itself; self-showing is stepping-into-appearance. The appearance into which something has stepped can be grasped, articulated, and understood by concentrating on it, naming it, and describing it. If this describing occurs under explicit recognition of the correlation—such that the correlation is reflected and the description is guided by this reflection—then it is phenomenological in the sense of a phenomenology that rests on the deictic understanding of phenomena.

This kind of phenomenological description is not tied to any specific objectivity. Anything can be a phenomenon for it; the only condition for an explicit phenomenal understanding of something is that the showing relation is determined by reflective attention to the correlation. Here the criterion for the discernibility of a phenomenon is given with the correlation itself; the deictic difference between showing and self-showing is divided onto the two relata of the correlation.

As we have already seen with regard to the expression, however, the deictic difference can also be actualized in one and the same thing. Living things are phenomenal in their expressive behavior; their self-showing need not be brought about by a showing that comes from outside, and it also does not require any external verification. Rather it is itself only revealing in connection with the showing that it is. Observation meets the full manifestation of what is otherwise only given in correlation.

The deictic difference does not become free in expressive behavior, however. In expression, a living being certainly enters into an appearance through facial expression, gesture, posture, or stance, but it ties all of these to itself and back into its factual life. It only shows *itself* in this appearance that it shows; joy or pain, fear, hesitation, contemplation, whatever can be shown through gesture or facial expression, are factual states of the living being that shows them and must be understood as such rather than as appearance. A living being's appearance in expression is never a pure appearance; it retains the weight of factual life, and in this lies its meaning. This is why a living being enters into an appearance without being completely in it; it does not dissolve into the appearance, but always remains reserved over against it—as a living being whose corporeal presence carries the play of facial expressions, gestures, postures, and stances by reserving itself from them without thereby being concealed. Quite the opposite; the potentiality of a living being belongs to its peculiar presence.[118] There is no expression without the expressionless. The latter is not simply opposed to the expression, but plays into it in such a way that facial expressions, gestures, postures, and stances are often not univocal in their showing—or not even univocally indicative. Gadamer once remarked that what the gesture says is "entirely its own being," and thus every gesture is "at the same time occluded in a mysterious way."[119]

Artworks are different. As appearing things, they are pure appearances, phenomena in the eminent sense. In them, the deictically understood phenomenality is liberated without any reservations. An artwork cannot even be reserved with respect to the appearances that it shows, for it is not alive; it is what it is, entirely without the occlusion of a potentiality comparable to corporeal presence. Artworks are unreservedly showing because they are unreservedly self-showing. In this way, they are beautiful in the Platonic sense of ἐκφανέστατον.

Artworks' unqualified showing initially lies in the fact that they unreservedly show *something*. This does not occur as a reference to something that lies apart from them, but, as with corporeal expression, as a presenting; yet in the case of an artwork, something is there that exists for itself and that is not identifiable as a property or a state of the artwork. While someone who expresses joy, for instance, shows this joy strictly as *his or her own,* such that he or she appears within it as one experiencing joy, in the artwork that which is shown is recognizable as such. It is not a state of the artwork. A painting like Henri Matisse's *Intérieur à la fougère noire*[120] shows what one sees and what one can point out: an interior, a room in which a woman sits in a high-backed chair, in front of her a round table, on this table a bowl containing lemons, behind this a vase with the black fern that lends the image its name. Even a so-called "abstract" painting shows *something.* A monochromatic painting from Gerhard Richter's series of paintings that all carry the title *Gray*[121] is not a flat, rectangular gray thing; rather, as the title states, it shows the color gray. Novels show the stories they tell, a poem like Goethe's "Over All the Peaks It Is Peaceful" [*Über allen Gipfeln ist Ruh*] shows the peacefulness that is named in its first verse. Pieces of music also engage in showing. A Bach fugue shows order as structure, as moving interweaving of moments. One need not know the title of a piece like Debussy's *Reflects dans l'eau*[122] in order to hear a soft, open striking, disappearing, and transformation. Even a tea bowl shows something. When the fired clay shows through the white Shino glaze, and when this glaze's flow appears at the unglazed foot of the bowl in irregular edging and soft droplets, the bowl shows a movement supplemented by the form's dissolution at its irregular edge. It shows the play of flowing and congealing; it shows transparency and matte opacity, movement in rest.

Since artworks' showing is not a pointing, one need not look for something pointed to beyond the artwork. Even if it were possible to find something of the sort, nothing depends on its actual givenness. That which artworks show is there in them in such a fulfilled way that any reference to other modes of its givenness abstracts from the experience of the work. This sort of external reference usually only arises if one attempts to elucidate the indicative character of artworks and thereby resorts to the possibility of indication, as Husserl does in his remarks on the "image-object."

Yet there is a familiar and everyday possibility of showing that comes close to the showing character of artworks: *demonstrating.* In demonstrating, what is shown is also not taken for something that actually exists in itself. It is only there through the person doing the showing, without being tied to that person as a state, like the expression is. A handshake, for instance, or a series of movements can not only be undertaken but also demonstrated—shown to another person. Both processes might appear similar to a superficial view; someone who hits a backhand in tennis does approximately the same thing as someone who demonstrates the backhand swing to another person in order that this person learns how to hit a backhand shot. Yet what occurs in each instance is different. In the first case, the point is to *do* something—whether in a match or in a test of one's own abilities. In the second case, the point is what one *can* do. It is to be made accessible as a *determinate possibility;* it is to appear as this possibility and is accordingly a *phenomenon,* even if it is not recognized as such.

Because the point is the appearance of the possibility, the person wishing to demonstrate a backhand will not simply execute the swing but will instead be intent on directing attention to the inner possibility of the swing, on making understandable its required posture and sequence of movements. To this end, it generally makes sense to take the posture more apparently than in a match or training, and perhaps even to exaggerate it a little. The sequence of movements will be more understandable if one slows it down and even breaks it up in order to discern its different stages. This, in turn, is easier if one does not actually take a shot, but only act *as if,* and demonstrates the swing without a ball.

The example immediately applies to art. One need only replace the tennis instructor with a mime. A mime concerned with tennis[123] will perform approximately the same movements as the tennis instructor, but what the former does is nevertheless distinct from what the latter does. For the mime, the movement of the swing without a ball has become normal; he can even do without a racket. For the mime, the doing *as if* has become the main point, and for this reason it is strictly speaking no longer a doing *as if.* The behavior of the mime is no longer measured according to the actual doing; it does not gain its meaning with respect to this actual doing. Instead, it makes the possibility—which is also actualized in the actual doing—accessible *as* possibility by setting it apart from its relation to reality and into appearance. The mime's behavior is *essentially* distinct from that of the tennis instructor. If one understands the behavior of a mime, it is clear that its enactment is concerned not with playing tennis, but with the showing of the playing of tennis.

The mime's showing can be grasped conceptually if one defines it as *presentation* rather than demonstration.[124] Demonstration is a veiled form of presentation. Conversely, the presentation that has been liberated and become recognizable is a showing for the sake of showing, a showing that is fulfilled in itself. What it is becomes all the more distinct the more clearly it is separated from the context of what is shown and the more different it is from that which is shown. Presentation is the showing of something *by means of something else;* this is how it can be a *pure* showing, which means a showing that is not related to the self-showing of what is shown in its factual existence. What is shown in a presentation is not present as itself. But this does not mean that it is there in an illusory fashion—as if its existence were merely a deception. This would only be the case if what is shown could *itself* be taken for *something,* and if one could accordingly be disappointed or sobered as soon as one sees through the deception. But this is not the case with a presentation. No one who watches a mime will be able to take his or her presentation of tennis for tennis. It is precisely for this reason that one understands so well the sequence of movements in the pantomimed presentation. One has not seen the sequence of movements on the tennis court as clearly as one does in the mime's presentation. On the tennis court, the sequence was factually enacted; in the pantomimed presentation, it came to appearance.

This fact of the matter could lead to the supposition that the mime has carefully studied the behavior of tennis players. The supposition could be supported with an elaboration of the concept of presentation. One could call the mime's presentation "mimetic," since "presentation" is an adequate translation of this term. This only makes sense, of course, if the term can be applied to the mime's behavior in its full meaning.

μίμησις, according to its canonical definition in Plato's *Republic*, does not simply mean "presentation." Rather, the word designates a presentation that arises when one "makes [oneself] similar" to that which one seeks to present.[125] μίμησις is presentation by means of making-oneself-similar, that is, through imitation. This only partially captures the behavior of the mime. To be sure, a mime wishing to present tennis playing must be able to execute the sequence of movements belonging to tennis. But his or her behavior is not determined by these movements. If this were the case, the mastery of these movements would lead to the art of pantomime. But that is not the case. One who masters the movements of tennis and can execute a backhand without a ball or racket is not therefore a mime. Presentation, in the sense of fulfilled showing, requires something else, namely the ability, by means of posture, gesture, and movement, to show more than just the sequence of movements. If one observes a good mime who presents a tennis player, one does not just see the movement of the swing, but also that which is not actually there and still belongs to it: the racket and the ball. One sees the game of tennis in its *possibility*.

This is not simply the case because the mime does not actually play the game. Even someone who wishes to demonstrate how a certain swing is executed does not play. But in order for the demonstration to fulfill its purpose, it is necessary, despite all modifications of the sequence of movements—slowing down, emphasizing specific moments—to keep to the movements of the actual game; the possibility of movement is directed here at its reality and thus also determined by this reality. In pantomime, on the other hand, in its fulfilled showing, the point is the possibility itself; it is to be recognized as possibility and not learned with respect to its actualization. Thus the mime will alter the movement he or she wishes to present to such an extent that one recognizes it particularly well. He or she will reduce it to what is characteristic, possibly exaggerate it slightly, and through the playful change rob the movement of its seriousness. Further, he or she will supplement the normal sequence of movements with moments that are unnecessary to the actual game of tennis and that might actually disturb it. Thus, among other things, a mime can follow the actually absent ball in order to allow it to be present.

Presentational showing is therefore not mimetic as such. Mimesis in the strict sense, taken as a presentation that becomes possible *through* making-oneself-similar, exists less in originary artistic showing than it does in art when it is interpretation in the sense of performance and in general in performance understood as interpretation.[126] Here it is the pregiven text to which one must make oneself similar in one's speaking in order to present it. The art of a speaker or actor is measured by whether this making-oneself-similar succeeds. This does not mean that the art of speaking or action would dissolve in the process of making-oneself-similar, in adapting one's own speaking to a text that is actualized like sheet music. A reflective and freely articulable understanding of the text certainly contributes to the success of the performance. There is also a certain space of freedom, not pregiven by the text, for the voice's pitch, speed, and mode of articulation. Yet with respect to the text, there is not the same possibility of free execution as in the art of pantomime, which is not bound to any text. At best, the art of pantomime contains mimetic moments that are subordinate to the showing that is fulfilled there.

The fact that mimesis does not belong to the essence of presentational showing becomes even clearer if one observes presentations that are not performed but instead exist as thing-like works. Accordingly, possibility comes to the fore even more clearly here as that which is shown. Myron's Discobolus, for example, cannot be taken to be mimetic, as the sculpture does not execute any sequence of movements. Nothing moves, the figure simply stands there. Nevertheless, one can see a movement—a movement in its possibility. The presented athlete is at the turning point of his motion; he has apparently wound up, and it appears that he will now bring his arm around forward in full swing, in a circular movement, and hurl the discus away. The sculpture shows the movement because its posture is open to that movement. Its posture has gathered the movement into itself. One sees that the figure cannot and could not remain that way. Yet this impossibility of remaining in place is perpetuated—as it never could be in an artless photograph that merely captures a given moment of motion. The sculpture shows movement precisely because it is not simply extracted out of the sequence of motions. It shows movement in its possibility and is thus a *figure of movement*. In its precarious balance and dissolvable tension, it is the figuration of a movement: it is movement, figuratively.

What is shown in such a way need not be revealed on the first glance. When one enters the room of the Museo Nationale Romano in which a Roman copy of the Discobolus is housed, one may immediately recognize the sculpture as a "discus thrower." Yet what is recognized in this way is not that which is shown. It is merely a *schema* that belongs to what is shown, to the sculpture's appearance, in a way that is initially unclear.

A schema, according to the meaning of the Greek word σχῆμα, is a form or outline, and is thus something only identifiable through perception. One who recognizes a schema need not necessarily know what that which is recognized even is. It suffices that a few characteristic elements are given in a certain arrangement, as with the schema of a face in the form of a circle, two dots, and a horizontal line. Conversely, nothing can be identified in perception without a schema. For a single thing to be identified as that particular thing, one must know in advance what it looks like. This, in turn, cannot refer to its individual givenness, but only to its look in general, to the schema within it. In this sense, Kant determined the schema as that which stands in the middle between concepts and the objects of experience in the form of perceptual images. Thus, Kant says, "no image of [a triangle]" could be "adequate" to its concept; no particular perceptual image reaches the universality of the concept, which applies not only to a specific triangle, but "for all of them, right-angled, oblique, etc."[127] This universality that corresponds to the concept is given through the schema. A schema is a "formal and pure condition of sensibility" (B 179, 135), special in each case, which means: a universal, concept-supplementing notion that allows one to identify something particular as something that fulfills a determinate form of appearing, of sounding, of feeling, etc., as this determined thing.

With respect to art, one aspect is important that Kant does not pay heed to, as he only discusses the imagistic givenness of objects of experience, not the relation between real objects and real images. Schemata allow one to recognize something as what it is, even if this is not given as itself but in a "depiction." What one might call "depiction" is nothing but the imagistic actualization of a schema that is really possible and possibly given. Someone pointing to Matisse's *Intérieur* and saying "this is a woman in a chair" has referred to the schema of the woman and the chair and has ignored that fact that this schema is not actualized here in a corporeal woman in a real chair, but in an image. In this respect, the image can be more or less exact; a few lines can suffice to make something identifiable as a woman who sits in a chair.

Schemata do not only exist for the visible, and also not solely for the perceptual. The meaning of descriptions that do not refer to anything real or actual are also not understandable without schemata. When there is talk, at the outset of Goethe's *Elective Affinites*, of a "rich baron in his prime,"[128] this must connect in one's understanding to a general, perhaps only diffuse conception. The more indeterminate a description is, the more schematic it is. If one took the description to be a reference, the notion connected to it could be confirmed through many actual people, even through those people who have been identified as "role models" of literary figures. Even if there is no reference being made, the immediate understandability of a presentation is bound to schemata. It is on the basis of schemata that one knows what a presentation is about.

Thus, schemata are possibilities of conception or of appearance that can be actualized in a variety of ways. But schemata are not phenomena. They lack the expressiveness for this. Schemata do not show themselves, and they are not shown. They are, rather, effective in their inexpressiveness. Insofar as they make possible, as concept or appearance patterns, the immediate and thus unproblematic identification of something factually given, they belong to the natural and not the phenomenological attitude. To be sure, schemata are significant for cognition, but not for the cognition of something that appears on its own. They have no deictic relevance.

Since art is deictic in the eminent sense, it does not simply retain the validity of schematic identification. Art robs schematic identification of its self-evidence. This identification either comes to nothing, is overfilled, set into abeyance, or partially suspended.

The fact that an artwork is not fully grasped by the capacity for schematic identification of its presentation can be shown in the case of the identification being entirely unproblematic and the artwork still demanding persistent and increased attention. Myron's discus thrower, for instance, can be schematically identified at first sight, and one's observation of it is thus less determined by the fact that it is a discus thrower as by the way the form of the discus thrower appears in its figure of movement. It often the case that the unproblematic identification is underscored through a work's title. This explains the banality of many titles that do not contribute anything to the interpretation of artworks, but are instead limited to what is schematically obvious. Cézanne's *Le garçon au gilet rouge* is an example of this. In the case of themes that are general but that might raise questions as to what precisely is presented or "depicted," the title often supplies the answer and thus first enables the observation of the image—as for instance with Monet's *La Cathédrale de Rouen, Le Portail* from the year 1894.

The schematic identification is set into abeyance when it is possible, but simultaneously relativized. Monet's *Intérieur*, for example, instantly shows the inside of a room in which one sees a table with a bowl of lemons, and next to it the black fern of the painting's title. The woman seated in the chair next to the table is also schematically identifiable. Yet through this woman, as with the other things in the room, that which is schematically identifiable appears in a way that is different from how it would appear in an actually given room. The woman is faceless; she is nothing but shape and is thus recognizable *as* the schema of a seated woman. At the same time, however, one's schematic view is disturbed.

The table is too large in relation to the woman and seems to float in the room, or else to stand with one leg on the woman's dress. Furthermore, the schemata that are recognizable in the image are combined with forms that withdraw from schematic identification. A surface filled with floral shapes, cut off at the painting's top and right edges, could be a window but also a painting. It is clearly recognizable *as* a surface, just as the floor in its glowing yellow and irregular dots seems to engulf the chair painted in the same yellow but with black stripes. The rear wall of the presented room does not retreat as it would in schematic spatial perception, but instead dominates as a surface, just as the floor does: as red rectangles separated by orange-colored gridlines. An interior, a table, a woman in a chair, a bowl with lemons, a plant—all this is schematically recognizable and at the same time set into another order that is determined by hues and compositionally inserted ornaments. It is decentered order, not one that can be captured through a schematic spatial view. The schemata that are set into the image are at once the occasion for its decentered order and at the same time part of that order. The image takes the schemata up so as to set them into the free play of its order. This order is that which the image shows. The latter can take up what is schematic and set it in abeyance because it is beyond the schematic.

The description of what the image shows is simultaneously a description of the image. It is only in this way that the description is even possible, for that which the image shows is only accessible in the image. It bears repeating that the image only shows by showing itself. The image, or more precisely the painting, is not simply there in actual givenness—as an "image-thing," as Husserl would say; rather, it has its own phenomenal character. It shows itself by way of itself, and this self-showing is revealed in the case that it shows in the same way that it is. The image's self-showing proves to be, ever anew, a showing, and this showing always turns back into the self-showing of the image. An image, and indeed any artwork as such, is transparent in its deictic difference without dissolving into two independent moments, the showing and the shown.

This transparency turns up in every experience with art. Artworks are present as artworks in their art forms. The *trompe l'oeil* is an exception among artworks. Poems and musical pieces are generally apparent as what they are. This manifestness stems from the essence of art. It is only in marginal cases that the experience demands the viewer's decision whether an artwork is an image, a poem, or a piece of music. In general, the recognizability of an artwork's form is made possible by the work itself. It is a part of art to more or less indicate that the image is an image, the poem a poem, and the piece of music a piece of music. Put differently, *reflectedness* belongs to the essence of art. Quite frequently, the image quality of an image is shaped into the image itself; poems brings their poetic character to language, and similarly music reflects music.

One can easily find examples of this in every art form. As concerns visual arts, one need only think of the presentation of images in images. These could be mirror images as in Monet's lily paintings, or paintings in numerous *intérieurs*, especially presentations of studios that show other images by the same painter, as is the case in Matisse's *L'atelier rouge*.[129] But images can do more than just show images, such that the image shows itself in what it shows. Reflectedness can also occur in the presentation of looking, as in Caspar David Friedrich's *Wanderer Above the Sea of Fog*,[130] or in the presentation of painting and the painter's gaze. One need only think of the self-portraits of painters with their brush and palette, of Max Liebermann for example, or of Picasso's countless variations on the theme of "painter and model." The most famous and most frequently philosophically discussed example would be Velasquez's *Las Meninas*.[131] If one observes the original,[132] one sees oneself positioned before the easel, into the painter's gaze, and thus into the model's place. The image draws the viewer into the depicted process of painting and thereby shows itself as the painting that it is.

The reflection of poetizing in poetry is no less common. It can articulate itself through the struggle with the "poet's vocation"—so the title of one of Hölderlin's poems—as occurs not only in Hölderlin but in Rilke's *Sonnets to Orpheus* as well.[133] Yet the reflection can also be limited to a pithy phrase, as in the opening sentence of Goethe's *Elective Affinities*. "Eduard—let that be the name we give to a wealthy baron in his prime"; a story that begins this way is immediately recognizable as poetic.[134] The literary narrator, who does not report facts, has every right to freely dispose of the figures in his story. Through the "we," which is not simply the *pluralis maiestatis*, he binds the reader into the literary game—as if there were an agreement between him and the reader to call the baron in his prime "Eduard."

Literary reflexivity of this sort is not limited to modernity. Accordingly, it is not an indicator that the poetic work has lost its appropriate social integration and has therefore become uncertain in its possibilities. Pindar's odes, set unmistakably into a social context as athletic honors, name the very song that they are, and do so in utter obviousness: "harp-dominating hymns / which god, which hero, which man should we sing?"[135] Or "Great city of Syracuse, realm of mighty / Ares, iron-joyed men and horses / divine seamstress / I come to you and bring from gleaming Thebes this song as report of the earth-shattering chariot / on which capable Hieron was victorious."[136] Even the oldest texts of European literature are poetic works that wish to be recognized as such. The invocation of the muses at the outset of the Homeric epics designates these muses as what they are. Even more obvious is the scene in the *Odyssey* in which Odysseus is at once both the hero of the story and its audience. At Alcinous' court, he hears his own story sung as an epic poem; the singer is a figure in the narrative song.[137] The scene reveals the power of song; the latter breaks Odysseus and stirs him to tears in a way that the recollection of his experiences never could have.

The reflexivity of music, like that of visual art and poetry, can reveal itself in the fact that a piece of music cites differently. One need only think of the military marches in Mahler's symphonies, of the intentional anachronism of the waltz in *The Knight of the Rose*. If this is joined by poetry, the possibilities of reflection are expanded and diversified. One could point to Wagner's *Meistersinger*, to Richard Strauss' *Ariadne on Naxos* and *Capriccio*—operas about music that reflect music's comical, unsettling, and enchanting possibilities as well as its limits. Yet the self-reflexivity of music can also consist in the fact that pieces of music—those of John Cage, for instance—bring their performative and experiential conditions to bear in especially obvious ways.

But artworks do not only show themselves in the aforementioned forms of reflexivity. They also show themselves in their perceivability insofar as they are eminently perceivable. An image experienced as an artwork makes possible a seeing that is distinct from normal, casual glancing, even distinct from everyday looking. In observing an image, seeing becomes the central matter. The image itself is something visible and something seen, in a special way—everything that is grasped and understood in it is subordinated to the being-seen.

The reason for this is that the image as such is invested in being-seen and is thereby placed in a special relation to seeing. The image is a visible engagement with seeing, and even more so with visibility as such. Anything that goes into the image as "content" is grasped in its visibility. Since art, in this case visual art, brings visibility into play from the outset, it can take what it shows out of its habitual perceptions and perceptual forms, and thereby allow a new, unbiased look at something.

The same is the case with the other arts. Music is not just heard, it is experience of the audible; literature, in different ways in various genres, shapes the speakable in its speakability; in dance, one openly experiences corporeal and lively movement. Architecture, when it is art, reveals the spatiality of visible and accessible space. It is spatial by virtue of showing itself as such.

In our considerations up until now, we have only circumscribed the self-showing showing of artworks—their showing self-showing. The outline should be clear enough, however, to see the possibilities of filling it out. If artworks show by standing forth and being more or less reflected *as* images, poems, or pieces of music, then their character of self-showing showing can be more finely determined in a clarification of art's various *forms*. What is to be clarified is the specific showing character that an image, a poem, or a piece of music possesses. One must thereby also raise the question as to how the multitude and diversity of these forms is to be judged. If there are *basic forms* of art, the showing character of artworks can be understood on their grounds. In that case, all other formal shapings of art can be taken as combinations that are certainly irreducible, but are only adequately determined in the specific combination of individual artworks.

But art does not only possess forms. Its perceivability allows it to be what we might preliminarily call "material" or "made of matter"; images do not only show themselves reflexively, but also in their colorfulness, the grain of the canvas, the softness or hardness of paper; the language of poetry, just as music, only exists in sounding. The forms of art are inscribed into the materiality or substantiality of works; they only show themselves, they only show as forms by belonging in the material or substance. One can only inquire into this belonging, however, once one has determined the forms of art. Without the forms of art, the material or substantial aspect of artworks would not be showing. Accordingly, it could not show itself in its belonging to the phenomenal essence of artworks.

THREE

Art Forms

Arts

One is acquainted in general with the forms in which art shows and shows itself. One encounters them along with artworks, and they seem tangible inasmuch as artworks fit into various genres. These allocations happen as if on their own. They arise as soon as one speaks and reflects about artworks. One can only determine what artworks are in any detailed sense by allocating them to a form. By calling a work a poetic piece, an image, or a piece of music, one is giving a formal designation.

It is easy to see that these genre designations are fairly unspecific. They can be further differentiated and supplemented by other designations. With differentiation in mind, instead of speaking of poetic works in a general sense, one would distinguish stories, poems, and plays. An image can be a painting, a drawing, or a photograph; a piece of music is a song, a symphony, an opera. In terms of supplementation, one would have to take sculpture, buildings, dance, and even tea bowls into consideration.

Yet even these designations are not exhaustive. The differentiation, as well as the supplementation, can be extended. At some point, these lead into confusion. One can introduce ever more detailed distinctions, for instance by dividing the story category into epic, novel, short story, or travelogue. One can also find art forms that cannot immediately be allocated to an established genre. Installations, for example, are neither buildings nor sculptures; the literary diary is neither essay nor story. Finally, there are transitions, connections, and crossovers. The relief is still an image and already a sculpture; one goes into the other. The combination of purportedly distinguishable art forms leads to difficulties that can only be surmounted by introducing new form concepts. An opera is just as much a musical as a literary work, which in its stage production also gains imagistic moments. A piece of calligraphy is an image and a poem at the same time. Crossovers lead very quickly beyond limits. Thus it would be quite difficult to even find a genre designation for a piece like John Cage's *4'33"* or Walter de Maria's *Vertical Earth Kilometer*.[1] The attempt at a designation here comes close to a description of the individual work. This issue combines with problems of judgment: As soon as a work can no longer be allocated to an established art form, the question arises whether it is an artwork at all.

This difficulty of allocating artworks to a univocally determined form could lead one to the conclusion that it is better to relinquish the definitive differentiation of art forms and only determine artworks in their respective individual givenness. In this case, one need not deny commonalities with other artworks, but they would remain partial. This approach would lead to a pluralism of art forms that could be engaged through Wittgenstein's concept of "family resemblance." Looking at individual artworks, one would see "a complicated web of similarities that overlap and cross each other"—"similarities in the grand and the minute."[2] But this is not clear. Family resemblance presupposes relation. This, in turn, can only exist if the relatives are recognizable in themselves and in their relation to each other. This is a conviction that accompanies the experience of art and that is continually confirmed. One assumes as self-evident not only that artworks are alike in infinite ways, but that they are fundamentally distinct from each other in their forms—*as* poetic works, *as* images, or *as* pieces of music. The deictic or presentational sense of art arises differently in different forms.

Of course, this is only an unclear supposition until the assumption of art forms can be verified. Toward this end, the individual forms must be determined as such; one must be able to say what the essence of such and such a formally determined artwork is. But the number of these essential determinations cannot be arbitrary; otherwise one would arrive again at the presumption of an infinite web of partial family resemblances. That is why one must limit the number of art forms and indicate why one only accepts this determinate number. Finally, one must determine the relation of these essential determinations to each other; one must be able to say how they connect in order to account for those works that cannot be univocally allocated to one genre. Put differently, one must be able to show why that which arises in each art form actually is art.

The attempt of such an essential determination of the arts is made difficult by the fact that the form that determines a work does not lie openly bare before one. To be sure, it is not concealed either, but one cannot tell just by looking at an individual work whether it is to be understood as an individual instantiation of a form, as a modification of this form, as a combination of various forms, or as a form *sui generis*. If one only starts from individual works, it is virtually unavoidable to assume the existence of infinite forms that are connected by way of family resemblance. Against this, there stands the intuition that there are different art forms; the assumption of established genres is a starting point for this intuition, but no more than that.

Because the forms of art are not simply evident, the attempts at determining them bear varying results. In this regard, the projects of Kant, Hegel, and

Nietzsche are especially revealing. They show in a paradigmatic fashion what is at stake in the determination of art forms, and they further demonstrate what stands in the way of an adequate determination. As all three projects confirm, the determination of the forms of art has to do with the presentational sense of art. Thus, in determining the forms of art, one should be guided by the question of art's presentational sense. What is more, the critical assessment of the aforementioned projects can make clear how one can miss this presentational sense, and this in turn indicates how one might do this sense justice.

Kant sees very clearly the difficulty of determining the forms of art. To meet this difficulty, he suggests orienting oneself by something outside of art that can serve as a model. There is "no more convenient principle" for the division of fine arts and thus for the determination of their forms than "the analogy between the arts and the way people express themselves in speech so as to communicate with one another as perfectly as possible, namely, not merely as regards their concepts but also as regards their sensations." This expression consists in "word, gesture, and tone," in "articulation, gesticulation, and modulation." Through the combination of these types of expression, "thought, intuition, and sensation are conveyed to others."[3] This results in the distinction of "three kinds of fine arts"; there is the "art of speech, visual art, and the art of the play of sensations" (B 205, 320–321).

Kant's division is easily graspable. By orienting himself along linguistic expression, the presentational sense, the deictic essence of artworks, comes into play. Kant also takes into consideration that visibility and audibility (yet not smell and touch) are important to this presentational sense. As Kant notes, plastic art is given "to two senses," namely "sight and touch," but to the latter "without regard to beauty" (B 207, 322). This addition is intelligible. Even if the surface texture of a sculpture is not inessential to it, the sculpture reveals itself primarily in visibility; one *sees* how it is textured, and this, not the factual touching, is significant for how one experiences its appearance.

This thought also makes Kant's broad understanding of visual art intelligible. Besides, sculpture and painting, visual art includes architecture and landscaping, although one could argue whether the latter is adequately categorized under the division of painting. It is indisputable, however, that a garden—just as a building—can be beautiful and thus be valid as an artwork apart from its usefulness, strictly for intuition.

It is another matter with the plausibility of Kant's understanding of the "art of speech" and the "art of the play of sensations." Precisely if one shares Kant's understanding of art in the full sense as fine art, then the division of the "art of speech" into oratory and poetry is not at all clear. Oratory may be an art, but it is most certainly not a fine art, for it lacks what Kant singles out as the foundational determination of all art forms: it is not a presentation of aesthetic ideas. The conception of the art of sensations is completely problematic, insofar as it is to encompass "music and the art of color" (B 211, 324). It remains open as to what distinguishes the "art of color" from the painting allocated to visual art.

This difficulty pertains to Kant's division as a whole. It is certainly not implausible to grasp music by way of tone and by way of the sensation that is expressed in tone. But as Kant himself must admit, the arousal of sensations is not specific to music. Expression in speech thereby loses its model character. If affects can also be induced through paintings and poetic works, then articulation and gesticulation must belong to the "beautiful play of sensations" as well. Thus, as art forms they would occur in other forms, and the whole division would lose its meaning.

Kant himself did not overestimate the integrity of his division of "fine arts." He emphasizes twice that it is merely a "design" and "attempt," not a "theory" or "decisive derivation" (B 204–205, 320). Other attempts, which "can and should still be made," are possible (B295, 320).[4] One might conclude from these difficulties in Kant's attempt that an analogous determination of art forms would be problematic as such. Despite all the difficulty associated with it, the determination must rather be gleaned from art itself. The presentation character of art can apparently only be determined in its various forms if one orients oneself according to the peculiar possibilities of art.

There are intimations of this in Kant. He distinguishes poetry, visual art, and music by determining them as different modes of presenting aesthetic ideas. The poetic work speaks, above all, to the understanding. Although it is a "play with ideas," it generates as much for the understanding as if the poet "had intended merely to engage its task."[5] In visual art, conversely, the "artist's spirit gives corporeal expression to what and how he has thought, and makes the thing itself speak, as it were, by mime" (B211, 324). In music, finally, aesthetic ideas are not to be bound to concepts, but are to be realized solely through the "form of the arrangement of [. . .] sensations" in "harmony and melody," although this arrangement could "be brought under certain rules mathematically" (B219, 329). The arts differ in that they bring the same thing, namely aesthetic ideas, to bear in different ways.

Kant's understanding of art forms includes an evaluative aspect. Since poetry speaks to the understanding, it is connected, in Kant's view, with the greatest clarity and freedom. Conversely, works of visual art are left to the associative power of the observer. The "thing itself," the "corporeal expression," only speaks "by mime," and thus it engages "the play of our phantasy, which attributes to lifeless things a spirit that corresponds to their form and speaks through them" (B 211, 324).[6]

Even in music, the aesthetic ideas are "not concepts or determinate thoughts" but merely associations that arise from the "proportioned attunement" of sensations—as the "idea of a coherent whole of an unspeakable wealth of thought [that aligns] in conformity with a certain theme that is the prevalent affect in the piece" (B 219, 329).[7] Since for Kant visual art and music are thoughtless in their forms and only vaguely induce thoughts, he wonders whether color and tone merely arouse "agreeable sensation[s]" or whether they carry with them "a liking for form in the aesthetic judgment" (B212, 324). Poetry is apparently free of such ambiguity. The "rules of euphony of speech [and of] propriety in the expression of ideas" are only mentioned with respect to oratory. (B 217, 327)

Kant's valuation is rooted in his understanding of aesthetic ideas. Because he sees in these ideas "tangential notions" that remain dependent on conceptual cognition,[8] they only come to their fullest fruition in the context of conceptual cognition. The articulation of such cognition is only to be found in poetry; it alone makes its objects cognizable in a conceptual fashion, in order to vary this cognizability in the "tangential notions" of aesthetic ideas. By this reasoning, only poetry possesses presentational sense. Kant rules out that the concept-less art forms could present aesthetic ideas. Visual art and music are like gestures and vocal modulations that lack articulation. Kant's determination of art forms leads to the paradoxical conclusion that only one art form corresponds to the model and standard given by linguistic expression.

This is not the case in Hegel's discussion of the forms of art. To be sure, Hegel remains close to Kant's project in many respects, not least in his understanding of music and his estimation of poetry. Yet as Hegel no longer takes his orientation from the model of linguistic expression, he can determine all the art forms he considers from the angle of art alone, namely under the aspect of their peculiar presentational possibility. In this way, he recognizes forms of art as such, and accordingly one can speak of them expressly in that way. Whereas Kant speaks of a division of "fine arts," Hegel distinguishes various "art forms." Hegel's division is at once systematic and historical. It is intended to take account of the development of art in a twofold sense—the genesis of art on the one hand, and on the other the possibilities, given through its forms, of fulfilling the essence, the presentational sense, of art.

Hegel's division of art forms is evaluative as well. The valuation, however, is not imposed upon art through some prior decision, but rather stems from the orientation by the presentational sense of art itself. Hegel's discussion assumes the possibility of a complete presentation, more precisely, the possibility of a form of presentation that would fulfill the essence of presentation itself. Complete presentation in Hegel's sense is the adequate appearance, in all respects, of an intelligible content. Art, Hegel states, has "the task of grasping and presenting existence as *true* in its appearance, i.e., in its adequacy to the content that is adequate to itself, and that exists in and for itself."⁹ This truth, Hegel adds, cannot be "mere correctness"; it is not an imitating realism that is required, but instead the external appearance of an essentiality merely cleansed of the particular, an appearance that brings what is presented to bear "in its universal character and its persisting peculiarity." Hegel designates this determination that hangs between universality and peculiarity as the "ideal" (206); the ideal is the middle in which presentation and what is presented meet, where they meet in such a way that only the presentation accomplishes the cleansing of the particular and thus lets what is presented appear as itself.

Hegel only sees this middle achieved in Greek sculpture as the presentation of the human form, insofar as the latter is no longer taken "merely as sensual existence, but just as the existence and natural shape of spirit" (110). Hegel divides the forms of art up in orientation along this example. Greek sculpture represents the "classical art form," from which the "symbolic" and "romantic" forms are distinguished. The symbolic form remains behind the classical in that it does not find a content adequate to it; it is the prehistory of art actualized in artistic fashion, "a *mere searching* of visualization" without the "capacity of true presentation." Hegel calls the content that is observed for itself an "idea" (107–11), and it is this content that remains indistinct in the symbolic form of art, and accordingly symbolic presentation is tentative, suggestive, and thus inadequate. The third art form, which Hegel calls "romantic," is characterized by the opposite failed relation. Here, the possible content of art, namely the existence unfolded in Christian religion, has become so rich and inwardly oriented that art can no longer do justice to it. In romantic art, "the indifference, inadequacy, and division of idea and shape—just as in the symbolic [form]—surfaces again, yet with the essential *difference* that in the romantic [form] the idea (whose deficiency on the symbolic level led to problems of shaping) is to appear in a *complete* way as spirit and mind, and because of this higher completion thus retreats from the corresponding unification with the external by only being able to seek and attain its true reality and appearance in itself" (114, emphasis in original). With the romantic form of art, the limitation of art as such becomes evident; its insufficiency shows that it is not adequate to the unfolded reality of spirit.

Hegel thus determines the three distinguished forms of art by finding realized in them three distinct possibilities of the relation between presentation and what is presented. He takes these three possibilities—adequacy of presentation and what is presented, indeterminacy of what is presented, insufficiency of presentation—to determinately exhaust art as presentation. If one follows Hegel's approach, there can only be these three forms of art. Yet they do not occur simultaneously, such that each form would determine the arts at any time. Hegel's image is that of a line of development; the three art forms stand for the prehistory, completion, and posthistory of art.

The sequence of art forms also marks the developmental stages of various arts. Art history in Hegel's sense is not a history that pertains to all arts more or less equally. In other words, none of Hegel's distinct forms applies to all arts; every art form is represented by particular arts. Although Hegel, in his discussion of the symbolic art form, goes extensively into poetic genres such as fable, proverb, didactic poem, and epigram, he sees the symbolic form represented especially well in architecture. The latter remains "of utterly symbolic type in its fundamental character" (vol. 14, 271); in the classical form its presentational pretentions, which Hegel takes to be actualized in the Egyptian pyramids, in steles and obelisks, are withdrawn for the sake of a pure purposiveness in which architecture—in the exemplar of the Greek temple—is reduced to being "an artistically formed surrounding [. . .] for the now independently actualized spiritual meanings" (vol. 14, 271). Over against this, romantic architecture breaks out of this limitation to pure purposiveness and develops through independent architectural shaping without the latter being related back to its purpose, as in the classical form. Here Hegel has in mind the ornamentation of a gothic cathedral, which cannot be subordinated to the pure purpose of giving a community a space of congregation. (vol. 14, 345) The cathedral is a building and, as a figurative presentation of religious inwardness, at the same time a prefiguration of painting.

Just as architecture represents the symbolic form of art, so sculpture represents the classical. Symbolic sculpture forms the prehistory of classical sculpture (cf. vol. 14, 446–453), and when Hegel deals with romantic, that is, Christian sculpture, he prefaces this with the remark that in the romantic form, sculpture cedes "to painting and music as the more adequate arts of inwardness and the free inwardly pervaded particularity of the external" (vol. 14. 458–459)—as if Michelangelo and Benvenuto Cellini did not exist. Contrary to sculpture, Hegel says, painting is no longer bound to "heavy material," but instead has "gleaming and the *shining of color*" as "sensual means of expression" (vol. 15, 205, emphasis in original); the painting does not stand over against one, and as a representation actualized for perception, it is thus better suited for the presentation of what is interior. The latter, to be sure, is also true of music. But music, in Hegel's view, is so "lacking in content" that it cannot delineate a "spiritual content" clearly enough. (vol. 15, 223) For this, it must call "for assistance to the more precise designation of the word" (vol. 15, 223–224). It is only "in the expression of thoughts and sensations" that music becomes "a more clear and more solid explication." The romantic art form becomes complete in poetry, not least because it unifies "the extremes of the *visual* arts and of *music* in itself" (vol. 15, 224). In poetry, as Hegel understands it, the inwardness of music combines with the formal determinacy of visual art. It is no wonder, then, that there is no talk of poetry in the classical form of art, nor of music or painting. What Hegel has to say about Greek poetry is found in the "system of individual arts" (vol. 14, 243), without any reference to the classical art form.

Yet this is no omission, for as Hegel believes, poetry is not only an exceptional art, as it was for Kant. Rather, it stands at the cusp of the forms of art; it still belongs to an art form, namely to the romantic, and yet it falls out of it at the same time. Poetry can absorb "the totality of content and of the forms of art" (vol. 15, 234); it is "the *universal* art that can shape in any form and express any content that is even capable of entering phantasy" (vol. 14, 243). Understood in this way, poetry is beyond art; in Hegel's sense, it is no longer a presentation, and thus no longer a sensual actualization of a spiritual content. In it, "the conjunction of spiritual interiority and external existence is dissolved to an extent that no longer even begins to correspond to the original concept of art" (vol. 15, 235). Accordingly, poetry is "that special art in which art itself begins to dissolve and attains for philosophical cognition that transition to religious presentation as such, as well as to the prose of scientific thinking" (vol. 15, 234). One must also add that Hegel considers the linguisticality of poetry to be inessential. The "work of poetry" can "be translated into other languages, transposed from verse form to prose, and thus brought into completely different circumstances of sounding, without a significant stunting of its value" (vol. 15, 229–230).

Through his understanding of poetry, Hegel puts his conception of art forms into a difficulty that is not solvable by means of that conception. Poetry is art yet no longer art; on the one hand, it is connected to the end of art belonging to romantic art, while at the same time also being actualized in every other art form. That is not simply a logical incongruity, but it further contradicts the line of development in which Hegel sees the three art forms he distinguishes. In poetry, then, art would have already met its end in the symbolic and classical forms as well. The complete presentation of classical (i.e., Greek) sculpture would have been undermined by Greek poetry.

The idea that poetry is to belong to the romantic art form and also not fit into it makes the weakness of Hegel's conception evident. As Hegel literally conceives of his three art forms in a spiritual-historical fashion and also allocates to them various representative arts, he cannot do adequate justice to the "simultaneity" of arts. Thus, his conception of art forms generates the constraint of allocating the arts (insofar as they are shaped by an art form) to a specific art-historical epoch. This requires Hegel to grasp the nonrepresentative arts as pre- or posthistorical. The "special arts" also reach "over and beyond their actual realms into the other forms of art." Yet "these branchings" are "partly only preparatory attempts of later beginnings, or they indicate an art's incipient breaching in which it [seizes] a content and mode of material treatment whose type [can] only be fully formed in a further art" (vol. 15, 232). In this way, architecture becomes the prehistory of sculpture, and painting its historical effect. Music only achieves validity romantically, that is, posthistorically, while sculpture loses its significance in romantic conditions, which serves to indicate the end of art. The spiritual-historical pressure continually forces Hegel into biases and stylizations. This leads to incongruities that are apparent to any impartial look at the history of art. With Hegel, one cannot comprehend that music, under the conditions of the classical art form, was a developed art with a high philosophical significance.[10] It is just as incomprehensible that Greek pottery painting should be a mere prehistory of "romantic" painting and that the gothic cathedral is a hybrid of a Greek temple, as it is that sculpture should only be fulfilled in Greek art.

Hegel's spiritual-historical conception of art forms is connected to a further difficulty. Through his determination of art forms, Hegel does not make clear *how* a spiritual content is present in the artwork. For Hegel, the art forms are not clearly distinguished forms of presentation but instead modifications of one presentation that is given through the complete congruity of materially actualized shape and spiritual content. Because of his imprecise and rigid comprehension of presentation, Hegel leaves unexplored the presentational and showing possibilities of art. Hegel does not help one understand *how* an image, a poem, or a piece of music presents or shows. It remains unclear in Hegel's *Aesthetics* what art forms are.

Nietzsche went further in answering this question. He distinguished two "art worlds" in his *Birth of Tragedy*[11] and by assigning the arts to these tried to make the arts comprehensible in their presentational sense. The "art worlds," dream and intoxication specify the imagistic nature of the Apollonian and the musical nature of the Dionysian as the two fundamental possibilities of art. The Apollonian and the Dionysian are the art worlds' respective "drives":[12] the drive to what is imagistic and the musical drive. Nietzsche seeks to determine the essence of art through these and what they bring to bear. Accordingly, the imagistic and the musical are the two art forms that Nietzsche distinguishes.

Nietzsche's approach might remind one of Kant's attempt at dividing the arts in orientation along linguistic expression. One could consider dream and intoxication to be possibilities of life that are not essentially, or not exclusively, realized in art, such that Nietzsche, too, would be determining art forms from beyond art. Yet for Nietzsche, dream and intoxication are not analogies and also not conditions for art, but instead are the "immediate art-states of nature," over against which every artist is an "imitator" (30). Dream and intoxication are the only modes of experience that can be articulated and formed in art. In that sense they are essentially artistic and in their articulation and formation make up the essence of artworks.

The meaning of this becomes more clear when one looks closer at Nietzsche's account of dream and intoxication. As the originary scene of the experience of images, the dream is pure observing. One is still, does not act, and does thus not need to take heed of anything that moves, changes, or bears surmounting; nothing is used, one does not reach a goal at the end of the dream, there is no result. In dream images, something is simply there—not in reality, but in such a way that it comes to appearance. Dream images are appearances, thoughts that one does not generate willfully, but that instead simply occur. If one follows Nietzsche, these thoughts have a peculiar consistency. In the dream, everything is of equal importance and equally comprehensible: "We enjoy the immediate understanding of shape, all forms speak to us, there is nothing of indifference or redundancy" (26).

The dream is contrasted with intoxication. The latter is a movement that expands boundaries and suspends limits, a happening that sweeps one along and captivates in distanceless unity. Intoxication is "self-forgetfulness" (29) being swept along affectively; it is dissolution in a whole that surrounds and pervades one, that is not recognizable, only experienceable.

When Nietzsche conceives of dream and intoxication as "art worlds" in this sense, he does not assign specific arts to them. The image art that stems from dreams does not only encompass visual art, but also "an important half of poetry," namely the epic. (26) Nietzsche's musical art of the Dionysian can certainly be explicated by means of music, insofar as the latter is characterized by the "shocking force of the sound," the "unified flow of the melody," and "the thorough incomparable world of harmony" (33). But not all music has to resound; the musical in Nietzsche's sense can be determinative in the art of words and images as well. In Nietzsche's view, every specific art arises through the *combination* of the two art worlds. Yet this combination does not stand on its own; taken in themselves, the art worlds are separate and distinct in their divisibility. The combination results from the fundamental artistic experiences being articulated and shaped.

Nietzsche uses the example of lyric poetry to elucidate what he means by this. To this end, he refers to a statement Schiller made in a letter to Goethe on March 18, 1796. Schiller, according to Nietzsche, admitted to "having before himself and in himself, as the preparatory state prior to the act of writing poetry, not a series of images with an ordered causality of thoughts, but rather a musical attunement." This is followed by a quotation: "My sensibility initially lacks any determinate or clear object; the latter is only formed later. A certain musical attunement of my feelings precedes this, and the poetic idea follows it in me" (43).[13] Nietzsche explains this observation by determining the musical-poetic occurrence as a double depiction [*Abbildung*]. The lyricist, "as Dionysian artist, first became completely one with the primordial unity, his pain and contradiction."[14] Then he produced "the image of this primordial unity as music," and only then did "this music become visible to him again under the influence of the Apollonian dream, as in an *allegorical dream-image.*" Nietzsche summarizes the idea once more: The "image- and concept-less reflection of the primordial pain in music, with its redemption in appearance," produces "a second reflection, as a single allegory or example" (44).

Nietzsche's interpretation of Schiller's letter deviates drastically from the letter. What Schiller describes is understandable; before the poem is finalized, its structure must be there—like an almost empty field that is determined only by a few determinations, into which the words that ultimately make up the poem can be entered. The preliminary form can also be taken as a movement that runs more or less quickly and that is more or less suspended, as the notion of a dark or bright sound for which the words are then found. Paul Valéry described the movement of poetry in this sense, which for him is also the movement of the reading of poems. The movement occurs from sound to sense, from what contains the meaning to what is contained, and the movement always returns to its verbal and musical starting-point.[15] Nietzsche, on the other hand, interprets the "musical attunement of feelings" in the sense of an "aesthetic metaphysics"[16] inspired by Schopenhauer, as that elemental movement of life and the world that Schopenhauer calls "will." Nietzsche calls it the "primordial unity," and with Schopenhauer he understands music as the direct depiction of life- and world-movement; "immediate objectivation" was Schopenhauer's term[17] for what Nietzsche calls the "image- and concept-less reflection." But the objectivation of which Schopenhauer speaks, the reflection in Nietzsche's sense, is the actually resounding music. Schiller had neither this nor the "metaphysically" understood will in mind, and he also did not wish to state that the poem is a "second reflection," in other words the depiction of a depiction. The poem that arises from out of a "musical attunement of feeling" does not need an actually resounding music as its preliminary form. It is musical in its preliminary form. This form, one might suppose, is that musical form of art that can be fulfilled in actually resounding music, but also in lyric poetry.

Although Nietzsche thus initiates a conception of art forms through his notion of the "art worlds," he does not develop it further. He is not clear on the peculiar intermediate stance of the art forms; he does not see that these precede artworks and are more determinate than the movement of life, however conceived. It is only because there are art forms that precede artworks that the artist's activity is even possible; it is only because the art forms instantiate themselves in the works that one understands the works in their presentational sense.

What Nietzsche did see is that art forms cannot be gleaned from established genres of art. Poetry can be derived from the musical form and be shaped by it without thereby being music. Yet while Nietzsche can only conceive of a musical condition for poetry, and not a poetic condition for music, by virtue of the subject matter one has to assume such a mutuality. Nietzsche's preference of music over against "Apollonian" poetry and imagistic art can be explained by the metaphysics of the will stemming from Schopenhauer and the supposition developed in its context that music is essentially to be conceived as movement and occurrence. That is one-sided—one need only think of the mathematical structure of music that Kant mentioned.[18] Art forms, it seems, extend beyond those arts determined by established genres. Art forms are found instantiated in works that belong to various genres, and the works apparently take part in different art forms. This would also explain why works refer to other genres and why these works can claim what is essential to or characteristic of these other genres for themselves. Debussy's *Images* and Manfred Trojahn's *Sea-Images* are examples, and so are Kandinsky's "compositions" and "improvisations." Finally, there is an image by Paul Klee titled *Old Sound*[19] and a poem cycle by T. S. Eliot named *Four Quartets*.

Nevertheless, Debussy's piano pieces and Trojahn's orchestral works are pieces of music, not works of visual art; Kandinsky and Klee made images, not pieces of music. Schiller's poems that "stem from a musical attunement of feeling" are linguistic artworks. This leads to the supposition that art forms do not always instantiate themselves in the same way, but rather in a way that they represent a certain form. If that is the case, one would be able to read a form especially well off of these works.

This thought seems to lead in a circle, however; one would need to derive the nature of an art form from the works, and this in turn appears to validate the established but unconfirmed distinction between art genres. A review of the conceptions just elaborated shows just how problematic that would be. Whereas Kant allocates architecture, sculpture, painting, and other arts to one art form, Hegel distributes these three main arts to three different art forms. Nietzsche, in turn, counts poetry among imagistic art, a move in which neither Kant nor Hegel would have followed him. Therefore, such divisions and distributions are to be avoided. The question of art forms that are instantiated in various genres and which affect these genres cannot be answered from the side of the genres themselves. One must go behind the genres.

This is precisely what Kant, Hegel, and Nietzsche had undertaken, yet in different ways, and in any case with problematic results. Nietzsche's approach is the least problematic; it is even quite promising if one modifies it. In his distinction of the two "art worlds," Nietzsche begins with the "experience of art" and shows that the experience of images differs from that of music. This difference need not be grounded in preartistic states like dreams and intoxication. In fact, the grounding is even quite unclear when the difference of art experiences can be retraced to the difference between experienced art forms. The latter only counts as demonstrated when the art forms as such are clarified. But one can count as probable that the art forms are correlates of the experience of art and that the variation in that experience indicates a connection to different art forms. Accordingly, one should set out upon an observation of various art experiences—in Nietzsche's sense—in order to glean insight into various art forms that are presentations—in Hegel's sense. Yet these presentational forms are only art forms if they are understood—in Kant's sense—as presentational forms for aesthetic ideas, more precisely, if their presentation shows something in a decentered order.

In this sense, the experience of images indeed seems as originary as Nietzsche supposes, that is, not reducible to another mode of experience. There is much to be said for taking the aesthetic experience of architecture, sculpture, or tea bowls as imagistic. Buildings, sculptures, and tea bowls are seen as images in aesthetic experience, and if the seeing of images is the originary aesthetic possibility of vision, the mode of their visibility could thus be an imagistic one. It is similar in the experience of music. It is not its audibility that refers to the musical form, but instead the peculiar listening experience of pieces of music. One can suppose that its clarification would also reveal the musicality of poems. Yet this does not mean that lyric poetry can be essentially clarified by means of an art form peculiar to music. That is just as unlikely as Nietzsche's attempt to allocate poetry to imagistic art. The peculiarity of poetry over against image and music stems neither, as Kant supposed, from the proximity to concepts nor, as Hegel thought, from its pure, nonsensual, notional character. Rather, what seems to be essential is its verbal character. The poem is open to a mode of access that is not captured by seeing or hearing: reading. Certainly, poems can be heard, and one can see them in their imagistic character. But the more complex a poem is, the more likely it is that one will only understand it in reading it.

Seeing, hearing, and reading may be the modes of experience that align themselves as if on their own with image, musical piece, and poem. But this does not mean that the essential forms of visual art, music, and poetry are exclusively accessible in these modes of experience. Otherwise, the references of various arts to each other would not be graspable. When Debussy and Trojahn name their pieces "images," they indicate that through them, one is to have an experience of imagistic character. Similarly, with an image like *Old Sound,* Klee seeks to make what is normally audible into something visible. The question of art forms that begins with the modes of experiencing art can thus only be a first step. When, through seeing images, the art form that shapes images becomes clear, one can inquire whether and how this art form can be instantiated in artworks that are not images in the usual sense. The same goes for music and for poetry. In other words, through eidetic variation with respect to artworks that belong to other established genres, one can observe and explore the art form that shapes the image, the piece of music. Only in this way can one explain that different genres can combine with each other, that a new genre label develops, as for example in the case of opera. With the forms of art clarified, the determinations of genre are also made transparent. Oriented by the individual plenitude of artworks, one can understand which of the genre designations are essential and which can be used more pragmatically.

Essential Determinations

It would be best to begin with the experience of images, as they are self-evident. Stepping into a room, one typically identifies an image as such immediately. It is as if images were cut out from their surroundings. Nearly everything else belongs to their environment and fits more or less into it. If not, it catches one's attention—as being useless, foreign, or bothersome. Images are different. They do not belong to the furnishings. If they do belong to the furnishing as a decoration, then it is obvious that they were not understood as images. Images are raised out in a peculiar way. A frame only underscores what belongs to the essence of the image.

The raisedness of an image has nothing to do with depiction, with something's schema showing up in an environment without that thing itself being actualized. Images that block or eschew such schematic identification have the same raisedness. They do not stand in relation to their surroundings either. The more recognizable one makes an image's severance, the more it comes to bear as an image. Images need a free space in a completely different way than other things. The so-called salon style of hanging certainly saves space. It may come across as decorative, but it does not do justice to any image.

That is because one is supposed to observe an image separately. When one recognizes an image in its separation from its surroundings, one has understood this. Observing the image means attending to the segment that the image is, and nothing else. When this succeeds, everything else that would be visible along with the image loses its significance. Sometimes it can feel as if nothing exists but the image that one is observing. The other images in the museum's room and the countless other people looking at images virtually disappear.

This kind of attention that is more or less exclusive, that is concentrated on the image, is an initial essential moment of images; in the observation of an image, all that matters is what is in the image and what belongs to it. Images are open to observation, but are essentially *closed*. Nothing beyond the image intrudes into it; nothing outside the image has significance for it. It is only when, in observing the image, one can disregard everything outside of it, that one understands the image as an image.

In their closedness, images are *exclusive*. They offer up to vision that which can be seen, and nothing else. An open window, such as those seen in some *Intérieurs* by Matisse, will never be closed. A woman's turned-away face, like that in Gerhard Richter's *Betty*,[20] will never be visible; it is invisible in a way unlike anything in the world. It is excluded from vision, not just from one's perspective, only thinkable as visible if one forgets the image as image. In a painter's studio, one could step before the easel and observe the painting that is in progress. Yet one will never know what the painter in *Las Meninas* is painting.

Just as images exclude, they also include. Everything that is visible in an image belongs to the image. That is why one does not understand an image if one views it selectively and only looks at one detail. The concentration on detail must always be tied back into the view of the whole; it is the view of the whole that the must determine the observation of an image. The image itself demands the view of the whole because it is one *totality*. It is the unified presentation of its moments, a plurality that is bound into a unity.

An image's totality is immediately present. It does not first need to be brought to consciousness by changing one's position and taking in various perspectives. It is not composed of several aspects. Nothing has to be presupposed or remembered. Everything is completely present; everything is simultaneous. Images are essentially *simultaneous*.

Closedness, exclusivity, totality, and simultaneity make up the essence of an image. One can call this essence "the imagistic" [*das Bildliche*], just as the term "the beautiful," as a substantivated adjective, does not only designate the beautiful thing, but also stands for the beautiful itself. The imagistic is always given when there is an image, regardless of its quality or its artistic significance. Of course, the essence of images is most recognizable in the masterpieces of art. Images that are artworks can be understood as "strong images";[21] they are more image than others—images that are not only recognized as such, but by virtue of which one knows what an image is. One sees this even if one cannot name the essential moments that make an image what it is.

The imagistic, however, is not only experienced in images that take the shape of paintings, drawings, graphics, or photographs. There are images without canvas or paper and that are not on walls, images that were not made by an artist. The cutout that they are is given immediately. Thus, a window can be imagistic. That which one sees when looking out a window has the same closedness, exclusivity, totality, and simultaneity as a painting. To be sure, one could leave the house and observe the tree in the garden from a perspective different than that of the window. But this possibility only pertains to the tree, not to the image that was given in the view from the window. By going outside into the garden, one loses this image. It is the same with images that are not so clearly delineated by frames as windows are. Even a landscape viewed from an elevation can be imagistic. Its totality is not marked as a segment, but it is certainly limited by being bound to a certain point of view. In the same way, it is possible that an image results not from limitation but from the collectivity of the manifold and different. That is the case with a group that is gathered at a table; all are there and visible in their collectivity, a family picture without photographer or painter.

This example hints at something that should be made explicit and grasped. Images need not be two-dimensional. Stage design is a good example of this. Even sculptures are imagistic; the boundary between the wall painting and the sculpture is fluid. The collage, the painting in which things are embedded (as in Rauschenberg or Anselm Kiefer), is already a relief. Conversely, many sculptures have a front side that is more for observation than other perspectives. The stele makes the space in which it is set up into an image. By circumventing that space, related to the sculpture in the center, one encounters a series of images.

Works of architecture were usually images or architects' drawings before they existed as structures. Thus it is little wonder that their image character remains after their completion. For instance, when one enters the convent chapel at Birnau on Lake Constance, one immediately recognizes a spatial image. The nave gradually narrows in its sweep toward the high altar; wall paintings and sculptures effortlessly join the lightness of the whole image. Of course, not all buildings reveal themselves to one's first look in this way. There are buildings that surprise one with every traversal and new room. In this way, they present a series of images. With every new angle and perspective, one sees a completely different totality of limitations and openings, of light and shadow. An image such as this is exclusive, too. To be sure, a change of perspective can make something visible that was not so before. But what is visible now belongs to another image. A building's sequence of images, however, need not consist of clearly delimited and thus distinguishable images. The transitions between images can be as continuous as the movement through the rooms, the transition from room to room. But in a building that is an artwork, there is always an image that appears to the attentive observer. It is no coincidence that, after visiting such a building, one recalls images.

With memory, another aspect of imagery comes into play. There are images of memory and fantasy, but if the essential determination of images presented here is correct, not every mental notion is an image. The aforementioned aspects determine whether something is an image. It does not matter whether something is seen or is present to one's power of imagination as if it were seen. Images need not be seen nor, as is often the case with the imagination, grasped by analogy to visibility. There are "thought-images,"[22] images composed of thoughts. If one follows Heidegger, thinking can even be particularly interested in the image form. In that case, "world-pictures" [*Weltbilder*] arise, and these, Heidegger stresses, are radically different from pictures or paintings. World-pictures are no representations of the world, but instead are the world itself in a certain form of accessibility. Heidegger elaborates on this accessibility by indicating the phrase of "being in the picture" about something. The phrase means that something stands before us precisely in the "way that it is." To "come to be in the picture about something" thus means "placing beings before oneself in the way that they are, and having them constantly before oneself." In the world-picture, "the world is grasped as an image"; "beings as a whole" are now "approached as that upon which humans arrange themselves and are "thus that which [humans] wish to bring before themselves, to have before themselves, and to thereby place before themselves in a decisive sense."[23] The talk of the world-picture is not metaphorical. World-pictures are real images; in them, the world—and not only the visible world—is brought into the form of the image.

The world-picture as Heidegger understands it goes back to "an essential decision about beings as a whole." He sees this decision at work particularly in modern technology and science. If one follows Heidegger's description, the "being of beings" is here "sought and found [in the] presentedness of beings."[24] Undergirding this understanding of the world-picture is the notion that the world as such is not an image, even if it is accessible in the image-form. The world is made into an image through a "decision" concerning the "being of beings." But in order for the world to be able to be "sought out" as an image, the possibility of its being an image must be known. This knowledge is attained through images, more precisely through the fact that these images are more or less explicitly understood by means of the image-form determining them. Yet it is crucial to this understanding to experience that, in general, images are not sought and found, but instead *arise on their own*. All at once, an image is there, and everything that is present accords to the image. One need not first shape the image, but can instead calmly observe it. Thus observation in thought as such—θεωρία, *contemplatio*—is founded upon the form of the image. Thought can accord with this form because it does not intrude, does not wish to change things, but instead leaves everything as it is. Observation leaves everything in its place within a whole that it has not created. If that is the case, then the volitional, systematically intrusive thinking that Heidegger describes must be dependent upon the originary observation; it is an attempt to regulate the possibilities that are given to this observation through the image-form. The attempt to be "in the picture" presupposes the image-form and the originary experience of it.

Even poetry can be imagistic, yet the case of the poetic image is different from that of the world-picture. The poetic image is not sought for the sake of regulation, but instead sets itself up as a concretion of observation, in such a way that the world is seen and presented in the closure of its contexts. Whenever poetry dedicates itself to the "totality of a worldview and life-attitude," as Hegel puts it,[25] it is concerned with the world *in* the image, with the world as it is imagistically given along with poetry. But the poetic image need not be a panoramic view as presented in the great novels of the nineteenth and twentieth centuries. Even the poetic description aimed at minute detail, as in Stifter or in Jünger's *Subtilen Jagden*, is imagistic. Any work is imagistic that actualizes totality and closure in the imagistic sense.

Music, too, can be imagistic in a comparable sense. There are pieces of music that are less essentially about progression than about a circling around recurring themes. Such pieces, as for example Debussy's *Images* or Ligeti's *Atmosphères*, resoundingly fill an image-space. The impression they leave is less that of a developing multiplicity than that of a closed and simultaneous whole.

It is more difficult to grasp the essential determination of music than of the image. There was a reason that Kant and Hegel, both of whom oriented themselves along visual art and poetry, struggled with music. But this does not mean that music refuses or eschews description. It belongs to music not to be graspable as images or poems are, and thus a description can use this as a starting point. Music initially appears un-thing-like; contrary to the poetic word, it has no articulated meaning. Furthermore, it lacks the still presence that an image possesses. Music is an art of time; as the time analyses of Augustine and Husserl show, music is an example par excellence of the experience of time.[26] Music occurs; in sounding, it is always only present in this occurrence. Part of what is played has already passed by after the first sounds, and another part lies ahead. Thus, one only ever has the present slice, and this one cannot hold onto; in sounding, even it passes by.

What is more, a piece of music stirs us differently than an image does. Music that resounds is not present across a distance such that one can quietly observe it. One must go along, one is taken along, sometimes even carried away. Music involves *movement*, and it moves affectively, puts one in an attunement or mood.

"Attunement" [*Stimmung*] is primarily a musical term. When Schiller speaks of a "musical attunement of feeling," he transfers the word denoting the tuning of an instrument, the setting of intonation, to experience. The attunement of "feeling" is the latter's harmony with something; it can also refer to the mutual harmony of affective powers themselves.[27] It is in this sense that music is attuning. In sounding, it is movement that moves and lets one be moved. This is why Nietzsche, in his early book, could primarily understand it as a Dionysian art.

Yet Nietzsche's understanding of music in the *Birth of Tragedy* is one-sided. Not all music is the Dionysian turmoil that Nietzsche illustrates by means of the closing choir in Beethoven's Ninth Symphony.[28] Even one of Bach's fugues or a string quartet by Webern induces movement, while there is nothing Dionysian about this music—no "shattering force of sound," no "unified flow of the melody" (33). Bach's music even makes clear that tone and tonality are not that important. The tonality of a modern concert piano is certainly different from that of a cembalo or a clavichord, but given a comparable interpretive approach, the attunement awakened by a Bach fugue will always be approximately the same regardless of what instrument it is played on. The peculiar musical movement is present in tonality and tone, but it is apparently not identical with it.

This confirms the supposition that musical movement and being-moved are possible without tonality and tone. This is how it is experienced in dance. The latter can often be physical movement that is awakened and led by resounding music. But dance does not require music that sounds; dance can be present strictly in physical movement and nevertheless be musical in its essence. In dance, the musical apparently arises from the movement and being-moved itself.

In his essay "Degas Danse Dessin," Valéry described a dance of this sort. He describes "beings of an incomparable, translucent, and sensitive substance; glassy, incredibly irritable skin; domes of flowing silk; vitreous crowns; long, living slings pervaded by swift waves; fringes and frills that enfold and unfold; all this while they turn, dissolve, retreat; fluid as the fluid mass that presses them, weds them, holds them, gives them space with the smallest inflection and takes the shape of their space."[29] What is described here are jellyfish (*méduses*): flowing, indeed fluid life-forms in the fluid element. They move and are moved, such that their movement exists in commutation with the element that surrounds them, pervades them, presses them, and at the same time leaves them space. The movement need not come from the jellyfish themselves; the water moves them. Yet in its streaming, the water does not wash them away. They work against the water's movement without resisting it. They take the movement up and return it as their own. Their form seems to exist solely for the purpose of this taking-up and giving back; they exist entirely within the movement that is both the water's and their own. Nothing solid prevents the movement of these "absolute dancers."[30]

Nothing stands in their way; there is nothing but being-moved and movement, such that Valéry can speak of an "ideal of being-moved."[31] Here there is no doing that affects anything; nothing here is univocally active or passive. All that exists is being-moved in the back and forth of movement. If this movement is a dance, and dance as commonly assumed belongs to music, then it is musical; it is musical without tone or tonality.

The musical movement as Valéry describes it can be grasped even more precisely by calling it "playful." Entirely in keeping with Kant's sense of the concept of play, it is a *free* occurrence that lets its moments come to bear unforcedly yet with all the intensity of their connection. The movement is *open*, that is, not directed toward completion. Its openness is actualized through interchange and reversal, in the back and forth. Playfulness is, in Gadamer's words, "the back and forth of a movement [. . .] that is not attached to any goal," but instead renews itself "in constant repetition."[32] In its openness, the movement of play achieves stillness. It is, as Gadamer puts it, "constant conversion, pure fulfillment, *energeia*" (118). Heidegger took the significance of this fundamental Aristotelian concept to lie in "movedness" [*Bewegtheit*] rather than movement, and saw the "pure unfolding of its essence" in the fact that "stillness does not mean ceasing or termination of movement; movedness instead gathers the *holding still* within itself, and this holding in does not exclude movement but includes it, does not merely include it, but reveals it."[33] The holding still or holding in of the movedness of play is to be found in "constant repetition," in the fact that it does not proceed toward an aim, but instead turns back on itself and thereby confirms what it has already been. Nevertheless, this turning back is not a postponement or halting, but is rather the still procession of movedness itself.

It is fitting that Gadamer does not elaborate his conception of play by way of games that people play according to rules; even if people's playful behavior does not fall under any serious purpose, they are usually not without some admixture of intention. The essential purposelessness of play is thus far better exemplified in the "play of light," the "play of waves," or the "play of forces." Play is "playing together," movedness that is always richer than its moments. As Gadamer states, play has a "medial sense."[34] It is an occurrence that results as if on its own, that cannot be attributed to an initiator; even when people play, the game is not effected by anyone. Rather, the game allows the "player to dissolve, as it were," and "thereby [takes] away the task of initiative." This is why play is experienced as "disburdening."

Yet the game can only be disburdening because, in its movement, it is not a Dionysian turmoil but an "order" (110). Dionysian turmoil rips one out of the context of activity without leading to another activity that is less founded upon initiative. The turmoil is self-forgetfulness, the "destruction of the *principii indi-*

viduationis."[35] Play, conversely, raises individual initiative into an ordered context that supersedes it, but without threatening individual life.

Gadamer speaks in passing about the order of play or its "ordered structure," as if it were obvious how this order is to be understood.[36] Yet it bears elucidating how one is to determine this order. The order of play must be described as the order of movement. In this respect, Valéry is more precise. There are many insightful observations about order in his essay *"Philosophie de la danse."* [One such observation is that] it is easy to notice that all automatic movements corresponding to the state of a living being—and not to an imagined or localized aim—would take on a periodic order.[37]

What Valéry wishes to describe here is the origin of dance. The movement that is not effective, that is, not directed toward an aim, would be diffuse and hardly executable if it did not find its way into an order. Effective movements are organized by the steps required to actualize their goals; they structure themselves according to the serial moments of this actualization. In contrast to this, the aimless movement falls back in itself, as it were. It is nothing more than the movement itself that must find its own way to determination. In this sense, Valéry speaks of dance as a "world" or a "system" without exteriority; here, there is no object that one could grasp or obtain that one could reject; nothing from which one would need to flee.[38] In dance, nothing exists outside the system that forms itself strictly through what belongs to it.[39]

Valéry's description is impressive, yet by conjuring an immanence that gives the (apparently Cartesian) philosopher occasion to rejoice at the sight of the dance,[40] it is not convincing. Valéry forgets the obstinacy of physical movement that he himself had described by way of the jellyfish, an obstinacy that is never entirely "systematic" but instead unfolds playfully. The musical order is no "system," and thus Gadamer's indication toward the "medial sense" of play gets closer to the matter. The ordered movement must be free so as to be musical; its freedom has to be confirmed in the musical order. As soon as the movement is free of any goal-orientation or direction, an order arises—however preliminarily—which, once it is there, carries the movement in a peculiar way. It determines the movement without robbing it of its freedom, for it arises out of freedom. A step, a gesture is repeated; the repetition needs the distance between the step, the gesture now—and now. The distance can be greater or smaller, the movement can accordingly be slower or faster. In addition, there is variation that swirls around what is repeated and allows one to better see it as repeated in the freedom of its play. By relinquishing itself to this order, it becomes at once free and ordered movedness.

The Greek word for the order that dwells within movedness is ῥυθμός. Rhythm is, as stated in Plato's *Laws*, the "order of movement."[41] Together with harmony, which is the ordered voice under the aspect of higher and lower tones,[42] rhythm forms the order of music—as sung.[43] Yet as we have seen in the case of dance, there is musical movement without tone. If this is so, all that remains of the determination of the musical, which is to be the essence not only of music in the narrow sense, is strictly the living rhythm, that is, the one which results from play. The musical, then, is *rhythmic play*.

This result can be confirmed by way of Nietzsche's thought, which is also interesting for its self-critical character. While Nietzsche, in the *Birth of Tragedy*, disparages rhythm as a "Doric architectonic in tones, but only in implied tones" to the benefit of the "shattering force of the tone" and the "unified stream of the melody,"[44] in *Vermischten Meinungen und Sprüchen* (1879, included in the collection *Human, All Too Human* II) he develops an understanding of music oriented entirely along rhythm. He refers in both cases to Richard Wagner's music, such that the shift in Nietzsche's understanding of music is easy to grasp as a turn from Wagner idolization to Wagner critique.[45]

The text in question carries the title "How the Soul Should Move, According to Modern Music." The question is answered quite clearly: The soul must swim. "Modern music" is like water in which, after a few steps, one loses the ground from beneath one's feet. Modern music is that "unified stream of the melody" still celebrated in *Birth of Tragedy*, "which is now, strongly but unclearly, designated as 'infinite melody.'" Nietzsche contrasts this with the type of movement found in "older music," in which one had to "*dance* faster or slower, in a delicate or celebratory or fiery back and forth." "The measure that was necessary for this, the maintenance of definite levels of tempo and energy, [forced] the soul of the listener into a constant *moderation*." "The magic of that music" lay in the "back and forth between this cooler breath that arose from moderation and the crazed breath of musical enthusiasm."[46] The "older music" permits what Plato (to whom Nietzsche implicitly alludes here) calls εὐσχημοσύνη: "grace," "elegance."[47] This goes together with moderation (σωφροσύνη), which consists in the form giving and thus limited order of life movement, and is thereby set over against the limitless desire for more (πλεονεξία). In moderation, the movedness of life has itself become measured. If one follows the *Republic*, this is precisely what is achieved through music. Musical education (ἐν μουσικῇ τροφή) relies on the fact that the music's order is absorbed into the "interior of the soul" (τὸ ἐντὸς τῆς ψυχῆς) and grips it. Music allows life to become graceful when the music itself is graceful, that is, of a free movement.[48]

Nietzsche takes this idea up, but he is concerned primarily with the measure of music itself and the danger in which music is threatened with dissolution in the fluidity of the "infinite melody." Wagner sought to "break all mathematical harmony of tempo and energy";[49] he feared "the ossification, the crystallization, the transition of music into the architectonic." Such a danger would constantly increase "if such music [relied] ever more closely on a completely naturalistic art of drama and gesture that was not raised or ruled through a higher plastic art" (435). That is precisely what Wagner demanded. The orchestra would "step into such an intimate relation with the motives of the action that, as embodied harmony, it [makes possible] on the one hand the definite expression of melody, and on the other [maintains] the melody itself in the necessary uninterrupted stream, and thereby [communicates] the motives with constant convincing intensity."[50] In Nietzsche's view, this process dissolves the music. Wagner would certainly not have agreed with him on this, but he would have accepted that rhythm was dissolved. This is shown by the fact that Wagner only recognizes melody as a musical form.[51] In the stream of melody, which in Wagner's conception is to adapt to the shifts of dramatic occurrence, music matches itself up programmatically to life and its possibilities of expression. It thus loses the possibility of giving a rhythmic form to life and thereby shape it in its movedness.

Nevertheless, Wagner's music remains art, and the rhythmic cannot have disappeared entirely from it. Nietzsche even admits this much to Wagner. Despite attempting to "break" rhythm's "harmony of tempo and energy," he does not entirely give up on rhythm but is instead "overabundant in the invention of those effects that [sound] to the older ear like rhythmic paradoxes and blasphemies." He sets a "three-beat rhythm over against a two-beat," frequently introduces "the five- and seven-beat," repeats "the same phrase immediately, but with an elongation such that it [gains] twice or three times the duration."[52] In this way, Wagner varies the rhythm. More than other composers before him, he introduces irregularity into it. In other words, he puts the playfulness and liveliness of rhythm to the test, thereby pushing the possibilities of the musical to an extreme that Nietzsche finds highly dubious. Yet as one could object to Nietzsche, that which Wagner musically explores lies within the musical itself. The merely uniform rhythm—that of the heartbeat or the ticking clock—is not musical; a rhythm like that is no rhythmic play. It belongs to the essence of the musical to measure the expanse of this play. Little wonder, then, that a composer like Stravinsky, who stresses rhythm and directs himself critically toward Wagner, can come after the latter.

It is noteworthy that Nietzsche, already in *Birth of Tragedy*, elaborates rhythmic form by means of concepts from visual art. If one takes this seriously, one must conclude that architectonic and plastic art are not foreign to music. Structure and order do not lead to the alleged "ossification" that Wagner feared, but instead allow the movedness of music to first be musical—whether it is in sounds or in the motions of a dance. Conversely, one may thus also infer that architecture and plastic art, and the works of visual art in general, can be musical. In this sense, Hegel speaks of the "eurhythmia" of gothic architecture;[53] the spirals and hatchings in Twombly's works from the late 1960s and early 1970s appear rhythmic.[54] They *appear* this way, along with the cathedral's vertically structured arches, towers, and embellishments, even though they are not in motion.

The impression could be traced back to a transference; thus, in observing a cathedral or a Twombly painting, an association with musical and rhythmic movement arises. As concerns Twombly's paintings, one might attempt to trace the rhythm of their lines back to the motion of painting itself; the painter accomplished a rhythmic movement, and the image retains the traces of this.

These attempts at explanation, however, do not refute the impression that architecture or painting themselves appear as rhythmic. The association with music can only arise if a building like the gothic cathedral gives the impetus for this, and thus the building itself must be rhythmic. In the same way, one would not be able to derive the movement of the painting hand from the painting if the movement were not itself in the painting—not as a trace, but as movedness. Accordingly, the latter is itself visible; in order to understand it as movedness, one need not think of the movement of the painting hand. After all, in sounding music, too, the movedness is in the sounds and not the pianist's hands that strike the keys. Yet sounding music is itself movedness; it occurs, whereas the cathedral is as motionless as the image.

The supposed paradox can be solved if one dissociates rhythm as musical form from movedness. It is not movedness that constitutes the form, but rather rhythm that is the form of movedness. As such, rhythm need not first arise with movedness, but can instead guide in advance, can be determined ahead of time. This type of guideline can be found in music in the form of notation. But this is not itself the guideline; it only indicates the "mathematical harmony of tempo and energy" that Nietzsche speaks of, in other words, the rhythmic order that organizes the sound.

There is a similar organization in the visual realm. It is especially obvious when the visible can be taken as an instruction for movement. This is the case with the steppingstones (*tobi-ishi*) that are set into the ground in the Japanese tea garden and which lead the way to the tea house.[55] The stones provide a rhythm for the path through the garden by being set in certain intervals. More precisely, it is these intervals that provide the rhythm for the path. They give each step its measure and thereby give the walk its time. This is not possible without the stones; the intervals are those of the stones. They provide the rhythm by being set in certain intervals. Just as the music in the *Republic* only makes one graceful by being graceful itself, the steppingstones can only provide the rhythm by being in a rhythmic order themselves. This order need not first be discovered in stepping on the stones and walking across the garden. If one looks closely, one can uncover the rhythm simply by observing. The case is the same with the cathedral's "eurhythmia" and the rhythm of Twombly's paintings.

Looking closely means *following* the order, *going along with* the order, letting oneself be led by it, and thereby measuring the matter in its in intervals with one's gaze. It means seeing the interval's repetition and transformation, evenness and change, both in sequence and at rest—all of which make the movement of vision into a movedness. The moments that are ordered through intervals do not first become rhythmic through their movedness, but they do relate to movedness. Rhythm is order that actualizes itself in movedness; this order is musical when it has the character of free play. As order, rhythm is not the reality given in movedness, but instead the form that makes the latter possible, and to which one must correspond in the actual movement of looking, moving, hearing, or playing. It bears recalling that the movedness is not a goal-directed proceeding. Even if it is realized in a process, it is nevertheless essentially determined by rest. This is how there can be movedness even in tarrying—in the pulsing of hues as experienced in close observation of Rothko's paintings, or as the advance and retreat of the black-outlined surfaces in Mondrian's paintings. These may appear static to a superficial look, but even here there is rhythmic play, and thus musicality and movedness.

The actuality of rhythmic order can be experienced in poetry as well. This pertains not only to the rhythm of spoken language, but to the structural sequence of the poetic work as well. In this sense, Hölderlin interpreted the action of a tragedy—in the example of Sophocles' *Antigone*—as a rhythmic succession in which "thought and sensation and reasoning develop in a poetic logic." The presentation of the various parts of action amounts to "a whole" whose "cohesion of the different faculties' *independent parts* [could be] called rhythm in a higher sense, or the calculable law."[56] Hölderlin's observation can be generalized: the plot of poetic works is rhythmically ordered in such a way that a plot's slow development can correspond to an acceleration in pace and again to an easing of it.

Over against this, the rhythmic character of poetic language is so obvious that one could take it for the essential mark of poetry. Nietzsche, despite having become self-critical and skeptical of the "infinite melody," could even be a role model for this. In the *Gay Science*, he identifies poetry with rhythmic language. Rhythm is the "origin of poetry,"[57] the latter is the dance of the speaking soul. Nietzsche only hints at this, while Valéry expressly compares poetry to dance and attempts to determine its essence with an eye toward dance.[58] In this, both Nietzsche and Valéry take the rhythmic and musical language of poetry to stand in opposition to prose. The good prose writer, according to Nietzsche, constantly avoids poetry. Every "abstraction" wishes to face "roguishly" up to poetry, and "all dryness and cool" is supposed to set poetry, "the lovely goddess," "in a soft desperation."⁵⁹ For Valéry, prose is determined solely by communication. In prosaic language, the form does not survive comprehension; it dissolves in clarity, it has had its effect, has allowed one to understand, and has thus lived.⁶⁰

The most proximate rejoinder to this conception of poetry can be mitigated by means of a conceptual clarification. The distinction of poetry and prose, as Nietzsche and Valéry state it, should not be taken as a distinction between metrically bound and free language, respectively. Even language that is not metrically bound can be rhythmic, and this allows for poetic prose while maintaining Nietzsche and Valéry's sense of poetry.

Yet the determination of the poetic in terms of rhythm is unsatisfying in two ways. On the one hand, it passes over the fact that the inflection of language with rhythm need not be poetic. It can be rhetorical and thus subordinated to usefulness, or it can be a characteristic of texts that are not poetic at all, but are instead quotidian, scientific, or philosophical prose. In these cases, a rhythmic order would in general characterize good style. On the other hand, the determination leaves out the fact that poetic language is not only spoken and read differently than normal "prose," but is instead a radically different language. Everything about it, even its way of meaning, is different. Valéry alludes to this notion when he stresses that poetic language is not communicative. Yet what is to be apart from this remains to be determined. The determination must go beyond language if the poetic, just as the imagistic and the musical, is not to be exhausted by one genre of art. Nevertheless, one must begin with that art in which the poetic is most proximately familiar. That which one takes to be poetic is first and foremost experienced in the linguistic artwork, in the work that is experienced most immediately as poetry: the poem.

Poems are not necessarily bound to meter, rhyme, or stanza form. There are poems that lack all these characteristics. Yet even such poems are recognizable as such; when one recognizes them as poems, one knows that this is a language that no one speaks. With its *parlando,* a poem such as Gottfried Benn's "People Met" ["*Menschen getroffen*"] only pretends to actually speak. It is too exact, too definitive to be spoken. In the poem, there is no probingly ventured phrasing that would require revision; nothing here belongs to that process of looking for words, even if the search for words is poetized and thus brought to language in the poem. What is poetized stands firm, and this means that it is essentially *that which is written*. In its earliest meaning, the verb "to poetize" [*dichten*] means as much as the Latin *dictare;* poetizing is a dictation for writing down. The poet *writes*. Even if, like Pindar, he is a singer, his verses do not come to him as song or in song, but need instead to be written beforehand.

The written character of the poem is more or less explicitly part of the experience of the poem itself. It is rare that a poem can be understood solely by hearing it; even if it is accessible in listening, one will understand it better by reading it. A relatively easy poem like Goethe's "Over All the Peaks It Is Peaceful" only shows the abundance of its moments in writing, and this is even more true of poems like Hölderlin's late hymns or Rilke's *Duino Elegies*. This is because a poem is a *fabric*. It is not a consecutive verbal expression that one follows, but is instead determined by a manifold of *correspondences*. The first line can correspond to the last; rhymes establish connections that do not exist in normal speech; a word can have a plenitude of correspondences in other words it resonates with. In a sonnet titled "Correspondences," Baudelaire poetized precisely such connections, thereby reflecting the poem back in its own appearance and making it comprehensible.

Through this poem, we conversely also see that the correspondences in a poem never simply pertain to lines, rhymes, and words, but apply to that which is said in itself. Things that would normally not be related to each other in everyday speech often stand, in a poem, in a relation that is both mysterious and illuminating, and which often remains suspended between the two. To be sure, allusions and analogies, similes and metaphors, belong to the essence of language and can thus be characteristic of stylistically sound and spirited speech. Yet with the poem it is different. The more poetic a poem is, the more the weight of everything said, of all that belongs to it, lies in its connection with something else. A simile thus no longer serves to clarify or elaborate a matter, but rather has the same status as that which is compared. When, in the third sonnet of the second part of the *Sonnets to Orpheus*, the mirrors are poetized as the "the interstices of time filled / with the holes of sieves," the notion of the mirror is combined with the almost conceptual language of time interstices and the object-like image of the sieve into a tense constellation. In the next stanza, a metaphor has a retroactive effect on that from which it takes its inception. The empty hall, extended by the mirrors, becomes "wide as forests when the dawn glimmers." Then "the chandelier goes through your [the mirrors'] inaccessibility / like a sixteen-pointer."[61] That the chandelier "goes" allows it to become that animal whose antlers the sweeping arms invoke. Hall and forest, chandelier and stag, the enterable room and the inaccessible but lit mirror-images of the room, are set into a context that only exists in the poem.

This state of affairs can be summed up in one word: that which becomes experienceable in the language of a poem is the *sense* of what is said.[62] Sense is something other than meaning. The meaning of terms used in a poem can be self-explanatory. When Rilke's sonnet speaks of mirrors, of sieves, of a hall, and of forests, these expressions mean the same thing that they mean otherwise. They are certainly not used to designate a thing or state of affairs, but remain in the state of possibility, without factual reference. Yet this possibility is that of normal language. The terms in the poem do not have any special meaning; otherwise, one would have to learn the poem's language as if it were foreign. The sense of the expressions used in the poem, however, is different from that of normal speech. They step into a special relational context and thus gain a special status. This context is their sense.

The sense of a poem has a peculiar intensity and incisiveness; it bears *more* sense than the context of the world experienced in everyday life, which is always open and is only disclosed through its respective modes of access. The world context is experienced as having sense insofar as one can actualize and fulfill one's own activity in it. It is through this that one's activity has sense; it has sense in a context that proves to be sensical with respect to the activity. In the poem, however, this connection to activity is dissolved. A poem's sense does not prove itself by validating, through a context, one's own possibilities of behavior and expectations. Rather, a sense context simply stands there in itself. It contains complex and unexpected connections that can only be accessed by understanding them. Since the sense only exists in the poem, it stands forth as such. The poem is therefore connected, as Valéry says, with the "sensation of a whole,"[63] a "tendency toward perceiving a world,"[64] which means a complete system of relations. In poetry, things, events, and actions are combined in such a way that they call each other forth and associate with each other in ways completely different from ordinary circumstances.[65]

The fact that such a heightened sensation of wholeness, an increased experience of sense, accompanies poetry may be familiar to us from everyday situations. When a situation is called "poetic," what is indicated is its particular coherence. It usually remains unclear, however, how this coherence comes to be. If it arises through the reading of a poem, then it can be described more precisely—as we partially attempted with respect to Rilke's sonnet. But what such a description alone does not yet make clear is what, in the essence of language, makes poetry possible. Thus, it also remains unclear whether and how the poetic can be actualized in other arts than poetry.

Heidegger concerned himself with clarifying this question unlike anyone else. His fundamental idea is that language itself is to be considered poetic. It is "poetry in the essential sense,"[66] that is, it is essentially a "naming" [*Nennen*]. By naming "that which is," language first brings "such beings to word and to appearance" (61).

The formulation is a late echo of the determination of phenomenology given in *Being and Time*. According to that definition, phenomenology is λέγειν τὰ φαινόμενα, and if λέγειν is to be understood as ἀποφαίνεσθαι, then phenomenology is ἀποφαίνεσθαι τὰ φαινόμενα.[67] Phenomenology, and according to the artwork essay, language as such, is a letting-appear, a showing. But this does not yet say wherein the peculiar linguistic possibility of showing lies.

The elaboration of λέγειν as ἀποφαίνεσθαι basically already gives the answer, however. In his engagement with Aristotle, Heidegger stressed that linguistic indication is a demonstration [*Aufzeigen*] and as such always occurs in the joining-together of various determinations. The propositional sentence (λόγος ἀποφαντικός) is connective, and this in turn is only possible because the determinations connected in it are at the same time held apart in their difference.[68] The sentence, more precisely the sentence that names something and gives it another determination—for example, stating of the table that it is made of wood—is, in Aristotle's terms, a demonstration of something with regard to something, the demonstration of the table with respect to its being made of wood.[69]

Heidegger later disconnects this relatedness as evinced in the propositional sentence from its Aristotelian roots and grasps it as the determination of language as such. Now λόγος is no longer just the sentence, the smallest linguistic unit that evinces connection and therefore sense. λόγος, as Heidegger delineates it in his essay "Logos (Heraclitus Fragment 50)," is the connecting, joining essence of language. Heidegger gleans this meaning of λόγος by orienting himself along the verb form of the word. λέγειν means "to read," and not only in the sense in the reading of writing; that is merely "one, albeit the prevailing mode of reading." The basic meaning of "reading" is "bringing together into gathered presence"; reading is a "carrying together" and "keeping safe," just as it occurs in the harvesting of grapes or the gleaning.[70]

Heidegger's elaboration is accurate. The word λέγειν indeed means a gathering of what is separate and different, in such a way that it is not the totality and unity of what is gathered that is stressed, but instead the belonging-together of the many; insofar as this belonging-together can also apply to individual moments, it is understandable why λόγος also means "relation" and "proportion." A determination of relation, too, is a gathering-together.

The gathering-together need not be linguistic; λέγειν can also mean "to count," since number, ἀριθμός, is nothing other than the determinate gathering of such-and-such a multitude.[71] When counting occurs not as the determination of an amount, but as addition and listing, it can in turn become a process bound to language, namely recounting [*Erzählen*]. It is not a coincidence that the word contains "counting," just as in the French "*raconter*" and the English "to tell." The latter basically means "to mention one by one or piece by piece."[72]

The linguistic collection in the sense just elaborated is not necessarily poetic. It can also be a referential speaking, an assertion about a certain state of affairs. If one were to take that as poetic, then poetry would be synonymous with indication, and the word would lose its specific sense. Nevertheless, the understanding of the essence of language gleaned from Heidegger's indication of λέγειν can be developed toward a determination of the poetic. Every speaking contains a connection, a gathering-together. But the latter need not be the *sense* of what is said. The sense of speaking, in other words, need not be fulfilled in linguistic sense, in the belonging-together of the manifold. Usually, the sense of speech consists in indication and communication, which means what is said joins together into the context of collective behavior. What is said gets its sense from this context; the context provides the sense of what is said. But speaking can also be about the context of what is said and what is sayable. In that case, the sense of what is said and the sense of speaking join together, and then speech has become poetic.

The poetic need not be actualized as great poetry. Every story is, in essence, poetic, because it is only about the sense of what is said; its sense is the context of events, people, and places that are brought into clarity through telling the story. If every story were not in essence poetic, then storytelling could not become poetry in the narrower and more emphatic sense. The simple story, just as a description that establishes an order of things and thus explores their sense, is essentially poetic. But it is not poetized. Poetry in the narrow sense only exists in writing. Only writing is capable of doing justice to the plenitude and complexity of sense. The more poetic speech is, the more pronounced its tendency toward writing.[73]

In order to locate this tendency toward writing in the essence of language, we can look once more to Heidegger's thoughts on the meaning of λόγος and λέγειν. Heidegger elaborates the term λέγειν as both "to read" and "to lay." The latter is, in turn, understood as letting-lie-before: "laying brings something to lie by letting it lie [there] together."[74] Heidegger does not specify how he wishes lying-there and letting-lie-before to be understood. He alludes to the fact that he is thinking of showing in the sense of the λόγος ἀποφαντικός, a showing that is less about ascertaining a state of affairs than about an experience of showing itself. That which "lies there together" is "placed, stored, set, deposited into unconcealment, i.e. it is sheltered in it" (216–217). The "lying-there-in-itself of what is deposited" is "the *presencing* into unconcealment of that which lies there" (217). If one understands the presencing here as appearing, then the sense of λέγειν, taken as laying, is its appearance; λέγειν is thus, as it was already determined in *Being and Time*, an ἀποφαίνεσθαι τὰ φαινόμενα.[75] Accordingly, the sheltering of which Heidegger speaks in relation to the letting-lie-before can only be understood as a preservation of appearance, more precisely as an unconcealment that ensures appearance. If the "reading that is part of [laying in λέγειν is] determined in advance by way of safekeeping,"[76] then reading is the taking-together and holding-together of phenomena in their phenomenality.

But reading, understood in this way, requires an adequate foothold in order to sustain the experience of "lying before" and in order not to seek its grasp in the matters and states of affairs that can be ascertained in speech. This foothold can only be adequate if it is adequate to the sense of reading, to the context of what is said. Writing bears this adequacy. Thus, the letting-lie-before in Heidegger's sense would have to be understood as being-written [*Verschriftlichung*]. The laying that belongs together with reading in the term λέγειν, and which determines reading to be a "safekeeping," is writing.

But how should writing be understood here? If the poetic in the essence of language refers to being-written, then writing cannot mean some linguistically external fixation in conventional symbols. Such symbols are only possible and can only be invented and developed because language, understood as λόγος, bears the fundamental trait of fixity within itself, and it is that trait by virtue of which symbolic notations are made. To reiterate Heidegger's point, language can only let that which is said lie before (in the sense of λέγειν) if language itself can lie before. Only when the λόγος itself lies before can one recognize etchings in stone, and traces of graphite or ink, as writing.

Language itself is helpful in grasping more precisely the lying-before of the λόγος. There is a Latin word that serves as a translation of λόγος: *textus*. The word, the basic meaning of which is "web" or "netting," initially designates the order of speech,[77] the context of what is said, inasmuch as this context is not vague and mutable but tightly interwoven. The interwovenness, the inner order of sense, certainly requires fixation in order to persist. But that which persists in the fixation is the inner order. In this persistence, the λόγος is a text. Accordingly, the poetic aspect of language is its textual character. Its validity is more distinctive the more clearly the language is textual.

It bears repeating that text is not synonymous with writing; a text can be instantiated in many different forms of writing. To a certain degree of complexity, it can even be maintained through memory. It can be stored in digital media. Texts are certainly dependent on finding particular possibilities of actualizing their persistence. But they are not exhausted by this kind of actualization.

The same goes for actualization in linguistic articulation and in written symbols. Texts do not have to be linguistic. Insofar as texts are solely defined as "networks" whose context lends sense to their individual moments, images and pieces of music can be taken as texts as well. They, too, are to be understood as contexts that embody the sense of their moments. Their essence, too, contains that persistence that can be actualized in one way or another. To use Heidegger's concepts, reading and laying have their effect in these [art forms]. They are coherent gatherings of the particular and diverse that have been brought to lie before. We can support this by way of a concept that is less frequently used with regard to poetry but is quite common with respect to images and music: the concept of composition. Images and pieces of music are arrangements. Something stands together in them that does not otherwise occur together, but which is now to be understood in the way that it is held together in the image or piece of music. This understanding, corresponding to the works, is a reading. Pieces of music and images are not merely heard or seen; they can and must also be read.

This should be obvious with respect to music. It is initially readable in the form of the score; it is impossible to fundamentally understand a piece of music without a thorough reading of the score. The clarity, coherence, and plausibility of a performance rests ultimately on the study of, and reflection upon, this score. In order for the piece of music to resound and be present in its sounding, one must know the piece [muß das Stück erkannt sein]. If this knowledge has an effect in the performance, then that which is known, the text of the piece, can also be experienced in the performance, and to a certain degree in hearing as well.

Buildings and images, too, must be read. In reading them, to use Gadamer's terms, the point is to "take part in the figure of sense that we encounter."[78] This occurs by getting involved with the text of the building or the image, and attempting to grasp it. Part of this entails not just experiencing the building as imagistic, as a series of images, but exploring its inner structure by walking through its rooms, seeing it in various perspectives, from near and afar. We must, as Gadamer puts it, "build it up for ourselves, as it were,"[79] in order to understand its shape. By walking through and around a building, one interprets it; one presents it—just as one presents a literary work for oneself in reading it.[80] In a way comparable to the study of a score, an engagement with the blueprint of a building can be helpful.

The reading of images occurs in a similar way, albeit in a way that appears less overtly to be a reading. The reading of a building is obviously a bringing-together and gathering, as is the reading of a literary work. In the image, however, everything is generally there in one glance. But it is not only the case with detailed images, such as Altdorfer's *Battle of Alexander at Issus*,[81] that the gaze must simultaneously go into the particular and gather it together in order to recognize the coherence of the whole, the text of the image. It is only by reading an image through observation that one can also describe it; only in this way can one understand the place of the particular in the whole—the sense of the individual in the context that is its sense.

The readability and necessity of reading pieces of music, buildings, and images should not be understood as an indication of their linguisticality. Any talk of the "language of music" or of the "language of images" is metaphorical.[82] At most, pieces of music or images are akin to language when they bear a signifying character, for example in the case of a military signal or when an image depicts the exit sign for a figure that is running toward it. The individual moments of a piece of music or an image, however, are not "signs" or "symbols"; they do not signify anything. For this reason, any attempt to grasp art in general through means of semiotic or symbolic theory will have little success; as artworks are not referential, one only ever has the possibility of grasping their moments as modifications or deviations from the normal function of signs,[83] and this ultimately requires one to state that they are not signs at all.

Nevertheless, the temptation to understand art as linguistic is not without its reasons. It stems from the textual character of art, from the fact that the artwork is always also a λόγος, and from the assumption that the λόγος is essentially linguistic. There is the resounding λόγος of music and the visual but "mute" λόγος of buildings and images.[84]

Mixtures

As has been shown, the art forms of the imagistic, the musical, and the poetic determine artworks in highly differentiated ways. Images and buildings are not only imagistic; they can also be musical and poetic; pieces of music are not only musical, but also imagistic and poetic; in poetry one finds, beside the poetic, the musical and the imagistic. The forms just elaborated, then, are not genres to which artworks could be assigned. Rather, art forms find many ways to instantiate themselves. They are mixed together in artworks in individual ways. To be sure, we have not yet established whether all artworks consist of a mixture of the three described forms. But on the basis of our description above, this supposition can count as highly likely. If one looks or listens more closely in the engagement with an artwork, if one reads in more detail and clarifies one's own experience, one will find the three art forms of the imagistic, the musical, and the poetic.

Yet with this insight, we have gained less than might appear at first glance. The art forms are not just forms of art. Every image is imagistic whether it is artistic or not. This includes images that one only sees for a brief moment—as perhaps the image of a gathered family or the image of a landscape—which, in order to be images, need not be beautiful and thus related to art. Many things are rhythmic. One cannot image life without rhythm: heartbeat, breath, ebb and flood, a bird's wings, the movement of jellyfish that Valéry described. It is not only an artwork that can be poetic in the sense elaborated above; one need only recollect that the concept of "text" is central for rhetoric and that Kant considers rhetoric to be part of poetry.[85] Philosophical thought, too, bears a textual character: the order of its thoughts lends it persistence and the ability to be fixated. By this measure, would one not have to call poetic any order that presents coherent sense? After all, it is to such orderings that poetic mood generally attaches, such that the orders, as the moods' possibilities, would bear the same essence. The concept with which the elaboration of the poetic began, λόγος, signifies for Heraclitus the order of the world.

If such is the case with art forms, then they are actually forms of world and life. As Plato puts it in the *Sophist* with respect to the "greatest categories" (μέγιστα γένη),[86] they pervade everything like a thread, such that without any one of them, it is impossible for unlike to combine with unlike.[87] This suggests conceiving of art forms themselves as "greatest categories." They are forms of accessibility and as such primarily *forms of appearance* that, as a third thing, connect that which appears with the experience of it in the appearance for someone. The forms of appearance are synonymous with the possibility of an appearance determined in a certain way. In them, the world can be present in a more or less restricted limitation and thereby be recognized. The connection of world and world-access is not least made possible by the fact that the forms of appearance are forms of order; they delimit, combine, and even allow order to exist and be experienceable in movement. By virtue of the order's determinacy, it is the thing in its appearance as well as the experience of it that is determinate. It is only through the imagistic that the world, or something in it, is there as a whole; it is only musically that its movement and the movement in it is structured in such a way that experience can join into it and disclose it in the enactment of its movedness; it is only poetically—namely, in the λόγος and the text—that a cohesion exists in such a way that the individual can sensibly fit into its context and indeed arise from this context as what it is.

As forms of appearance, the elaborated forms are not reducible to anything further. They are beginnings, ἀρχαί, or *principia;* conditioned and determined by them, everything else has its inception in such a way that it is an appearance, comes into appearance, and is experienced as appearance. Insofar as art allows things to appear, it can rightly be traced back to the three elaborated forms. One does not need an explanation of the form-character of artworks through a regression to the human capacity of communication, to the material realities of spirit, or to experiences like dreams and intoxication. These grounding attempts actually rely on individual forms of art. Kant's attempt to clarify art by means of communication leads just as much to an eminence of the poetic as does Hegel's conception of art as spiritual shaping. Nietzsche's understanding of art as a manifestation of life's movement aligns with an elevation of music. Heidegger, in his grounding of art, goes directly back to a definite art form, the poetic that Kant and Hegel had already distinguished. "All art is essentially poetry";[88] poetry in the narrow sense is just one way "of poetizing in this broader sense" (60–61). Yet it remains unclear why only poetry should make up the essence of art. Since he only considers poetry, and not the poetic, as an art form, his attempt to determine the essence of art falls back into an unfounded elevation of poetry. The "building and shaping" is said to "always already and only [occur] in the open of the saying and naming" (62). Music is simply forgotten, and Heidegger does not say how the "building and shaping" as such are to be possible. By presupposing poetry prior to "building and shaping," and yet not attempting to derive the latter from the former, he silently admits the latter's irreducibility.

Yet even if one were to prove the unavoidability and irreducibility of art forms, it would remain open how they become *art* forms, and do not simply apply to art as they do to all other things. It is not enough simply to indicate that the forms were elaborated through orientation by artworks. The finding that certain forms take shape in artworks is only an initial step. This is true even if these manifestations appear especially connected to the forms—to such an extent that they can be named according to definite arts that are conventionally taken to be genres. If the works of visual art, of music, and of poetry respectively and evidently disclose one art form, this indicates these forms' proximity to art, as well as to the primacy of art in the experience of these forms as such. But this does not yet clarify *how* these forms take shape in the artworks. For this, one needs a more precise observation of the artwork that attends to the manifestation of the forms.

By combining with the determination according to which artworks are objects, this manifestation can be more precisely designated as an *objectivation*. When the forms are objectivated, they stand over against one as something other. As one otherwise finds oneself held *within* the forms of the imagistic, musical, and poetic, they can now be experienced as such. It is only in this way that they have become *deictic;* they show in such a way that the artwork in which they manifest themselves shows itself in them and does so in a more or less reflected way.

The outline of this notion is developed in Gadamer's determination of art as play. To be sure, he does not speak of objectivation. Once play no longer simply occurs and is played as occurrence, but instead becomes art, there is a "turning" that Gadamer calls the "transformation into structure." Through this transformation, play gains "its ideality" in such a way that it shows itself "as if detached from the presentational activity of the player."[89] What is now experienced is the "truth that remains"; everyone asks themselves "what that is supposed to be, what is 'meant' there" (117).

Gadamer's considerations strike in a decisive way at the objectivation involved in art. That which has become an object, what Gadamer calls a "structure," now no longer only has its actuality in occurrence, activity, and action. It stands forth, and that means, among other things, that it is expressly there for an audience, and only in that way can it possess the character of showing. While a game can be played in obliviousness and without the observation of others, the structure in Gadamer's sense is there to be experienced and understood.

The "transformation" that Gadamer wishes to describe is that from the merely occurring game to the "spectacle" [*Schauspiel*] (114); thus it is only logical that Gadamer illustrates his thoughts by means of the "example of the tragic" (133–139). What occurs in this case can indeed, in Gadamer's terms, be called a "transformation." That an observer joins onto play does not change the game to such an extent that its existence would be altered. To be sure, after the transformation that which was there "is no longer" (116–117). Nevertheless, *something* has changed that, as itself, is still recognizable in its new shape. This, as Gadamer proposes, is the "truth that remains" of the game, that which was not graspable as itself in the simply occurring play.

Despite their plausibility, Gadamer's considerations are not without their problems. Not only do they leave unconsidered the fact that not all artworks are transformed games, they also do not do justice to the games themselves. No simply occurring play can ever become an artwork that would be understandable to a viewer or listener in the selfsameness of its "ideality." For this, one would need repetition in various situations and through different players, which would only be possible on the basis of an identical text. The text, in turn, seldom arises on its own; it must, in some way or another, be fixated. Gadamer forgets the artist—the poet, the composer, the painter—without whom the structure would not be present. That which is forgotten is certainly there indirectly; Gadamer confirms its presence when he says of the structure that it "has the character of the work, of '*ergon*' and not only of '*energeia*'" (116). Yet what a work is, and how it comes into being, is not explained in Gadamer's considerations on the "transformation into structure."

In their incompleteness, Gadamer's thoughts refer to that determination of art of which they are clearly a variation: Heidegger's determination of art as the "setting-into-work of truth."[90] Yet although Heidegger gives a thorough treatment of the "being-made" of the work, he basically does not contribute anything to the clarification of the concept of the work. While the being-made is supposed to essentially determine the experience of the work, the artwork bears "its peculiarity [in the fact] that it is produced along into what is made" (52). But this manifestness of "being-made" is only elaborated by reference to "what is extraordinary" about the artwork; this abnormality consists in the "impact that the work, as this work, is." If one inquires further about this abnormality of the work, Heidegger simply refers one to that which is set into the work, namely the truth. One does not find out from Heidegger, however, how the being-set or "being-set-in-place" [*Festgestellt-sein*] (53) of truth in the work, and therefore the work as such, is to be understood.

While Gadamer merely evades this question through the notion of the "transformation into structure," Heidegger openly indicates why it is so difficult to answer. The difficulty lies in the concept of the work itself, more precisely in the fact that this concept is not peculiar to art in the sense of fine art, but belongs instead to the context of art in the sense of τέχνη. Even if art indisputably entails artisanal capacities, it cannot be solely determined by them, and accordingly the artwork cannot be a work in the sense of τέχνη. Nevertheless, it is no coincidence and not entirely inappropriate that both the work of τέχνη and the work of fine art should be designated with the same term. The process of production or bringing forth that is peculiar to τέχνη is not foreign to the essence of fine art, indeed so little so that the Greek term for this process, ποίησις, can also designate the art of poetry. The designation seems insightful enough that it established itself in other languages as well.

The relation between the essence of τέχνη and fine art speaks for the process of taking τέχνη as a guide to answering the question of what occurs when art forms take shape in the work. It is only in the precise distinction of fine art from τέχνη that this question can be answered. This theme has occasionally been touched upon, but it has not been taken up explicitly because the contexts did not lead anywhere. Thus, Kant's distinction between "purposive" production and beauty "without purpose" was central to the determination of beauty.[91] Yet since it stopped at this mere opposition of purposiveness and lack of purpose, it does not help one proceed into an understanding of the artwork as a work.

The decisive determination of τέχνη, which also oriented Heidegger's considerations, was developed by Aristotle. There, τέχνη is construed very broadly, not only as a technical production but as the general accomplishment of something that is external to the process of accomplishing. The activity does not, as ἐνέργεια, fulfill itself in itself, but instead in its ἔργον.[92] Yet despite its externality, the goal is connected to the activity that accomplishes it. The connection is given through the εἶδος that, as the εἶδος in the soul of the producer,[93] guides the accomplishment and thereby determines the shape of the work. Since the εἶδος is the same for both the accomplishment and the work, it can be designated with the same name. In the case of medicine, the εἶδος of both is health, in the case of building it is the house, and thus Aristotle can say that, in a certain sense, health comes from health, and the house from the house.[94] With respect to both the accomplishment and the work, the εἶδος is a form in the sense that it is the inner order of that which can be known and actually given. Insofar as the actual givenness of the order goes back to knowing, the accomplishment guided by knowledge can be understood as a transfer of the form from knowledge into reality. In this vein, Heidegger elaborated production [*Herstellung*] literally, namely as the "setting-there" [*Her-stellen*] of the εἶδος. It is "not actually the individual table [that is] produced; rather, what is set out and placed into visibility and tangibility is the 'essence'—understood in the sense of εἶδος."[95]

This elaboration is exaggerated in that it ignores production in the narrower sense, namely the fact that an actual table is produced. Yet with respect to the εἶδος, it hits upon what is essential. That which is brought into validity through production in the work has already been there in advance. It was not there as an ability or capacity on the part of the producer, such that production could be a creative process to be traced back to this skill. Rather, it is the form, the order, that was there in advance, and which as such first determined the producer. It is more the case that the producer acts *within* the form than that it is at his or her disposal. Accordingly, the work is less his or hers than it is the form's work. It belongs to the form, for the work is bound to it, while the work is not bound to this specific work. The form can even exist in ways other than visibly and tangibly. It is only because of this that a work can arise.

Now, one can also comprehend the artwork and its production. Just as τέχνη, fine art too is a setting-there, and like τέχνη fine art has to do with forms. Yet the forms in which it is accomplished are not the particular forms of producible things, but instead the forms of appearance—the imagistic, the musical, and the poetic. Whatever peculiar talents an artist might have, what is essential is that he or she be directly subordinated to the forms of appearance and understands his or her action by way of these forms, as something that belongs in them. The artist's action—the shaping, painting, composing, and poetizing—is the setting-into-place of the forms of appearance that through this setting-down first reveal themselves to be the forms of art.

The setting-there can be understood, with Heidegger, as a "setting-into-the-work." The artist sets something into the work, but not the "truth" understood as openness, which is too unspecific to allow a more precise grasp of the work. If what is set into the work are the art forms, then the artwork is the imagistic, musical, and poetic that has been set into the work. Of course, the identity and homonymy of the form as Aristotle delineated it with regard to τέχνη is only partially valid here. Certainly the imagistic can be set into the image, the musical into music, and the poetic into poetry. But when the imagistic is also found in music and in poetry, when the musical is in poetry as well as images, and when the poetic is in the image and in music, the allocation loses its univocity. Then an artwork reveals itself to be determined by several art forms. It is a *mixture* of these forms. The work as work, viewed formally, *is* this mixture.

Yet the work is thereby not merely a work; it is an image, a piece of music, a poem, or more precisely a building, sculpture, vessel, painting, drawing, symphony, opera, quartet, sonata, novel, epic, drama, elegy, haiku, epigram. These distinctions, however, do not concern the essence of the artwork. They are certainly not arbitrary, but they are generally only introduced for pragmatic reasons. Thus, the distinction between architecture and sculpture has more to do with the difference in artistic competence than with some essential difference between the works. There are buildings that are distinctly recognizable as sculptures,[96] and there are sculptures—as those of Per Kirkeby—that look like buildings.[97] The sculpture and tea bowl are both sculptural, but in distinction from the installed sculpture, the tea bowl can not only be observed, it can also be put to use. Painting and drawing, conversely, differ in the materials employed. A distinction such as that between orchestral and chamber music merely concerns the number and arrangement of instruments and thus the conditions of performance, whereas the distinctions between sonnet, elegy, and haiku refers to various forms of poem without designating anything about the essence of a poem. Distinctions only concern the essence of art when they refer to art forms in their mixture. Even then, however, there are no permanent divisions. It is always crucial how exactly one wishes to grasp an artwork and determine it in its commonalities with other works. Divisions that do not concern art forms as such do not serve the purpose of knowing the essence of art, but serve instead to describe, and these divisions must accordingly demonstrate their usefulness through description.

Frequently, one art form will dominate the mixture that is a work. Since the forms of art take shape in such diverse modes of clarity, they can be recognized and rediscovered in other works. This also makes the designation and allocation of artworks easier; for instance, if the imagistic form dominates, this suggests calling the work an image. In this way, the distinction of the three art forms suggests distinguishing three art genres: visual art, music, and poetry.

Yet in contrast to the distinction of the art forms themselves, this latter division is not obvious; there are poetically dominated images, imagistic poems, poetic music, and musical poetry, just as there are imagistic pieces of music and musical images. The best example of the latter is film. Besides, the division of art into three genres is not sufficient; it does not exhaust the realm among which it distinguishes. It is not always the case that one art form dominates in a work. There are works whose determinacy of form hovers, as it were. Thus, calligraphy is just as much poem as it is image. A ballet is at once both music and image, an opera with a literarily convincing libretto is just as much a poem as it is a piece of music. If it is performed, it also gains the imagistic dimension that belongs to it. Ambiguous mixtures like these make it difficult to allocate the work to an established genre. One result of this may be the creation of a new genre. In the case of opera, it is not a coincidence that the Italian term for "work," *opera*, has won out as a makeshift solution. The more manifest the mixture of a work is, the more it is simply just a work.

This state of affairs suggests that an artwork is *essentially* a mixture of all three forms of appearance. This would clarify, conversely, why genres combine so effortlessly with each other and transition into each other as if one their own. Further, it would explain the recurring difficulty of univocally allocating works to art genres. The supposition can be confirmed by recapitulating the three forms once more and considering the way they belong together.

No artwork is possible without the exclusivity and totality of the imagistic. Pieces of music and poems do not take up anything that does not already belong to them, and that which one experiences in them is only there in the way that the work presents it. Every artwork is a totality; one only understands a work if one tries to attend equally to everything that belongs to it. This ultimately also means that every artwork is simultaneous. To be sure, pieces of music or poems cannot be grasped at once, and one might hesitate to call them simultaneous. Yet as an image, they are there at once. Even if the performance takes time—just as the observation of an image takes time—that which one reads or hears is the work as such. No part of it has passed or lies ahead; rather, whatever one reads or hears in a given moment is determined by the whole of the work. The work itself is present in every moment with all of its moments. That is why artworks reveal themselves all the more, the better one knows them and keeps them present as wholes. Their simultaneity is there, but it must be experienced, even achieved. But only because it is there can this experience and achievement even be possible.

The complete presence of a work is not only imagistic, but also poetic. Just as with the closedness and simultaneity that belongs to the imagistic, the poetic, too, is given along with the text of the work as the meaningful context of its moments. Every work has a text. This text can be written, musically notated, painted, chiseled in stone, formed by hand, or drawn. In the form of the poetic, the presence of a work is structured in such a way that what differs is woven together, as it were. The structure of an image is poetic, as is the harmony in a musical *melos*—as we have had cause to underscore, λόγος also means "relation" or "proportion." But in order for such "logical" moments to belong to the poetic form of art, they may not just be defined mathematically; they must give sense to the sounds that they order and thus themselves be moments of a meaningful context.

Through the structuring of a work, we also get the rhythmic play of its moments. The text of a work is more and less dense, and accordingly it provides a possibility, like the steppingstones in the tea garden, of following it. The same is true of visual art. A detailed image must be viewed differently than one with a large surface; a dense jointure holds the gaze differently than an open line that clearly gives a direction; a spacious building has a different order of movement than one with small rooms. Likewise, Proust's multiclause sentences with their recurring caesurae differ greatly from the lapidary prose of Goethe or late Ernst

Jünger. An author's style, the individuality of his or her work, is grounded less in the author's choice of words than in the rhythm of his or her language.

The musical form thus already contains the free play that is never forced, that is never merely steady, and that makes a work beautiful and accordingly a work of art. Yet the playful rhythm of the musical does not exist on its own in the work; it exists only along with the form of the text. Without the poetic fabric of various moments, there is nothing there that one could follow. But the text does not exhaust itself in the fact that one can follow it. Through the text, each individual part is set into relation to others in such a way that every moment is only meaningful and given in its sense through its belonging-together with others. As the art form of the poetic, the text is essentially decentered and thus, like the playful rhythm of the musical, fulfills the criterion of beauty.

Just as there is no rhythm in the work without text, the decenteredness of the text does not stand on its own. It is not just that it must be rhythmic and therefore open to being followed; the text's decenteredness is impossible without the closedness of the imagistic. A text that is not structured by central moments must be closed. Otherwise it will become diffuse instead of unfolding the intensity peculiar to the fabric of the poetic. It is only imagistically that the poetic and musical forms gain validity in the totality of a work. Without the imagistic, the decentered order of the beautiful fails to become an object, such that it is not there as something lifted out. In order for the imagistic to be actualized in a work, it needs the textual fabric in the playful openness of the musical, in which one can become involved and which one can follow.

Thus, a true artwork is only a work by virtue of the mixture of art forms; this mixture is itself in each case an individually actualized decentered order. Viewed formally, an artwork is all the more beautiful the more intimate the connection of art forms is within it. There is no predefined measure for the mixture. Like opera, a work can set various art forms into a kind of hovering and allow them to supplement each other. Another work, such as a monochromatic Richter painting, is entirely imagistic and almost completely absorbs the rhythm and text into the uniformity of its gray. An artwork can also dominate by making the other forms subservient. Thus, for example, the poetic and musical forms can submit to the imagistic. This is not only the case with artworks that are painted, and thus visible, images. Insofar as Stifter's story "Granite" is subservient to the imagistic, it represents an imagistic artwork.

Accordingly, it is not possible to derive a strict allocation of art forms to the modes of access entailed by vision, hearing, or linguistic comprehension. We already witnessed the difficulties associated with such allocations in Kant's attempt at dividing the arts. The forms of appearance claim and foster the modes of access to the world in different ways. Thus, the closedness and simultaneity that belong to the imagistic are evinced most easily in sight, while the rhythmic play of the musical is accessible to the ear no less than to the eye. The poetic's fabric of sense is certainly not bound to language, but it is recognized easier in language than in visibility or audibility.

What is decisive, however, is not the mode of access one has to artworks, but the way in which they show themselves. This determines the access one has to them. With regard to the showing, the works' perceivability and readability bear a decisive significance. What this significance is can best be stated in connection with a summarizing observation on the deictic character of artworks, insofar as it is determined by the art forms.

The works show in the art forms of which they are a mixture; they allow that which they show to present imagistically, musically, and poetically. As artworks' showing is not a pointing to something factually extant, the art forms themselves take on validity in a more or less obvious way. The possible that the artworks show joins into the bridge-function of art forms as the connecting {element} between intention and the factually given correlate of this intention. Through the art forms, the work is a phenomenon in the phenomenological sense, a possibility lifted out of factual existence. As something possible, however, it is shown *in the possibility of its appearance* and thus not only recognized but, in Kant's terms, seen in the possibility of "cognition as such." Everything that artworks show is shown *in its form of appearance,* such that it is experienceable how it can be present imagistically, poetically, and musically. It is experienceable because artworks show themselves in the forms, and these forms show themselves.

The explicit experience of appearance, made possible by artworks, is connected to artworks' object-character. One only experiences the imagistic's form and mode of appearance if one does not stick directly to the imagistic or remain caught up in it; the connecting element of λόγος only comes to bear when λόγος has the consistency of a text and stands forth in this; likewise, the rhythmic play must become a drama in the widest sense in order for one to not only join into it, as occurs in Gadamer's description of play and its medial character. The imagistic, the poetic, and the musical can only stand over against us insofar as they *are thing-bound,* which means are *perceivable.* The visibility and audibility of artworks, without which their readability would not exist, is a condition of their object-character. Without visibility and audibility, the art forms cannot show themselves; they can only appear in their perceivability for the senses.

The perceivability of works is that aspect of them that is there as if on its own. The mixture of forms of which the works consist can and must be set in place, but the perceivability of what is set in place exists on its own. An artist that paints a picture, composes a piece of music, choreographs a dance, or writes a poem has always already accommodated this perceivability. Artworks are *simply there* in their perceivability. This simple existence, the appearing for which the forms of appearance exist, is that which allows artworks to look "like nature."[98] To inquire into the appearance of artworks thus means to investigate nature with respect to artworks and the nature of artworks.

FOUR

Nature

Oppositions

When Kant states that art is only beautiful insofar as it appears at the same time to be like nature, he is referring to the irregularity of the beautiful formation. To be sure, a "product of art" must be made according to rules of its craft, such that it can attain "all *exactitude* in the accordance with rules"; a composer should have mastered composition, a painter should know how to mix colors, a poet who wishes to write a sonnet must know its form. But "exactitude" means that precision in regularity must be "without *strain*," that is, as Kant says, without "the taught form showing through"; the "product" must not show any "trace" that "the rule hovered before the artist's eyes and constrained the faculties of his mind."[1] An artwork must appear to be spontaneous; even though it is made, everything about it must exist as if by its own impetus. In this way, it is like nature.

This notion should be intelligible, both with respect to art and with respect to nature. A work is only an artwork if it is ordered in a decentered way, not reducible to a "rule." It appears in its decentered order, and its appearance as such is never created or effected, but at most only occasioned. That which appears shows itself. It is not pointed to, not even in the sense of setting-in-place; it is not reducible to its being produced. It shows *itself* as that which it is—as image, poem, or piece of music, by standing in view or being heard. The imagistic aspect of an artwork, as well as its text and its rhythmic play, are set into the work. But the work stands forth on its own; it *shows* itself. Precisely this "on its own," the spontaneous, is what is named with the term "nature." *Natura*, from *nasci*, "being born," has the fundamental meaning of "birth." φύσις comes from φύειν, "to grow," such that it designates "growth." But even when an artwork appears as if it has been grown, it has not. Yet it shows itself in the way that something grown shows itself. In its spontaneous self-showing that is not compelled by anything, it is like nature without being nature.

That the artwork is "like nature" does not mean that one takes it to be something natural. When artworks shows themselves as such, the experience of them is not deceptive. A stele by Ulrich Rückriem does not appear aesthetically as an erratic boulder, which it could at most be for a superficial or distant gaze. It is the sparse yet unmistakable traces of workmanship that make the stone into an artwork. Just as nature, according to Kant, only appears "beautiful" when it looks "like art" (B 179, 306) and is nevertheless recognized as nature, so art is only beautiful *as* art and yet at the same time appears to be like nature.

In their relatedness to each other, art and nature are nevertheless distinctly separate. One can imagine that nature itself is absent in art. Insofar as the artwork is like nature, its peculiar appearance merely *reminds* one of nature in such a way that art comes to stand in for nature. This is how Adorno described the relation of art and nature: "The artwork, θέσει through and through, something human, takes the place of what would be φύσει, a thing in itself, to use Kant's term, that would not merely exist for the subject."[2] If nature is determined in this way, it *must* come to be substituted through something else. For as long as there is a foreign access to it that shapes it in its foreignness, it cannot be what it is. Nature, as nature, cannot exist "for the subject." As itself, it is not an appearance in the Kantian sense. Rather, it is in and for itself, in the sense that one means when one speaks of the "nature of a matter." The nature of a matter, in this sense, is its own essence that is independent of any appearance, the matter itself.

In its essence, this determination might be convincing, especially if one does not yet quite understand it. By speaking of nature in a "Kantian" manner, however, Adorno makes it disappear almost as soon as he addresses it. As a "thing in itself," it is unknowable. That which, in the Kantian sense, "appears" as nature is not nature. Thus, as Adorno believes, art stands in for nature's being-in-itself, whereas the self-showing of nature itself is deferred to an indeterminate point of salvation: "Thus the artwork impinges on the subject as something so identical to [the thing in itself] that it is as nature would have to be" (99).

Such an eschatology of nature, however, not only empties its concept, it also fails to do justice to the artworks. If one considers the thing-like character of artworks, it is a strange idea that they would "collapse into the subject" or be "something human." The marble or granite sculpture is nothing strictly human, not even something that is a placing (θέσις) "through and through." The stone must be there in order for the sculptor to shape it into a sculpture, and what stands there as a sculpture stands in stone and of stone. Yet the stone is, in an admittedly still unclarified sense, natural. The resounding tone and the visible color are natural in this sense as well. Voice is natural, and even when it is trained and capable of great artistic achievement, it is the voice of a natural being. As we have mentioned above,[3] Kant even determined artistic talent—that which is not exhausted in the craft of an art—as natural: genius, understood as an "innate disposition (*ingenium*)," is "the talent (natural gift) that gives art its rule."[4] Certainly not everything is nature, but nature is everywhere, it is in everything, to such an extent that one often does not recognize it as nature. The natural is connected, indeed frequently fused, with all that is not nature. The natural is in the unnatural and is thus not immediately experienceable as such. In this sense, one could state with Heraclitus that nature loves to hide.[5]

This hiddenness of nature certainly does not make plausible the opposition that Adorno sets up with the notion of the substitution of nature through art, but it does make it understandable. It seems that nature can only appear in contrast, and this contrast can seemingly only be effected by something detaching itself from nature, stepping out of it and becoming different from it, only by completely integrating the natural into the nonnatural form, or by removing it. This is how Adorno understands art. It has incorporated "what the older aesthetics accorded to nature"; in the "ideological religion of art in the nineteenth century," the claim of beauty was only still valid for art.[6] The reason for this is the radical emancipation of art. In order to truly be art, it freed itself from the "heteronomy of materials, especially of natural objects"; it no longer tolerates nature as its precept, role model, or standard. Only once "the rawness of what remains unmediated into spirit has been extinguished" (99) does art reach that radical independence that returns it into relation with nature. In order to be able to serve as a substitute for nature, art must thus be as independent as nature; in its independence, it must be like something natural and at the same time radically different. Through its "spiritualization," art has not "alienated itself from nature, but instead [approached] it according to its own shape." "Artworks' pure expression liberates from the materially bothersome, from so-called natural material," converges "with nature, just as the pure tone in Anton Webern's authentic formations, the tone to which they [are reduced] by virtue of subjective sensibility," reverses "into the natural sound" (121).

Adorno's considerations are easily recognizable as commentary on Hegel's supersession of the "older" (i.e., Kantian) aesthetics through the philosophy of art.[7] His opposition of art and nature, too, thrives on earlier ideas; it contains resonances of older oppositions. When Adorno takes art to be θέσις, a human positing that leads to independence over against growth or φύσις, one hears in this the opposition of νόμος and φύσις that the sophists made famous and that Plato took to be a challenge to philosophical thought, especially in relation to politics.[8] In this opposition, νόμος is the conventional institution that solely satisfies human interests, which can change according to power relations and which is only ever binding as long as it exists. νόμος is thus also the realm of that which is not predefined, of the malleable, and of that which stands within the assessment of reflection and decision. This, in turn, brings another opposition into play that Adorno addresses by reference to the "heteronomy of matter." According to this opposition, nature is not simply that which exists as it is on its own. Rather, it is the foreign, the ἕτερος νόμος, the law that is distinct from one's own. That which stands opposed to nature as the realm of natural laws is freedom, decisively conceived by Kant as autonomy.[9]

Kant's opposition is radical. Law stands over against law, and this means that the supersession of nature is only possible under the condition of equal ranking. This presupposition also grounds Adorno's thesis of substitution. Art can only stand in for nature if, as nature, it can stand on its own. It is precisely in its non-naturalness that art is to be like nature, but for itself. Yet this raises the question how art is to even still relate to nature. The "being-in-itself" of artworks in which the "being-in-itself" of nature, "which does not exist yet," is to be substituted, could also be conceived independently of nature simply as the "pure expression" that has become "spiritual" and from which all naturalness and any resonance of nature has been eradicated. Adorno merely asserts the "reversal" "into the natural sound," and this can only be asserted if the "being-in-itself" of nature is that of an "unknown"[10] that is simply conjured up.

Adorno's determination of the relation of art and nature thus fails on the point that they are not determined in their relation; the opposition based on the demand of equal ranking inadvertently becomes a nonrelation, an indifferent juxtaposition. If nature is to be discoverable in and through art, their opposition must possess the character of an alteration; it must allow nature to be recognized in the modification of something common, in such a way that nature is at once repeated and set apart.

It is in this sense that Kant developed the guiding question of the *Critique of Judgment*, the question of the relation of art and nature. He grasps this relation neither from the side of freedom as autonomy, nor with respect to the lawfulness of nature, but instead by locating the possibility of a relation between nature and human freedom in the "free formations" of nature. This possible relation still remains distant; it can only be intimated, not understood. Even when art, as the art of the genius, is traced back to a "natural gift," art can only be related negatively to nature; what allows the artwork to look natural is the unintentionality that can be read off of its irregularity. Art only looks like nature by absence of intention. But this absence could also be coincidence, and taken in itself, coincidence does not imply nature. Nature, as such, is not coincidental; the coincidental can just as easily be natural as unnatural. It is not like nature, but simply just coincidental.

Thus, the relation of art to nature cannot consist simply in the deviation from rules. If the natural is not exhausted by the coincidental, it must, despite all difference from art, be ordered or ruled in a way comparable to art. It is recognizable as nature in that it is ordered in a different way than the product of art.

Aristotle determined the relation of art and nature in this way. To be sure, fine art does not play a role in this determination; Aristotle orients himself instead along art in general, along τέχνη. Yet even fine art is art, and in this way Aristotle's determination is helpful in understanding the relation between fine art and nature. In his discussion of art and nature, φύσις and τέχνη, Aristotle goes beyond mere analogies and relations of substitution. His determinations are specific enough to show what art and nature have in common.

Aristotle wanted to show that nature and art are equal in the respect that they fall under the same structural conditions and that they only differ in the ways that these conditions respectively pertain to them. In this way, they are opposite to one another. For Aristotle, this opposition evinces the possibility of depicting art and nature in mutual relation; art is to be disclosed by way of nature, and vice versa. On the basis of this mutuality, it could also become clear why Kant's account describes art appearing as nature. Of course, since fine art is certainly art, but not τέχνη, this clarity will only be possible once we develop a more precise distinction of fine art and τέχνη in the context of the relation to nature.

For Aristotle, τέχνη is simultaneously independent from nature and bound to it. τέχνη's independence from nature consists in the fact that τέχνη can bring something to completion that nature could not achieve. It is bound to nature, however, in that it takes nature as its role model; since it does not complete nature, τέχνη imitates it.[11] This determination brings to mind the fact that every production deals with natural processes and conditions. A doctor can ultimately only bring about the health of his or her patient in the way that it would have returned naturally if nature alone were producing it. If the patient does not return to health on his or her own, the doctor, in a sense, initiates the natural process of convalescence by bringing about that which nature omitted. When such a supplementation of nature is not necessary, Aristotle thinks that production still occurs on the model of natural processes. To elaborate this notion, he points out that production and natural generation bear the same structure. Both cases involve a goal-oriented process in which the earlier and serial steps occur for the sake of some aim. If a house were not built by hand, but were generated by nature, the process would still unfold as it does through the use of τέχνη.[12]

The elaboration that Aristotle provides here rests on his definition of nature. Nature is a beginning and an initiation of self-movement and rest for that which possesses it incipiently and not accidentally.[13] Nature, or φύσις, is thus the term that especially applies to living beings. It designates the possibility of moving or resting of one's *own* accord. As Aristotle notes in an earlier passage, this concerns the movement from one place to another, and accordingly of not just being in one place, but of tarrying there. Yet it also pertains to growth and decay that, in the case of a natural being, come about from within it.

Aristotle's determination of φύσις is very specific. It certainly does not exclude nonliving natural beings, but it really only applies directly to living beings. As concerns these, Aristotle's elaboration is enlightening, and it is enlightening because it merely grasps more precisely what is already contained in the term φύσις; Aristotle himself indicates this.[14] Only what lives grows, whereas the artificial must be produced and, instead of growing, proceeds through various stages of completion.

Yet, taken in itself, Aristotle's discussion says less than it first appears to. Aside from the fact that Aristotle understands the movement of the natural as stemming from itself, he leaves its naturalness undetermined. He only grasps it in more detail when he orients himself by τέχνη. Then the movement of the natural appears as the manifestation of a form (εἶδος) in material. Aristotle believes that nature itself must be this form, for one does not primarily designate a generative process by way of what is merely possible, but rather by way of the form through which something possible can become actual. That is how it is with τέχνη; if something were only a bed frame by way of possibility, and did not possess the form of a bed frame, one would not say that it falls under τέχνη. The same is the case with what is "naturally assembled."[15] Neither flesh nor bone possesses its nature before it has taken on the form appropriate to its structure and according to which one defines what flesh or bone is; nor do flesh or bone exist through nature without this form.[16]

The forcefulness of this comparison would not have been lost on Aristotle. He was certainly aware that a living being is not assembled out of flesh and bone in the same way that a bed frame is made of posts and boards. Yet Aristotle apparently saw no other way of making natural generation comprehensible. How could he? Once φύσις has been grasped in its model character for τέχνη and make understandable through the similarity of φύσις and τέχνη, φύσις can only be understood according to the image of τέχνη. Unlike φύσις, τέχνη is apparent in its structure. How could it be otherwise, as τέχνη is a form of knowing?

The similarity of φύσις and τέχνη results, as if on its own, in the understanding of natural becoming, especially the generation and growth of living beings. It is the becoming of one form from another; humans come from humans, Aristotle avers,[17] and this can only mean that when a human is generated, the human form manifests itself in a material, however this material is to be thought. Although the natural comes into existence from itself, whereas the artificial must be produced, the structure of becoming is the same in each case. Just as humans come from humans, so the house is generated from the house: the material house comes from the house that is without material.[18]

That this determination of natural becoming is problematic is less due to the notion of form; it may ring true that a human is generated from the form of a human that every human fulfills, however this form is to be grasped. Where there are forms, there must be an organizing, formal principle at play. The genetic code is a kind of form. Yet what is problematic is the notion that in natural generation, there is a material that lends form for the possibility of real existence. What is problematic is thus the thought of a form distinct from material, and the attempt of relating this distinction to natural becoming.

The difficulty can be clarified by way of the term Aristotle uses and which we have rendered with "material." ὕλη means "wood," more precisely "wood for building." The expression thus indicates building material, making "material" a better translation than just "matter"; whereas the term "matter" can be used neutrally, "material" fits solidly into the processes of production and manufacture. In order for something to be understood as material, it must be taken into view according to a form and grasped with respect to this form. This view upon something—according to a form and with respect to it—is the *view of production* by means of which something is discovered as being suitable for production. The understanding that guides production is characterized by the prudent search for suitable material, which in turn is accomplished with respect to the form that is to be produced. This search is necessary because the form that is to be produced is not real in itself; it is not present, is not within view. It is in need of production in that one needs something present and visible in which the form can be placed and upon which or in which it can be present. The production of the form is not, as Heidegger described it,[19] a setting-in-place of the form, but instead a setting or forming of the form into the material.

Just as the form to be produced is immaterial as such, there is no material that corresponds to it in every respect. Most forms are realizable in various materials, and it is necessary in each case to find and use the material suited to their production. That is always a violent process. Material does not exist in nature; that is why Aristotle is correct in rejecting the determination of φύσις as an unordered stuff that dwells within each thing.[20] There is no formless material that is simply lying around. Everything natural, and especially living, is present in a form that must be taken from it in order for it to become material; it is altered, damaged, or killed. Trees are felled to be cut into beams and boards; animals are hunted or butchered so their skin can be processed into leather for the production of bags and shoes.

As thoroughly as this processing into material may change something, one can frequently still recognize the origin of the material. Accordingly, the difference between form and material that is essential for production and materializing in general still remains recognizable. However successful the processing is, it is still the case that the connection of form and material is effected and forced more or less obviously. It is unnatural.

It would certainly not have entered Aristotle's mind to make the processing of material into the guiding notion for natural becoming and for nature as such. After all, it is primarily form that is nature or φύσις for Aristotle, not the material. Nevertheless, the idea of manifesting forms in a material lends the possibility of seeing what is formal and graspable in nature as something that has been brought to it. The "Copernican turn" that Kant suggests with respect to modern natural science lies in the wake of this idea; it is the assumption that "the objects" must "conform to our knowledge," instead of us trying to measure knowledge according to the standard of the objects."[21] If that were the case, reason would not need to "let itself be led along" by nature's leash, but could instead require nature "to answer its [reason's] questions." In that case, reason would relate to nature "in order to be taught by it, but not in the way that a student repeats what the teacher wants, rather in the manner of a judge who demands that the witnesses answer the questions that he presents to them." The decision that answers would count would be decided by whether the judge understands them, for reason only has insight into that which "it presents according to its own design" (xiii).

Yet the distinction between form and material that makes such a cognitive demand upon nature possible is not really adequate to the natural. The form of a tree is not realized in wood; rather, the solid yet pliable consistency of the tree can only be designated as wood under the guise of a foreign form that, in distinction from the tree's form, requires materialization. The distinction between form and material simply does not apply to the natural; it slips off.

Valéry had an experience of this slippage when he observed a shell washed up on a beach. The observation tests the adequacy of any orientation guided by production. It carries all the more weight as Valéry took the orientation along production to be the sole possibility of understanding anything. One only understands what one is capable of *making*.[22] The notion of making is the most primary and most human; to explain something is none other than to describe the process of making and to make it again in thought. (891) Whoever understands something knows its inner makeup and structure, and accordingly knows how it is assembled or could be assembled. Consequently, the limits of understanding are to be grasped as the limits of being able to make. Whatever can only be understood inadequately, or not at all, is thus made in an opaque manner. This is the case, Valéry believes, with the natural. Nature is the maker and generator to whom we relegate the production of everything that we do not understand how to make and which nonetheless appears to us as made.[23] Yet how it is made remains incomprehensible.

Valéry carries this idea out by comparing the natural with that which is produced. Two things are decisive for the incomprehensibility of the natural: the indivisibility of form and matter, and the variability that both of them lack. Valéry's development of this notion reads like an interpretation of Aristotle's conception of τέχνη. The material for production must be selected, and that means that it can be distinct from what is factually chosen and used. Moreover, the form one wishes to actualize can be any size one wishes. Anything that can be produced can be larger or smaller than it actually is.[24] After all, the ability to make something is not limited to a certain form. One can only actualize a certain form because one can also bring forth others. If one were only capable of making a single thing and making it in a singular way, it would be as if the thing made itself. Producing it would not require thought, and thus one would not understand it. (895)

To sum up Valéry's considerations, making and producing only exist in a space of possibilities of decision. It is only in such a space that a form—as a possibility distinct from other possibilities—is determined. Further, the fact that a thing at hand is an actualization of a form can only be recognized if one can distinguish between thing and form. One knows that thing and form are not congruous by knowing that the thing, as realization of this form, could have also ended up differently—larger, smaller, better, or worse—and that there are accordingly many possible realizations of this one form that may even be made of various materials. How exactly a thing is to look and be constituted is decided through production alone. The latter sets the thing in place, and that is only possible because it is accomplished in a space of determinate but not fixed possibilities. This space is opened through the distinction between form and material. It is only because the form, as not yet actualized, is accessible—as Aristotle says, it exists in the soul of the producer[25]—that it can be compared to other forms with respect to their actualizability. It is only when the reality of the form is not yet determined that one has the possibility of varying its size, quality, and manifestation. Only then does one have the possibility of choosing between various materials.

None of this has any relevance anymore as soon as one is dealing with the natural, for instance with a seashell that has washed ashore. The seashell need not be anything special, no Pacific prize piece; an ordinary shell suffices. Observing it, one knows that there are no reconstructible possibilities of its being different. It is simply the way it is. It would be the same case with a shell that had a different form, shape, or constitution. It would not be a variant of the one first observed, but instead another shell, just as unique. It, too, would be just as it is. Just as the first shell, as every shell that one could observe, it would be incomprehensible within the space of producibility.

Valéry eyes a single way of avoiding capitulation to this incomprehensibility. He compares the seashell to an artwork, or more precisely asks himself whether an artwork is not the human approximation to the simply being-thus of a seashell. Is perhaps that which one calls the perfection of art nothing other than the feeling of seeking and finding in a human work that certitude of execution, that necessity of inner origin, and that indissoluble mutual connection of shape with material that the most minute of seashells makes visible?[26]

Valéry's consideration leads art as close as possible to nature. Nevertheless, the two do not become congruent. This is prefigured in the concept by which the approximation of art to nature is to be made comprehensible. The perfection of which Valéry speaks still belongs in the realm of producibility. The French word *perfection*, as the Latin *perfectio*, is related to the word for "making," *facere, faire*. At the same time, however, the concept of completion leads beyond the sphere of producibility. Whatever is perfectly made is certainly produced under the consideration of alternatives; unlike the thing that Valéry considered in his thought experiment, which someone could make without thinking, the perfect thing does not have to be as it is. But as it now appears, it looks necessary; it can no longer be different, even though it could have. In this way, the completion of art brushes up along simple being-thus; at its apex, in its completion, art is almost like nature.

Nevertheless, even the complete artwork does not attain the natural. Even if there were no εἶδος of the artwork in the soul of the artist according to which the work was produced, one can still, in distinction from the natural, speak of materials in the case of art. Whereas no tree is made of wood and no shell is made of calcium, one can say of the sculpture that it is made of marble. The marble sculpture could, in principle, have been made from granite. The oil painting could have—as in the case of some works by Cézanne that were done in a thin glaze—been executed with watercolors. An artwork lies a great distance away from the simple being-thus of a seashell.

Accordingly, Valéry can only express the proximity of the artwork to the natural by transgressing the boundary between the two and describing the natural in artistic terms: the certitude of execution, the necessity of inner origin—thus not an origin that stands in advance as an aim. The mutual connection of shape and material are not visible in a "most minute" of seashells; they are only visible in a work of art. Although Valéry, unlike Aristotle, avoids grasping the natural as structurally analogous to the producible, and although he, conversely, underscores the incomprehensibility of the natural, he still sees nature and art as joining together in an infinitely distant vanishing point. He can think this because for him, nature is the producer, the generator, *"la Produisante ou la Productrice."* Understood in this way, nature is art, but an art that humans, limited to their human art, cannot comprehend.

The notion that the natural world may be assembled as if through art does not stem from Valéry. It goes back to Plato, who developed the idea in his *Ti-*

maeus. If the natural world, as appearing order (κόσμος), was created, it must have arisen out of a cause (αἰτία).²⁷ Without further justification, this conclusion becomes the occasion for presupposing a demiurge (δημιουργός) whom the narrator of the dialogue, Timaeus, and with him the reader, observe in his work. Yet through his narrator, the author leaves no doubt that the κόσμος is not really to be understood this way. What Timaeus tells is not a λόγος in the sense of a conceptually determined and established clarification, but instead an εἰκὸς μῦθος, a story that, measured according to the constitution of the natural world, only depicts probable things about this world's makeup. To go beyond such a μῦθος is improper, (29d), for as was already stated, it is difficult to find the creator and father of the whole, of the universe, and it is impossible to speak to all about him.²⁸ The creator and father of the whole cannot be known or communicated as other things can; even the language of a "creator" and "father" is mythical, a narrative transposition of humanly known things onto that which is not known as things in the world are known. Nothing about this changes even when one replaces the mythical notion of a demiurge with the notion of a "naturing nature," *natura naturans*, which is to be distinguished from "natured nature," *natura naturata*.²⁹ For this, too, is thought from the side of causality, even if it is the causality posited in nature itself, such that nature appears as "la Produisante" or as "la Productrice." The notions are mutually conditioned; if nature is conceived from the side of art as production, then art, in its relation to nature, must be referred to the natural mode of production. Yet art always lags behind this mode as something complete, but never natural.

But it could be that the connection between art and nature is simply covered over in the attempt to bring art into proximity with nature. Nature would thus hide itself the most where one thinks to recognize it most clearly. The reason for this is not difficult to understand. Nature seems to possess its most evident recognizability through the notion of τέχνη. Yet as soon as one takes this as one's orientation, one only finds τέχνη instead of nature and transposes τέχνη onto nature. That is the case with Valéry: he promises himself the greatest approximation to nature from an art that is nothing but perfected τέχνη. Yet perfection, as we subsequently saw with Kant, is not beauty; beautiful art is not simply art. It exceeds τέχνη at the very least by the fact that nature can show itself in it.

Limits and Inclusions

The natural always occurs in τέχνη as well. To be sure, forms that are produced are invented, but in the end the material is always natural; the series of manipulations always leads back to something natural: to the skin of an animal, to the tree, to the stone, to the ore, or to the earth that can be made into clay for the forming and firing of vessels. Whatever became material was initially simply there; it had to be found in its simple being-thus, just as the seashell that Valéry describes.

Since the natural that is present in this way does not entirely lose its naturalness even in the process of manipulation, one could suppose that it was nature as such. For the sophist Antiphon, cited by Aristotle, the wood of the finished bed frame is nature. If one were to bury the bed frame and let it rot such that a sprout formed, it would not produce a bed frame but wood. The arrangement that was undertaken according to a conventional rule (νόμος) (i.e., art) is only present as something supplemental, while that which suffers the manipulation and remains in place is beingness (οὐσία).[30] Yet Antiphon merely forgets that the buried and rotting bed frame is not itself the sprout from which a new plant grows. To this extent, Aristotle can rightly respond that the form from which something arises is not derivable from that which can be material. Nevertheless, along with the form, there is always already something present in nature that, under the maker's guise, becomes material. Frequently, its naturalness remains preserved even if it loses the form that was originally its own. One can certainly not play the naturalness of what is discoverable as material off against form in such a manner that the latter is merely understood as an addition—as accomplished in the sophistical contrast of φύσις and νόμος. There are natural forms. With regard to these, Aristotle's critique of Antiphon, and thus of all natural philosophers that view nature as material undergirding everything—fire, earth, air, or water—is on target. (17–28) Yet the naturalness does not lie in the form alone; the natural that was once material is even more tenacious, and for this reason its naturalness is more easily recognized. In this respect, Antiphon remains correct.

Of course, the naturalness of the factual or possible material is not always recognized or experienced. One observes it just as little during production in the sense of τέχνη as one does when ultimately using that which is produced. Here the aspects of suitability, usefulness, and durability maintain priority. If, within the space of producibility—which is also always the space of usefulness—one were to call attention to the naturalness of the processed material, one could not expect denial, but perhaps a certain perplexity. In just as irrefutable and ungroundable a manner, and thus in an unclear way, one knows that this wood, stone, or clay is natural. But one leaves this knowledge be; it is not important, and one cannot do anything with it in the realm of production and use. The natural that is to be found in τέχνη and likewise in the usefulness toward which τέχνη is directed does not come to hold sway *as* natural. Accordingly, there is no reason to seek an understanding of its naturalness.

It bears repeating, however, that the natural is there *in* the space of producibility and *in* the space of usefulness. One need not seek it beyond or outside of these spaces in the hope that it will reveal itself as such if one only distances oneself far enough from producibility and usefulness. It suffices that the things with which one deals are not *simply* works of τέχνη, and that they are not exhausted in their use.

Architecture is a good example of this. It is a τέχνη, and for Aristotle it is even the example of a complex art that integrates a series of subsidiary arts.[31] Its works are in general designated for use, and accordingly they must meet its conditions and demands. Yet they need not be exhausted by this. A house that is designed and built according to all of the rules of architecture can simultaneously be an artwork, and this changes the experience of the natural. The experience then exists in a way that no conventional work of architecture can offer.

The house that allows one to experience and describe this is miles away from other houses. It is built in a wooded area, on a slab of rock on a hill that lies above a small river. The looming walls are made of stone, and the large yet not dominating windows and glass doors are encased in red metal frames. Four terraces and a flat roof, all in concrete painted in an ochre color, determine the shape of the house that is defined by horizontal lines. The large masonry fireplace wall, together with a narrower parallel front wall, offer a vertical counterbalance to this. One of the terraces juts out from the front of the house. Two others, on the ground floor and second story, protrude quite far and define the long side of the house that faces away from the hill. The terrace on the ground floor juts out further with the narrower end of its rectangle than the terrace on the second floor, which is aligned perpendicular to the long side of the house. This emphasizes the looming, stretching character all the more. Both of these terraces jut out over the small river right where the river falls over a slab of rock and becomes a waterfall. This lends the house its name: Fallingwater.

The house is a masterpiece of architecture, not least because the construction of the two terraces over the waterfall involved extremely difficult statical problems, which supposedly even gave the architect, Frank Lloyd Wright, nightmares.[32] Yet the house, designed in 1935, built in the subsequent two years, and supplemented by a guest house in 1939, is also an artwork. It is beautiful, and it is showing. It shows in a manifold way, and it especially shows nature. It shows this by showing itself as natural.

One experiences the house's showing when one spends time in its rooms. The large windows, undressed with any blinds or curtains, lead one's gaze into the forest surrounding the house and to the river. This is partly the case because the ceilings are relatively low. Even without curtains or blinds, one feels secure and can therefore follow the line of sight through the openness of the windows all the more readily. If one opens the windows, the rushing of the wind in the foliage joins together with the forest view that changes with the seasons and the play of light in the trees, and one hears the soft burbling of the river that can swell to a raging flow in the corresponding weather. The terraces are viewing platforms from which the gaze moves into the depths of the forest without one's being able to survey the house's landscape as if from a lookout point. The house sits *in* the landscape and is open to it, just as the most beautiful Japanese buildings, like Katsura Rikyu, a gracefully staid royal country house outside of Kyoto, belong into the garden to which they lead one's gaze. Frank Lloyd Wright only explicitly demonstrated his reverence for Japanese architecture through the red color of the steel window frames. A Buddha sculpture on the terrace of the narrow side of the house strengthens the association.

Yet the house does not only show nature by giving the gaze free rein upon something that can be immediately recognized as nature. Nature is present *in* the gaze itself. Cornices, closets, shelves, and tables are all made of black American walnut. The quarry stones that make up the walls of the house are flat rocks of varying sizes that are layered haphazardly and remain unplastered. The floors, too, of the terraces as of the home itself, are irregular stone slabs that look like cross-sections of rocks. This stone stands out even more in contrast with the concrete ceilings and the windows and glass doors with their red metal frames.

The impression that one gets inside the rooms of the house is intensified even more when one views the house as a whole, ideally by going a short distance downstream. Then, one not only sees that the stone of which the walls are built is the same stone as the riverbed and the surrounding rock. One also sees that the terraces and the flat roof adopt the layerings of the river bed, especially of the mighty slabs that form the waterfall under the house and another smaller waterfall further downstream. The roof, the terraces, and the slabs form a rhythmical structure and yet are clearly separated from each other. The light ochre of the terraces certainly takes up the lighter colors of the rock, but the clear and smooth shapes of the roof and terraces are sharply distinct from the irregularity of the rock formations. The house is clearly recognizable as a work of architecture; it does not try to ingratiate itself to the formations of the river's course and the double waterfall. It defines the river and the waterfall by looming over them both, and at the same time it integrates itself into them. It is a concentration and a continuation of the natural shapes and thus steps into a tense harmony with them. The house shows the natural as such, and accordingly shows nature.

We can describe in more detail how this occurs. First, it happens by virtue of the natural being set into an image through the windows and glass doors that function as frames. Nature around the house is not merely a natural surrounding but is a *landscape;* through determinate and emphatic sections of perspective, it is experienceable in an imagistic way. Furthermore, the natural that is built into the house is recognizable as such through its having been fashioned and shaped, more clearly recognizable, in fact, than if it had simply been found as natural; the layered stone slabs in the walls and the irregular floor pieces stand out more in their naturalness than do the rocks in the riverbed. Finally, the house shows nature by being set into it. It joins into it and lets it come forth by raising itself off within the inclusion.

None of this would be possible if there were no clear *boundary* between the house and its natural surrounding. The house itself is this boundary. It is a boundary and a bounded area that stands for itself and is withdrawn from the immediate influence of that which surrounds it. It is only through the limitation that forest and river, wind and rain, light and darkness, become *external;* they are only external because they are beyond the boundary.

Yet that which is beyond is at the same time on this side of the division. It is simultaneously incorporated into the area from which it is excluded: as incident light, as the imagistic view granted by windows and glass doors, as stone in walls and floors. The house itself is this inclusion, just as it is itself the boundary. It exists only in the inclusion; there would be no inclusive area without the stone of the walls and floors. The rooms are what they are by virtue of the view they have and especially through the light that falls into them.

The inclusion would not be possible without the setting of the boundary. That which has entered the bounded area of the house can only have *entered* because it comes from beyond the boundary and initially belongs to the external that lies beyond the boundary. The house is simultaneously limitation and inclusion; it is limiting and inclusive, and it is a boundary through inclusion, an inclusion through limitation. The house's limitation only arises through inclusion; it is established through stone and concrete, and thus through cement, sand, water, and sediment, as well as glass, metal, and wood. By virtue of these natural things being included, they become the boundary. The boundary, then, by which the natural can become external and experienced as such, is not possible without the natural itself. But the boundary itself is not natural, just as little as the inclusion is natural—unlike that which is included. The house's limitation and inclusion only exists in that nature into which it is built. Yet it is only through limitation and inclusion that the natural is there as such; it is only through these steps that nature comes to be distinct from the mode of enactment of limitation and inclusion. The classical term for this mode of enactment is τέχνη, art. Understood in this sense, art is limitation and inclusion of nature.

Every house is a boundary and inclusion in the sense just elaborated. But not every house, in its inclusion of nature, draws a boundary to nature in such a way that nature itself is experienced. One might see nature by looking through the windows; one might take the exclusion of sun, wind, rain, and cold to be comfortable; one may notice built-in quarry stones or wooden beams in their naturalness. But houses do not normally show. They only do this when they are artworks.

Fallingwater is an artwork. It is even an especially beautiful work of fine art. This stems from the fact that the house is an artwork *as* a house. The architect did not borrow from other arts like sculpture or theater in order to actualize the art-character of his work. The house is not hidden beneath sculptural exaggerations, nor is it, like many a palatial complex, staged as a representative view according to the model of set design. Rather, Fallingwater is a house, the essential moments of which—boundary and inclusion—are shown in their possibility. Here boundary and inclusion are determined through art's forms of appearance: the house's rooms allow for imagistic views, they allow everything external to the house and included within it to be interrelated in a meaningful order and, through their sequence of views and moments of order, place everything into a rhythmic play. This is especially actualized by virtue of the house's boundary being open and allowing something to be seen. Thus the terraces, protruding as they do, are emphatic spaces of interpolation that mediate between the boundary and that which is beyond it. They belong to the house, and this belonging is evinced by the fact that they share the same floor as the rooms; they are once beyond the boundary, in the open, and yet are not exhausted in that external space.

Additionally, many interior walls continue as exterior walls without any visible interruption. In order to achieve this, Wright set several windows directly into the stone without frames; horizontal metal stays prevent this from creating the impression of a cavernous opening. The house is a limitation that precisely through its limit makes evident that it is not exclusionary, but instead revealing. The boundaries of the house are always already crossed and thus crossable in observation. Anyone who moves from room to room within the house experiences ever-new crossing of interior and exterior in the rhythmic sequence of images.

But the house is not merely openly limiting; it is also openly inclusive. It freely shows the natural in which it exists and of which it is made. This reveals that its limitation is an inclusion. This is especially clear in the living room in front of the fireplace, where three massive stones jut into the room from the floor and thus make the house's foundation visible. The stones stand in open correspondence to the stone built into the walls, such that the unfinished stone makes especially clear that the natural is included into the building.

Just as the house shows its foundation, it allows nature as such to come forth. It leads one into nature and indicates it, and thereby also leads one back to the house itself. This occurs in stages. The house *connects* in ever-new and surprising ways. There are transitions and contrasts: stages of openness and of closure, stages of naturalness and processing. In the rhythmic play of transitions, the house shows nature both by opening itself to nature and offering a reprieve from it, as well as by getting close to nature and distancing itself from it: from the stone that is simply there as itself all the way to the windowpane and monochrome concrete wall. With Fallingwater, the natural is not present through contradiction but as something that is recognizable in the modifications of its mere being-thus.

In this way, the house itself is recognizable in its naturalness and in the modifications and transformations of it. It shows nature solely by *showing itself naturally*. It comes to appearance on its own in the transitions and contrasts we have described here. Fallingwater does not simply stand erected in nature; such a placement could be executed in entirely different ways, in such a way, for example, that a house is no more than a foreign object where it stands. Rather, the house in this case comes from out of nature. If growth were not an exclusively natural process, one could even speak of "growing" out of nature here. But it would be a growing that goes beyond nature, and in that case it would no longer be growth. The nonnatural aspect of its clear lines and smooth surfaces makes it evident as a placement, as a building. The rhythmic play of the riverbed and its stone slabs continues in the terraces and the roof, and at the same time the house is clearly recognizable as a work of architecture. The house comes from out of nature and leaves it; it stands outside of nature, marking a boundary, and has at the same time taken nature up into itself. The house comes to appearance in this open transition. In the latter, it shows itself as natural and yet not as nature.

On the one hand, the house's appearance rests on the fact that in it, the natural and the nonnatural are gathered together in an overarching order. This is the decentered order of the beautiful that is shaped through transitions, contrasts, and correspondences and that is shown in the mixture of these aspects as the self-showing of the work. This order is free of any predetermined, factually actualizable or actualized form. It is an order of appearance; that which belongs to it only comes to bear in its possibility of appearance.

Yet this order's appearance also rests on the thing-like presence of the work. As the order in which it is gathered is decentered, that which is circumscribed does not bear the character of a functional moment, but can instead show itself in its peculiar complexion. The house's stone shows itself as stone, the wood shows itself in its graininess and in its warm hue. With such presence, the decentered order would be absent. It can only be decentered by letting the thing-like things in which it is present be what they are. As a decentered order, it *arises* from out of that which it includes and which does not belong exclusively to it. It rests in and upon that which it delimits. Accordingly, it only shows itself as an order when that which is delimited and included by it shows itself. The beautiful order allows the natural to show itself, and only in this does beauty show itself.

Insofar as the self-showing or appearance of an artwork like Fallingwater is involved in and bound to the natural in this way, the work itself can be designated as natural. Its natural self-showing involves that being of artworks that Kant had addressed when he spoke of them as being "like nature." But as the experience of Fallingwater shows, the naturalness of artworks need not only be made by way of comparisons. It is not limited to the natural elements of a work in the strict sense. The artwork appears natural in the sense that one also deems a person's behavior to be "natural." Natural in this sense means a behavior that is not contrived or forced, but that comes from the person whose behavior is being designated as such. This still counts even if the behavior was learned or intentional and thus was not a natural process to the same degree that one's circulation is. The naturalness of the behavior lies in the fact that it arises *on its own*, and therefore does not rest upon an effort of the will nor an outside force. It possesses an effortless consistency and harmony that could not be experienced and appreciated if it were a natural process. This is also the case with the appearance of a work like Fallingwater. The naturalness of this appearance can encompass the nonnatural, because the latter, even if it is not there of its own accord, results as an appearance from the interplay with the natural. It appears from out of the natural and remains determined by it.

The notion of such a broad conception of naturalness may remind one of Heidegger's consideration of an understanding of φύσις that is not, like Aristotle's understanding, gleaned from an orientation by natural things, the φύσει ὄντα, and thereby especially by living beings. For this reason it is helpful to go into Heidegger's considerations in more detail. Moreover, his considerations stand within a context that will allow us to critically assess and further develop the determinations we have made in the description of Fallingwater. Heidegger's considerations on φύσις also have to do with the question of the relation of artworks and the natural.

φύσις in Heidegger's sense is "self-revealing" and, as such, is the "coming-forth into unconcealment" that is first secured "in its essence as such an unconcealment" by way of "self-revealing." "Unconcealment," and thus the "truth" understood as "unconcealment," is not a state of nonconcealment,[33] but instead an openness that has resulted from concealment. In this way, it can only be understood by means of the occurrence of "self-revealing," of φύσις.

On the one hand, Heidegger's understanding of φύσις as "originary," not overdetermined by metaphysics, is as broad as one can conceive—so broad that he can even equate φύσις with "being."[34] This, of course, severs any relation between nature and the natural, even though the word φύσις cannot be understood without this relation. However one might object to Aristotle's conception of φύσις—φύειν simply means "to grow," φυτόν is the plant, such that φύσις cannot be synonymous with "being" or ἀλήθεια, "unconcealment."

Through this synonymy, Heidegger on the other hand narrows the meaning of φύσις in a problematic way. If the occurrence of φύσις is taken as a "self-revealing," there must be a movement from concealment to revealing, and accordingly everything that undergoes this event would have to possess the basic quality of concealment. This is certainly the case for all growth and development. But appearance is not always of this kind. Everything that belongs to an appearance can simply be there, and then the notion of φύσις as something self-revealing can only be retained if one interprets some part of that which is present as an appearing of something concealed.

We can elaborate how this is to be understood by addressing once more the description of the Greek temple Heidegger includes in the "Origin of the Work of Art." The temple, as an example of "the truth set into the work,"[35] does not only set up a world by opening the "shape of its destiny" for a "historical people," it also sets this world "back upon the earth." The earth is "that into which the rising [shelters] all that rises as such." It is "that which shelters," that is, that concealment from which self-revealing arises and which this self-revealing in turn "clears" (28).

It is not easy to see what exactly is meant by "earth." The term is supposed to encompass everything that is not part of the historical world and at the same time to merely designate that which is essentially characterized by inaccessibility. The latter is certainly the case for the "stone ground" out of which the "resting of the work" (i.e., of the temple) raises "the darkness of its unusual and yet unforced carrying" (28). For Heidegger, the stone's grounding goes together with its impenetrability. If one splits the stone, it "never shows in its pieces anything interior or opened," but instead retreats "again into the same dullness of weight and mass of its pieces." This, Heidegger believes, makes evident the peculiarity of the earth. Earth as such is the "essentially unfathomable," "that which closes itself off" (33).

What goes for the stone must therefore count for everything that is considered part of the earth. Heidegger had previously elaborated the earth, which one mistakes as the "environment" (29) of the temple, by indicating "humans and animals, plants and things" (28). In the first draft of the artwork-essay, he states that earth is "the harmony of mountains and sea, of storms and air, of day and night." The word indicates "the trees and the grass, the eagle and the horse."[36] Earth, it appears, does not merely designate the planet with all of its plants and living creatures, but instead—including the sky through day and night—the natural in general in contrast to the historicality of the world, such that the "strife" of world and earth[37] that art accomplishes proves to be an echo of the contrast between φύσις and νόμος.

Yet Heidegger has considerable difficulties in coherently elaborating this concept of earth. What was true of the stone is no longer true of color. As Heidegger himself states, color glows "and wants only to glow." Its essence is appearance that does not include any aspect of reticence. Heidegger's attempt to clarify the "earth-like" inaccessibility of color by indicating that it disappears when one divides it "through measurement into quantities of vibrancy" (33) is not convincing. In distinction from the splitting of the stone, the measurement of color does not confirm its impenetrability, but instead destroys its appearing. This appearing's possibility is distinct from the unfathomability and impenetrability of earth. Unlike the latter, appearing is common to all natural things, be it stone, living being, or star, be they opaque or transparent.

Yet the concept of earth in Heidegger's sense is not only unconvincing with respect to the natural in general; it also fails to adequately grasp the natural as one encounters it in art. When Heidegger speaks of "earth" with respect to the artwork, it is with the intention of distinguishing the artwork from the work of τέχνη. The work of τέχνη is accordingly merely recognized as a usable thing, as "equipment" [Zeug]. That of which the equipment consists, namely its "material" or work-stuff, disappears "in usability" and is "all the better and more suited, the less resistantly it [dissolves] in the equipmental being of the equipment." Over against this, a work of art like the temple allows the material "to initially come forth." The stone comes "to carry and rest" and "so first becomes stone"; the metals come "to flash and glimmer, the colors come to glow, the sound comes to resonate, the word comes to voice." All this is said to occur by way of the work setting itself back "into the bulkiness and weight of stone, into the firmness and flexibility of wood, into the glow and opacity of color, into the resonance of sound, and into the naming power of the word."[38]

The state of affairs as described is uncontroversial, but Heidegger's account does not make clear how it arises. What does it mean that the artwork "sets itself back into" the earth? Heidegger's formulation gives the impression as if the work were present initially and then somehow enters into earth—as if it were a form conceived in advance that need merely be actualized. Yet while this notion thereby becomes identified in a problematic way with τέχνη, the actual proximity to τέχνη remains unaddressed. Heidegger leaves open precisely *how* an artwork has its existence in stone, in wood, in color, in sound, or in the word. The reason for this may well be that Heidegger takes the openness of the artwork not to be that of its own order, but instead that of the historical world opened up by the work. The artwork is a "producing," a setting-into-the-open of the earth, in that it moves and holds this earth "into the open of the world."[39] Yet an artwork can only be in the "open of the world" by including that out of which it is made. The work of art is not a "strife" in the sense that it carries out a confrontation of the openness of the historical world and the "self-enclosing" (35) of the earth; rather, it is a free play of limiting order and enclosed naturalness. It is a free play in the sense that the order both allows the natural to appear in itself and itself appears in the natural.

This notion offers an occasion once again to hold onto the distinction between fine art and τέχνη: whereas every τέχνη is determined by forms that are known in advance and actualizes these forms in something that must be discovered as material for them, art moves in an interplay in which there cannot be any forms determined in advance. Art's forms of appearance do not determine the natural as material, and thus the work can come to appearance in the natural and out of it. It does not grow, but it is natural in its appearance. In fine art, the point is to find within limitation an adequate possibility of appearance for the natural. With respect to the natural that art encloses in itself, art is without violence. Adorno's understanding of art as a "construction" that is an "uncompromising subordination not only of everything that comes to it from the outside, but of all immanent and partial moments," is thus inaccurate. No art "tears the elements of the real out of their primary context and changes them to the extent that they are once again capable of unity."[40] Rather, art only exists inasmuch as the peculiarity of the natural is not only respected with regard to an intended work, but is respected in itself. The processes of production may be so similar as to be mistaken for each other. Yet in the one case someone shapes vases out of clay according to a form that is determined in advance, whereas in the other case there results a vase that is beautiful in its individuality and irregularity and is thus not a vase made out of clay, but is clay as a vase. It comes from out of the natural and shows the natural by showing itself naturally. "Ceramics," according to the artist Sozan Kaneshige, "is born out of nature, out of the landscape. I am only its helper."[41] If one looks at this artist's work, for instance a "tea bowl with traces of fire,"[42] one understands what he means.

The artist's "helping" can be more or less intrusive. It includes careful work that is executed with experience and deftness and yet will always rest upon the insight that what can be attained through intention is limited in art. What is essential, namely the appearance of artwork, retreats from intention; it cannot be brought about, but only occasioned. Nevertheless, the inclusion of the natural within artworks, and through this the appearance of the natural, is possible in a multitude of ways. This diversity, in turn, essentially depends upon how the artwork's limiting is accomplished in each case. There are three fundamental possibilities conceivable here.

As concerns the first, an artwork's limitation can be focused on showing something natural in its naturalness. In this case, the natural is not changed. It remains as it is and is merely placed into appearance through enclosure, such that it is emphasized or intensified. The artwork then essentially consists in the natural that it shows in the limiting enclosure. Second, the act of enclosure can also show something by raising it from inconspicuousness into appearance. In this case, the natural is more evidently modified through the inner order of the work or with respect to the special demands of an art. Finally, the enclosure can pertain to just one aspect of the natural. In this case, the natural only counts in a reduced way, such that it is shown especially in the naturalness of the order in which it is enclosed.

The first of these possibilities can be seen especially well in the placing of stones in Japanese Zen gardens, the most famous of which is the garden of Ryoan-ji in Kyoto. The north garden of the temple of Daisen-in, in the temple complex of Daitoku-ji, also in Kyoto, is smaller and more concentrated but no less beautiful. There are two groups of stones in a rectangular raked surface of gravel. The first group consists of two stones, of which the first almost disappears in the gravel, the second of three stones of various shapes and heights. The middle stone juts up and is emphasized by a smaller stone in its proximity over which it clearly towers. A further stone lies some distance from the others. It is more squatted, rounder, and with an obvious recess.

The stones in a Zen garden, which are often transported from a great distance to find their place in the garden, are not processed. They are not sculptures, but were rather discovered to be beautiful just as they are, in their shape and surface texture. Their placement in the garden is to show them as the stones that they are. Yet they are not simply exhibited; in the garden they become moments of a decentered order that for its part consists in the stones. Whereas the stones, in their location of discovery, are merely themselves, in the garden they enter into correspondence to one another. Their shape, size, and condition appears in more detail here in the distance, size, similarity, and contrast that is precisely determined through their placement. In this, the garden is precisely what its name indicates: enclosure, bounding.[43] In the case of the Japanese stone garden, the boundary is created through the rectangular surface covered in raked gravel. This delimits the decentered order that shows itself as that of the placed stones. The order is that of the garden, just as the stones are the stones of the garden.

Comparably to the stone garden, works like Robert Long's stone circles are formed and also have their existence in found natural objects. There is something similar in Wolfgang Laib's pollen fields.[44] Yet no field of flowers can glow as intensively as these works of art. It is only the patient collecting and sifting of pollen in an irregular rectangle softly dissolving at the edges that lends the pollen its appearance. Nothing about it is changed. In this sense, the glowing, almost blinding yellow that is shown in the pollen field by showing itself is a natural color. Yet the color becomes an appearance by being concentrated in an unnatural, almost supernatural fashion. The pollen fields show the color because this color shows itself as natural yet enclosed into the artwork.

These works of Laib's are a limit case. The pollen in which they have their existence is found; and yet, unlike the stones in the Zen garden and Long's stone circles, it is no longer what it usually is. Through collection and sifting, the pollen was certainly not modified, but nevertheless changed in a way that can be taken to be a preliminary step to processing. In contrast, the stones that make up the walls of Fallingwater are obviously processed, and any stone that has been made into a sculpture is processed. Often, this manipulation first brings out the appearing quality of the stone or the wood of which the sculpture is made. The veining of marble, for instance, can only be seen in a polished surface. The grain of wood is concealed in the tree and is only revealed through the cut; furthermore, its color only comes out through the application of oil. Manipulations of this sort, however, do not make the stone or the wood unnatural. The veining of the stone is just as natural as the grain and color of the wood. There are qualities of the natural that are not openly manifest. Yet they are not concealed or self-enclosing in Heidegger's sense, but are instead, taken in themselves, simply inconspicuous. Art brings them to appearance. In contrast to τέχνη, the manipulations of art are essentially concerned with this appearance.

Taken in itself, the human voice too is inconspicuous. To be sure, it co-determines a person's presence in some way. Yet under normal circumstances, one hears it less as a voice and focuses more on that which it articulates or that which finds expression in it. Over against this, the voice that speaks poetry—even more so the voice that sings—evidently stands forth as a voice. Even if it articulates words, its actuality lies in sounding. In this way it is natural, simply there on its own, not subordinated to any communicative function. The naturalness in its articulation, in the melodic flowing and in the warm or metallic force of its sound, however, is connected to the condition of its schooling and training. It is natural without simply being naturally what it is.

In general, it is rare that the musical note is a natural sound. The sounding of music, even more so than the human voice, is recognizable as art when its possibility demands instruments; according to the name *instrumentum*, they are a type of use object the sole purpose of which is the production of notes that underlie a determinate, prefixed order that makes them notes and not sounds. The decentered order of a piece of music is more or less heavily prefigured by this prior order.

To be sure, instruments are the results of historical development, such that the modern orchestra of the Western musical tradition is a highly differentiated cultural product. Nevertheless, such an orchestra can sound natural. The harmonious sounding is natural—in the sense we have elaborated—by virtue of the fact that it lacks anything forced or willed. This is how the essence of the sounding comes to bear. Every sound is natural simply by the fact that it is a sound. The vibration of a string or of breath in a resonating body, the vibration of a drumhead or a struck metal pipe is a natural process. The naturalness of this process is experienced in the fact that it is sounding in an emphasized and delimited way. It is certainly effected in a determinate way that is connected to complex conditions, but still occurring on its own and thus without intention, as the rushing of wind of the murmur of water. Beethoven's Pastoral Symphony—ignoring for a moment the ironical exception of the cuckoo—does not imitate natural sounds, but is instead natural in the intention-less sounding flow of its music.

Pure notes only occur seldom and by chance in nature. In this way, every musical note is artificial, as if distilled from the infinite manifold of that which could sound. Yet if the analogy is correct, the musical note is accordingly a sounding in an especially intensive way, the essence of sounding as it were. In its intensity, a musical note is like the intense yellow of Wolfgang Laib's pollen fields. What distinguishes it from the color of the pollen are the special possibilities of production that are not given in nature. Still, what makes the musical note like a color is that the color is made in order to be nothing but color in the image.

Color essences of this sort can be found in the later paintings of Piet Mondrian. One only sees local colors that are shaped into rectangles through black bars. In the lattice created by these bars, in a light gray area, the fields of color lift each other out and, despite the strict composition of the image, form a floating order. The images contain nothing that could directly appear to be natural. Even the application of the paint is smooth without a trace. There is no possibility for any association with water, earth, or raked sand to take hold. Nevertheless, there is nature here, too. The images' color brings the naturalness of color into its elemental state.

Thus, however pure or "abstract" a color or note may be, even if it connects in any recognizable way with the natural, the purity or abstractness does not preclude naturalness. It lies in the spontaneity of the order, and especially in the fact that the color and note are simply there. They offer themselves to perception *of their own accord*. They are shown in the order that encloses them and allow this order to show itself to perception. This prompts the supposition that the natural reveals itself more easily, perhaps even less distortedly, to perception than it does to the understanding. Accordingly, the experience of the natural in art, too, would stem primarily from perception. In order to verify this, we need to precisely describe the perception of the natural and its accompanying self-showing in nature and art.

Primordial Appearance

The natural is always there, but it is not always perceived as such. If directed toward something's naturalness, one would not dispute it, nor even wonder at it. It would be a matter of fact that the rock and the tree are natural, just as the formation of clouds in changing light. It would be even more of a matter of fact to assert that this rock on the path presents a hindrance or that the tree that comes into view around the bend indicates the goal that one wishes to reach. The cloud formation indicates rain and the expectation of bad weather.

Everyday perception is, in a word, *orienting*.[45] It belongs in the context of purposeful behavior in such a way that it perceives this context along with action. Accordingly, everyday perception is always already connected to those meanings in which everyday life finds itself and orients itself. Perceiving in an everyday sense, one discovers that which is perceivable insofar as it accords with those meanings; be it that the perceivable indicates these meanings or that these meanings attach to the perceivable. Things are perceived under the inflection that they are meaningful for life; to use a Heideggerian term, they are perceived in their significance [*Bedeutsamkeit*].[46] Under everyday conditions, one can hardly separate the bare perception of something from its significance. As *Being and Time* elaborates, one would need "a quite artificial and complicated attitude in order to 'hear' a 'pure sound.'" Yet the fact that we "initially perceive motorcycles and cars" instead of pure sounds counts as "the phenomenological proof for the fact that Dasein, as being-in-the-world, always already [tarries] *with* what is ready-to-hand within the world."[47]

The fact that everyday perception is tied to significance helps explain another basic trait: everyday perception is always *directed*; in this perception, the abundance of the perceived is structured in such a way that one thing is always more important than something else and thus stands in the foreground, while the other forms the backdrop or the environment of what is primarily perceived. In Husserl's terms, it forms the "horizon of inauthentic 'co-givenness' [*uneigentlicher 'Mitgegebenheit'*]."[48] In such a horizon, perception is related to something or engaged by something. It is, in some form or another, more or less strongly *attentive*; which means it is directed toward something that is significant for the present action, be it that one attends to this thing for the sake of the action, be it that this thing has claimed our attention and is investigated more closely. This is usually connected to the question of how one is to behave with regard to the object; yet it can also be motivated by the intention, irrelevant to action, of exploring the perceived in more detail. When one calls perception *intentional* in order to highlight that it is always the perception *of something*, then this is merely a formal determination that can be concretized either in the sense of purposeful directedness toward something or in the sense of an engaged attentiveness to something.[49]

The bond between perception and significance can be broken. This usually occurs in quiet, undemanding situations, so in situations that are neither determined by intentions nor interrupted by anything affectively claiming us. Accordingly, they are situations of decreased attention. In these situations, the difference between the given and the merely "cogiven" either pales or disappears entirely; one is not directed at anything in particular and thus perceives a situation as a whole.

Peter Handke describes one such mode of perception as a tiredness that has become a "friend." One does not want to do anything, nothing needs to be done, and one therefore no longer needs to "fight off" the tiredness that overcomes one. Simple existence takes the place of purposeful action: "Far into the evening, I did nothing more than sit and look; during this time, it was as if I need not even draw breath. No conspicuous, pompous breathing exercises or yoga postures: however you sit and breathe in the light of tiredness now is incidentally correct."[50] Through the randomness of the gaze, one's own attitude to things loses its significance; one is not concerned with any attitude and certainly not with any position toward things: "For the one who gazes in this way, as if by a wonder, tiredness has taken away the self, that which is always causing mayhem: all usual distortions, habits, ticks, and cares fall away; nothing more than unfettered eyes."[51]

As with the perceiver, so too that which is perceived is changed; it is no longer viewed *from oneself* in a peculiar way that is determined by oneself or meaningful only to oneself. Instead, it is simply there: "Earlier in the history of thought, there was the notion of a thing 'in itself,' a notion that has passed because the object can never show itself in itself, but is always in conjunction with me. These tirednesses that I mean, however, renew in me the old notion and make it evident" (53). Yet no single thing appears as "thing in itself"; what arises is rather the interwovenness of all things: "In such fundamental tiredness, the thing never appears for itself, but always together with others, and even if it is only a few things, in the end everything is together" (68).

Heidegger saw such an experience of totality in moods. It is especially in the "fundamental mood" of anxiety, elaborated in *Being and Time*, that the world is experienced *as* world as a whole; this occurs in a way comparable to tiredness, when the things in the world lose their significance. In anxiety, so Heidegger states, the world possesses the "character of complete insignificance."[52] Yet this insignificance is not simply taken as it is. The experience of not being able to act is connected with the oppressive certainty of the unavoidability of acting. In anxiety one's "being-in-the-world" is threatened (250), and it is therefore the uttermost intensification of self-relation. In anxiety, one is far from the possibility of simply letting things be there and "together."

Against this, the tiredness that Handke describes leads one to reconsider the relation to things: there is an experience of things that is not dominated by predeterminations on the part of the one experiencing. This does not mean that one need consider the experiencing subject to be absent in order to reach things in themselves. The appearance that is distinguished from the thing in itself is not an appearance by virtue of being at knowledge's whim, however disposed it may be. That there are appearance in this sense is rather tied to *the act of knowing*. Taken in this way, appearance is everything that is there for a perceiver from the perceiver's point of view or direction, and which can only be described in its being from this angle. Such appearances, as Nietzsche already saw,[53] are the result of accentuations, emphases, and selections. They follow from distinctions made according to certain criteria, and from comparisons undertaken according to definite viewpoints. Thus, everything that exists by way of certain interests' viewpoints is also an appearance. It appears as desirable, detrimental, or beneficial, as needing preservation or change, without *itself* being these things when taken solely as itself. Appearances of this sort are not phantasms; they can be shared, for no one possesses concepts solely on his or her own. They can also be fulfilled in actions and thus prove to be saturated with reality. What appeared as useful proves to actually be such, and what was taken in advance to be a hindrance can turn out through engagement to actually confirm this. Yet the appearance that is distinguished from the thing in itself is always present according to the measure of the cognizing *subject,* the subject in the more precise sense of *subiectum* or ὑποκείμενον that is the foundation of appearances.[54]

If appearances in this sense are dependent on the respective perspectivally bound modes of intuition and the meanings accorded to things, then these appearances cease to exist once the perspectival position toward things—as the more or less intentional relation to something—ceases. To be sure, it is still the case that one only perceives what one *can* perceive. Yet what is perceived in the frame of this possibility is simply there. In Kant's words, one is without all interest and leaves that which is simply to exist. The question of what one thing is in distinction to another no longer plays any role. The possibility of targeting something for perception is without meaning. Accordingly, things are calmed in a peculiar way. They no longer lack anything, for no one wishes to change them. They no longer stand in relation to anything that a perceiver wants and can thus simply be affirmed. Handke again: "The way the thing shows itself in the moment, that is not simply as *it is,* that is how it *should* be."⁵⁵ The thing can simply *show itself* as that which it is. Since one no longer wishes to change or remove it, since one no longer wishes to possess it and since one does not wish it away, its factual existence no longer matters; it instead is an appearance, now in a different sense. Freed from the respective particular subjective appearing, it is liberated into pure appearance.

As this liberation coinheres with the disappearance of an attention that is always directed at something, what shows itself in this way also no longer stands on its own. The pure appearance pervasively harmonizes all things. Things move together in such a way that "everything is together" (68).

Handke illustrates this togetherness of things by using an example in which art and nature combine. He names "those flower still lifes of the seventeenth century, typically Dutch, in which a lifelike beetle, snail, bee, or butterfly sits on the blossom, and though perhaps each does not know of the other's presence, in the moment, in *my* moment, all [are] together." Despite the emphasis on the moment, this togetherness does not indicate a chance meeting, but rather a belonging-together, "the whole" (69).

Nature must be such a whole, at the very least when everything in the end is natural and its naturalness can only be hidden under the surface of perspectival, intention-bound meaning. The distinction between "natural" and "artificial" shrinks back in light of this meaning. Something is no longer viewed with respect to an imagined form that is determined by purposes, and thus what is created, shaped, and changed steps forth in its naturalness. In joins together with everything that is there of its own accord. In this instance, a house is "together" with stone, tree, and body of water. Everything shows itself together in a gaze that is no longer directed, that is involuntary, and that passes over distinctions and emphases.

It is no coincidence that Handke, in describing tiredness, opts for paintings as his illustration of this togetherness. Although the undirected gaze is not "aesthetic" in the narrow sense and thus not bound to the beautiful, the simultaneity and totality of the image aligns with this gaze like no other. In the image "everything is together" in an especially apparent and meaningful way. Conversely, one can only experience an image as such if one observes it in an undirected fashion related to tiredness. One must have it in view as a whole. Whoever concentrates on particularities or leaps from one detail to the next might see something *in* the image, but not the image itself. This allows one to surmise that images as artworks do not only need the undirected gaze, but in fact owe themselves to it. In a general sense, then, artworks would already be impossible without undirected perception simply because of their essentially imagistic nature.

If that is the case, then the undirected perception that Handke describes by way of tiredness cannot be tied to such involuntary states. To be sure, states like tiredness are "not planned" and can therefore "not be an aim in advance" (77). But not all states of undirected viewing must be like tiredness—moods in which one "finds oneself,"[56] such that one cannot deliberately adapt to or practice them. If it is not just images, but artworks in general as determined by the imagistic that cannot exist without states of undirected perception, then it must be possible to *take* this position. Certainly, the initial experiences of undirected seeing or hearing must have occurred in states akin to those that Handke describes. But art cannot be dependent on such states; it has too much to do with ongoing effort, discipline, and work. So the opposite is more obvious: if art is not dependent on states of undirected perception that arise on their own, and this perception nevertheless belongs to art, so the possibility for this perception must essentially lie within art itself. In that case, the possibility of training this perception belongs to art in a way much like Ernst Jünger describes by observing and describing orchids: "My practice consists in observing them for a long time with a thoughtless gaze, until through some primal creation, as it were, the word sets in that is adequate to them."[57] The essence of the natural opens itself to the intention-less gaze that is at once the condition of art and, here, of the poetic word.

We may generalize the result: If the totality as such that opens itself to the intention-less gaze is nature, and if this gaze belongs essentially to art, then art and nature are connected more deeply that it initially appeared. The experience of nature and of art would have a common root. In the undirected perception belonging to it, art would always go together with the experience of nature, and thus the experience of nature could come to itself in art. Nature and art would be the *same;* they would not be identical to each other, but would together form a state of affairs. Accordingly, one could only understand this state of affairs because nature and art are distinct; it is only through their difference that the situation in which they belong together would become evident.

Cézanne described this belonging-together of art and nature. In the conversations with Cézanne that Joachim Gasquet recorded,[58] one comes to know what painting is for Cézanne, especially open-air painting that takes place before the subject in the landscape. If one follows Cézanne, then art cannot succeed without a lack of intention. The painter, he says, need not be anything more than a receptacle for sensations.[59] Only then will the landscape mirror itself in the artist. It will become human and think itself in him.[60] In order for this to be possible, the artist must avoid any intervention.[61] He must retreat completely, his will must become mute, and all prejudicial voices in him must be silenced. The painter must stay silent, and become a complete echo.[62] Then the whole landscape will inscribe itself on his sensitive photographic plate. In order to fix the landscape on the canvas, in order to externalize it, the craft of manipulation enters the game; but it is a craft full of respect, ready for nothing but obedience.[63]

The description is extraordinarily precise. Insofar as this precision is what matters, it is far less important whether the description stems from Cézanne's own transmitted words or was formulated more freely by Gasquet on the basis of Cézanne's expressions. The descriptions capture the conditions of painting as an interplay of intention-less seeing that is no longer determined by the will, a silence or forgetting, and obedience. The silence does not pertain so much to speech as it does to the "voices of prejudice," and that can only mean the linguistic meanings that form judgments about what each perceived thing is. The point is to forget that here is a house, and that there is a bridge; one is not to observe this any longer. Only in this way can the will be silenced and the gaze become intention-less. When the meaning of the perceived is forgotten, the perceived no longer bears any importance and in this sense no more meaning for the perceiver. The muting of meaning leaves behind only one thing: seeing itself. Instead of following prejudices, the point is to obey vision, to submit all of one's doing to it. The painter is to be guided by vision. The point about painting is captured by what the architect Bruno Taut noted after his visit to Katsura Rikyu: "The eye thinks there."[64]

The meanings do not disappear by being silenced; but they are put in abeyance such that they no longer determine perception. In this way, one can understand the muting phenomenologically as an ἐποχή, even if it is an ἐποχή of a peculiar kind. One does not only bracket the orientation according to factual existence that is given in the natural attitude.[65] Rather, in Husserl's terms, we are dealing with "a peculiar kind of thematic ἐποχή." This latter concerns everything that can be led back to the "constitutive achievements of an intentionality immediately or indirectly related to foreign subjectivity."[66] These, in turn, are not just produced items "whose origin and sense refers to subjects, and in general to foreign subjects and their actively constituting intentionality." Rather, the ἐποχή concerns the "objective world" in general insofar as it is revealed through mediated meanings that we share with others. As Husserl says, this reality has the "experiential sense of *being-there-for-everyone*" and is thus "objective."[67]

Merleau-Ponty interpreted Cézanne's painting as a suspension of this "being-there-for-everyone," and relied for this interpretation on Cézanne's conversational statements to Gasquet. What is essential to Cézanne's art, according to Merleau-Ponty, is the "severance" (*coupure*) of "the spontaneous order of things from the human order of ideas and the sciences."[68] Cézanne wanted to paint the "primordial world,"[69] the "basis of 'nature' upon which we construct our sciences."[70] Insofar as Cézanne goes back to the "foundations of mute and solitary experience upon which culture and the exchange of ideas" is erected,[71] his paintings give the "impression of nature at its origin."[72]

When Merleau-Ponty calls the theme of Cézanne's painting the "primordial world," he does so in connection with Husserl, but with a silent correction. For Husserl the "primordial world" is the world as it is given in one's "own" perception that one does not share with others. It is the correlate of the "sphere of ownness"[73] [*Eigenheitssphäre*] or "primordial sphere" (139)[74] in such a way that it is only revealed by these and thus remains completely enveloped by them. Over against this, Merleau-Ponty appears to consider the primordial world as being foreign to perception; it is a "strange world," a world in which one does not feel well, since it forbids any "effusion of the human."[75] Yet when Merleau-Ponty sees the primordial world as given with the "foundations of mute and solitary experience," it is clear that he remains oriented by the "sphere of ownness" as Husserl conceived it. Accordingly, he can understand Cézanne's art—which in his reading offers access to the primordial world—as an expression of Cézanne's own [*eigenheitlichen*] experience. In the *Phenomenology of Perception*, which appeared simultaneously with the Cézanne essay, Merleau-Ponty had already expressed the view that art is essentially expression.[76] The artist thrusts out his work as a human once voiced the first word, without knowing if it was something other than a scream and whether it could sever itself from the flow of individual life and persist as a work.[77] Insofar as the artworks that owe their existence to this eruption of expression convey "the impression of nature in its origin,"[78] the experience of the expression must itself be that of this original nature.

Here, too, Merleau-Ponty follows the Husserlian description of the sphere of ownness. As Husserl states, the thematic ἐποχή that brackets the "objective" world that we share with others makes us realize that a "bare nature," experienced through embodiment, belongs "to my ownness." In bodily perception, one experiences "all of nature [. . .] including one's own embodiment, which is related back to itself in this nature."[79] For explication, Husserl refers to a state of affairs he had already described earlier in *Ideas* II[80]: The fact that the body is related back to itself is made possible by the fact "that I *can* perceive one hand *by means* of the other, an eye by means of the hand, etc.; whereby the functional organ becomes an object and the object must become a functional organ."[81] With this state of affairs, primordial nature shows itself; in Merleau-Ponty's words, we see nature at its origin. It is nature not as "thematic for the natural scientist," who for his understanding of nature must bracket "anything psychical in addition to the personally arising predicates of the objective world" (127). It is nature as one's own [*eigenheitlich*], as only present to *me*, and which—as is shown in touching oneself—*incorporates* me. Merleau-Ponty developed this idea in his last fragmentary volume by attempting to think primordial nature as the "flesh of things."[82] "Flesh" is thus the dense mutual transitioning, the "interwovenness,"[83] the "chiasm,"[84] or the "reversibility"[85] of perceiving and perceived in which it is shown that both are a "being with two sides"[86]—one is always already also the other.

Such an all-encompassing, enveloping nature that moves between perceiving and perceived does not exist for the artistic perception as Cézanne describes it. He does not speak of ownness and experience; instead, he talks of a radical self-forgetting that includes forgetfulness of the body. There is a reason Cézanne calls his capacity to perceive a sensitive photographic plate; following this designation, artistic perception is a mere reception that no longer has anything essential in common with a living being's embodiment in the natural world. The artist, as Cézanne says, is nothing but a "receptacle for sensations, an apparatus that registers."[87]

This nonnaturalness of artistic perception cannot lie in perception itself, which after all is a natural process. It occurs by virtue of art, which delimits the painter from the nature that he sees. It is only on the basis of this delimitation that the painter sees the landscape *as* nature. He sees it without intentions, without human perspectives that cover over its naturalness. The painter does not belong into the landscape he paints, nor does he, as Merleau-Ponty at one point expresses it, lend the landscape his body.[88] Rather, the landscape stands over against the painter. Only in this confrontation is it nature. It is on the other side of the easel and the stretched canvas, and the more the painter is determined by the placing of the canvas and thus by painting, the more clearly he sees himself as separated from the landscape. Under the condition of painting, the painter begins, as Cézanne says, to separate himself from the landscape and to see it.[89] It is only first by way of the separation from nature that the painter sees the landscape as such. He sees it as landscape and thus as nature, for what he sees has lost all binding to institutions, conventions, and inhabited human forms."[90]

The canvas before the painter, which forms a boundary between him and the landscape, is the possible image. Accordingly, the painter's activity is conditioned by the image, by the work. His behavior is a *being-at-work*, but of a completely different kind than that designated by Aristotle's concept of ἐνέργεια. The Aristotelian concept designates an activity that is "at work," ἐν ἔργῳ, in such a way that it itself is the completion that lies in the work's production and that therefore no longer needs a distinct work. The painter's activity, on the other hand, is subordinated to the work. It belongs within the ordered arrangement that, from the start, is effective as the work's possibility. This not only counts for the activity of painting, but for perception as well, yet without excluding

Cézanne's understanding of this activity. The possibility of intention-less perception that registers things like an apparatus is given to the painter in the ordered arrangement of the possible work. The possible image, in other words the stretched and empty canvas, marks the boundary that delimits the painter from that which he sees. Beyond this boundary there is nothing for him to do, and his gaze that surpasses the limit can therefore be free of any willed determinacy. It is a disembodied gaze that is nothing but reception. The painter sits or stands behind his easel as if tied down; he does not step into that which he sees.

Cézanne's description of artistic activity confirms that the canvas is a boundary. The craft determined by respect must be prepared to obey and "translate in an unconscious manner."[91] This self-forgetting perception fulfills itself in painting. It is by translating that what is perceived becomes an image.

Translation is always a crossing of boundaries. In translating one language into another, one must have entered into the other, foreign language in order to bring something from it into one's own language and thereby understand it. In this sense, Heidegger literally took translation to be a setting-*over* [Über-*setzen*]. Every understanding of something spoken is a translation in which the said initially must have "set [us] *over* into another truth and clarity, or else into questionability."[92] Yet this displacement into alterity does not fully determine the translation. There must, according to Heidegger, be a movement in another direction. Heidegger calls it "setting-back" [Herübersetzen]. Translation is only complete when the alterity into one was displaced is "set back"[93] into that which is one's own. Translating is the process of understanding that accomplishes and demonstrates that one can *say* something *differently*.

Heidegger's description is also illuminating for the understanding of painting as translation. What occurs in painting is comparable to saying differently. In it, the seen landscape becomes an image. The painter experiences a displacement into the foreign by finding his way out of his own familiar gaze that is determined by "prejudices." This occurs by way of the foreign, the landscape beyond the canvas, "inscribing"[94] itself in him and engaging his capacity for perception. By inscribing itself in the painter, "becoming human" and "thinking"[95] within him, the landscape transposes the painter into the foreign. Yet the external, the natural landscape beyond the canvas that is viewed without intention, does not transform into the painter, just as little as the painter transforms into the landscape. The occurrence of perception and the process of painting are translations and not, as Merleau-Ponty believes, "transsubstantiations," transformations of body into natural world and of natural world into imagistic color.[96] The painter does not go out; he does not cross the boundary beyond which lies the external past the canvas. It is only for this reason that there is such an outside that, in its externality, the painter can allow to affect his perception.

Because everything depends on this externality, the translation can naturally not be a "setting-back" in the sense of an appropriation. Rather, it must have the character of an alienation; to fix the seen landscape on the canvas means to externalize it—*extérioriser*.[97] The landscape remains in the painter's perception as if shrouded, kept in the dark like an exposed photographic plate that cannot be exposed to light without destroying it. That which was seen is first evinced in the artwork, to which perception in its self-forgetting was subordinated from the start. The perception that had forgotten itself, along with the perceived, are set into the work.

The setting-into-work of what is perceived remains subordinated to it. The setting-into-work does not humanize by somehow making the perceived understandable or commensurable with the human "prejudices" of which Cézanne spoke. Instead, the process of painting and the craft (*métier*) that it puts in play confirms the perceived as the externality that it is. *The externality of the landscape can only come to bear in the externality of the painting.* Insofar as the landscape is perceived in a self-forgetting manner, its externality certainly has an effect, but in perception it is not there as externality.

The image first reveals the externality, and this in a twofold way: first, by functioning as a boundary and delimiting something external beyond the limit; second, by enclosing and repeating the externality of the external. The landscape's externality only shows itself in this repetition, and painting has its meaning in this. As art, it is a "harmony parallel to nature,"[98] as Cézanne put it, thereby capturing all of these considerations here.

Following his understanding of painting as translation, Cézanne designated this parallelism as that of two texts; in thus taking nature to be a text, he reached back to the traditional conception of the "book of nature."[99] The craft of painting knows its language well, nature as seen and sensed, nature that is there in the green and blue surface and nature that is here in the painter's head, as it were.[100] The "inner nature," nature in the head, should not be thought as a finished image that is introspectively accessible and thus able to be depicted in the process of painting. This is already contested by the designation of artistic perception as a photographic plate. It can only mean perception together with the "respectful craft" subordinated to it, in other words the painter's ability to set the perception into an image, just as the photographic plate only becomes a photographic image through the process of developing. Thus, that which Cézanne calls the "language" of painting is precisely speaking not a text. A "text" parallel to nature can only first exist in the image, such that the "sensed text" is nothing but the "text" in its possibility. It is the possibility of development given in the "language" of painting, which, understood according to the "text" of nature, is a translation. It is a translation in which that to be translated, the landscape, "thinks" itself by being thought in art as a "respectful craft" and being set into the image in a conjoined play of eye and hand, hand and brush, brush and paint, paint and canvas.

Cézanne described the result of this process very clearly. Be it "right, left, here, there, everywhere," he takes these hues, these shades, these nuances and fixates them, brings them closer to each other. The hues and shades form lines; they become things, rocks, trees, without the painter thinking about this. They take on volume; they have a value. If these volumes and values on the canvas correspond in the painter's sensibility with the surfaces and spots that he possesses—which are "there before our eyes"—then it is good. In that case, the canvas folds its hands like someone who has done his work and is allowed to rest.[101]

What Cézanne describes here can be seen in the painting *Montagne Sainte-Victoire,* created between 1904 and 1906, and displayed in Zurich's Kunsthaus. The painting is one of Cézanne's latest depictions of this theme, with which he was always intermittently engaged. This painting shows the engagement particularly well, showing the massif near Aix-en-Provence whose shape sets itself against the sky. The mountain looms over a plain in which one can recognize, on closer glance, trees and even houses. Most of them are partially covered, such that only their roofs are open to view. There are a few highlighted spots, no sun, and no recognizable light source. One sees clouds in a gray sky. The weather is hazy.

This description already looks beyond the image as it is seen, for in the painting there is no illusion of a landscape. To be sure, one can see a landscape, but it lacks the spatial depth that a landscape usually possesses and which landscape paintings quite often present. Yet here there is no foreground or background. The massif does not lie far in the back, as it would be in a real landscape or a realistically painted one. Rather, it is just as close to the viewer as the plain. The painting almost has a two-dimensional effect; as a viewable surface, it is evidently recognizable as an image.

An additional reason for this evident superficial status is the way in which the paint is applied. The oil paint is forceful but not pastose, applied in broad strokes between which the unpainted canvas appears in some places. The resulting color spots thus form a more or less dense pattern that fills the entire surface of the painting. With its gray-blue tones, the sky behind the massif is certainly set apart from the darker gray-blue tones of the mountain and the greens and ochres of the plain, yet one still finds the plain's green in the sky. The painting is paint *all over* and visible as paint.[102] Just as Cézanne describes, the forms appear more or less clearly from out of the diffuse pattern of colors, such that some can be more evidently recognized than others, and some, like the shape of the mountain, are raised out significantly. The mountain's sky-bordering contour is even strengthened by a few sparse dark blue strokes. Yet in no part of the painting does a contour have a prominent enough placing that the color would be subordinated to it as a mere quality. The form comes out of the color; it arises from the colors' diffuse structure.

If that is the case, then this confirms what Cézanne's description of painting suggested: that one cannot understand this structure as a "text." To be sure, a text's moments need not always be capable of being differentiated clearly; it is possible to have vague passages and diffuse transitions. Yet the opacities cannot dominate. A text is only that which can be read and understood. However interwoven its moments may be, they must result in an order and be graspable and describable in their mutual reference when one goes through this order. In contrast to this, the pattern of colors in Cézanne's painting is certainly visible, but not readable. It is too ambiguous for this. As Cézanne puts it, everything in the painting is "dense and fluid at the same time";[103] every moment passes into others and belongs to these others in such a way that it is barely or not at all distinct from them. The interweaving of colors in Cézanne's painting is not a text. It is a *texture*.

Textures are formations that are not clearly recognizable orders. The streaks or drops of a liquid, the spikes of a crystal are structures of this kind. The graininess of sand and the damp weight of clay are textural as well. One recognizes a certain consistency. Something is neither uniform nor consisting of separated parts. There are lighter and darker grains in sand; there are pieces that are close to dust, and also small stones. A texture can be mixed, but it entails that the elements are densely or chaotically woven together in each other or with each other, in a way that cannot be reconstructed.

Textures are difficult to describe, for descriptions distinguish different parts. If one describes the surface of the sand at the beach or the interconnected green, blue, and gray tones of the water, then the individual element is already there as such; everything in the description is differentiated. But what is differentiated is not everything that is there. One always perceives more than one can descriptively grasp, such that textures are primarily given in perception. What one calls "green" in one's description of the sea is, for one's eye, an innumerable plenitude of gradations. The same is true for the rushing of the wind in the trees, which brings the leaves to rustle, the bows to creak, and the trunks to groan. Taste, too—for instance of a fruit—is textural. How is one to exhaustively describe the taste of an apple, the manifold of aromas, the distinctive and yet barely graspable element of firmness and freshness, acidity, and sweetness? In the green of the sea, the rushing of the wind, and the taste of the apple, everything is, as Handke put it, "together." What is together cannot be clearly distinguished and is, in this sense, dense [*dicht*].

Nevertheless, the density that one perceives is a togetherness of the different. Perception, as Aristotle already knew, is perception of what is different. One perceives the light and the dark in vision, the high and the low in hearing, the bitter and the sweet in taste, the warm and the cold, dry and wet, rough and smooth, hard and soft, in touch.[104] If these differences and their gradations did not exist, one would not perceive anything; everything would be the same.

Yet perception does not hold onto what is different as such. Vision as such does not fixate; in hearing, one does not lift the particular groaning of the tree trunk out of the rushing of the wind in the trees. The sweetness of the apple is always there together with its sourness, with its freshness and firmness. Even when a particular quality determines perception, this always belongs within the plenitude of what is perceived.

This plenitude, its textural essence, is always there. It forms the realm in which the particular, for instance this distinct bright color, can take hold of our attention. As soon as this occurs, the plenitude of what is perceived retreats. It is there, but not perceived as such; one only perceives it along with the particular, just as one only hears the rushing of the wind and the murmur of the stream along with the birdsong when one focuses on the latter. The birdsong stands out from the background sound of the wind and the water and yet still belongs within this background, within the audible texture.

Cézanne's *Montagne Sainte-Victoire* clearly shows what mattered to the painter as he sat before his subject and gazed. He wanted to see the texture of what is perceivable and to translate this into the painting. To this end, he had to gaze "like a dog," "without any nervousness or ulterior motives," as the painter Mathilde Vollmoeller put it when observing Cézanne's work.[105] He had to gaze until the houses and trees of the plain, the mountain massif and the clouds in the sky changed into color. As soon as that occurs, Cézanne claims, an airy, colorful logic suddenly takes the place of the dull and stubborn geometry. Whereas the gaze determined by geometry was fixated upon nothing but lines, planes, and shapes, now everything organizes itself differently. Textural difference replaces fixed distinctions. "I see through spots," Cézanne claims. Now, as he puts it, there are only colors.[106]

By seeing color as such, vision arrives at itself, as it were. Seeing *is* the seeing of colors; Plato and Aristotle recognized this,[107] and Goethe strengthened it in the Introduction to his *Theory of Colors*. "The eye does not see a form when light, dark, and color together make up that which distinguishes one object from another, and one part of an object from another, for vision."[108] Yet whereas in an everyday attitude the lightly and darkly graded color differences are immediately perceived schematically as forms, in the painter's gaze they remain preserved *as* colors in the inexhaustible plenitude of their nuances. The painter's vision as Cézanne practices and describes it is *primordial vision;* it is a seeing that aims at vision itself.

Yet painting is no performance of vision. The painting is not an expression or a document of it. When the painterly vision is set into the image, it is not vision but the visible that holds sway: color *as* color. This does not mean, however, that the visible is taken out of reality and brought closer to the interiority of sensation. Even when painting, as Hegel says, selects for itself "the shining and the *shining of color*" instead of remaining satisfied, as sculpture does, with "the heavily formed, unparticularized matter that is only to be grasped according to its *shape*,"[109] painting is not concerned with the mere shining that is lifted off of "living reality," not even when painting "develops into a magic of spreading color [*Kolorit*], in which the objective already begins to hover away, as it were" (133). Insofar as the color in the painting stands over against one as the landscape did to the painter behind his easel, it does not have the character of illusory shining [*Scheinens*]; rather, it is *appearance* [Erscheinung]. It is really there for perception. In the painting, that which is there for primordial vision can be experienced *as* primordial appearance, because the painting has the character of being a thing and thus itself presents the appearance. The painting as such is a primordial appearance. In contrast to Hegel, Goethe clearly saw this peculiar intensifying of visibility that occurs in the painting. In his words, painting is capable "of bringing forth on a canvas a much more complete visible world than the real world can be."[110]

What Goethe here calls "completeness" can be elucidated in more detail by way of Cézanne's description of the painting process, and especially by looking to a late painting like *Montagne Sainte-Victoire*. Cézanne's painting is not an illusion of a landscape, but instead the visible evidence of the state of affairs that Goethe described, namely that visible forms are present strictly in the paint. The painting makes this state of affairs evident by letting the forms—clouds, mountain massif, trees, and houses—*result* from the color. At the same time, the texture of Cézanne's painting clears up; its density loosens. But it does not dissolve into clearly delineated forms. Rather, it becomes visible as the possibility of the text, as a text-bearing possibility. In observing the painting, one sees that something must initially be a perceivable appearance in order to be distinguished and understood as something determinate and distinct from other things.

This can only become evident in Cézanne's painting because the painting is not only a correlate of perception. One need not bracket the understanding of that which one sees, as if one were strictly involved with the visible to which, in Merleau-Ponty's view, one must return in abstraction from the "human order of ideas."[111] There is no abstraction in Cézanne's painting. One sees the mountain massif in front of the sky, one sees it looming over the plain with its trees and houses. Yet if one observes the painting as a painting, one will not grasp schematically what one sees, but will instead see how the identifiable forms rise out of the color and are simultaneously embedded in it. The text of the image becomes visible and is held in possibility as a text in its visible textural embeddedness. At the same time, the texture appears as the possibility of a text; it can allow the latter to arise in a visible way. In this way, too, the painting's appearance is primordial. Through it, the visible is made visible in an originary way, namely by way of the paint, while what is understandable in the painting is tied into the visibility. In the primordial appearance, what is understandable cannot be separated from the color in which it is present.

Primordial appearances also exist in the everyday whenever something is understandable in its being perceived. Yet typically, everyday primordial appearances are covered over by orientations of utility or productivity. They remain philosophically unexamined when one orients oneself according to the model of τέχνη and thus according to a notion of forms dissolvable from perception. Yet on the other hand, primordial appearances are seemingly so unavoidable that one encounters them as soon as one begins to analyze perception. This is how Aristotle came across them, by determining the correlate of perception as εἶδος; it is not the stone that is in the soul, but its εἶδος.[112] Since he is discussing perception, the "idea" in question cannot be meant in the modern sense, that is, a pure presentation in thought.[113] But one should also not translate the word as "form," as is common in Aristotelian contexts. Qualities of sensation, tones, and colors are not forms like something's essential determinations that can be detached in thought from what is perceived (τὸ τί ἦν εἶναι), nor are they like what lies beneath (ὑποκείμενον) and can take up or lose various properties. What is in perception must rather have the character of an appearance. That is precisely what the word εἶδος addresses; the word can also mean "appearance."[114] Insofar as it concerns perception, it cannot mean *mere* appearance, but instead only the manner in which what affects perception is present for it. If one considers that the word εἶδος especially designates something's essential determination that is detachable in thought, then Aristotle's determination is certainly conceived by way of the understandability of what is perceived; yet it cannot avoid grounding what is understandable in what is perceived. The form must be a perceivable appearance in order for it to be detachable in thought.

Aristotle phrased this even more clearly in another passage of *De Anima*. The example that he uses, not coincidentally, is that of hearing a voice. The latter is taken to be a sounding-together (συμφωνία). It is not a noise and not a uniform sound; it is articulated. Yet as Aristotle states, the sounding-together of what is articulated in the voice is λόγος. Provided that the voice and hearing are one—after all, they belong together inasmuch as the voice is received and appears in hearing—then hearing is necessarily also a λόγος. Since this is the case, any excess in height or depth of sound destroys hearing. The excess does not fit into the joint sounding and can thus not actually be heard. It does not appear, but instead disappears when it becomes too quiet, and when it becomes too loud it only causes pain. This, Aristotle adds, is also the case with taste, with smell, and with sight, where anything too bright or too dark destroys vision. Thus, perception is a λόγος.[115] Taken in the already delineated sense of an understandable order, λόγος is a *text*.[116]

This determination may be confusing. Yet when Aristotle calls perception a λόγος, he does not mean that it is a language or thought that distinguishes conceptually. Rather, the context clearly shows that λόγος means "relation" or "proportion" here. The visible colors make up something like a structure, audible sounds resonate together, and the tone that is too high or low exceeds this joint sounding. What is perceived is not scattered, but instead forms a context. Within this context, it is in a more or less harmonious relation, and since the perceived is present in perception, the perception itself must itself be such a relation.

Nevertheless, the resonances with reason and language in Aristotle's account are probably intentional. Otherwise he could have avoided the term λόγος and limited himself to the term συμφωνία to designate the perceived context. He might have also chosen a different example than that of the voice. The latter makes the inner cohesion of thinking and perceiving graspable as that of understanding and hearing. The voice that articulates a sentence must be heard in its articulation in order for an understanding of the sentence to even be possible. What is said and understood, the λόγος as text, must always also be something audible or, in the case of reading, something visible. That which is communicated in a graspable way belongs together with the perceivable, just as two matching parts of a broken identification token can be brought together again. Thus, Aristotle calls vocal articulations σύμβολα.[117] If the audible and visible were not itself λόγος, in other words a harmonious sounding-together, then spoken language would be impossible. Its understandability must stem from perception.

In its perceived understandability, vocally articulated language is primordial. Everything that can be understood or thought must be perceivable, be in some way tied to perception and thus be experienced through perception as an appearance. The thinkable, so Aristotle claims, is within the perceivable appearances,[118] and no one can learn or understand without perception.[119]

Despite this insight, Aristotle described the perceived, in the example of the voice, by way of the understandable. He does not advance to the insight that perception is richer than intelligibility, such that the latter can glean its abundance solely from perception. Aristotle views the texture of the perceivable as a text

Nature

and thereby remains with the notion of a "symbolic" and thus symmetrical conjunction of perceivability and intelligibility.

One reason for this might be that Aristotle does not take his orientation from art but from everyday speech. In everyday language that is directed toward communication and comprehension, one overlooks the primordiality of the audible. Language first becomes obvious in its deficiency, when articulation becomes unclear or too quiet, or in any case is difficult to comprehend. Otherwise, the voice can be heard along with the audible in such a way that it sounds pleasant or unpleasant, or pleases us because it is the voice of someone we love. It is only present *as* voice, however, if one attends less to what is said and more to the sounding itself, and thereby experiences how that which is articulated is woven into the dense texture of the sounds. Then, one hears the text of what is said and understood from out of the texture. Then, the text is always already inscribed in this texture. Conversely, one could also say that the texture clarifies itself into a text here, just as seemingly separate puffs form out of the nebulous clouds that hang in the sky like cotton and yet nevertheless still belong to the clouds.

When the texture proves in this way to be a dense, still imprecise λόγος, it becomes clear why a text can form out of it. Despite all clarity, that which one experiences remains ambiguous, like a puzzle. What is experienced can be textural or textual. The textural can be grasped in the direction of a text, just as one can weaken one's understanding and let the text sink back into the density of the texture. Yet because this play of text and texture rests upon the texture and always returns to it, the text in its intelligibility cannot be separated. It is only on the basis of the texture that the play is a primordial appearance.

This close belonging-together of the intelligible and the sensible, as it is capable of being experienced in the play of text and texture, cannot as such be created. It is there on its own and is thus recognizable as the "indissoluble and reciprocal connection" that Valéry conceived as the bond between "shape" (*figure*) and "matter" (*matière*) and thus sought in vain to understand.[120] The belonging-together remains incomprehensible if it is at all taken to be a "connection" (*liaison*)—as if the seashell's shape and its chalky substance had needed to be joined together. No explanation will be able to grasp that the seashell is there as a living being. But one can see and describe that its shape rests in the texture of the chalk and only thus appears as a shape at all, without any vexation through the pointless question of how the shape got into the chalk. The question reveals itself as pointless when one gives up the attempt to detach the form from what is perceived. One must trust in perception and let what is perceived be free in it, such that it can enter into a free play with the intelligible. The intimate belonging-together of text and texture that one experiences as this free play is natural in art, which is parallel to nature, as well as in nature itself. Nature as such is a primordial appearance.

This becomes all the more clear the more the belonging-together appears as such. The experience of nature in its naturalness is tied to the vividness and conciseness of primordial appearance. The latter is more vivid and concise the more it is recognizable as play, in other words, the more evidently the readable and intelligible text belongs *into* the texture and at the same time results *from* it, without being detachable from it. That is the case with those free formations by means of which Kant exemplified his conception of what is naturally beautiful,[121] the formations that cannot be decisively determined, but which are instead de-centered orders. In their beauty, one can experience nature *as* nature.

The primordial appearance in the artwork is even more explicit than in the natural. The naturalness in Cézanne's later *Montagne Sainte-Victoire* painting lies in the fact that the text of forms arises in and out of the texture of color. Yet in art, this resulting of the text is itself set into the work, which means that it is specifically made possible by the art forms of the imagistic, poetic, and musical. To be sure, Cézanne does not create the texture of his painting; in order for the textural essence of the color to be set free, anything willful or intentional, as Cézanne underscored, had to be bracketed. But that simply means that the color could not be subordinated to some predesigned particular form. Only in this way can the form arise from the color in its dense and ambiguous togetherness. In a comparable fashion, the composed structure, the text of a piece of music, results from the togetherness of the notes, which is realized no less in Bach's polyphony than in the tone-colors of the *Tristan* prelude. Only here, the realization is different, closer to the text or closer to the texture. Even the plot threads, character depictions, settings, and objects in a novel result from the dense context of what is capable of being narrated, which in its togetherness must be experienced without intention. Here the texture from which the text results is the language that holds the narration together and, as Proust shows in his novel, comes to the text from itself. It is the words that resound against each other, such that the structure of the story can arise from them, the names too, which are full of narratability and can be developed into descriptions. Over and above this, the poem becomes a text, a readable order, out of the dense togetherness of allusions, relations, pauses, and depths of meaning, which are not so much understood as unintentionally heard.

The texture is primary. If a painter, composer, or poet does not engage the texture in an intention-less manner, his or her work will merely be constructed and thus not an artwork at all. Yet in art, the texture is enclosed within the work. To stay with the example of color, we can say that it is the painting's color; it is set into the boundaries of the painting and accords with its totality. The color is to be visible with regard to what is shown in the decentered order of the painting. The paint's texture is set into the painting in such a way that the painting's text can rest in and result from it. The textural self-showing of the painting belongs together with that which the painting shows in its decentered order. If the showing were lost, it would no longer be a painting. Thus, even the coincidental application of color, as for example in Jackson Pollock's drip paintings or in the ink drawings of Julius Bissier and Yu-Ichi, remains in relation to an imagistic text. Even the natural forces of fire to which the clay of bowls and vases is subjected in the furnace are kindled for the sake of the vessels' decentered order that results as a text from the texture. Art is not something natural; it is, to borrow once more Cézanne's nice phrase, "parallel to nature." In the artwork, the text's arising from out of the texture comes to appearance imagistically, poetically, and musically. It is made accessible in the forms of appearance, through limitation of the perceivable and by embedding forms into the perceivable, in other words through objectification. In contrast to the natural, the artwork's text becomes recognizable in its possibility from out of the texture, and thus it becomes evident that the texture bears within it the possibility of the text. Whereas one encounters beauty in nature as simply being groundlessly possible, in art the beauty is revealed *as* possibility in the work. The artwork is the imagistically, poetically, and musically delimited area in which the play of text and texture can be experienced as a play of the possible that has been set free.

This setting free of the possible occurs within the boundaries of the work, a work that is a boundary as such and that can therefore include something and unfold its order in and from this inclusion. In doing this, the work seals off the observer, reader, or listener in the same way that the possible painting sealed the painter lost in observation from the landscape before him. No one has anything to do in the work, which is how it becomes visible, hearable, and readable. By placing the observer outside itself in this way, the artwork is spatial. Insofar as it can essentially not be entered, its spatiality may well be incomparable. But it will only be by clarifying this spatiality peculiar to the artwork that we will adequately grasp its character of appearance and its mode of being an object.

FIVE

Space

Places

There are artworks whose spatiality is obvious. Buildings are rooms, and as such they are in space. Rooms are formed by walls that open onto exteriors through windows, doors, or sliding walls. Sculptures need space around them so that one can move around them and observe them. They are not set up in collections, but placed instead in public spaces or landscapes, where they protrude into the sky or, like Eduardo Chillida's *Wind Combs (Peine del viento)*,[1] reach like iron claws into the distance. Images, too, are spatial. Like wall paintings, they can belong to a room or, like sculptures, simply require space. Images only show themselves in the right distance.

The spatiality of music is no less evident. Music resounds in space; the consistency of the space is essential to a piece of music having the adequate effect. Only in the proper space can the sounds resonate and unfold. Yet if that is the case, they sound in a spatial manner. To be sure, the performance of a piece of music takes place in time, but the piece only comes into its own through the distinction of its sounds, through the proximity and distance of its voices. Its successiveness is held together by the uniformity of its spatial sound. Every occurrence that is experienced temporally is in space temporally, such that time is seemingly a possibility of space.[2]

Things appear to be different with regard to poetry. To be sure, the dramatic performance needs its space just as the musical performance does, and that is also true of poetry insofar as it is spoken, and certainly any fixation in writing is spatial, being either here or there. Yet in distinction from the musical piece, the poem seemingly does not lose anything when it is not read or spoken aloud, but is instead learned by heart and meditated upon. A poem like Goethe's "Over All the Peaks It Is Peaceful" does not appear to be anywhere in space. And yet it was not only conceived, but also inscribed on the wall of the hunting cabin on the Kickelhahn, a mountain in the Thuringian forest. One also refers to a poem in a spatial manner when one indicates a word or verse and states: "Here, it says . . ."

Even with artworks whose spatiality is readily apparent, it initially remains unclear how to understand that spatiality. It is evident, and thus it is clear that it is not intended to be metaphorical. The artworks appear in real spaces, and not in an inner realm, however it is to be understood.³ This real space possesses a peculiar self-evidence—indubitable, but at the same time difficult to grasp. One stands in front of or within this self-evidence, or imagines it, but one cannot find elucidating words for what is obvious about it. It is the obviousness itself that prevents the description and grasping. Language slips off of what is obvious, especially when one cannot think of an alternative. Concepts and descriptions always distinguish. But how should a building be otherwise than spatial? Something that has no alternative—in this case, the spatiality of buildings, sculpture, images, music, and drama—is almost as unpresentable to thought as something that is unimaginable as such.

That spatiality is difficult to conceive and describe does not mean that there is no language for it. But this language does not describe spatiality; it articulates it. This language of spatiality is especially given in expressions that designate spatial relations. "Here" and "there," "near" and "far," "close" and "distant," are expressions of this sort, just as "above" and "below," "next to," "within," and "outside of." There are many more such expressions. Upon closer inspection, we would even notice that expressions without a clear spatial reference still have a spatial sense. If one speaks of fullness or emptiness, of openness or closedness, then this refers to something spatial. We would seem to get closer to grasping spatiality if we pursue the meaning of the expressions just listed. But this meaning only reveals itself by way of an experience of what is meant. In order to clarify it, one must begin with the experience of spatiality.

There is strong evidence that spatiality is experienced in an exemplary way with works of art. We have already seen that in art, everything that occurs in it is capable of being experienced in a special way: the possibilities that artworks show through their decentered orders, the forms of appearance in which this showing takes place, and the naturally perceivable, the texture of texts realized as art. Accordingly, one would expect the spatiality of artworks to be especially distinct. It would then be a key to an understanding of that spatiality in which the spatiality of artworks conceptually reveals itself.

In order to grasp to the spatiality of artworks, one should begin with what is obvious. In this sense, the distinct spatiality of a building as an artwork should be obvious. A house such as Fallingwater allows one to experience spatiality in its subtle play of opening, crossing, and limiting. It shows space by structuring it, by indicating the outside from the inside, and allowing both to step forth in their belonging-together. The outside lacks as much arbitrariness as the inside. It is not only the inside of the house that belongs to the overall order; this order does not end at the outside walls. The external walls belong just as much to the house as they do to that which is beyond the house, to the landscape into which the house is built. The house looms into this landscape, closing itself off against it and opening up onto it, by raising itself on the rock above the stream and looming over the stream with its terraces. These reach out, as it were, and thereby reveal themselves to be distantly related to Chillida's *Wind Combs*.

It is in the belonging-together of the interior and the exterior that the spatiality of the house comes to bear—just as much inside, when one remains in its rooms or on the terraces, as outside, when one looks upon or into the house. In this belonging-together, the interior and exterior are not given abstractly, in some generality. The measurable extension of the house is of no concern for the visitor. To be sure, it played a role for the architect when he designed the layout, but even for him it was not of primary concern. What initially strikes the visitor must have also been most important to the architect: the *setting*, the *situation* of the house. This situation is precisely what he brought into the work: the house in the middle of the forest, far away from other houses, set on the rock above the stream whose rocky bed is taken up, repeated, and thus brought to exceptional visibility in the house's terraces. The house could not stand anywhere else. The house belongs so intimately together with the rock, the stream, the waterfall that lends the house its name, with the forest that surrounds it, that the house would be unthinkable in any other location. The house has its *place* here and nowhere else. It belongs together with this place in a situative manner, such that it can only be what it is there, and at the same time determines the place in a peculiar way. Insofar as the experience of space opened by the house is determined by its place, it must essentially be an experience of place.

With respect to architecture, there are reasons to think that a building's art-character cannot be conceived with its character of place. Whereas standard living houses that merely have to fulfill their purpose can be erected nearly anywhere, houses that are artworks belong closely together with their surroundings. In the case of Fallingwater, that is obvious. Le Corbusier, too, saw his Notre-Dame-du-Haut chapel in Ronchamp as a response to the place in which it was built—"réponse au site."[4] As Tadao Ando conceptualized a museum of modern art for Naoshima, a small island in Japan's Inland Sea, the most important question for him was where the museum was to be built. As Ando writes, he traversed "the whole island" in order to take in "as deeply as possible the landscape's expression": "And then, completely unexpectedly, like a spontaneous reaction to my encounter with nature, I saw before me the form that the museum should take. I transferred this vision back upon nature there and repeated this communication with the landscape several times."[5]

Heidegger was the first to formulate philosophically the idea of the spatiality of artworks as the determination of a place. In his dense 1969 essay "Art and Space"—which nevertheless still remains a mere sketch—Heidegger calls plastic art "the embodiment of places"; shortly thereafter he specifies it as "an embodying bringing-into-the-work of places."⁶ Heidegger's use of plastic art as his point of orientation can be explained on the one hand by the fact that he wrote the essay with an eye toward Eduardo Chillida's art. On the other hand, the relation to plastic art stems from the matter itself. Plastic art is bound to place much in the same obvious way that buildings are. Chillida's *Wind Combs* determine the rocky Basque coast near San Sebastián just like Fallingwater determines the Bear Run valley or Ando's museum determines the hill on the island of Naoshima. Heidegger's characterization of plastic art sets the latter into an essential relation to space. The "interplay of art and space"⁷ is thereby to be understood by way of place, because place, in Heidegger's estimation, is the primary givenness of space. This strengthens the supposition that the spatiality of artworks is primarily to be grasped as their character of place. In the course of Heidegger's development of this idea, he introduces a thought that is helpful in clarifying artworks' character of place.

In order to understand this thought of Heidegger's, one should first note that his considerations are directed against the "physical-technical" understanding of space. (205) Space, according to Heidegger, is not "that space which, since the time of Galileo and Newton [has received] its initial determination [as the] uniform expanse that is not distinct in any place, that possesses the same value in all directions, and which is nevertheless not perceivable" (204–205). In other words, space is not to be the measurable extension of length, breadth, and depth as Descartes defined it.⁸ This determination is abstract because it neglects the primordial givenness of space. That which is measurable is not primarily present as an unqualified extension. It is instead, in Heidegger's terms, "the free," more precisely "the open,"⁹ which, "among other things, allows for the appearance of present things" and gives them the possibility "of belonging to and appearing from out of their respective whence." This open, in turn, is only to be experienced by way of a place. The belonging-together of things results from a place, such that the openness that is peculiar to the belonging-together is to be thought on the basis of a place. In Heidegger's view, the place "in each case opens a region by gathering the things into a belonging-together within the region" (207).

The key word in this determination of place is "gathering." It reminds one of Heidegger's development of his understanding of λόγος. Similarly to the sense of λόγος as gleaning [*Lese*], so the gathering here is a bringing-together of a plurality into a totality.¹⁰ Yet "gathering" here does not refer to language; rather, it refers to that which can come to language, to the context of what is sayable. In Heidegger's later thought, this context is not, as in *Being and Time*, given as a sphere of "significance" for Dasein,¹¹ a connectivity of things in a plurality of pragmatic perspectives. As Heidegger now realizes, the context of what is sayable lies in the things themselves. The thing is not gathered, but instead *is* a gathering, a "thing" in the old Saxon and old Frisian sense of the word, though it is not, as Heidegger surmises, "old high German."[12]

We can ignore here the fact that Heidegger considers the thing's gathering in general as the gathering of a world conceived as "fourfold," more precisely as the gathering of "sky" and "earth," "the divine" and the "mortals."[13] In "Art and Space" there is no mention of this conception of gathering. In his latest works, Heidegger liberated himself from the narrow determination of gathering as the "fourfold" and thus also from the contrast of "world" and "earth" that echoed "The Origin of the Work of Art." Here things are no longer allegorically overloaded, in contrast to the bridge described in "Building, Dwelling, Thinking," which was to be a gathering as a "swinging crossing before the divine."[14] Now every thing, as thing, simply opens the gaze or path to other things. One is to let this opening of things by things to simply be as it is. Heidegger's term for this is "granting" [*Einräumen*]. Granting is not to be understood as the setting up of things in a room, but instead as that retreat of the self that one means when one grants someone a seat, an extension of a deadline, or a right. Granting in Heidegger's sense is a "release"[15] [*Freigabe*], the leaving-be or allowance of a place that in turn leaves space for things.[16] As Heidegger says, it gives "things the possibility of belonging to their respective place [*Wohin*] and, from this, to each other," without any need of bringing them together in any way.

The belonging-together of things, as Heidegger describes it, always arises from a thing. In order to experience it, one has to begin with a thing. This thing for Heidegger is the place that gathers and thereby opens a "region" for other things. This "region," the "free expanse" as Heidegger also calls it,[17] is space, insofar as it is no longer conceived abstractly as extension but by way of the place as its open expanse. Space, conceived by way of place, is always a particular space, one space among many. Places, Heidegger states in "Building, Dwelling, Thinking," "always first allow spaces." The spaces receive "their essence from places and not from space 'as such.'"[18]

Heidegger's considerations are understandable. If the expanse of space is not to be grasped abstractly, as extension, by looking away from what it contains, it must be secured to something capable of being experienced, which opens the expanse on its own. This, in turn, occurs by way of a thing referring to other things. In this reference, the thing is no longer, as in *Being and Time*, an object of use that belongs into the referential totality that is delivered over to Dasein's behavior. Rather, it is a place. As a place, it refers to other places. This can be elucidated through the example of the bridge Heidegger describes in "Building, Dwelling, Thinking": As a place at which one can gather, the bridge also leads into an expanse; it leads the street over the river, and it lets the crossed river come from and go into its distance. The bridge, in Heidegger's terms, thus opens a "mutual play of places," a "locality" [*Ortschaft*], as he calls it.[19]

Yet upon closer inspection, Heidegger's ideas turn out to be problematic. They rest upon the notion "that the things themselves are the places and do not simply belong to a place" (208). Heidegger had already spoken in "Building, Dwelling, Thinking" of things that "are places,"[20] and held onto the idea that one "never [finds] places, i.e. things like the bridge" in mathematically constructed space. (158) This determination exceeds the distinction of thing and place that is given in every process of locating a thing. If, for example, one says that the vase is on the table, this does not designate a relation of two things. To be sure, the table is a thing just like the vase. But when it is addressed as the vase's place, its character of being a thing retreats in a peculiar way. Insofar as the table is the vase's place, it is not seen *as* a table. If one designates it as the place in which the vase stands, this occurs from the side of the vase. It is only through the vase that rests upon it that the table proves to be a place. If the table were empty and one did not take it to be a possible place for another thing, then one would just see it as the thing that a table is.

It is just this relation of thing and place that Heidegger has in view. In "Building, Dwelling, Thinking," he states that places are not simply "ready to hand." Referring to the bridge example, Heidegger concedes that there are certainly "many spots along the river that can be occupied by something." Yet only "one among them" proves to be "a place, and this *by way of the bridge*"; the bridge does not first come "to stand in a place, rather the bridge itself first [brings] a place" into existence. But this precisely does not mean that the bridge is something like a place. (156) It would only be a place for someone who crosses it or for something that is placed upon it. Yet insofar as the bridge itself "occupies" a place that Heidegger, with some difficulty, calls a "spot" [*Stelle*], it reveals it to be a place. Since the place is thus a "result" of the bridge, the latter cannot itself be a place.

Heidegger's confusion of thing and place is all the more understandable the more intimate the relation of the two is. Since a house like Fallingwater, like Notre-Dame-du-Haut, or like Ando's museum on Naoshima could not stand anywhere else, one could imagine that it stands in and as its place. The place where Fallingwater was built in the Bear Run valley is designated quite simply by the name of the house itself: Fallingwater; the place Ando's museum occupies is seemingly enveloped by this structure, such that one could designate it by describing the museum.

The buildings just mentioned are, in fact, more than a marking for the place in which they stand. They characterize their place so decisively that one first sees this place by virtue of them. It is only through the buildings that Bear Run valley, the mountain of Ronchamp, and the gentle south slope of Naoshima have become what they now are. Yet just as this designation indicates, the places are distinct from the buildings. They are places for the buildings and were there before them. But the way one knows them now is first determined as a place by way of the buildings. Everything that belongs to these places can be viewed by way of the building, insofar as the artwork shows it. In attempting to understand the place-character of artworks and, through them, the essence of place, one has to pay heed to both of these aspects.

The first aspect can already be grasped by observing a building like Fallingwater in its place. The valley, and especially the slab of rock at the waterfall, allow the house as such to have its effect. The house appears in the place at which it was erected; it shows itself in this place. The house can only show itself at this spot. It is only possible at this spot for it to stand out from the trees of the forest and to loom over the river and its waterfall. For this reason, one can say that the place allows the building to show itself. It permits this self-showing, releases it.

One should not suspect any metaphorical attribution of agency on the part of the place in this "release." That would be a senseless notion. Rather, the release simply occurs by virtue of the place being a place. A place is only ever capable of being designated as such if it is a place *for* something; otherwise it is only a possible place that is grasped through its potential of being a place for something. A place is a place for something by taking this something up as different from itself and, keeping it more or less distinct, allowing it to show itself. Self-showing *is* precisely the standing-forth and being-distinct that is made possible by the standing-back of what is receptive. This standing-back that allows something other to come into effect is the release that is essential to the place. Places, one might say, are the *phenomenally giving,* while that which shows itself in a place is the *phenomenally given*. The giving and being-given do not thereby have the character of events.[21] They belong to a relation that is only possible as a spatial one.

In an artwork like Fallingwater, the receptive essence of the place, which Plato already indicated in the *Timaeus*,[22] is especially obvious. Whoever descends into Bear Run valley and moves toward the house will be drawn to the house as soon as it comes into view. The landscape retreats. Yet the landscape, in its retreat, does not remain invisible. By virtue of the house coming into view, the landscape is simultaneously perceived as that which remains behind. Along with the house, one sees the landscape as the house's place. If, conversely, one lets the house direct one toward the landscape, such that, for example, the house's terraces allow the rock slabs in the river to be seen, then one no longer sees these as a place. At that point, they belong to the decentered order of the artwork. Here the observation of the house in its landscape is a deictic play in which something is shown in one moment and then a place in another.

Aristotle's determination of the essence of place indirectly captures place's retreating mode of existence as well as what is present in this place. The place (τόπος) is defined as the delimitation that something possesses by way of its surrounding body.[23] Put differently, place is the containment by something that surrounds, at which or upon which or in which something else is located. If the place were congruent with that which is at it, one would not experience it as a place. In order to be perceivable as a place, the surrounding body must extend beyond what is contained, just as the tabletop extends beyond the vase that stands upon it and surrounds it.

Accordingly, Aristotle hit upon something essential with his determination of place as a "surrounding body." But he did not take account of the fact that the essence of place that surrounds and extends beyond that which is contained does not exist without that which is surrounded and delimited. That which receptively surrounds and extends beyond what is surrounded can only be such if there is something there that is delimited. It is by way of that which is delimited that it (the surrounding body) is capable of being experienced as surrounding and extending beyond that which is delimited. In Heidegger's terms, it is released or granted as such by way of that which is delimited.

One can reinforce this matter with an example. If one observes Fallingwater, one definitely sees the landscape in which the house stands. One sees it without it having any quality of appearance comparable to that of the house. If the landscape appears—as when the rock slabs appear together with the house's terraces—then it has its appearance by way of the artwork, within the work's own decentered order. Even when it is seen as a place, it does not fully retreat. It is not only perceived along with the house, as something that lies at the edge of one's actual perception. Rather, one sees the landscape *as a place*, in the manner that the house that stands at this place grants it. House and landscape are not equivalent moments in a play of self-showing, such that now one stands out, now the other. What one sees is the building in its place—the building as that which is phenomenally given by its place. And it is the place as that which gives, which is such only by way of the building. What one sees is the building's self-showing by way of that which comes to show itself by virtue of the building.

This transparency of self-showing exists because Fallingwater is an artwork. Only in artworks can something that belongs to a place at the same time be something shown. Of course, that is not always the case. Not every artwork shows the place that phenomenally gives it. Thus, the empty wall is certainly the phenomenal place of a painting, but the painting does not show the wall. Over against this, the matter of self-showing in a place is essential for artworks, indeed it is not even limited to artworks. The case is always the same whenever something shows itself more or less clearly, for instance as a book that lies on the table.

In this case one can certainly direct attention toward the book because the table surface lets it show itself. But one will hardly perceive and grasp the table, on its own, as the book's place. That would immediately change if, instead of the book, there were a vase on the table that is an artwork, for instance a hanaire in the Iga style, whose clay is covered in a free-form glaze of ash as a result of several days' firing in a wood oven. The vase as artwork does not show the table, but instead merely grants it as its place. For this reason, the table must be made in such a way as to tolerate this granting. For instance, it would have to be clear of any stuff, like a flowered wax tablecloth, that would impede or destroy its place-character. If the table's surface, by whatever means, were to assert itself too strongly, it could no longer be the phenomenally giving place for an artwork. An artwork is never phenomenally giving, although it can be a place. If one were to put a wild flower into the aforementioned Japanese vase, the vase would not stand behind the flower, but would show the flower from itself. By way of the vase, the flower would become a moment within a beautiful, that is, a decentered order.

The examples indicate an essential characteristic of places that we have not yet directly named but that is easily recognized as a result of Aristotle's determination of place. If places are only recognizable as such insofar as they are not congruent with that which is located at them, they must themselves have an *expanse*. The table surface on which the Japanese vase stands has this expanse, as does the river valley in which Fallingwater stands, as does the Ronchamp mountain and the south slope of Naoshima. Places are thus not spatial elements that, as Heidegger puts it, "allow" for spaces, but are themselves spaces.[24] Spaces do not first result from one place indicating others and, in a "mutual play," "gathering" these into a "locality" [*Ortschaft*]. If a space is "something granted, released,"[25] then the openness too, in which something can show itself and that lets this be itself, must be a space. In Heidegger's terms, a place is itself a "locality." If that is the case, then a place need not necessarily refer beyond itself.

It is certainly possible, as Heidegger's example of the bridge illustrates. Plurality belongs to the essence of place. Spatial determinations, as they are given in such expressions as "next to," "under," "above," "near," or "far," articulate things' relation to each other, things that are at difference places; thus they also articulate a "mutual play" of different places. Each of these can be related to others, and in this way a place reaches beyond itself. There are infinitely many places; they can be expansive or narrow. The table surface is one place, but so is its right or left side, or one of its corners. A place is anywhere that something is or could be. The more differentiated the relation to things in their places, the more complex the determination of place becomes, and thereby also the network of places.

But the web of places can also become indifferent. Anyone who observes an artwork like Fallingwater will hardly think about the fact that the house's place is connected by roads to other places, such that one can reach these more or less quickly. These connections exist; otherwise one would not have been able to reach Fallingwater's place. Yet when one sees the house in the river valley, these other places become a matter of indifference. They contribute nothing to the experience of the house's beauty; the latter does not refer to them. Just as one does not relate the house's place to other places, one does not segment the place into many places that make it up. One may certainly notice that there is an especially old tree "there" and a stone in the riverbed "there," but these are not understood as particular experiences of places. If one observes the house, one sees it in a place. This place includes everything that surrounds the house insofar as it lets the house show itself and is granted by the house as a place. Everything that belongs to the house's place forms a totality. In this, the house can show itself; it grants and releases it.

The totality—everything that surrounds the house—belongs to the expanse of its place. This expanse is contained in a peculiar way. Not that it is bounded in any obvious manner. One knows when observing the house, however, that one is in it and that one has left it as soon as the house is no longer in view. Then one knows that one was in a special place.

The result of these considerations deserves to reiterated and secured. Artworks like Fallingwater can only show themselves by being at a place that lets them show themselves. This place, in turn, is an expanse that is released and determined as such (i.e., granted) by the self-showing artwork. As such a granted expanse, the artwork's place is a space, namely the space of this space-granting artwork [*Raum einräumended Kunstwerks*]. Insofar as self-showing is essential to artworks, the place that lets them show themselves *must* be a clear expanse, an obviously experienceable space. Accordingly, an artwork cannot take this space up all for itself, or fill it up. It grants the expanse and only thus gleans the space of its self-showing, in which it can also be showing. Yet the artwork's space is strictly determined as such by self-showing. It is a *deictic* or *phenomenal space* that is always to be understood only by way of the artwork that it allows to show itself.

Heidegger does not take account of this peculiar significance of space for an artwork. According to Heidegger's premise that places are to be understood as things, the artwork becomes the embodiment of a thing and thus a tautology. But even if one corrects this aspect of Heidegger by grasping places differently—as Plato and Aristotle do—the determination remains problematic. Heidegger assigns artworks to the opening of space that occurs by way of places, and thus lets them serve as mere affirmations or confirmations of an openness independent of art. Heidegger explains that sculpture can be an "embodiment of places" by stating that the places "hold something free gathered around them, opening a region and keeping it safe." This "something free" is to be such that it "accords the respective things a tarrying, and grants humans a dwelling among things."[26] Here there is an echo of Heidegger's determination of art as he had formulated it in "The Origin of the Work of Art," but the aspiration of the earlier piece is distinctly retracted. The artwork, as Heidegger now sees it, no longer opens the world of a "historical people,"[27] but instead *embodies* being in the openness of the region, which, understood as "dwelling," "protects" this openness and allows it to exist as such.[28]

But an artwork like Fallingwater is more than the marking or emblem of a region to be settled in this way. Even if the house were still occupied, as an artwork it would not "embody" an openness that "grants" dwelling. Its art-character would still consist in a showing that shows itself, in the fact that, through the play of limitation and inclusion, it shows its spatially extended, decentered order and thereby reveals a special possibility of dwelling that includes aesthetic experience and is opened up by it. This is only possible in space, and thus at this artwork's place.

Even when artworks like Fallingwater are spatial in their self-showing showing, this would not need to be the case for all artworks. It may therefore seem doubtful whether all artworks are like Fallingwater. Sculptures like Chillida's *Wind Combs* certainly have a place that is spatial in the sense just elaborated. The iron formations that reach into the distance do not belong precisely to that location on the rock where they are affixed. That which allows them to show themselves is the expanse of the rocky shore, in which the sculptures allow the rocks—which would otherwise just be there in themselves—to be related to each other. The *Wind Combs* need the expanse of the sea and the sky; in showing, they release the gaze toward the sea and sky.

In a manner different from but comparable to buildings or sculptures, wall paintings like Giotto's frescoes in the Scrovegni or Arena chapel in Padua belong situationally together with their space. Here the mutual belonging is even more intimate, for the chapel space that allows the frescoes to show themselves is not only granted or released by these, but is constituted by them as an image-space. It is a space that owes its peculiar expanse solely to painting, in such a way that the painting opens the space with its star-strewn heavenly structure on the ceiling that repeats itself more or less clearly in the wall pictures. The experience of the chapel space, the gazing measurement of its expanse, is entirely determined by the sequence of frescoes. These lead one's gaze into the space's depths, toward the central depiction of the final judgment, and into its heights, from the grisaille depictions of the virtues and vices to the life of Jesus, the life of Mary, through the life of Mary's parents, all the way to the depiction of God in the lunette, sending his angels to earth. If, following this depiction, one traces the sequences of frescoes in the opposite direction, they present a visual history of the Incarnation that leads to the level of the observer. The space in which these images reside is an image-space, and the latter is a space of a history that is spread out and structured in it and in the space of that history's meaning. That which is shown here in its harmony only exists by virtue of space, which gives the images and, as the giving, stands in the images themselves.

The Rothko Room in the Phillips Collection in Washington, D.C., is not an image-space in the sense just described, but it is a space that was specifically conceived for images. The room, established in 1960 by the owner of the collection, Duncan Phillips, and renovated in 2006, allows four large-scale paintings to show themselves. In the center of the small room is a simple wooden bench from which, by changing the direction of one's gaze, one can observe the four paintings in their correspondence. The room does not only definitively set these four paintings into relation with each other, it also determines the distance in which the paintings offer themselves to the observer. The fact that one sits or stands quite close to the images makes these less easy to survey. One dives into their surfaces of color, as it were, in a way that their depth and luminosity have a particularly strong effect.

The room, which incidentally received the artist's praise,[29] predetermines a distance for the observer in which the images show themselves in an especially impressive manner. But unlike the frescoes in the Scrovegni chapel, the paintings were not painted expressly for this room. One could exhibit them elsewhere, and then it would be a matter of finding a room that is suited to them and arranging it adequately. Thus, in contrast to Giotto's frescoes in the Scrovegni chapel, the relation between image and space is reversed. One can imagine that Giotto proceeded in a manner similar to Ando as the latter looked for the best place for the museum on Naoshima. Giotto may have observed the chapel for a long time, and it may have become clear to him how he would paint the frescoes. With regard to a transportable flat image, however, the artist can seek out particular places. In this sense, Rothko wished for small rooms like chapels, spread across the United States, in which a traveler could meditate on a single image for an hour.[30] Yet taken for itself, the flat painting is apparently placeless. It does not seem to have a space unique to it.

But that is not the case. When images like Rothko's have their effect in certain rooms, while they are cramped or lost in others, these images have their spatiality, namely their deictic or phenomenal spatiality, in themselves. This spatiality is always present as a possibility. It belongs to the images, even when these are deposited out of sight in storage. The images' phenomenal spatiality is thus not affixed to particular, real rooms, but can instead be realized in various situations. This realization is the respective installation of the phenomenal space that belongs to the image.

Every image, every sculpture, and every building that is an artwork has a phenomenal spatiality that is unique to it. It is just that this spatiality does not come to bear as frequently if it coincides with artworks' factual spatiality. Unlike Fallingwater in the middle of the landscape, a Rothko painting, in the best scenario, merely grants the space that allows it to show itself for the sake of looking at the painting itself. Rothko's desire for rooms that exist only for one painting demands a realization of phenomenal space that is as unimpeded as possible, a space that dissolves in letting an artwork show itself.

The installation of such phenomenal spaces faces the difficulty that no factual space is an exclusively phenomenal space. Accordingly, the installation must take care to structure the space visibly granted by the artworks in such a way that it approximates the works' phenomenal space as much as possible. That is the challenge for any installation of a sculpture that is not created at a specific place (like Chillida's *Wind Combs*), and likewise for the hanging of any image. It is especially a challenge for museum architecture. If the installation of phenomenal space is successful, the artwork's own spatiality comes into effect; if it fails, this spatiality juts out by way of the room not redeeming it. Yet the redemption is not dependent on whether the installed room completely retreats for the sake of phenomenality. The realization of phenomenal spaces need not always occur according to the model of the Rothko Room, namely through hermetic exclusion. The visible inclusion of a landscape or a park—as in Renzo Piano's structure at the Fondation Beyeler in Riehen or in Richard Meier's Museum Frieder Burda in Baden-Baden—can definitely have the sense of a phenomenal space. Whether and how that is the case can only be revealed through the setting up or hanging of artworks. In this regard, Piano's structure is more successful. While Piano's is a room for images, Meier's structure does well without images.

The installation of phenomenal spaces does not only pertain to visual art and especially painting, but to music as well. Pieces of music carry phenomenal spaces in them, which can be measured, for example, by what instruments or arrangements the pieces are written. And, like museums, the performance spaces for music are not phenomenal as such. The curator's task of setting up an exhibit is repeated for the performer, and especially the conductor, with every performance. Each time, it is a matter of the space allowing the work to show itself. This occurs on the basis of the space's possibilities. The phenomenal space of music is, after all, not the visible chapel or the visible concert hall. It is the space insofar as it is audible, the acoustic space in which the sound unfolds itself in one way or another. Unlike visible space, acoustic space is hardly capable of being experienced as granted. The resounding music pervades it; it fills it, and for this reason the space is usually only identifiable through the type of sound: its dryness, its reverb, its brilliance, or its blurriness. Of course, that the expanse or narrowness of the acoustic space is granted by the piece of music need not remain concealed. It comes to bear the more evidently a piece of music audibly shows the spatiality. That is the case in Monteverdi's *Vespro della Beata Vergine*, when choirs and soloists do not stand facing the audience but are instead distributed throughout the space, approximating the instructions given by the composer for the performance in the San Marco in Venice. Luigi Nono's *Prometeo* is also like this; during the performance the music resounds from around the audience.

Even poetry needs phenomenal spaces. This is immediately evident in the case of drama; it needs a place of performance, which the word θέατρον designates. The theater is a deictic space par excellence. It allows the drama's play to show itself, which, by showing itself, at the same time grants the space of the theater as an audience-space. The entire granted space is thereby directed toward the play's occurrence; its only role is to let the play show itself. To this end, the space has to be delineated from the actual stage. Drama only occurs in clear separation from all other behavior and speech. The stage, as the delineated area in which the play occurs, is at the same time open to the audience-space. Stage and audience-space are two sides of the same space, which, as this space, is established through the delineation. The drama is only possible because it exists for the audience, just as the audience is made possible by the drama. Accordingly, the delineation can be regarded from two sides: as separation of the stage, the free space in which the play occurs, or as separation of the audience-space, the free space for observation. In the theater, the artwork's self-showing has an adequate place for each of its two moments. The *self*-showing of the work on the stage is evident as a self-*showing* for an audience. That which Gadamer sought to grasp as the "transformation into structure," namely art's openness for the observer,[31] proves to be the spatiality of art.

Just like the space of the image and the acoustic space of music, theater should not primarily be understood as a structural work. Architecture only creates the more or less constant conditions for the staging place that results from the interaction of play and audience. The staging place as such results from the diversity of actors and audience members, and from the spatial essence of these. For this reason, every observation—no matter how banal—forms an audience-space. Goethe, upon visiting the Roman amphitheater in Verona, described such an elemental audience-space in his *Italian Journey*: "Whenever anything worth watching occurs on flat ground, and everyone flocks toward it, the rearmost seek to elevate themselves by any means possible above those in front: one stands on benches, rolls barrels over, brings the wagon and lays boards across it, occupies the nearest hill, and very soon a crater is formed. If the performance occurs frequently in the same place, one builds light scaffolding for which people can pay, with the remaining masses doing whatever they wish." Insofar as the audience-space is formed by the audience, Goethe adds, an architect can certainly form "such a crater by way of art." But the aim here is for "its embellishment to be the people themselves." Accordingly, a theater-structure like the one in Verona should "not be seen empty, but instead full of people."[32]

The theater as it is described here is a *public space;* the audience is literally a *publicum* [*Publikum*]. Those who individually observe something "worth watching" do not form a theater. They do not need the more or less artistic installation of such a space. This installation only results from the public nature of observing that, like any public gathering, requires and receives its respective space because it itself is spatial.

Yet the theater is not only a staging place. It does not only allow something to be seen, but also heard, such that the theater-space is also an acoustic space. Besides, a drama is also a play of language, and should be understood as such. Thus, the theater is a *hermeneutic space,* or more precisely, a respective public concretion of hermeneutically determined space to which every understanding whatsoever belongs.[33] As a hermeneutic space, the theater is first and foremost a space of language, not in the sense that this space would only be found in language, but in the sense that language essentially determines it. The language that connects an audience and thus first makes it possible as an audience allows the work to show itself in its intelligibility. And the work, by showing itself, grants the public language-space in its own way.

It is not only publicly performable dramas that are spatial in this way, but poetic works in general. They belong to a respective special language-space that they are nevertheless not sealed into, as the possibility of translation shows. This language-space, too, requires a kind of installation. It does not exist without writing; the places at which works show themselves in it are handwritten or printed, especially books.

That books are places is made evident by the fact that when one indicates a passage in a literary work, one points to the book: "here it is." This is different from pointing to a spot on a canvas. The mountain's contour line, for instance, only exists in the Zurich version of the *Montagne Sainte-Victoire*. Whoever wishes to show the spot must seek out the painting in its place where it can show itself. If one were to point at a reproduction, that would merely be an indication [*Anzeige*]; one would state which spot of the painting one meant if one were to stand in front of it. Just like the actual painting, the indicated spot on the painting only exists in the original paint on this unique canvas. Conversely, the book one holds in one's hands, this individual exemplar of a special edition of a literary work, is not the work itself. It is a place and thus just one of many possible places. Pointing to the opening sentence in an edition of Goethe's *Elective Affinities*—"Eduard—so we shall call a wealthy nobleman in the prime of life"[34]—one means the work, but can only point to one of its possible places. Which of the possible places it is might not be significant in relation to the work. The personal copy that has been filled over the years with markings and marginal notes could also be replaced with another given copy. It is different with the edition that one refers to. One decides upon it and its way of organizing the work because it allows the work to show itself in a certain way. For this reason it is also important that, referring to the work, one cites it.

The phenomenal spaces that artworks allow to show themselves are generally determined in multiple ways: as optical, acoustic, or hermeneutic spaces that are also usually public. Their respective consistency could be described in more detail with respect to various art genres. Even that, however, would remain at the level of typology. Ultimately, every artwork has its own space, not necessarily the way a building or a painting has its place, but in any case the phenomenal space of its self-showing, which it alone grants. That this space belongs to the artwork itself leads one to surmise that an artwork not only grants a space, but is itself spatial. By clarifying this spatiality that belongs to the artwork itself, the deictic character of space will become all the more evident.

Emptiness

Artworks require distance, and it must be the distance appropriate to them. An image only shows itself in a distance that, while determinate, is not measurable, for it is never precisely determined. If, for example, one steps too close to an image like Monet's *La Cathédrale de Rouen, Le Portail au Soleil*,[35] one only sees a chaotic mixture of oils; one only sees texture. One would have a similar experience if one were to hear Mahler's Sixth Symphony while sitting in the orchestra; the complex, layered themes of the first movement would become a confused din. Similarly, a reading of poetry that attaches itself to the word and ruminates on the meaning of a single sentence without letting the work unfold as a whole will remain without comprehension. One cannot get too close to the works, for one literally cannot do anything with them; one can and should simply observe them, and observation requires distance. The boundary that the possible work represented for the artist and that assured the artist the manner of perception belonging to art—as for instance Cézanne's easel with its canvas in front of the mountain-subject of the Sainte-Victoire—is drawn for the viewer by the completed work. Of course, here there is no longer anything that would be observable beyond the boundary, on the other side of the canvas. There is no more subject; there is nothing but the work. Yet if the work is still a boundary, it must simultaneously be that which is observable beyond the boundary. In that case, it seeks distance in the phenomenal space that it grants and thereby shows itself as the work that it is.

The fact that the boundary belongs to the essence of artworks is confirmed when the distance to a work becomes too great. For in that instance, the work no longer serves as a boundary. It loses its phenomenal space and is merely an object in space. Thus, a large-format painting like Barnett Newman's *Cathedra*[36] would become a mere blue surface that is divided by a wide, white line to the left of center and a thin, barely visible light blue line toward the right side. What would be lost is the image's expanse, its spreading, barely nuanced cobalt blue that at once draws one in and makes one recede. The boundary that the image is only has an effect when there is at least the possibility of disregarding it and getting too close. Like Rothko, Newman did not wish to have his large-format works viewed from too great a distance.[37] If one stands close enough to a painting such as *Cathedra*, it can no longer be grasped in a single gaze without losing its boundedness. At this proximity, the image is no longer a flat object in space, as it might appear at a greater distance. Rather, it itself proves to be spatial. Its image-character itself, its totality that lets everything belonging to it be there together, has a spatial essence. An image's simultaneity is an especially obvious form of the simultaneity belonging to the essence of space as such.[38]

If the image in its image-character is spatial, one can assume that the same holds for any formation of the imagistic as an essential determination of art. In that case, every artwork that takes part in the imagistic would itself be spatial, even if it did not evoke spatial notions.[39] If spatiality belongs to the essence of artworks, then artworks must be spatial in themselves even without this qualification, namely insofar as they are determined by the art forms of the musical and the poetic.

Yet one can grasp the inner spatiality of other artworks better if one has first completely determined that of images. The latter, after all, do not merely consist in the described expanse that is obvious in large-format works like *Cathedra* that have to be viewed from the right distance. If one stands in front of this image, the color does not just expand in such a way that the vertical lines prevent one from losing oneself in it. At the same time, one's gaze goes into the color and one experiences the painting's depth.

This depth is something other than a spatial sense evoked through an image. The latter is an imagistically achieved schema, whereas the depth at issue here is a determination of the image itself. Accordingly, the image-depth would have to come to bear all the more strongly—as in Newman's painting—the less it is covered over by the schematically identifiable presentation of a space. It is questionable whether image-depth really is, as Merleau-Ponty claims, a privilege of modern painting and a result of its effort to free itself from "illusionism."⁴⁰ If image-depth belongs to the art-character of painting, it will always be present in one way or another. Contrary to Merleau-Ponty's thinking, it can then no longer serve as an alternative to a definite understanding of space, as for example that understanding represented in Renaissance painting. It thus cannot be an alternative to Cartesian space, determined strictly by extension and "without refuge."⁴¹

However, Merleau-Ponty's considerations are not merely problematic due to the epochal schema that undergirds them. His conception of image-depth itself is difficult to follow. Unlike Heidegger, Merleau-Ponty identifies the spatial depth of images with their thingness; for him, that is their spatial depth. He thinks that a "global locality" has taken the place, in modern painting, of perspectival constructions, a locality in which "everything exists at once, and height, width, and distance are abstractions from a voluminosity that one expresses with one word when one states that there is a thing there."⁴² It is not entirely clear if this means the thingness of the image itself or the things represented in it. The reference to Cézanne—who, Merleau-Ponty claims in quoting Giacometti, sought depth for his entire life⁴³—seems to indicate the latter. Cézanne, it is said, goes directly toward that which is solid, toward space, and he has noted that things in this space move color against color and adapt to each other in their instability. Since that is the case, one has to look for space and its contents together.⁴⁴ The latter point is indisputable—how should space ever be experienceable without that which is contained in it? But it does not follow from this that space as such consists in things' textural coloration. By describing this as a texture, one has not yet grasped its spatiality.

As concerns this spatiality, Rothko has made more progress in his considerations on the inner spatiality of images. Like Merleau-Ponty, Rothko begins by inquiring into the "plasticity" of images. Even his mode of questioning is similar. In the debate between Bernhard Berenson and Edwin Blashfield concerning the spatiality of Giotto's painting, Rothko takes the side of Berenson, who took this spatiality to lie not in the production of a spatial illusion but in the tangibility of figures in Giotto's images. For Rothko, that these figures, in Berenson's terms that Rothko cites, "awaken the tactile sense,"⁴⁵ stems from the fact that they appear to step forth and recede in space. Plasticity is to be defined as "the sensation of reality imparted to us by means of the sensation of things moving back and forth in space" (47). This could still be grasped as the generation of an illusion and thus in analogy to a perspectivally constructed sense of space. Yet Rothko immediately makes it clear that he does not mean this, but instead the play of image-elements, especially that of color values: "Color advances and recedes" (48). Color itself generates the feeling of movement into the image and toward the image from the outside.⁴⁶ The colors open themselves up in various degrees. They can be more transparent or more dense, closer to the front or further back.

Rothko's paintings do the best job of showing what this means. In an image like *Orange and Red on Red*, for instance, which is in the Rothko Room of the Phillips Collection, the horizontal orange rectangle in the top half of the image takes a distinct frontal position.⁴⁷ It covers over a red strip at the top margin, which for its part stands out from the darker red of the background. But these designations are not unambiguous. The red surface beneath the orange rectangle is brightened to an extent that it enters into correspondence with the orange. It is as if both together form a color chord in which the orange evinces its brighter luminosity in a floating interplay with the red.

Qualifying his earlier considerations, Rothko later found the term *breathingness* to describe such subtle differences in depth. He apparently took the term to be better than any talk of space in the image, perhaps because this still reminded him too much of the imagistically achieved illusion of space.⁴⁸ Nevertheless, the talk of a space in the image is appropriate. The density and transparency of the color is not a "story," but rather constitutes the self-showing image. Distinct moments, surfaces of color arise out of the dense texture of color. The difference of text and texture is played out in the density and transparency of color.

This certainly has to do essentially with the colors' brightness. It is the more or less strong "inner light" of color that allows it to come forward luminously or recede dully.⁴⁹ But this approaching and receding, a color's more or less determined "front" or "back," can be explained neither through the color itself nor through the light at play in it. It must reside in an openness that allows the color and light values their interplay by first giving them the self-showing of color and the showing in the play of their values; it must lie in space, more precisely in the inner space of the image. The play of color and light values is thus itself spatial, determined in each of its moments by the space in which it resides. It first becomes evident in the *distance* between the color and light values, by virtue of one color's luminosity distancing it from a darker color. That which thus exists in the distance between colors is not itself a color; it is also not light, if the image's light is in the colors. It is not anything special or particularly determinable, but just *emptiness*.

Rothko's description of experience in the inner space of images confirms this fact that there must be emptiness in the image. "The artist invites the spectator to take a journey within the realm of the canvas. The spectator must move with the artist's shapes in and out, under and above, diagonally and horizontally; he must curve around spheres, pass through tunnels, glide down inclines, at times perform an aerial feat of flying from point to point, attracted by some irresistible magnet across space, entering into mysterious recesses—and, if the painting is felicitous, do so at varying and related intervals. [. . .] Without taking the journey, the spectator has really missed the essential experience of the picture."⁵⁰

One could take this attempt at describing the experience of the image in its spatiality as a series of metaphors. In this case, it would not be the image that is spatial, but the attempt, oriented by obvious as well as chaotic notions of space, to grasp the experience of it. Nevertheless, it is difficult to deny that one often executes an acrobatic feat of flying from one point to another when observing an image. One part of an image does not always lead to another, such that the shift of one's gaze would be inevitable. Rather, despite all rhythmic predeterminations, one is always free within the image's space and must be free in order to relate all of the various moments of the image to each other in their simultaneity, and thereby to explore the image's decentered order. This, in turn, is only possible if the realm of the image is open like a space in which one can move from one place to another; that means that it must be empty.

Rothko's considerations are not limited to images. In his view, pieces of music are explored in ways similar to images. "An auditor can lie back in his chair and be overcome by the sensuous waves of tone which are aphrodisiac or narcotic. He may even find the pleasure of beating with his foot, enjoying each momentary change of interval. Yet if this is the sum total of his reaction, then he has not experienced the piece of music. Unless he has traveled with the composer up and down the scales and through the corridors of polyphony, and has sensibly observed the relationship of the elements in this journey to one another, he has simply experienced a sensual pleasantness not far removed from the kind induced by the spilling of a bottle of perfume" (48).

What is described here is the λόγος of music, its text, that which is poetic in it. Rather than simply being subjected to a mass of noise, one hears music when one follows this text. Yet its moments must be recognizable as such, and that is only possible if there is no transition between them. It is only when they are separated from each other and distinct from one another that they can correspond. Thus, the text of music and, presumably, the text of poetry cannot exist without the respective work's inner space. This space, in turn, does not exist without emptiness.

It is due to emptiness that space is so difficult to grasp. Emptiness is present somehow, but apparently neither visible nor audible. Perhaps that is the reason for the tendency to take the conception of emptiness-based space as an abstraction, as the construction of a pure extension that can take up anything determinate but is itself nothing. To be sure, no space is experienced as pure extension. The emptiness is not there by itself; it always comes to bear along with things. But that does not mean that it can be understood by way of things. The essence of emptiness would only be met indirectly through such an approach; one would not miss it, but one would not hit upon it either.

A good example of this is Heidegger's consideration of emptiness. While the concept did not yet factor into his conception of space in *Being and Time*, in "Art and Space" emptiness is considered to be "related to the peculiarity of the place." It is not taken to be a "lack" or "privation," but instead a "bringing-forth." In its relatedness to places, emptiness must have the character of being opening and gathering. Heidegger elaborates this notion by elucidating emptiness [*Leere*] by way of the verb "emptying" [*leeren*], and this in turn by its proximity to "gathering." Emptying, according to Heidegger's audacious assurance that is in no way covered in everyday usage, is a gathering. Even the cited examples are unconvincing. To empty a glass means "to gather it into its being-emptied as that which grasps"; to "empty the gleaned fruit into a basket" means "to prepare this place for it."[51] While the latter example turns the emptying—presumably of the container with which one has gathered the fruit—into a filling, the former example presents a case of emptying, but not of gathering. In Heidegger's sense, "gathering" always applies to a manifold or plurality, such that a glass cannot even be "gathered."

Yet these examples are revealing precisely because one cannot immediately follow them. By grasping emptiness via gathering places, Heidegger misses the fact that the gathering that belongs to the essence of places is impossible without emptiness. Emptying is not gathering; instead, gathering presupposes emptiness. Thus, one can only "prepare a place" for the gathered fruit that Heidegger mentions if the basket is empty. In emptying a glass, it proves to be a possible place to once again take in wine.

Heidegger elaborated emptiness in this way in his lecture "The Thing," using the example of a jug. Here, Heidegger's thoughts are less self-conscious, presumably because his considerations of the jug are not made in the context of spatial questions and thus do not confront him with the problematic conclusion of conceiving space by way of emptiness. In "The Thing," emptiness is even determined to be the essence of the jug: "Emptiness, this nothingness as part of the jug, is that which the jug is as a holding container."[52] The emptiness itself is that which holds. In a quiet allusion to the Platonic definition of the χώρα, it is "receptive and retentive." But the holding, we learn in a surprising phrase, consists "in pouring out." "Holding is what it is" in pouring out. This is partly because the essence of jug, according to Heidegger, lies in "serving" (173). Yet the emptiness can only prove to be what it is by not retaining indefinitely what it holds, but in taking it up only to pour it out again. If what was taken up stayed in the jug, such that it were filled with resin rather than wine, then its emptiness and its essence would disappear.

Heidegger comes quite close to the essence of emptiness. It is determined as that which first allows places to become what they are: as the possibility of taking something up and releasing it again. Yet it still remains ungrasped what emptiness is in itself. It only enters the frame as a temporary state: as the no-longer or not-yet filled. The jug as Heidegger describes it is empty because it has not yet been filled, or is no longer so. Heidegger does not inquire into that which is itself present in this in-between state—presumably because he does not wish to determine the essence of the jug as emptiness, but as the "donation of the pour" (174) in which emptiness certainly plays a role, but not an enveloping one. The unmentioned but highly likely source of Heidegger's considerations concerning the jug, however, determines emptiness as that which first gives the jug its utility in pouring: "Clay is fashioned into vessels, but it is on their empty hollowness that their use depends"—so Lao Tzu states in the eleventh section of the *Tao Te Ching*.[53] If the vessel is comprehended by way of its utility, the giving aspect recedes. Then it is radically inconspicuous.

Yet this inconspicuousness does not lie in the essence of emptiness. The latter comes to bear even more evidently than in Heidegger's and Lao Tzu's example of the jug when it is not an in-between state, but instead remains in effect. That is the case in an *interstitial space*. The essence of space is especially evident in interstices. It is no coincidence that in many languages, the word for space goes back to the Latin *spatium*, interstice. "Space," "*espace*," "*spatio*" are examples of this.

Husserl tries to describe the essence of emptiness by way of the interstice. The example he uses is that of "two spheres that are raised off from an empty background, the sky." There is "empty space" between these.[54] As Husserl explains, this space is experienced as such because each of the two spheres is continually given in a different way. Thus, for instance, one of them can be blocked by the other and, if one changes one's point of view, be seen as a whole; whereas the appearance of the blocking sphere is continually "extending," meaning that it fills the time in which it is given and seen.[55] There is always "empty space" between two "distant" things, that is, those "constituting themselves in discrete extensions."[56]

That is an accurate but still indirect description of emptiness, as if the latter had to be derived from the separation of two things existing independently of each other. In order to make emptiness as such comprehensible, Husserl indicates the possibility of filling out the interstice, and in this regard his considerations are similar to Heidegger's. One sees a "corporeality"—a sphere here and a sphere there—but it leaves open "infinitely many possibilities for further corporealities," namely "in the 'in-between.'" Where there is nothing, something could be. It becomes understandable that nothing is there when one imagines that something could be there. Yet Husserl is not satisfied with this response. He knows that the interstice need not—indeed cannot—be made comprehensible by way of the possibility of its being filled. Husserl summarizes his thoughts by noting that "we would already have here the in-between as an empty but continually fillable space, as the possibility of real investigations that are lawfully determined, even if we cannot say that the empty space is seen" (261).

Nevertheless, in Husserl's description the interstice is *seen* as an empty space. One need not put one's hand between two things in order to convince oneself that there is space between them. Also, the experience of space does not require one to first investigate the things' various "extensional discretions." Somehow, prior to any descriptive or elaborative attempts, space is mysteriously just there. In order to grasp its essence, one has to let it be there. The attempt at making it comprehensible has to begin with its simple existence, even if it is initially unclear what "existence" means in this case. After all, it cannot be the existence of a thing. Emptiness is, to repeat Lao Tzu's notion, that which makes something useable. More generally, this means that emptiness is that through which something can be what it is. That which exists must thus be thought on the basis of emptiness. Art shows how this is possible.

Emptiness' capacity to make possible is especially evident in images, whose moments are clearly separated from each other. The later Matisse created images like this in his scissor collages,[57] as did the later Kandinsky, for example in *Bleu de ciel* from 1940,[58] which depicts bird-like figures together with others that consist only of colorful tubes, dots, and slightly bent forms, all in front of a fluffy sky-blue background. The figures are floating. They seem to tumble and turn. Their relation to one another is not capable of being constructed; it is open. Thus, the relation can only consist in the airy interstices that bring the figures close to one another and keep them apart. In observing the painting, one does not try to fill in the interstices in order to make them comprehensible as in-between spaces. One understands them immediately, in the first glance, by noticing the lightness and liveliness of the image. The interstices lend the figures their floating character. One only sees this floating because it exists by virtue of the interstices.

There are interstices in acoustic space as well. No music can resound without rests. Yet a rest is no mere interruption. It also not a gap in which something is missing, as if the quarter rest in the sheet music indicated a possible but not factually written quarter note. The rest is *not a sound*, not even a possible sound. From the perspective of musical play, it is a pause that is not a mere stop. Yet it is also not a quiet transition from the last sounded note to the next one, as if the last note resounded and announced the one that is coming. Rather, what comes to bear in the rest is the stillness that makes sound possible. Rests allow the notes, phrases, and movements to be recognizable as such. Rest contains the stillness of the space that lets sound be structured and thus first makes music possible in distinction from ongoing noise.

Even language has rest indicators: the period, which in English is labeled with the nicely emphatic *full stop*, the semicolon, the comma, the dash, and the paragraph for larger breaks. All of these rests are visible as interstices in writing. Period, semicolon, and comma mark a boundary and note the distance to the next word or sentence. Poems contain even more interstitial space: the limits of verses often set rests in the middle of sentences, by which they are no longer normal sentences but are instead transposed into the flotation of their moments. By virtue of the verse boundary, a word that in everyday speech or in prose is nothing more than a meaningful moment that joins into the whole now stands forth. Its relation to other things remains open; it moves into emptiness, and in this emptiness can be all the more relational. Let us attend to this poem's interstices of rests and verse limits:

> Rowing, Conversation
>
> It is evening. Two inflatable
> Boats glide by, in them
> Two naked young men. Rowing side by side
> They talk. Talking
> They row side by side.

If one were to write the four sentences of Brecht's poem[59] without verse boundaries, or if one were to speak them without attending to the verse boundaries, the sentences would still be recognizable as poetic. The play of twos—"two inflatable boats," "two naked young men"—would be just as recognizable as the chiasmus of their speaking and acting: "rowing [. . .] they talk. Talking they row." In reading or hearing the sentences in prose form, one would also arrive at the notion that the "side by side" of the young men, their unselfconsciously natural nakedness connected with the ingenious device of the inflatable boat, is an implicit togetherness that lies in the speaking itself: "Rowing side by side they talk. Talking they row side by side." But in this way, one would have to lift out of the heard or written form that which is readily apparent in the poetic form. In the latter, one recognizes what belongs to the poem as such: how a floating interstice results from the separation of what is said. The initially reference-less number two—"two inflatable boats," "two naked young men"—becomes comprehensible, through the act of rowing, as a side-by-side proximity. This proximity determines the talking and is in turn determined by it.

Talking is the center of the poem. In it, the side-by-side elements are joined together and yet remain next to each other. It must remain a side-by-side proximity in order for one young man's talking to reach the other. One sees the proximity in the proximity of talking: "They talk. Talking." The repetition of the word "talking" is no mere doubling. The period in the middle of the verse, which as such is no sentence, orders the talking into a symmetry that is hardly disturbed by its grammatical deviance. The interstice indicated by the period is both a conclusion and a new beginning. Like a mirror, it allocates the "Rowing side by side" to the "They row side by side" and thus makes clear that the poem structured by this interstice is itself a speaking on the part of the interstice. The poem brings into a linguistic picture the openness of talking in a side-by-side proximity. It holds onto a fleeting scene—"Two inflatable boats glide by"—without turning this into an imagistic presentation. At its outset, the poem announces that there is barely any possibility of such an imagistic presentation, perhaps even none at all. There is no bright image in "It is evening." The gliding-by of the boats on the unnamed water is perhaps more of a sound, just as the splashing of the oars, and certainly the talking. The imagistic aspect of the poem is only present in language, just as the rhythm of this language does not arise from its being like music, but from its belonging entirely to language.

The interstices of the poem lend it its poetic order. This order—the playful structure of correspondences from which the poem's text arises—would become even more clear if the poem stood on a page for itself. Then the process of reading it would not be disturbed by the other poems (which certainly belong together with it in the *Buckow Elegies*, but are nevertheless independent poems). Its form—the symmetry of its five verses, the middle of which, as a symmetrical axis, is twice as long as the others—would also stand forth more clearly. One would especially recognize more clearly the significance of interstices and rests: the sparing use of words, the verse boundaries unbound to any syntax. It would become obvious how the poem as such stands in its openness, which arises in peculiar ways through the poem's interstices. On the page dedicated to the poem, one would see that the interstices, the rests or empty spaces between textual moments, belong to a space that is determined by emptiness.

As long as one is dealing with the poem as a linguistic work and thus with its intelligibility, one cannot see this space. One experiences it in the limitation of what is poetically written, in the fact that the poem, as what is said, stands within the *unsaid;* the latter, which includes the pause in talking, is the emptiness in the poem. The poem stands within this unsaid in a different way than an everyday sentence, which can also only be spoken as this determinate sentence. But the everyday sentence is capable of being supplemented by other sentences; one can distinguish each other sentence's further determination. This possibility of extension does not exist with respect to the poem. The poem requires its emptiness, its pauses, in order to unfold in the rhythmic sequence of its moments. In this sense, Hölderlin spoke of a "counter-rhythmic disruption," which, as the "pure word," interrupts the "transport" of poetic presentations such that "the presentation itself," the unified composed poem, can appear apart from the transport.[60]

The poem's empty spaces are recognizable as such, not because they can be filled in one way or another, but because they are final. In this way, they reveal the unsaid as that emptiness in which the poem's saying stands. The emptiness is what becomes evident if one prints or writes the poem on its own page. Then one sees the poem's proximity to a haiku which, written in ink, lies in the delicate order of its symbols on paper. And one also sees the rests that speaking must adhere to if the poem is to come to bear as the poetic order that it is. The emptiness of the unsaid, the emptiness that lies between the visible elements and symbols, and the emptiness in what is heard; these are one and the same. The intelligible, the visible, and the audible belong to the same space that is merely experienced in different ways.

Of course, the empty page on which the written signs stand presents this space in an especially evident manner. The empty paper gives the symbols space into which they can step forth, and thus it gives the symbols that raise themselves off against the paper in black on white. The paper seems to be nothing but a giving. There is virtually nothing to it.

Yet this nothingness is not a condition for something to be giving, and thus it is not a condition for emptiness. The sky blue in Kandinsky's painting is not by any means void. One sees it in the first glance at the painting, whereas one can easily overlook the whiteness of paper on which symbols are written or lines are drawn. The painting's sky blue is not even monochromatic, but slightly cloudy, covered in the margins by a slight white veil. The image's sky blue is not a void, but is rather emphatically textural. Nevertheless, it is giving; the colorful floating and tumbling beings in the image are clearly lifted off from the blue. An image's giving element can be even more obvious than the sky blue in Kandinsky's painting, as in Matisse's *The Red Studio*.[61] What is giving in this large-format painting is the brown-red, almost monochrome surface from which the paintings and sculptures in the depicted studio lift off. The furniture, conversely, is only outlined with bright lines on the red surface. The furniture at once steps forth from the surface and disappears back into it. The furniture thus belongs more to the giving than to what is given. What is given in the image are especially the paintings.

In *The Red Studio*, the giving emptiness is easily recognizable despite its colorful dominance. The monochromatic red is empty to the extent that it is barely formed. It is undifferentiated and uniform and thus makes up what one might call the textural *ground* of the image. It is from this ground that the furniture-outlines step forth, and it is from it that the depicted paintings and sculptures, such as a painted plate and a vase with a creeping vine, also step forth. The image makes its textural ground visible as such. It is with this ground that the emptiness in which something can be given comes into effect. What is depicted in the image stands in front of emptiness. That which one calls the image-ground is at once both texture and emptiness—texture in its perceivable density and emptiness inasmuch as something can lift itself off from it.

This lifting-off can be more or less pronounced, a coming-forth from the texture, as with the studio's furniture, or a clear standing-forth, as with the artworks depicted. The image's most bare possibility consists in the giving and the given to be factually the same. One of Gerhard Richter's *Grey Paintings*, for instance, or a *White Painting* by Robert Rauschenberg is the texture as which it shows itself and the emptiness from which its texture can show itself.[62] As an image, it is a play within the same, simultaneously giving and given. It is only in this play that it is an image, just as John Cage's *4'33"* is only music in this play.

These works just mentioned are attempts on the part of art to reach its own depths. Their appearance tries to get at the possibility of appearance. They make it clear that this possibility is emptiness, and they can only do this by giving shape to emptiness. They draw back the given as far as possible in order to get at the giving. This reduction, of course, can only succeed if the image or the piece of music has a minimal amount of depth. By showing itself, an artwork must show *something*, be it the textural surface of brushstrokes, the length of performance and thus the determination of how long the silence should last. The risks entailed in such works is clear: the attempt to assure oneself of emptiness as one's ground only ends up making this emptiness into an integral moment of the work. The distinction between giving and given can thereby become so slight that it risks being leveled. If this disappears, one loses the essence of artworks: appearance.

This consequence is instructive. It makes clear *ex negativo* what was present in the considerations of the artwork's emptiness, but which deserves to be grasped explicitly: the artwork's appearance is not just a play of self-showing and showing, and thus of texture and text, but is instead *a play of self-showing, showing, and emptiness*. The emptiness is at play between texture and text. It lets the textual elements stand in front of the density of the textural.

This does not mean that the text raises itself off from the texture as if from a background. Emptiness need not be an extended uniformity, and thus the paintings by Kandinsky and Matisse are especially clear but by no means representative examples of emptiness in an artwork. Emptiness can play with texture in any moment. It is that which pauses and recedes, which dominates in the monochrome surface and in silence, but can also be the barely noticeable pausing and receding in the language of a poem—almost inaudible and invisible. Yet emptiness need not even be a rest or an interstice. It can also consist in the *neutrality* of color, of sound, or of speech, or as an appearing empty space in the middle of color, sound, or speech. An empty space is something insofar as it is *not shown*. It can be seen and heard and is present as a word in the poem, but in such a manner that it leaves the way open for other elements to show themselves and be shown. Empty space of this sort can, upon second glance or listen or reading, be something shown or self-showing. Thus, the matte red at the margins of Rothko's *Orange and Red on Red* is an empty space insofar as it is giving for the orange and the brighter red. If one looks in a different way, it can step forth as the boundary of the more glowing colors and be viewed as textural and as a moment of the shown image-order. The latter, in turn, can only be seen if one is directed toward the self-showing texture of the image.

Nothing is empty in itself. There are no fixed moments that, belonging to an order or being perceptually relevant to an order, exist in a diffuse and intangible emptiness.[63] Emptiness pervades everything in a more or less evident way. It can therefore be everywhere. Wherever there is something given, emptiness appears more obviously the more the given appears. There is only appearance because emptiness grants it. Since emptiness is at play in appearance, the latter also includes depth.

The depth of appearance, and with it the appearance itself, is unfathomable. There is no ground to which it can be traced. What appears as ground in the image is the texture, which, belonging to the artwork as appearance, is itself given. As soon as something steps out of the texture or lifts itself off from it, emptiness proves to be antecedent. In Schelling's terms, one might call it "immemorial."[64] But emptiness is not a dark or abyssal ground. It is the absolutely groundless, ungrounded, neither grounding nor groundable. It allows for appearance, and that is all it does. Where emptiness can play in an undistorted manner, appearance is entirely itself. Free appearance, that is, beauty, thus stems from emptiness. It is also for this reason that emptiness can be called "the beginning of the terrible."[65] It is close to the abyss that could mean downfall, whereas beauty is often—barely—a floating. In beauty, as groundless and purposeless as it is, one comes as close as possible to emptiness. That is because the experience of the beautiful is an experience of the distant.

Here

The space of an artwork is distant; it is not capable of being trespassed. The space in which one experiences it, the space that grants the artwork, always only permits one to look into the work's depth, to listen into it, or to experience it in the play of what is said and unsaid. Even buildings that are artworks possess this inability to be trespassed. They are beautiful in that they open themselves up and are opening. As soon as one enters a room, one's gaze is led into the depth of the play of appearance, which disappears immediately if one tries to pursue it. Perhaps a new depth would open up in that case, but the result would be the same. That is why the sequence of rooms in a building that is an artwork cannot be grasped in a complete image. To be sure, one can find one's way in it. To use Husserl's terms, one can comprehend the building as a unity that stands in a "continuous unified context of appearance,"[66] such that the unity unfolds within this continuity of appearance. As Husserl elaborates, it belongs "to the sense of this unity that we call a thing to be a unity in a manifold of appearance," and to appear as a unity in this manifold, in infinitely many possibilities of givenness. (cf. 189) But an artwork is no simple thing; it is an appearing thing. It *is* the play of its appearance that, in a building that is an artwork, is experienced in the ever novel showing and self-showing of every room of the building. In its decentered order, the appearing thing has no unity. Its depth is confirmed with every new experience.

The untreadable and immeasurable depth of an artwork makes it distant. It is not closed off, but literally inaccessible, never where one is oneself. But this distance does not have the character of an indifferent externality that does not concern one. One is peculiarly affected by artworks in their distance. It is only for this reason that one observes them, listens or reads in that unintentional way that already proved to be essential for the artist's experience and that is now made possible by the works themselves by virtue of their distance erasing any intention. Due to this effect, Walter Benjamin spoke of the distance of artworks as an *aura*. The latter, according to Benjamin, is the "unique appearance of a distance, as close as it may be."[67] It is an appearance that has an effect precisely in its unavailability. Benjamin elaborated on the notion of aura thus: "Resting on a summer day and following a mountain range on the horizon, or a twig that casts its shadow on the viewer, until the moment of hour takes part in the appearance—that is what it means to breathe the aura of these mountains, of this twig."[68] What Benjamin grasps here in the image of the shadow is addressed another way in the Greek word αὔρα. The latter is the breath of wind, the fresh breeze that blows over one. That is the effect of distance; what is distant does not touch one, but instead wafts over.

Benjamin also described the aura in another manner. While considering photography in his study "On Several Themes in Baudelaire," he returns to the topic of the aura as, in his work on the history of photography, he had accorded it a central significance in the disappearance of the aura in modernity. The description is revealing, as it clarifies the aura's essence. Someone or something's aura rests upon the fact that the gaze that falls upon someone or something is returned. Where this occurs—no matter whether it is an "intentional gaze of attention" or a "glance in the simple sense"—"there occurs the experience of the aura in its fullness."⁶⁹ Accordingly, the aura has the sense of something looked at, insofar as it returns the gaze that falls upon it. The aura of things that can neither look back "intentionally" nor "in the simple sense" thus, according to Benjamin, merely consists in transferring "the form of reaction common in human society" to "the relation between humans and the inanimate or nature": "To experience an appearance's aura means according it the ability to break open the gaze." This investment, as Benjamin adds in a footnote, is "a source of poetry": "Wherever a poet invests a human, animal, or inanimate thing in this manner, and it breaks open his gaze, it also draws him into the distance" (646–647).

One may doubt whether the aura can really arise from a transference or investment. After all, the experience of the aura as Benjamin describes it is something that befalls one and can therefore not rest upon one's own doing. The experience of standing in someone or something's gaze is, in fact, quite a self-evident experience. One cannot avoid the other's gaze by moving aside, and in this way the experience of being looked at cannot rest upon one's own gaze. It may reveal itself in one's own looking; one looks at someone and sees them look back, such that one experiences oneself as standing in the gaze. But there is an experience of being looked at even without one's own gaze. One need not see the other or the other thing that one knows is looking at one. The gaze that one feels looking can come from out of the dark or, as Sartre describes it in his phenomenology of the gaze, from a house up there on the hill that conceals the one that I know is looking at me.⁷⁰ The feeling of being looked at in this way could certainly rest on pure fantasy. Perhaps there is no one in the dark that sees me; perhaps the house up on the hill, from which I feel looked at, is empty. Yet that would not change anything concerning the priority of the other's gaze over mine, but merely confirm it. In order to feel looked at, one need not look at anyone. Even the notion of another's look can put one in the peculiar mood that is related to the factual situation of being looked at. As soon as one has this feeling, one is no longer "master of the situation," as Sartre puts it.⁷¹

Of course, Sartre's phenomenology of the gaze is meant to be a description of the human. It is to make clear how another person is immediately experienced as such and is not something in the world that one must first discover to be human. Yet the description of the gaze's effect also counts for anything that is auratic in its appearance, in Benjamin's sense. Thus anything would be auratic that affects one from a distance and in that distance, such that one is no longer master of the situation—being able to determine what one encounters by way of one's own intentions and interests. This accords well with what Benjamin says about the aura's decay. When this decay coincides with the tendency "to bring things 'closer' to oneself in a spatial or human way"⁷² by passing over their uniqueness and making them available in the most effective manner, the aura decays or disappears in the attempt to once again become master of the situation. One no longer lets oneself be drawn into the distance, but instead insists upon things' proximity to oneself. And when Benjamin traces the aura back to a transference or investment, he insinuates that one actually is master of the situation and can suspend this in poetic distances of every sort.

Yet the primacy of this appropriative position in Benjamin is easily refuted. The drawing-closer is not possible without distance; the independence of things precedes their appropriation. This is confirmed by an analysis of primordial experience. The "source of poetry" that Benjamin mentions can only be identical with the experience of nature as Cézanne described it for his painting. Insofar as something has an aura, the distance that is essential to the natural comes to appearance. This can be repeated "parallel to nature" in the artwork, in the appearing thing.

Sartre's formulation that one is no longer "master of the situation" captures well the experience of artworks. The latter cannot be dominated or appropriated as such; their effect is uncontrollable. They are thus auratic, essentially distant and thus unapproachable, if, as Benjamin puts it, "the *essentially* distant [is] the unapproachable."[73] What is more, the "mechanical reproduction" that Benjamin discusses in his essay changes nothing about this state of affairs. A sculpture may exist in several castings, an etching can be printed in large numbers. If the sculpture and the etching are artworks, however, one is not dealing with multiple instantiations of a type; rather, every casting or print is an artwork in itself, unapproachable and auratic.

Yet even if artworks affect one like the gaze of another, their effect need not be one of a gaze. One cannot glean the gaze character of artworks from Sartre's thoughts on the gaze of the other. Even if the experience of being looked at by another need not be limited to the perception of this gaze, the experience remains dependent on the fact that the other can indeed really look at me. The house on the hill that one sneaks around can only be the point of reference for being looked at if one supposes someone to be there who can look. But artworks do not gaze; they do not have eyes and are not capable of the intentional attention that Benjamin mentions. To be sure, an artwork can depict a gaze. In that case, the eyes in a portrait seem to look at the observer of the image. The observer can even find him or herself in the position of the subject, as in Velasquez's *Las Meninas*. But this observation of a gaze cannot be equivalent to the experience of the artwork's aura. For in that case, the experience of the aura would only be possible by way of represented gazes, and that cannot be.

Although it is paradoxical that it is not only living beings that gaze, the thought is nevertheless suggestive. Valéry, a thinker completely innocent of obscurantism, writes in "Degas Danse Dessin" that things look at us and that the visible world is thus an ongoing impulse that first makes the comprehension of things possible. Everything awakens or nurtures "the instinct to appropriate the figure or the modeled aspect of the thing that the gaze" constructs.[74] Merleau-Ponty takes the idea up by designating the seer as being taken in by what is seen. The seeing that one enacts is also experienced by things, and thus one feels, as many painters have said, looked at by things, one's own activity at the same time a passivity.[75] The latter is easy to agree with; even Aristotle already described perception in this way.[76] Yet the πάθος of perception need by no means be comprehended as the experience of an activity that one exerts by oneself; that things affect the perception of them, "construct" them as Valéry says, does not mean that the things themselves perceive. Accordingly, one has to elucidate this thought's suggestiveness in another direction. One must clarify what can be gleaned as being-seen from Sartre's description of disempowerment.

A poem of Rilke's is revealing in this regard; as the artwork that it is, it brings to language an artwork that gazes. Yet any possibility of taking this gaze in the sense of a living being's look can be ruled out. The artwork brought to language here is a torso, a headless and eyeless sculpture, an "Archaic Torso of Apollo":[77]

> We did not know his incredible head
> In which the eyes ripened like fruit. But
> His torso still glows like a lamp
> In which his gaze, merely dimmed,
>
> Holds still and gleams. Otherwise, the breast's bow
> Could not daze you, and the quietly turning
> Loins could not contain a rippling smile
> Toward that center that carried the conception.
>
> Otherwise, this stone would stand distorted and short
> Under the shoulders' translucent slump
> And would not glisten like beasts of prey
>
> And would not burst out from all of its seams
> Like a star; for there is no place there
> That does not see you. You must change your life.

The torso that comes to language here is not the preserved remainder of an artwork, but instead its withdrawn and concentrated appearance that is seemingly independent of the complete shape. It is something that "glows" and "gleams," "like a lamp" or "like a star," that which glows and shines of its own accord, the beautiful in the Platonic sense of the ἐκφανέστατον. Nevertheless, what comes to language is still a torso: a shape whose past completeness is fully known to be conclusively past. The poem does not name that which is visible and can be described; it names what is missing, that which escaped any memory and is lost, that which is completely unrecognizable: "We did not know his incredible head."

That which is past and lost is the complete artwork, the plastic shape of Apollo named in the poem's title, a lifeless work of stone. But this lifeless thing is described as if it were alive. The "eyes [. . .] like fruit"; those are not the eyes of everyday speech that have devolved into a metaphor, but instead "ripened" fruit. What has been lost or destroyed in the "center" is not the male sexual organ but the "conception," the vitality that endures in the offspring. The formerly whole artwork is like a living being, or more precisely, its pastness reveals what is lost with any artwork, even complete ones: the vitality that is present in living beings.

Yet this lost vitality is at the same time present in a mysterious way. It "glows," like a lamp, to be sure, and thus like an artificially produced thing; it "glistens," but like the fur of "beasts of prey," so not like the fur of a living animal, but like the stripped skin of a dead one. What glistens in this way is the stone. The ecstatically heightened vitality that the poem brings into play with its allusions to Dionysus—such that the apotheosis of life from Nietzsche's book on tragedy is readable in its lines—has gone into the stone, "dimmed" as the poem states in technical sobriety. Yet at the same time, the vitality bursts from it like a glowing star. This glowing and shining, the artwork's beauty, is the transformed vitality. It is entirely withdrawn into the artwork, while in a living being it moves and reaches outward as movement, gesture, and expression. The shining is the vitality transformed into structure, a structure of appearance.

The torso's "gazing" or looking becomes comprehensible on the basis of this transformation. The gazing "holds still" in its glowing and gleaming. It lies in the beauty of the artwork. But the artwork as Rilke poetizes it does not appear "blissful in itself"; the artwork of the torso-sonnet is not inconspicuous in its shining; it does have the petty bourgeois living room feel like the shining in Mörike's poem "To a Lamp." The artwork's beauty goes outward; one experiences it as directed toward oneself, just as another's gaze can be directed at one: "for there is no place there / That does not see you." There is no direction in it, as with a gaze that is fixated upon something. It affects one by way of its lack of direction, its directionless, radiating appearance. It comes from a distance and remains distant, unapproachable. In that way, it is auratic.

The artwork's radiating and thus emerging appearance is no representation and certainly no imitation of a living gaze that aims to deceive. As a torso, the artwork Rilke sets into poetry cannot be a representation of that sort. The appearance that it is does not stem from anything else to which it would owe its existence. It is simply just itself. For this reason, the torso is also not measured over against a complete human form. It is not "distorted and short," but complete in its appearance.

Rilke elaborated this notion in his thoughts on Rodin's torsos *La Méditation* and *Voix intérieure*. There, he states that a "human body had [never] been so gathered around its interior, so bent by its own soul," being nothing but the "strained listening into its own depths."[78] "Nothing essential" is lacking in this concentrated figure of movement. One stands before the sculptures "as if before something whole, complete, [admitting] of no addition." "The feeling of incompleteness [stems] not from simple looking, but from circuitous thinking, from petty pedantry" that states "that a body is supposed to have arms and that a body without arms can absolutely not be complete."[79]

Like the figure in an image, its perceivable, thing-like appearance is not something borrowed that refers to a living being, such that the impression of vitality would have to be sought by way of deceptive effects. That which stands for the vitality is the stone's textural appearance. In his art, Rodin wanted to explore the human body's surface, and he discovered that it consists "in infinitely many encounters of light with the thing." He discovered "that each of these encounters was different and peculiar," remarkable and astoundingly in play with the other encounters: "At this point, they seemed to take each other up; at another, [they appeared] to hesitate and greet each other, at yet another [they appeared] to pass each other by." "Infinitely many places, and none at which nothing occurs."[80] This play of the surface in the light and of the light at the surface is found in the sculpture. Its surface is to be a dense texture of appearing "places," such that there are "no symmetrical surfaces, that nothing repeats itself, that no place remains empty, mute, or indifferent" (416). There is no place that does not belong to the textural appearance and that would be "empty" in the sense that it drops out of the texture of appearance. Thus, Rilke can say the same of Cézanne's painting: "It is as if every place knew about the other."[81] Every place radiates; there is none "that does not see you."

The artwork does not imitate life, and it is precisely for this reason that one experiences it, in all impossibility of confusion, just as one experiences a living being. If one follows the poem, it contains the challenge of art: "You must change your life." The demand within the poem is succinct, stated without any further elaboration. The poem leaves open what the demanded change consists in. It passes the demand on to a "you" that is at once the observer of the poetic torso and the listener or reader addressed by the poem. The change of one's life that is demanded in art goes beyond art. It reaches from art into life. It is life that is intended, not the artwork. That is certainly what the demand consists in. It intends life by way of something that is beyond life: by way of the artwork that *stands over against* the viewer. The artwork *does not confront*. It is not a person and not a living being. It stands in the object and simply there as the object, even if it is performed as a piece of music or stands on the page as a poem. It is thing-like, not a manifestation of life, not an expression; it is a thing, an occurrence that is merely possible as a thing, like a sound. But the fact that a thing is there like a living being, that is the challenge that art poses, to which one is to respond by changing one's life, as Rilke's poem states. It is the mystery of art that one encounters in the vitalization of artworks. That is when one says that they gaze.

In his torso poem, Rilke radically poetized this experience back into the thing-like appearance of artworks. What one calls the feeling of being looked at proves to be the radiative shining of appearance, over against which one is indeed not the "master of the situation." But this does not yet say why one self-evidently grasps this shining as a being-looked-at. It remains to be clarified what, in the artwork's appearance and in its shining, is like the encounter with a living being.

For this, Sartre's phenomenology of the gaze is helpful once again. The irritation that, according to his account, coincides with the appearance of another stems from the fact that the other overrides the self-evidence of one's relation to the world. To be sure, an other that one encounters is aligned into one's present *world context;* someone is standing there, next to a car that might be his, and clears the snow from the windows. Sitting at one's desk, one sees him through the window, in a familiar surrounding. But the surrounding is also *his;* he sees the same trees, looks along the same street, over to the window behind which one sits. All of this belongs to one's own surroundings, but not the fact that the surroundings are also his. Sartre calls this a "pure disintegration of relations that one apprehends between things of one's universe."[82] The other disappropriates one's own world. The other's appearance is synonymous with the fact that the world slips from one's grasp without anything happening. With this appearance, the central perspective of one's own experienced horizon dissolves. In this sense, it can be considered a "decentering" that "undermines the centering that one undertakes at the same time."[83]

The state of affairs described here should not be conceived as a threat on the part of the other, even if Sartre's account might make that impression. The disintegration and decentering that Sartre diagnoses still takes place even if the encounter with the other is friendly. It is grounded in the other's spatiality. The other brings something to appear in the world that otherwise belongs inextricably to oneself and thus cannot be seen in one's own world: the center of spatial allocation around which everything else gathers. As one is such a center oneself, so is the other, but the latter steps into one's world and thus stakes a claim to it. The other takes up space; an entire space "gathers around him or her," and this space is, in Sartre's terms, "made up of mine."[84]

Two of the most important expressions that make spatial allocations can help elaborate how we should understand the center of spatial allocation. Everything that is distant, that is, at an obvious distance from oneself, is *there*. Conversely, the fact that something is *here* means that is it close to oneself, so close that its distance is negligible. It is within reach, at hand, in the proximity that Heidegger determines as essential to the spatiality of human Dasein in *Being and Time*. In Dasein, he states, there is "an essential tendency toward proximity."[85] This tendency can only exist, however, because one is oneself the center of every possible proximity to something. Something can only be here because one is oneself here in an exceptional way.

This being-here is not identical to the self-localization that is enacted in the expression "here." Localizations like "in this room" and "here at this desk" are only ever possible because one understands oneself, however clearly, as being-here. Wherever one is, one is here, because one is essentially *here*. One can never be *there*. If one went *there* and remained at the place that is there from here, one would once again be *here*. The reason for this would not be that, in standing in the other place that has now becomes one's own, one relates to things in the world. Rather, the other place is one's own because the relating to something begins with it. The *here* thus lies in this relating, or rather, in the possibility of relating to anything, which is only lent to the place in which one finds oneself.

Of course, one could not lend any place this *here* if one were not really there. One is only ever *bodily here* in a place. *Here* is every place at which one physically finds oneself, for instance the table at which one sits, in distinction from the chair over there. Because the being-here is never experienced without one's corporeality, one could imagine that the body makes it possible. But the body does not exhaust the being-here. One's own body is what it is by virtue of the possibilities of being alive, the possibilities of understanding, perceiving, sensing, and acting, whether in motion or at rest. These possibilities that are characteristic of living beings, which Aristotle combines under the heading of ψυχή, distinguish the form of life of a living being.[86] Through the body, they have the possibility of being located. They can be realized in different places, and they are always realized at the place in which a living being is physically present. But the corporeal localization of the possibilities of being alive is determined by these possibilities. It is only by virtue of these that the body is more than an arbitrary object in space. (392–398) It is strictly on their basis that the body is not simply a place, but a *here*. Its being-here lies in its vitality, and thus also in the fact that spatiality belongs to the essence of its vitality.

Husserl spoke of the body as a "center of orientation" in this sense. By relating to something, this is always perceived "in a certain orientation." It is closer or farther away, above or below, left or right, always in relation to one's own bodily existence. For this reason, the body bears "for its ego the singular distinction of [carrying] in itself the *zero point* of all these orientations." "One of its spatial points," even if it is "not one that is actually seen," is "always characterized by the mode of the ultimate central here." This is a here that has "no outside itself in relation to which it would be a 'there.'"[87]

What Husserl calls the "zero point" of orientations is that which cannot be an identifiable point in any orientation. It is the nonplace of relating oneself to something, or more generally, the nonplace of vitality, which as such certainly has its bodily place, but cannot itself be localized. Nevertheless, vitality is not unspatial. It has the character of an "ultimate central here" that cannot be localized as a *there* from any possible perspective. It is an *absolute here* that is not localizing but instead first makes localization possible. It reveals the openness of space in the possibilities of localization and orientation.

Husserl's notion of the ultimate central here makes it clear why the experience of the other can be described in Sartre's terms. To be sure, an other can be localized in one's own sphere of orientation; someone else stands there in the street. But the fact that *this there* is another can only be comprehended by grasping it in its relational and orientational possibilities, namely in its spatially realizable vitality. These possibilities of orientation, in turn, are not localizable. One can certainly say that someone *there* relates to me, for example in such a way that he looks at me. Yet the looking as such is not *there*, but *absolutely here*. In the spirit of Sartre's account, it does not belong to one's own horizon, but stems instead from the possibility of a horizon, from the ability to perceive that radiates into visible space. This possibility communicates itself in the other's gaze, in his or her absolute here.

The other's absolute here need not be perceivable in his gaze. The other need not even relate to oneself. His being-here can communicate itself in an oblivious activity; he can be sitting there in thought, doing nothing. Yet insofar as one recognizes the other's vitality, one understands that this doing-nothing falls within the possibility of a life that is spatial insofar as it has space of its own accord and, in this sense, has *its own space*. A living being can experience this space in its expanse within the framework of the possibilities of its life that are structured in many ways; it can reach out into this space and pause within it: perceiving, holding itself at rest or in motion, understanding. The possibility of life is recognized in each instance in the way that it realizes itself in space and thus determines space. In this way, the possibility of life cannot be identified without spatiality. It has the spatiality of the absolute here.

The spatial determination that stems from an absolute here need not be a human one. All living beings that perceive and possess mobility live the possibility of their life in the space that they determine and that is thus theirs. Accordingly, the experience of other living spaces is not necessarily antagonistic and as disturbing as Sartre's account would have it. Another living being's space is not necessarily "made out of mine" in such a way that, in experiencing the being in its space, I lose my own. Living beings' spaces overlap. The same terrain is generally discovered without competition by many, frequently diverse, living beings, such that the various spatial determinations that arise from an absolute here exist as if in abeyance. The various spaces are not clearly allocated in this abeyance. Insofar as one is oneself in the space of others (who are themselves in one's own space), a common space has always already formed in the mutual interplay of spatial life, a common space that springs from and is held open by the many absolute heres of living beings.

The space around the absolute here that one is—although it is that which is most familiar—usually remains unknown. It is similar with the spaces of other living beings. In general, through the many intersections with other spaces, these remain indifferently common space. It is another matter when the absolute here around which a space is formed is not that of a living being. In that case, the expanding space is no longer a possibility of common space. The mutual vitality in which living beings recognize each other is interrupted. Space is just space.

Artworks determine space in this way. Every artwork is an absolute here in that it is an originary possibility of spatial determination. It is the appearance that exemplifies this possibility and thus the being-here of the artwork. The appearance is not derived from anything beyond itself and is thus comparable to the vital expressions of a living being. Nevertheless, an artwork's appearance is radically different. It does not stem from a possibility that can articulate itself anew and differently in various situations of life. Unlike a living being's potential, the artwork's possibility is fixed. Through the work, it is determined for all time.

The artwork's possibility is its depth. Thus, it is by nothing but space itself that the artwork determines the space that it grants. The space into which one is placed by the artwork is the artwork's own space. As the space that the artwork is, it is inaccessible, just as inaccessible as the possibility of life, the absolute here into which no other can enter. Yet the here of the artwork is open in its inaccessibility. Unlike the possibility of life, one sees or hears into this space and can know it by reading it. This space, the artwork's open depth, stands over against one. It is there for anyone who sees themselves as placed within the artwork's granted and determined space. While one only knows a living being's absolute here by way of its expressions—which stand in relation to it like iron shavings to a magnet—the absolute here of the artwork is the here of its appearance. It can contain anything that the artwork shows in its self-showing. Anything that can be experienced by way of the artwork is thus *here* in a way usually reserved only for the innermost possibility of life. The possibility of life, with its possibilities of articulation, can itself be placed into the here of the artwork. In this way, a living being that is able to perceive and understand can encounter its own possibility in the artwork. Yet that is different than when a living being meets other living beings and recognizes what it is in the mutual encounter. The mutuality of living beings belongs to common space, whereas an artwork's space remains protected from any transgression or fusion. As the object that it essentially is, the artwork simply stands there and allows itself to be recognized by a perceiving and understanding living being in the absolute otherness of an absolute here. Anything that could otherwise only exist for such a living being in the space that it determines stands present in the artwork. This independence of the artwork is irreplaceable. No cooperation supplants it in any way. This is confirmed by what Kant emphasizes about the sociality of aesthetic experience. If cooperation as such could uncover the possibilities of life as well as the experience of art, one would not turn together to works of art. The success of such community even attests to an especially strong and intimate cooperation.

If one takes the artwork seriously as the object that it is, this has the radical result that is voiced at the end of Rilke's torso-poem: "You must change your life." Not in this or that manner, but in such a way that life is no longer merely understood from itself. In this way, it gains a different direction. It becomes an objective life with possibilities of recognizing itself that are not achieved in self-referential attempts at self-knowledge. Goethe's words about "objective thinking" in general are especially applicable to artworks: "Every new object, well observed, reveals a new organ within us."[88]

It thus becomes obvious how little thought is separated from the things of the world. Not that thinking would be derivable from a physics of things or inserted into a general living, perceiving world of things that returns the thinker's gaze. Every thinking must have that which is thinkable and thought over against it. But that which is capable of being experienced in thought can, in its standing-over-against thought, also be something that one encounters, as it were. Not a mirror, but also something not foreign. Rather, it is absolutely other, in such a way that it bears the possibility of living thought in its own manner radically distinct from life. All beautiful things possess this basic trait of independence. They are not dissolved in any integration or allocation. Yet it is especially beautiful things as artworks that show what Kant saw in them as the fundamental theme of philosophical aesthetics: that humans fit into the world.[89]

There is a sculpture by Barnett Newman that shows the peculiar objectivity of art in its highest concentration. The sculpture is a column of stainless steel, a strip that is not very wide, but more than three meters high. It stands on a pedestal that seems to hover slightly above the ground and rise into a conical shape above a narrow, flat base. If one approaches the column, one has to look up. If one walks around it, one can view it from its narrow side or again from its wide side. The column does not divulge much. Its surface is smooth, almost repellent. It only shows the figure that it is. The sculpture is that which stands there. Its title is *Here*.[90]

Newman's sculpture can be interpreted in several ways. It may remind one of the upright posture of a human, of a tree trunk, of an architectural column. It can be compared to Giacometti's extremely slight human figures; one can even establish an association to totem poles. The second of three total version of *Here*[91] consists of three columns; here an association with Golgotha is unavoidable.[92]

None of the interpretations can be definitively ruled out, but none is compulsory either. Newman's sculpture is something like the quintessence of all columns, steles, figures, and towers that mark a standing-over-against; for this reason, it cannot be determined as any one version of such standing. Yet it does not stand *there*, but instead in the *here* that its title indicates. It is not subject to a spatial order that derives from a living center, but is rather essentially decentered, beyond any view with a central perspective, without thereby representing another view. The sculpture does not stand for another, living, absolute here. It is *here* without one's being able to attribute to it the possibility of life. Since it is not *an* other of the same essential kind as oneself, but something other, it decentralizes in a way no other in Sartre's sense, no living being, would be capable. It draws one out of one's own absolute here without offering another place where one could be. It does not take one up. Rather, it opens the opportunity of understanding oneself *out of* an absolute here in its unavoidability, rather than *by way of* an absolute here. Thus, it suspends the self-evidence of a life lived from the central perspective. It puts one in abeyance such that one can grasp oneself without any self-reference. By showing itself as a sculpture, Newman's sculpture shows the artwork's possibility into which anything can enter, such that one experiences it otherwise than usual, distant from oneself, decentered and decentralized; one experiences it as an appearance in its possibility, in a bindingness that lacks any proof, but which cannot be surpassed in its evidence: here it is, for here is the work.

NOTES

1. Art, Philosophically

1. Friedrich Nietzsche, *Vom Nutzen und Nachtheil der Historie für das Leben (Unzeitgemäße Betrachtungen II)*, in *Sämtliche Werke*, critical edition (hereinafter cited as KSA), ed. Giorgio Colli and Mazzino Montinari (Berlin: de Gruyter, 1980), vol. 1, 243–334, here 243.

2. Cf. Plato, *Republic*. Plato's works will henceforth be cited according to *Platonis Opera*, ed. John Burnet (Oxford: Oxford University Press, 1900–1907); Aristotle, *Nicomachean Ethics*, ed. Ingram Bywater (Oxford: Oxford University Press, 1894).

3. Cf. Aristotle, *Metaphysics* I, 2; 982b11–28, ed. William David Ross (Oxford: Oxford University Press, 1924).

4. Cf. Aristotle, *Metaphysics* I, 2; 982b17–18.

5. Heraclitus, VS 22 B 40, 160, in Hermann Alexander Diels and Walther Kranz, *Die Fragmente der Vorsokratiker*, 7th ed. (Berlin: Weidmannsche Buchhandlung, 1954), vols. 1–3.

6. Heraclitus, VS 22 B 42, 160.

7. Cf. Plato, *Republic*, 377c–d.

8. Cf. Plato, *Sophist*, 242c–d.

9. Plato, *Apology*, 22b–c.

10. Cf. Günter Figal, "Die Wahrheit und die schöne Täuschung: Zum Verhältnis von Dichtung und Philosophie im Platonischen Denken," *Philosophisches Jahrbuch* 107 (2000): 301–315.

11. Cf. Gorgias of Leontinoi, VS 82 B 11, 294–303, in Hermann Alexander Diels and Walther Kranz, *Die Fragmente der Vorsokratiker*, 7th ed. (Berlin: Weidmannsche Buchhandlung, 1954), vols. 1–3.

12. Immanuel Kant, *Kritik der Urteilskraft*, B 181, *Kant's gesammelte Schriften* (hereinafter cited as AA), Volume V (Berlin: Königlich Preußische Akademie der Wissenschaften, 1913), 166–485, here 307.

13. Kant, *Kritik der Urteilskraft*, B 184; AA V, 309. [English translation cited from Immanuel Kant, *Critique of Judgment*, trans. Werner S. Pluhar (Indianapolis: Hackett, 1987).]

14. Friedrich Nietzsche, *Die Geburt der Tragödie*, KSA 1, 9–156, here 14.

15. Cf. Plato, *Republic*, 514a–517a.

16. Friedrich Nietzsche, *Die Fröhliche Wissenschaft*, 301; KSA 3, 343–651, here 540.

17. Cf. Günter Figal, "Was ist Wissen? Die Frage des Sokrates," in *Verstehensfragen: Studien zur Phänomenologisch-Hermeneutischen Philosophie* (Tübingen: Mohr Siebeck, 2009), 159–166.

18. Cf. Nietzsche, *Die Fröhliche Wissenschaft*, 299; KSA 3, 538: "*wir* aber wollen die Dichter unseres Lebens sein, und im Kleinsten und Alltäglichsten zuerst."

19. Nietzsche, *Die Fröhliche Wissenschaft*, 301; KSA 3, 540.

20. Cf. Richard Rorty, *Contingency, Irony, and Solidarity* (Cambridge: Cambridge University Press, 1989).

21. Cf. Joachim Ritter, "Landschaft: Zur Funktion des Ästhetischen in der Modernen Gesellschaft," *Schriften der Gesellschaft zur Förderung der Westfälischen Wilhelms-Universität zu Münster* 54 (1963). Reprinted in Ritter, *Subjektivität: Sechs Aufsätze* (Frankfurt am Main: Suhrkamp, 1974), 141–163.

22. Cf. Aristotle, *Metaphysics* III, 1; 1003a21–22.

23. This position, decisively represented in modernity by Husserl, is critically discussed in Figal, "Hermeneutik und Phänomenologie," in Figal, *Verstehensfragen: Studien zur phänomenologisch-hermeneutischen Philosophie* (Tübingen: Mohr Siebeck, 2009), 177–188, here 184–186.

24. Cf. Hans-Georg Gadamer, "Lob der Theorie (1980)," in *Gesammelte Werke* (hereinafter cited as GW), vol. 4 (Neuere Philosophie II. Probleme—Gestalten) (Tübingen: Mohr Siebeck, 1987), 37–51.

25. Johann Wolfgang von Goethe, "Bedeutende Fördernis durch ein geistreiches Wort," *Sämtliche Werke nach Epochen seines Schaffens*, Munich edition (hereinafter cited as MA), vol. 12 (Weimarer Klassik 1798–1806), ed. Karl Richter (Munich: Hanser, 1986), 306–309, here 306.

26. Cf. Stephen Addiss, *Japan und der Westen: Die Erfüllte Leere* (Cologne: DuMont, 2007), 22–23 and 26–27.

27. Edmund Husserl, *Formale und Transzendentale Logik: Versuch einer Kritik der logischen Vernunft*, Husserliana XVII, ed. Paul Janssen (The Hague: Nijhoff, 1974), 254–255.

28. Kant, *Kritik der Urteilskraft*, B 176–177; AA V, 304–305.

29. Cf. recent works on the *querelle*: Joan DeJean, *Ancients Against Moderns: Culture Wars and the Making of a Fin de Siècle* (Chicago: University of Chicago Press, 1997); Levent Yilmaz, *Le Temps Moderne: Variations Sur les Anciens et les Contemporains* (Paris: Gallimard, 2004).

30. G. W. F. Hegel, *Vorlesungen über die Ästhetik I, Theorie-Werkausgabe*, based on the *Werke* of 1832–1845, ed. Eva Moldenhauer and Karl Markus Michel, vol. 13 (Frankfurt am Main: Suhrkamp, 1970), 25.

31. Hans-Georg Gadamer, *Hermeneutik I—Wahrheit und Methode: Grundzüge einer Philosophischen Hermeneutik*, GW 1 (Tübingen: Mohr Siebeck, 1986), 293.

32. In a later work, Gadamer himself elucidates the concept in this way. Cf. Hans-Georg Gadamer, "Wort und Bild—'So Wahr, So Seiend' (1992)," in *Ästhetik und Poetik I—Kunst als Aussage*, GW 8 (Tübingen: Mohr Siebeck, 1993), 373–399, here 375–376.

33. Cf. Søren Kierkegaard, *Philosophische Brocken*, in *Gesammelte Werke* (hereinafter GW), vol. 10 (*Philosophische Brocken: De Omnibus Dubitandum Est*), trans. Emanuel Hirsch (Düsseldorf: Diederichs, 1952), 52–107.

34. Gadamer, *Wahrheit und Methode*, GW 1, 293.

35. Theodor Wiesengrund Adorno, *Ästhetische Theorie, Gesammelte Schriften* (hereinafter GS), ed. Rolf Tiedemann and Gretel Adorno, vol. 7 (Frankfurt am Main: Suhrkamp, 1970), 272.

36. Gadamer, *Wahrheit und Methode*, GW 1, 291.

37. Adorno, *Ästhetische Theorie*, GS 7, 58.

38. Richard Wagner, *Das Kunstwerk der Zukunft* (Bibliothek der Deutschen Literatur) (Leipzig: Wigand, 1850). Cf. Ludwig Feuerbach, *Grundsätze der Philosophie der Zukunft* (1843), in *Werke in Sechs Bänden*, ed. Erich Thies, vol. 3 (Kritiken und Abhandlungen II: 1839–1843) (Frankfurt am Main: Suhrkamp, 1975), 247–322.

39. Adorno, *Ästhetische Theorie*, GS 7, 17.

40. Søren Kierkegaard, *Der Begriff der Angst*, GW 11/12, trans. Emanuel Hirsch (Düsseldorf: Diederichs, 1952), 1–169.

41. Gadamer, *Wahrheit und Methode*, GW 1, 295.

42. Friedrich Schlegel, *Lyceums-Fragmente*, in *Kritische Friedrich-Schlegel Ausgabe*, vol. 2 (Charakteristiken und Kritiken I: 1776–1801), ed. Hans Eichner (Darmstadt: Wissenschaftliche Buchgesellschaft, 1967), 147–163, here 149, n. 20. Cited in Gadamer, *Wahrheit und Methode*, GW 1, 295.

43. Gadamer, *Wahrheit und Methode*, GW 1, 293.

44. Adorno, *Ästhetische Theorie*, GS 7, 37.

45. On the hermeneutic circle, cf. Günter Figal, *Gegenständlichkeit: Das Hermeneutische und die Philosophie* (Tübingen: Mohr Siebeck, 2006), 95–97.

46. Cf. Aristotle, *Nicomachean Ethics* I, 4; 1095b2: ἀρκτέον μὲν γὰρ ἀπὸ τῶν γνωρίμων.

47. Cf. Jacob Grimm and Wilhelm Grimm, *Deutsches Wörterbuch* (Leipzig: Hirzel, 1873), vol. 5 (K), 2680–2682.

48. Alexander Gottlieb Baumgarten, *Aesthetica*, unaltered reprographic reprint of the Frankfurt 1750 edition (Hildesheim: Olms, 1961), §1.

49. Cf. chapter 3, 97–110.

50. Cf. Wolfgang Wieland, *Urteil und Gefühl: Kants Theorie der Urteilskraft* (Göttingen: Vandenhoeck & Ruprecht, 2001), 25–46.

51. Kant, *Kritik der Urteilskraft*, B xix–xx; AA V, 175–176. [Translation by Pluhar emended.]

52. Kant, *Kritik der Urteilskraft*, B 258–259; AA V, 353.

53. Immanuel Kant, *Logik*, AA XVI, 127.

54. Cf. Alfred North Whitehead, *Process and Reality: An Essay in Cosmology*, ed. David Ray Griffin and Donald W. Sherburne (New York: Free Press, 1979), 36.

55. Hegel, *Vorlesungen über die Ästhetik I*, Werke vol. 13, 13.

56. Cf. F. W. J. Schelling, *System des Transcendentalen Idealismus*, Sämtliche Werke (hereinafter SW), ed. K. F. A. Schelling, division 1, vol. 3 (Stuttgart: Cotta, 1858), 327–634, section 6, §§1–2.

57. Conrad Fiedler, "Über den Urprung der Künstlerischen Tätigkeit" (1887), in *Schriften zur Kunst* I. Reprint of the Munich 1913–14 edition, with further texts from journals and the estate, ed. Gottfried Boehm (Munich: Fink, 1971), 183–367, here 192.

58. Cf. John Dewey, *Art as Experience* (New York: Penguin, 1958), 58–81.

59. Cf. Baumgarten, *Aesthetica*, §§18–20. One can easily recognize the three rhetorical categories of *inventio, dispositio,* and *elocutio* in Baumgarten's distinction of the beautiful.

This is because Baumgarten reaches back to poetics that lie in close proximity to rhetoric. In antiquity, the two were not always clearly distinguished. When Gorgias, for instance, describes the force and power of speech in his encomium to Helen, this includes poetry.

60. Hegel, *Vorlesungen über die Ästhetik I, Werke* vol. 13, 85.

61. On the history of this concept, cf. Konrad Cramer, "Erlebnis," in *Historisches Wörterbuch der Philosophie*, ed. Joachim Ritter, vol. 2 (D–F) (Darmstadt: Wissenschaftliche Buchgesellschaft, 1972), 702–711.

62. Martin Heidegger, *Beiträge zur Philosophie (Vom Ereignis), Gesamtausgabe* (hereinafter GA) vol. 65, ed. Friedrich-Wilhelm von Herrmann (Frankfurt am Main: Klostermann, 1989), 129.

63. Martin Heidegger, *Nietzsche: Der Wille Zur Macht als Kunst*, GA 43, ed. Bernd Heimbüchel (Frankfurt am Main: Klostermann, 1985), 101.

64. Gadamer, *Wahrheit und Methode*, GW 1, 72.

65. Wilhelm Dilthey, *Studien zur Grundlegung der Geisteswissenschaften*, in *Gesammelte Schriften*, 2nd ed. (hereinafter GS), vol. 7 (Der Aufbau der Geschichtlichen Welt in den Geisteswissenschaften) (Göttingen: Vandenhoeck & Ruprecht, 1958), 24–69, here 27.

66. Gadamer, *Wahrheit und Methode*, GW 1, 87.

67. Cf. Arnold Gehlen, *Zeit-Bilder: Zur Soziologie und Ästhetik der Modernen Malerei*, 2nd rev. ed. (Frankfurt am Main: Klostermann, 1965), 47–51; André Malraux, *Le Musée Imaginaire de la Sculpture Mondiale* (Paris: Gallimard, 1952–1954).

68. Gadamer, *Wahrheit und Methode*, GW 1, 87.

69. Rüdiger Bubner, "Ästhetisierung der Lebenswelt," in *Ästhetische Erfahrung* (Frankfurt am Main: Suhrkamp, 1989), 143–156 (originally appeared in *Das Fest* (Poetik und Hermeneutik XIV), ed. Walter Haug and Rainer Warning (Munich: Fink, 1989), 651–662.)

70. Heidegger, *Beiträge zur Philosophie*, GA 65, 126.

71. Something like this occurs when, by abstractly exaggerating the "moment," one passes off the "experience of presence" in sports and pop culture as the essential core of aesthetic experience. Cf. Hans Ulrich Gumbrecht, *Diesseits der Hermeneutik: Die Produktion von Präsenz*, trans. Joachim Schulte (Frankfurt am Main: Suhrkamp, 2004); Karl Heinz Bohrer, *Plötzlichkeit: Zum Augenblick des Ästhetischen Scheins* (Frankfurt am Main: Suhrkamp, 1981).

72. Gadamer, *Wahrheit und Methode*, GW 1, 90.

73. On this experiential quality, cf. 60–82 below.

74. Hegel, *Vorlesungen über die Ästhetik, Werke* vol. 13, 142.

75. Cf. 17–27 above.

76. Martin Heidegger, "Der Ursprung des Kunstwerkes (1935–36)," in *Holzwege*, GA 5, ed. Friedrich-Wilhelm von Herrmann (Frankfurt am Main: Klostermann, 1977), 1–74, here 27.

77. Cf. Jacques Derrida, *La Verité en Peinture* (Paris: Gallimard, 1978); Meyer Shapiro, "Theory and Philosophy of Art: Style, Artist and Society," in *Selected Papers* (New York: Braziller, 1994), 135–151.

78. Martin Heidegger, "Der Ursprung des Kunstwerkes," GA 5, 31.

79. Cf. Plato, *Phaedrus*, 250d. For an elaboration of this passage, cf. 60–82.

80. Heidegger, *Nietzsche: Der Wille Zur Macht Als Kunst*, GA 43, 242.

81. Cf. Figal, "Gadamer als Phänomenologe," in *Verstehensfragen: Studien zur phänomenologisch-hermeneutischen Philosophie* (Tübingen: Mohr Siebeck, 2009), 277–290, here 282–285; Gadamer, *Wahrheit und Methode*, GW 1, 442.

82. Gadamer, *Wahrheit und Methode*, GW 1, 481.

83. Hans-Georg Gadamer, "Die Aktualität des Schönen: Kunst als Spiel, Symbol und Fest (1974)," GW 8, 94–142, here 106.

84. On this concept, cf. Gadamer, *Wahrheit und Methode*, GW 1, 113.

85. Gadamer, "Die Aktualität des Schönen," GW 8, 119.

86. Gadamer, "Wort und Bild—'So wahr, so seiend' (1992)." GW 8, 391. Cf. Günter Figal, "Kunst als Weltdarstellung," in *Der Sinn des Verstehens: Beiträge zur Hermeneutischen Philosophie* (Stuttgart: Reclam, 1996), 45–63.

87. Gadamer, "Die Aktualität des Schönen," GW 8, 107.

88. Hans Robert Jauß, ed., *Die Nicht Mehr Schönen Künste: Grenzphänomene des Ästhetischen* (Poetik und Hermeneutik III) (Munich: Fink, 1968).

89. Hans Sedlmayr, *Verlust der Mitte: Die Bildende Kunst des 19. und 20. Jahrhunderts als Symptom und Symbol der Zeit*, 11th ed. (Salzburg: Müller, 1998).

90. Gehlen, *Zeit-Bilder*, 185–187.

91. Adorno, *Ästhetische Theorie*, GS 7, 31.

92. Cf. Jean-Francois Lyotard, *Die Analytik des Erhabenen* (Kant-Lektionen; *Kritik der Urteilskraft* §§23–29), trans. Christine Pries (Munich: Fink, 1994).

93. Adorno, *Ästhetische Theorie*, GS 7, 78. There are similar notions in Elaine Scarry, *On Beauty and Being Just* (Princeton, N.J.: Princeton University Press, 1999); Arthur Coleman Danto, *The Abuse of Beauty: Aesthetics and the Concept of Art* (Peru, Ill.: Carus, 2003).

94. For a critical discussion of this thesis, cf. Birgit Recki, "Herabkommen ins Sichtbare: Eine Apologie der Schönheit in Pragmatischer Hinsicht," in *Das Leben Denken—Die Kultur Denken*, ed. Ralf Konersmann, 176–196 (Freiburg: Alber, 2007).

95. Rainer Maria Rilke, *Duineser Elegien*, in *Werke*, Kommentierte Ausgabe in vier Bänden (hereinafter KA), vol. 2 (Gedichte 1910–1926), ed. Manfred Engel und Ulrich Fülleborn (Frankfurt am Main: Insel, 1996), 199–234, here 201. [English translation cited from William H. Gass, *Reading Rilke: Reflections on the Problems of Translation* (New York: Basic Books, 2000), 66.]

96. Gehlen, *Zeit-Bilder*, 187.

97. Cf. Pseudo-Longinus, *Peri Hypsous: De Sublimitate Libellus*, 3rd ed., ed. Johannes Vahlen (Leipzig: Teubner, 1905); Schelling, *System des Transcendentalen Idealismus*, SW I, 3, 621: "For if there are sublime artworks, and the sublime tends to be contrasted with the beautiful, then there is no true opposition between beauty and sublimity; the truly and absolutely beautiful is always also sublime, the sublime (when it is truly such) is also beautiful."

98. Cf. Kant, *Kritik der Urteilskraft*, B 76; AA V, 245.

99. Cf. Friedrich Schiller, *Über das Erhabene*, in *Sämtliche Werke* (hereinafter SW), based on the original prints, ed. Gerhard Fricke and Herbert Georg Göpfert, vol. 5 (Erzählungen. Theoretische Schriften) (Munich: Hanser, 1959), 792–808, here 796–798.

100. Kant, *Kritik der Urteilskraft*, B 104; AA V, 261.

101. Cf. chapter 2, 42–60.

102. Aristotle, *Nicomachean Ethics* I, 4; 1095b2–3: ἀρκτέον μὲν γὰρ ἀπὸ τῶν γνωρίμων, ταῦτα δὲ διττῶς. τὰ μὲν γὰρ ἡμῖν τὰ δ᾽ἁπλῶς.

2. Beauty

1. The concept of taste was primarily employed in this sense in the moral philosophy of the seventeenth and eighteenth centuries, notably by Gracián and Shaftesbury. Cf. Baltasar Gracián, *El Discreto*, ed. Miguel Romera-Navarro (Buenos Aires: Academia Argentina de Letras, 1960); Anthony Ashley Cooper, Third Earl of Shaftesbury, *Characteristics of Men, Manners, Opinions, Times*, ed. John M. Robertson (Indianapolis, Ind.: Bobbs-Merrill, 1964), vol. 1, 89–93; Gadamer, *Wahrheit und Methode*, GW 1, 40–47.

2. On the development of Kant's thoughts about the concept of taste, the following work still remains helpful: Alfred Baeumler, *Das Irrationalitätsproblem in der Ästhetik und Logik des 18. Jahrhunderts bis zur Kritik der Urteilskraft*, reprint of the second, expanded edition of 1967 (Darmstadt: Wissenschaftliche Buchgesellschaft, 1981), 261–274.

3. Kant, *Kritik der Urteilskraft*, B 15; AA V, 210.

4. Cf. Kant, *Kritik der Urteilskraft*, B xxvi; AA V, 179.

5. Immanuel Kant, "Logik," in *Logik, Physische Geographie, Pädagogik*, AA IX, 3–150, here 91, comment 1.

6. Kant, *Kritik der Urteilskraft*, B 25; AA V, 216.

7. Cf. Plato, *Philebus* 52a.

8. Kant, *Kritik der Urteilskraft*, B 17; AA V, 211.

9. Translation by Pluhar.

10. Cf. Immanuel Kant, *Kritik der Reinen Vernunft*, A 124; AA IV, 91: "We thus have a pure faculty of imagination as a fundamental capacity of the human soul, which lies a priori beneath any knowledge. By means of this, we bring the manifold of intuition, on the one hand, into connection with the condition of necessary unity of pure apperception, on the other."

11. Kant, "Logik," in *Logik, Physische Geographie, Pädagogik*, AA IX, 91, comment 1.

12. Kant, *Kritik der Urteilskraft*, B 31; AA V, 219.

13. Gadamer took up these determinations for a reason. Cf. Gadamer, *Wahrheit und Methode*, GW 1, 40–47.

14. Wolfgang Wieland gives an incisive and concise defense of this quite pervasive interpretation of the judgment of taste. In his view, judgments of taste are not capable "of determining objects in their content in a differentiated way"; they agree "that the place of the predicate is always only [occupied] by the same element, namely always by one and the same specific feeling" (Wolfgang Wieland, *Urteil und Gefühl: Kants Theorie der Urteilskraft* [Göttingen: Vandenhoeck & Ruprecht, 2001], 228). Similarly, cf. Bubner, *Ästhetische Erfahrung*, 37, and John H. Zammito, *The Genesis of Kant's* Critique of Judgment (Chicago: University of Chicago Press, 1992), 113. The cognitive character of aesthetic experience, conversely, is underscored by Rodolphe Gasché, *The Idea of Form: Rethinking Kant's Aesthetics* (Stanford, Calif.: Stanford University Press, 2003).

15. Kant, *Kritik der Urteilskraft*, B 31; AA V, 219.
16. Bubner, *Ästhetische Erfahrung*, 37.
17. Hermann Schmitz, *Was wollte Kant?* (Bonn: Bouvier, 1989), 166.
18. Adorno, *Ästhetische Theorie*, GS 7, 22.
19. Kant, *Kritik der Urteilskraft*, B 14; AA V, 209.
20. In this regard, cf. Birgit Recki, "Intentionalität Ohne Intention: Die Praktizität der Urteilskraft," in *Akten des Siebenten Internationalen Kant-Kongresses*, ed. Gerhard Funke, vol. 2.2, 165–178, here 172 (Bonn: Bouvier, 1991): Aesthetic judgment deals with concepts "without the aim of [bringing] the presentation to a *determinate* concept."
21. Kant, *Kritik der Urteilskraft*, B 11; AA V, 207.
22. Immanuel Kant, *Grundlegung zur Metaphysik der Sitten*, AA IV, 385–463, here 438. Cf. Figal, *Gegenständlichkeit*, 211.
23. Kant, *Grundlegung zur Metaphysik der Sitten*, AA IV, 435.
24. Kant, *Kritik der Urteilskraft*, B 32; AA V, 220.
25. Translation by Pluhar.
26. Martin Heidegger, *Der Satz vom Grund*, GA 10, ed. Petra Jaeger (Frankfurt am Main: Klostermann, 1997), 62.
27. Heidegger, *Der Satz vom Grund*, Ga 10, 77.
28. Plato, *Gorgias* 503e–504a: εἰς τάξιν τινὰ ἕκσαστος [τῶν δημιουργῶν] ἕκαστον τίθησιν ὃ ἂν τιθῇ, καὶ προσαναγκάζει τὸ ἕτερον τῷ ἑτέρῳ πρέπον τε εἶναι καὶ ἁρπόττειν, ἕως ἂν τὸ ἅπαν συστήσηται τεταγμένον τε καὶ κεκοσμημένον πρᾶγμα.
29. Kant, *Kritik der Urteilskraft*, B 49; AA V, 229.
30. Cf. Kant, *Kritik der Urteilskraft*, B 71; AA V, 242.
31. Gadamer, "Die Aktualität des Schönen," GW 8, 111; on Gadamer's relation to Kant, cf. Dennis J. Schmidt, *Lyrical and Ethical Subjects: Essays on the Periphery of the Word, Freedom, and History* (Albany: State University of New York Press, 2005), 7–18.
32. Gadamer, *Die Aktualität des Schönen*, GW 8, 111.
33. Kant, *Kritik der Urteilskraft*, B 49; AA V, 229. [Translation by Pluhar emended.]
34. Cf. Birgit Recki, "Die Dialektik der ästhetischen Urteilskraft und die Methodenlehre des Geschmacks," in *Immanuel Kant: Kritik der Urteilskraft* (Klassiker Auslegen 33), ed. Otfried Höffe, 189–210, here 204 (Berlin: Akademie Verlag, 2008).
35. Kant, *Kritik der Urteilskraft*, B 48; AA V, 229.
36. Translation by Pluhar.
37. Translation by Pluhar emended.
38. Kant, *Kritik der Urteilskraft*, B 72; AA V, 242; for a work that is independent of Kant, but agrees with him on the subject matter, cf. So͞etsu Yanagi, "The Beauty of Irregularity," in *The Unknown Craftsman: A Japanese Insight into Beauty* (New York: Kodansha, 1972), 119–126.
39. Kant, *Logik*, AA XVI, 127.
40. Kant, *Kritik der Urteilskraft*, B 248–249; AA V, 348. [Translation by Pluhar.]
41. This is a critical reversal of the topical considerations that I made in Günter Figal, *Theodor Adorno: Das Naturschöne als spekulative Gedankenfigur. Zur Interpretation der 'Ästhetischen Theorie' im Kontext philosophischer Ästhetik* (Bonn: Bouvier, 1977). At the time, I

held it to be necessary, with regard to the agreement of freedom and nature, to adhere, along with teleological judgment and especially with Schelling, to the notion of a "real autonomy."

42. Kant, *Kritik der Urteilskraft*, B 247; AA V, 347.

43. George Steiner, *Real Presences: Is There Anything in What We Say?* (Chicago: University of Chicago Press, 1989).

44. Cf. Aristotle, *De Anima* III, 2, 425b26–27: ἡ δὲ τοῦ αἰσθητοῦ ἐνέργεια καὶ τῆς αἰσθήσεως ἡ αὐτὴ μέν ἐστι καὶ μία, τὸ αὐτό αὐταῖς; cited from *De Anima*, ed. William David Ross (Oxford: Oxford University Press, 1956).

45. Cf. Plato, *Republic* 507c–508a.

46. Johann Wolfgang Goethe, *Faust. Der Tragödie zweiter Teil*, in Munich edition, vol. 18.1, ed. Gisela Henckmann and Dorothea Hölscher-Lohmeyer (Munich: Hanser, 1997), line 4727.

47. Cf. Henry George Liddell and Robert Scott, *A Greek English Lexicon*, vol. 1 (Oxford: Oxford University Press, 1951), 499.

48. Cf. Gadamer, *Wahrheit und Methode*, GW 1, 485.

49. Plato, *Symposium* 211e: αὐτὸ τὸ καλόν.

50. Plato, *Phaedrus* 250d.

51. Cf. Plato, *Symposium*, 211b: αὐτὸ καθ' αὑτὸ μεθ' αὑτοῦ μονοειδὲς ἀεί ὄν.

52. Friedrich Schiller, *Über die ästhetische Erziehung des Menschen in einer Reihe von Briefen*, SW 5, 570–669, here 657.

53. Kant, *Kritik der reinen Vernunft*, B 69; AA III, 71. [Translation by Pluhar.] Martin Seel follows this conception of appearance with aesthetic intentions by designating the "appearance of an object" as that which "can be recognized about it in observational perception." Seel, *Ästhetik des Erscheinens* (Munich: Hanser, 2000), 82. If aesthetic experience is to be conceived as a perception that only differs from normal perception by the fact that in it, the "being-so" of things is to be disregarded in its determinacy, then it is a deficient state that does not permit one to see how it could be connected to insights, let alone with insight into "cognition as such" in Kant's sense.

54. Schiller, *Ästhetische Erziehung*, SW 5, 656.

55. One variant of this notion seems to be present in Georg Picht's thesis, according to which artworks are phenomena that, "in their appearing [*Schein*], also [make] the phenomenality of other phenomena transparent"; Georg Picht, "Kunst und Mythos," in *Vorlesungen und Schriften*, ed. Constanze Eisenbart, vol. 2 (Stuttgart: Klett-Cotta, 1986), 210. The considerations we develop here, however, differ radically from Picht's thesis. Picht takes phenomena to be something that does not require the mediation of words and concepts (cf. Picht, "Kunst und Mythos," 162). Thus it is only consistent "to dissociate [those] forms of experience in which phenomena show themselves as they appear from those other forms that are imprinted in advance by the structures of the logos" (Picht, "Kunst und Mythos," 129). But this conclusion is purchased at the price of vaguenesses and frequently also through exchange of conceptual clarifications for suggestions and evocations. As Picht himself states, what he aims at, and only achieves in fragments, has nothing to do with phenomenology. Thus Picht believes that he can ne-

glect an engagement with phenomenology's concept of phenomenon. Cf. Picht, "Kunst und Mythos," 127.

56. Cf. 19.

57. Husserl, *Formale und transzendentale Logik,* Hua XVII, 253.

58. Elsewhere, Husserl elaborates this notion by developing the mutual dependence of the "field of perception" and the "thing-field." Edmund Husserl, *Die Krisis der europäischen Wissenschaften und die transzendentale Phänomenologie. Eine Einleitung in die phänomenologische Philosophie,* Hua VI, ed. Walter Biemel (The Hague: Nijhoff, 1962), 165.

59. Husserl, *Krisis,* Hua VI, 169–170, note 1.

60. Husserl, *Formale und transzendentale Logik,* Hua XVII, 255.

61. Edmund Husserl, *Zur Phänomenologie der Intersubjektivität. Texte aus dem Nachlaß. Dritter Teil: 1929–1935,* Hua XV, ed. Iso Kern (The Hague: Nijhoff, 1973), 434. Cf. also Dan Zahavi, *Husserl's Phenomenology* (Stanford, Calif.: Stanford University Press, 2003).

62. Cf. Husserl, *Formale und transzendentale Logik,* Hua XVII, 255–256.

63. Edmund Husserl, *Die Idee der Phänomenologie. Fünf Vorlesungen,* Hua II, ed. Walter Biemel (The Hague: Nijhoff, 1950), 44. Cf. also Figal, *Gegenständlichkeit,* 150.

64. Husserl, *Die Idee der Phänomenologie,* Hua II, 14.

65. Edmund Husserl, *Ideen zu einer reinen Phänomenologie und phänomenologischen Philosophie. Erstes Buch,* Hua III.1, ed. Karl Schuhmann (The Hague: Nijhoff, 1976), 105.

66. Cf. Husserl, *Ideen I,* Hua III.1, 104.

67. Husserl, *Formale und transzendentale Logik,* Hua XVII, 257.

68. Husserl, *Krisis,* Hua VI, 169–170, note 1.

69. Husserl, *Ideen I,* Hua III.1, 147.

70. Husserl, *Formale und transzendentale Logik,* Hua XVII, 255.

71. Husserl, *Ideen I,* Hua III.1, 148.

72. "Brief an Hugo von Hoffmannsthal vom 12. 1. 1907," in Husserl, *Briefwechsel,* ed. Karl Schuhmann (Dordrecht: Kluwer, 1994), vol. 7 (*Wissenschaftlerkorrespondenz*), 133–136, here 133. On the biographical context of the letter, cf. Rudolf Hirsch, "Edmund Husserl und Hugo von Hofmannsthal. Eine Begegnung und ein Brief," in *Beiträge zum Verständis Hugo von Hofmannsthals* (Frankfurt am Main: Fischer, 1995), 273–280.

73. Husserl, "Brief an von Hofmannsthal," *Briefwechsel* VII, 135.

74. On the concept of ἐποχή, cf. Husserl, *Ideen I,* Hua III.1, 61–66.

75. Cf. Husserl, *Ideen I,* Hua III.1, 62.

76. Conversely, cf. Roman Ingarden, *Das literarische Kunstwerk* (Tübingen: Niemeyer, 1960), 260, where he states that the literary object appears as "putatively 'real;'" the object tries, "as it were, to cover over the corresponding real and represented object, by [pretending to be] this latter object."

77. Husserl, *Ideen I,* Hua III.1, 104. Cf. 76.

78. Ironically, Illiers has meanwhile adopted the name "Illiers-Combray," and thus tied the pure appearance back to reality. One could also say that reality is lending itself the gleam of pure appearance.

79. Cf. William Howard Adams, ed., *Prousts Figuren und ihre Vorbilder* (Frankfurt am Main: Suhrkamp, 1988), 121–124, 134–135, 136–139, 142–145.

80. Husserl, *Ideen I*, Hua III.1, 146.

81. Cf. Aristotle, *Poetics* IX, 1451b5–7; in what follows, the book will be cited according to *Poetics*, ed. Ingram Bywater (Oxford: Oxford University Press, 1987).

82. Cf. Aristotle, *Poetics* IX, 1451a36–38: Φανερὸν δὲ ἐκ τῶν εἰρημένων καὶ ὅτι οὐ τὰ γενόμενα λέγειν, τοῦτο ποιητοῦ ἔργον ἐστίν, ἀλλ'οἷα ἂν γένοιτο καὶ τὰ δυματὰ κατὰ τὸ εἰκός ἢ τὸ ἀναγκαῖον.

83. Cf. Aristotle, *Poetics* IX, 1451b5–7: διὸ καὶ φιλοσοφώτερον καὶ σπουδαιότερον ποίησις ἱστορίας ἐστίν. ἡ μὲν γὰρ ποίησις μᾶλλον τὰ καθόλου, ἡ δ'ἱστορία τὰ καθ'ἕκαστον λέγει.

84. Cf. Husserl, *Ideen I*, Hua III.1, 147.

85. Johann Wolfgang Goethe, "Wiederholte Spiegelungen," in *Tag- und Jahres-Hefte als Ergänzung meiner sonstigen Bekenntnisse*, Munich edition vol. 14, ed. Reiner Wild (Munich: Hanser, 1986), 568–569.

86. Husserl, *Ideen I*, Hua III.1, 147.

87. Cf. 61–64 above.

88. Husserl, *Krisis*, Appendix III, Hua VI, 371.

89. Cf. Figal, *Gegenständlichkeit*, §13, 126–141.

90. Cf. catalog for the exhibit from November 27, 2005, to February 26, 2006, at the Fondation Beyeler: *Wolfgang Laib. Das Vergängliche ist das Ewige* (Ostfildern-Ruit: Hatje Cantz, 2005).

91. Cf. catalog for the exhibit from November 26, 1993, to February 20, 1994, at the Kunsthaus Zurich: *Joseph Beuys* (Paris: Editions du Center Pompidou, 1994), 189–191.

92. Merleau-Ponty already emphasized this. Cf. Maurice Merleau-Ponty, *Phénoménologie de la perception* (Paris: Gallimard, 1945), 176: "En ce sens-là, comme toute oeuvre d'art, le poème existe à la manière d'une chose et ne subsiste pas éternellement à la manière d'une vérité."

93. Cf. Aristotle, *Metaphysics* VIII, 6, 1045b2; IX, 10, 1052a11.

94. Edmund Husserl, "Phantasie, Bildbewusstsein, Erinnerung. Zur Phänomenologie der anschaulichen Vergegenwärtigung," in Hua XXIII, ed. Eduard Marbach (The Hague: Nijhoff, 1980), 489. Cf. also the manuscripts on aesthetics and the following clarificational text: Gabriele Scaramuzza and Karl Schumann, "Ein Husserlmanuskript über Ästhetik," in *Husserl Studies* 7, no. 3 (1990): 165–177.

95. Husserl, "Phantasie, Bildbewusstsein, Erinnerung," Hua XXIII, 491.

96. Cf. Jean-Paul Sartre, *L'imaginaire. Psychologie phénoménologique de l'imagination* (Paris: Gallimard, 1940), 233.

97. The image exists in many variations, the first of which was exhibited in 1915. Cf. the catalog for the exhibition from March 23 to June 10, 2007, in the Kunsthalle Hamburg: *Das Schwarze Quadrat. Hommage an Malewitsch*, ed. Hubertus Gaßner (Ostfildern-Ruit: Hatje Cantz, 2007), 25.

98. Yet if this is the case, then the image that no longer depicts, or the abstract image, cannot be a thing-like illusion in the sense of a "mirage revealed to be mirroring air." Cf. Hans Rainer Sepp, "Crisis Imaginis: Sartre zur Lösung des Bildes vom Ding im Kunst-

werk," in *Kunst und Wahrheit. Festschrift für Walter Biemel zum 85. Geburtstag,* ed. Madalina Diaconu, 249–268, here 260 (Bucharest: Humanitas, 2003).

99. Husserl, "Phantasie, Bildbewusstsein, Erinnerung," Hua XXIII, 491.

100. Maurice Merleau-Ponty, *Le visible et l'invisible. Suivi de notes de travail,* ed. Claude Lefort (Paris: Gallimard, 1964), 195: "au lien [. . .] du visible et de l'armature intérieure qu'il manifeste et qu'il cache."

101. Merleau-Ponty, *Phénoménologie de la perception,* 177: "un noeud de significations vivantes."

102. Merleau-Ponty, *Phénoménologie de la perception,* 177: "Un roman, un poème, un tableau, un morceau de musique sont des individus, c'est-à-dire des êtres où l'on ne peut distinguer l'expression de l'exprimé, don't le sens n'est accessible que par un contact direct."

103. Edmund Husserl, *Ideen zu einer reinen Phänomenologie und phänomenologischen Philosophie. Zweites Buch,* Hua IV, ed. Marly Biemel (The Hague: Nijhoff, 1952), 144–147.

104. Merleau-Ponty, *Le visible et l'invisible,* 176: "Ceci ne peut arriver que si, en même temps que sentie du dedans, ma main est aussi accessible du dehors, tangible elle-même, par exemple, pour ma autre main."

105. Merleau-Ponty's term is "recroisement"; Merleau-Ponty, *Le visible et l'invisible,* 176.

106. Cf. Husserl, *Ideen II,* Hua IV, 148: "I do not see myself, my body, in the same way that I touch myself. That which I call my seen body is not a seeing-seen like my body, as touched body, is a touching-touched."

107. Cf. Merleau-Ponty, *Le visible et l'invisible,* 177.

108. Merleau-Ponty, *Le visible et l'invisible,* 204: "vérité ultime."

109. Cf. the explications of perception and λόγος on page 138.

110. Cf. Maurice Merleau-Ponty, "Le Philosophe et son Ombre," in *Signes* (Paris: Gallimard, 2008), 259–295.

111. Merleau-Ponty, *Le visible et l'invisible,* 183: "deux séries indéfinies d'images emboîtées qui n'appartiennent vraiment à aucune des deux surfaces, puisque chaucune n'est que la réplique de l'autre, qui font donc couple, un couple plus réel que chaucune d'elles."

112. Martin Heidegger, *Sein und Zeit,* GA 2, ed. Friedrich-Wilhelm von Herrmann (Frankfurt am Main: Klostermann, 1977), 38.

113. Martin Heidegger, "Die Idee der Philosophie und das Weltanschauungsproblem" (1919), in *Zur Bestimmung der Philosophie,* GA 56–57, ed. Bernd Heimbüchel (Frankfurt am Main: Klostermann, 1987), 1–117, here 87.

114. Heidegger, *Sein und Zeit,* GA 2, 42.

115. On this point, cf. Günter Figal, *Martin Heidegger. Phänomenologie der Freiheit,* 3rd ed. (Weinheim: Beltz Athenäum, 2000), 258–269.

116. Heidegger, "Der Ursprung des Kunstwerkes," GA 5, 53.

117. For a detailed account of this, cf. Figal, *Gegenständlichkeit,* §23, 233–242; Figal, "Zeigen und Sichzeigen," in *Verstehensfragen: Studien zur phänomenologisch-hermeneutischen Philosophie* (Tübingen: Mohr Siebeck, 2009), 200–210.

118. In this sense, Gottfried Boehm speaks of the "background potential of corporeal presence." Gestural showing comes from "out of the *interpretationless* off of a bodily

presence that is full of possibilities but never completely externalizes them through action." Gottfried Boehm, *Wie Bilder Sinn erzeugen: Die Macht des Zeigens* (Berlin: Akademie Verlag, 2007), 24. On the potentiality of a living being, cf. also Figal, *Gegenständlichkeit*, 389–390 and 397.

119. Hans-Georg Gadamer, "Bild und Gebärde," in Ästhetik und Poetik I. Kunst als Aussage, GW 8, 323–330, here 328.

120. The painting is held by the Fondation Beyeler, in Riehen near Basel.

121. Cf. Götz Adriani, ed., *Gerhard Richter. Bilder aus privaten Sammlungen* (Ostfildern-Ruit: Hatje Cantz, 2008), 95–97.

122. The piece is the first in the cycle *Images I*, written for piano.

123. Cf. the closing sequence of Michelangelo Antonioni's film *Blow Up* (1966).

124. On the concept of presentation [*Darstellung*], cf. Figal, *Gegenständlichkeit*, §11.

125. Plato, *Republic* 393c: Οὐκοῦν τό γε ὁμοιοῦν ἑαυτὸν ἄλλῳ ἢ κατὰ φωνὴν ἢ κατὰ σχῆμα μιμεῖσθαί ἐστιν ἐκεῖνον ᾧ ἄν τις ὁμοιοῖ.

126. On this, cf. Figal, *Gegenständlichkeit*, 85–91.

127. Kant, *Kritik der reinen Vernunft*, B 180, A 141; AA III, 136.

128. Johann Wolfgang Goethe, *Die Wahlverwandtschaften*, in *Epoche der Wahlverwandtschaften 1807–1814*, MA 9, ed. Christoph Siegrist et al. (Munich: Hanser, 1987), 283–529, here 286.

129. The painting is in the Museum of Modern Art in New York.

130. The painting is in the Kunsthalle in Hamburg.

131. Cf. Michel Foucault, *Les mots et les choses. Une archéologie des sciences humaines* (Paris: Gallimard, 2007), 19–31. Bernard Lypp, "Spiegel-Bilder," in *Was ist ein Bild?*, ed. Gottfried Boehm (Munich: Fink, 1994), 411–442.

132. The painting is in the Prado in Madrid.

133. Heidegger called Hölderlin the "poets' poet" and said that his poetry poetizes "the essence of poetry itself." Martin Heidegger, *Erläuterungen zu Hölderlins Dichtung*, GA 4, ed. Friedrich-Wilhelm von Herrmann (Frankfurt am Main: Klostermann, 1981), 34.

134. Goethe, *Die Wahlverwandtschaften*, MA 9, 286. [*Elective Affinities*, trans. David Constantine (New York: Oxford University Press, 1994). Translation emended.]

135. Pindar, "Zweite Olympische Ode." In *Siegeslieder*, Greek/German, ed. and trans. Dieter Bremer (Munich: Artemis & Winkler, 1992), Second Olympian Ode, 17–25, here 17, 1–2: Ἀ'ναξιμφόρμιγγες ὕμνοι, / τίνα θεόν, τίν' ἥρωα, τίνα δ' ἄνδρα κελαδήσομεν;

136. Pindar, "Zweite Pythische Ode." In Pindar, *Siegeslieder*, Greek/German, ed. and trans. Dieter Bremer (Munich: Artemis & Winkler, 1992), 120–127, here 121, 1–5: Μεγαλοπόλιες ὦ Συράκοκσαι, βαθυπολέμον / τέμενος Ἄρεος, ἀνδρῶν ἵππων τε σιδαροχαρ—/ μᾶν δαιμόνιαι τροφοί, / ὕμμιν τόδε τᾶν λιπαρᾶν ἀπὸ Θηβᾶν φέρων / μέλος ἔρχομαι ἀγγελίαν τετραορίας ἐλελίχθονος, / εὐάρματος Ἱέρωον ἐν ᾇ κρατέων.

137. Cf. Homer, Odyssey VIII, 72–79.

3. Art Forms

1. For an analytical discussion of John Cage's *4'33"* in the philosophy of music, cf. Stephen Davies, "John Cage 4'33": Is it Music?," in *Themes in the Philosophy of Music* (Oxford: Oxford University Press, 2003), 11–29.

2. Ludwig Wittgenstein, *Philosophische Untersuchungen*, in *Schriften*, vol. 1 (*Tractatus logico-philosophicus. Tagebücher 1914–1916. Philosophische Untersuchungen*) (Frankfurt am Main: Suhrkamp, 1969), 279–544, here 324.

3. Kant, *Critique of Judgment*, B 204–205; AA V, 320. [Translation by Pluhar.]

4. Cf. also John Sallis, *Transfigurements: On the True Sense of Art* (Chicago: University of Chicago Press, 2008), 41–54.

5. Kant, *Critique of Judgment*, B 205–206; AA V, 321. [Translation by Pluhar.]

6. Translation by Pluhar emended.

7. Translation by Pluhar emended.

8. Cf. 61–64.

9. Hegel, *Vorlesungen über die Ästhetik*, Werke vol. 13, 205.

10. Cf. Plato, *Republic*, 397b–403c; Plato, *Laws*, 652a–667b and 796d–802e.

11. Nietzsche, *Die Geburt der Tragödie*, KSA 1, 26. On the following discussion, cf. Günter Figal, *Nietzsche: Eine philosophische Einführung* (Stuttgart: Reclam, 1999), 63–102.

12. Nietzsche, *Die Geburt der Tragödie*, KSA 1, 25.

13. Nietzsche is quoting inexactly here. The beginning of the quotation actually runs: "In me, sensibility . . ." (*Briefwechsel zwischen Schiller und Goethe in den Jahren 1794–1805*, MA 8.1, edited by Manfred Beetz [Munich: Hanser, 1990], 167).

14. Nietzsche, *Die Geburt der Tragödie*, KSA 1, 43–44.

15. Cf. Paul Valéry, "Propos sur la poésie, in *Oeuvres*, vol. 1 (Paris: Gallimard, 1957), 1361–1378, here 1373–1374: "observez alors que le mouvement de votre âme, ou de votre attention, lorsqu'elle est assujettie à la poésie, toute soumise et docile aux impulsions successives du langage des dieux, va du *son* vers le *sens*, du contenant vers le contenu, tout se passant d'abord comme dans l'usage ordinaire du parler; mais il arrive ensuite, à chaque vers, que le pendule vivant soit ramené à son point de départ verbal et musical."

16. Nietzsche, *Die Geburt der Tragödie*, KSA 1, 43.

17. Arthur Schopenhauer, *Die Welt als Wille und Vorstellung* I, *Sämtliche Werke*, ed. Wolfgang Freiherr von Löhneysen, vol. 1 (Stuttgart: Cotta-Insel, 1960), 359.

18. Kant, *Critique of Judgment*, B 218–220, AA V, 329. Cf. 100.

19. The image is in the Basel Kunstmuseum. On this topic, cf. Michael Baumgartner, ed., *Paul Klee: Melodie und Rhythmus* (Ostfildern-Ruit: Hatje Cantz, 2006). A reproduction of the image is on p. 121.

20. The image is in the Saint Louis Art Museum. It is reproduced in Robert Storr, *Gerhard Richter: Malerei* (Ostfildern-Ruit: Hatje Cantz, 2002), 225.

21. Boehm, *Wie Bilder Sinn erzeugen*, 245–248.

22. Walter Benjamin, "Denkbilder," in *Gesammelte Schriften* (hereinafter cited as *Schriften*), vol. IV.1 (*Kleine Prosa, Baudelaire-Übertragungen*), ed. Tillman Rexroth (Frankfurt am Main: Suhrkamp, 1972), 305–438.

23. Martin Heidegger, "Die Zeit des Weltbildes" (1938), in *Holzwege*, GA 5, 75–113, here 89.
24. Heidegger, "Die Zeit des Weltbildes," GA 5, 89–90.
25. Hegel, *Vorlesungen über die Ästhetik* III, *Werke* vol. 15, 393. It is entirely in this sense of Hegel's that Lukács speaks in his early work of the "extensive totality of life" in regard to the novel. Georg Lukács, *Die Theorie des Romans: Ein geschichtlicher Versuch über die Formen der großen Epik* (Berlin: Cassirer, 1920), 31.
26. On these analyses of time, cf. Figal, *Gegenständlichkeit*, 319–338.
27. Cf. Jacob and Wilhelm Grimm, *Deutsches Wörterbuch*, vol. 10 (Leipzig: Hirzel, 1941), 3130.
28. Nietzsche, *Die Geburt der Tragödie*, KSA 1, 29–30.
29. Paul Valéry, "Degas Danse Dessin," in *Oeuvres* 2 (Paris: Gallimard, 1960), 1163–1240, here 1173: "des êtres d'une substance incomparable, translucide et sensible, chairs de verre follement irritables, dômes de soie flottante, couronnes hyalines, longues lanières vives toutes courues d'ondes rapides, franges et fronces qu'elles plissent, déplissent; cependant qu'elles se retournent, se déforment, s'envolent, aussi fluides que le fluide massif qui les presse, les épouse, les soutient de toutes parts, leur fait place à la moindre inflexion et les remplace dans leur forme."
30. Valéry, "Degas Danse Dessin," in *Oeuvres* 2, 1173: "danseuses absolues."
31. Valéry, "Degas Danse Dessin," in *Oeuvres* 2 1173: "idéal de la mobilité."
32. Gadamer, *Wahrheit und Methode*, GW 1, 109.
33. Martin Heidegger, "Vom Wesen und Begriff der φύσις. Aristotles, Physik B, 1 (1939)," in *Wegmarken*, GA 9, ed. Friedrich-Wilhelm von Herrmann (Frankfurt am Main: Klostermann, 1976), 239–301, here 284.
34. Gadamer, *Wahrheit und Methode*, GW 1, 109.
35. Nietzsche, *Die Geburt der Tragödie*, KSA 1, 28.
36. Gadamer, *Wahrheit und Methode*, GW 1, 110.
37. Cf. Paul Valéry, "Philosophie de la danse," in *Oeuvres* 1, 1390–1403, here 1401: "c'est un fait aisé à observer que tous les mouvements automatiques qui correspondent à un état de l'être, et non à un but figuré et localisé, prennent un régime périodique."
38. Cf. Valéry, "Philosophie de la danse," in *Oeuvres* 1, 1398: "il n'y a pas d'objet à saisir, à rejoindre ou à repousser ou à fiur."
39. Cf. Valéry, "Philosophie de la danse," in *Oeuvres* 1, 1398: "Rien n'existe au-delà du système qu'elle se forme par ses actes."
40. Cf. Valéry, "Philosophie de la danse," in *Oeuvres* 1, 1398: "Le philosophe exulte. Point d'extériorité!"
41. Plato, *Laws* 665a: κινήσεως τάξις.
42. Cf. Plato, *Laws* 665a: τῆς φωνῆς, τοῦ τε ὀξέος ἅμα καὶ βαρέος συγκεραννυμένων.
43. Cf. Thrasybulos Georgiades, *Der griechische Rhythmus: Musik, Reigen, Vers und Sprache* (Hamburg: von Schroder, 1949).
44. Nietzsche, *Die Geburt der Tragödie*, KSA 1, 33.
45. The following considerations refer strictly to the result of Nietzsche's confrontation with Wagner. Christophe Corbier has shown how this result takes shape in the thorough

engagement with rhythm: Christophe Corbier, "*Alogia* et eurhythmie chez Nietzsche," in *Nietzsche-Studien: Internationales Jahrbuch für die Nietzsche-Forschung* 38 (2009): 1–38.

46. Friedrich Nietzsche, *Menschliches, Allzumenschliches: Ein Buch für freie Geister*, vol. 2, KSA 2, ed. Giorgio Colli and Mazzino Montinari (Berlin: de Gruyter, 1980), 367–704, here 434.

47. Cf. Plato, *Republic* 401d; Plato, *Symposium* 196a.

48. Plato, *Republic* 401d.

49. Nietzsche, *Menschliches, Allzumenschliches* II, KSA 2, 434.

50. Richard Wagner, "Zukunftsmusik," in *Sämtliche Schriften und Dichtungen. Volks-Ausgabe* vol. 7, 6th ed. (Leipzig: Breitkopf & Härtel, 1912), 87–137, here 130.

51. Cf. Wagner, "Zukunftsmusik," in *Sämtliche Schriften und Dichtungen* 7, 125: "Let us begin by stating that *melody is the only form of music*."

52. Nietzsche, *Menschliches, Allzumenschliches* II, KSA 2, 434–435.

53. Hegel, *Vorlesungen über die Ästhetik* II, *Werke* vol. 14, 332.

54. Cf. Richard Leeman, *Cy Twombly: Malen, Zeichnen, Schreiben*, trans. Matthias Wolf (Munich: Schirmer, 2005), 166–185.

55. Cf. Wolfgang Fehrer, *Das japanische Teehaus* (Sulgen: Niggli, 2005), 111–115.

56. Friedrich Hölderlin, "Anmerkungen zur Antigonä," in *Sämtliche Werke und Briefe* (hereinafter cited as *Sämtliche Werke*), ed. Michael Knaupp, vol. 2 (Munich: Hanser, 1992), 369–376, here 369.

57. Nietzsche, *Die fröhliche Wissenschaft*, 84; KSA 3, 439.

58. Cf. Valéry, "Propos sur la poésie," in *Oeuvres* 1, 1370–1371.

59. Nietzsche, *Die fröhliche Wissenschaft*, 92; KSA 3, 447.

60. Cf. Valéry, "Propos sur la poésie," in *Oeuvres* 1, 1373: "En d'aures termes, dans les emplois pratiques ou abstraits du langage qui est spécifiquement *prose*, la forme ne se conserve pas, ne survit pas à la compréhension, elle se dissout dans la clarté, elle a agi, elle a fait comprendre, elle a vécu."

61. Rainer Maria Rilke, *Sonette an Orpheus*, in *Gedichte* 1910–1926, KA 2, 237–272, here 258.

62. On what follows, cf. Figal, "Sinn: Zur Bedeutung eines philosophischen Schlüsselbegriffs," in *Verstehensfragen: Studien zur phänomenologisch-hermeneutischen Philosophie* (Tübingen: Mohr Siebeck, 2009), 148–158.

63. Valéry, "Propos sur la poésie," in *Oeuvres* 1, 1363: "sensation d'univers."

64. Valéry, "Propos sur la poésie," in *Oeuvres* 1, 1363: "une tendance à percevoir un 'monde.'"

65. Cf. Valéry, "Propos sur la poésie," in *Oeuvres* 1, 1363: "Ils s'appellent les uns les autres, ils s'associent tout autrement que dans les conditions ordinaires."

66. Heidegger, "Der Ursprung des Kunstwerkes," GA 5, 62.

67. Heidegger, *Sein und Zeit*, GA 2, 46.

68. Cf. Martin Heidegger, *Logik: Die Frage nach der Wahrheit*, GA 21, ed. Walter Biemel (Frankfurt am Main: Klostermann 1976), 135–142.

69. Cf. Aristotle, *On Interpretation* 6; 17a25: κατάφασις δέ ἐστιν ἀπόφασις τινὸς κατὰ τινός; ed. Lorenzo Minio-Paluello (Oxford: Oxford University Press, 1949).

70. Martin Heidegger, "Logos (Heraklit, Fragment 50)," in *Vortäge und Aufsätze*, GA 7, ed. Friedrich-Wilhelm von Herrmann (Frankfurt am Main: Klostermann, 2000), 211–234, here 215.

71. Cf. Aristotle, *Physics* IV, 11; 219b6–9, ed. William David Ross (Oxford: Oxford University Press, 1936). On this, cf. Figal, *Gegenständlichkeit*, 308–309.

72. *Webster's New International Dictionary of the English Language*, ed. Philip Babcock Gove, vol. 3 (S–Z) (Chicago: Merriam-Webster, 1986), 2351.

73. As a supplement to the following considerations, cf. Figal, *Gegenständlichkeit*, 286–299.

74. Heidegger, "Logos," GA 7, 216.

75. Heidegger, *Sein und Zeit*, GA 2, 46.

76. Heidegger, "Logos," GA 7, 217.

77. Cf. Figal, *Gegenständlichkeit*, 68–69.

78. Hans-Georg Gadamer, "Über das Lesen von Bauten und Bildern (1979)," in *Ästhetik und Poetik I: Kunst als Aussage*, GW 8, 331–338, here 337.

79. Hans-Georg Gadamer, "Über das Lesen von Bauten und Bildern (1979)," GW 8 (Tübingen: Mohr Siebeck, 1993), 334.

80. On the notion of interpretation as presentation, cf. Figal, *Gegenständlichkeit*, 92–104.

81. The painting is located in the Alte Pinakothek in Munich.

82. In this sense, Kant calls music "a general language of sensations, as it were, that is comprehensible to *any* person." Kant, *Kritik der Urteilskraft*, B 219; AA V, 328.

83. This also goes for Nelson Goodman's concept of "semantic density." Cf. Nelson Goodman, *Languages of Art* (Indianapolis, Ind.: Hackett, 1976), 127–130.

84. On the latter point, cf. Gottfried Boehm, "Der Stumme Logos," in *Leibhaftige Vernunft: Spuren von Merleau-Pontys Denken*, ed. Alexandre Métraux and Bernhard Waldenfels, 289–304 (Munich: Fink, 1986).

85. Cf. 99.

86. Plato, *Sophist* 254d.

87. Cf. Plato, *Sophist* 253a: οἶον δεσμὸς διὰ πάντων κεχώρηκεν, ὥστε ἄνευ τινὸς αὐτῶν ἀδύνατον ἁρμόττειν καὶ τῶν ἄλλων ἕτερον ἑτέρῳ.

88. Heidegger, "Der Ursprung des Kunstwerkes," GA 5, 59.

89. Gadamer, *Wahrheit und Methode*, GW 1, 116.

90. Heidegger, "Der Ursprung des Kunstwerkes," GA 5, 65.

91. Kant, *Kritik der Urteilskraft*, B 179; AA V, 306. Cf. 50–59.

92. Cf. Aristotle, *Nicomachean Ethics* VI.

93. Cf. Aristotle, *Metaphysics* VII, 7, 1032a32–1032b1.

94. Cf. Aristotle, *Metaphysics* VII, 7, 1032b11–12: ὥστε συμβαίνει τρόπον τινὰ τὴν ὑγίειαν ἐξ ὑγιείας γίγνεσθαι καὶ τὴν οἰκίαν ἐξ οἰκίας.

95. Heidegger, "Der Wille zur Macht als Kunst," GA 43, 219.

96. Cf. Friedrich Teja Bach, *ArchiSkulptur: Dialoge zwischen Architektur und Plastik vom 18. Jahrhundert bis heute*, ed. Markus Brüderlin, and published on the occasion of the exhi-

bition from October 3, 2004, to January 30, 2005, in at the Fondation Beyeler (Ostfildern-Ruit: Hatje Cantz Verlag, 2004).

97. For example the *Brick Sculpture* (1994) in Humlebæk, Denmark. The sculpture is depicted in Juul Michael Holm and Paul Erik Tøjner, eds., *Per Kirkeby* (Humlebæk: Louisiana Museum of Modern Art, 2009), 141.

98. Kant, *Kritik der Urteilskraft*, B 179; AA V, 306.

4. Nature

1. Kant, *Kritik der Urteilskraft*, B 180; AA V, 307.
2. Adorno, *Ästhetische Theorie*, GS 7, 99.
3. Cf. 11.
4. Kant, *Kritik der Urteilskraft*, B 181; AA V, 307.
5. Heraclitus, VS 22 B 123, 178.
6. Adorno, *Ästhetische Theorie*, GS 7, 98.
7. Cf. 82–96.
8. Cf. Plato, *Gorgias* 483e–486c; *Republic* 358b–362c.
9. First described in Kant, *Grundlegung zur Metaphysik der Sitten*, AA IV, 440.
10. Adorno, *Ästhetische Theorie*, GS 7, 121.
11. Cf. Aristotle, *Physics* II, 8, 199a15–17: ὅλως δὲ ἡ τέχνη τὰ μὲν ἐπιτελεῖ ἃ ἡ φύσις ἀδυνατεῖ ἀπεργάσασθαι, τὰ δὲ μιμεῖται.
12. Cf. Aristotle, *Physics* II, 8, 199a9–13.
13. Cf. Aristotle, *Physics* II, 1, 192b20–24: ὡς οὔσης τῆς φύσεως ἀρχῆς τινὸς καὶ αἰτίας τοῦ κινεῖσθαι καὶ ἠρεμεῖν ἐν ᾧ ὑπάρχει πρώτως καθ' αὑτὸ καὶ μὴ κατὰ συμβεβηκός.
14. Cf. Aristotle, *Metaphysics* V, 4, 1014b16–17.
15. Aristotle, *Physics* II, 1, 193a35–36: ἐν τοῖς φύσει συνιοταμένοις.
16. Cf. Aristotle, *Physics* II, 1, 193a34–193b3.
17. Cf. Aristotle, *Physics* II, 1, 193b12.
18. Cf. Aristotle, *Metaphysics* VII, 7, 1032b11–12: συμβαίνει [...] γίγνεσθαι [...] τὴν οἰκίαν ἐξ οἰκίας, τῆς ἄνευ ὕλης τὴν ἔχουσαν ὕλην.
19. Cf. 133–134.
20. Cf. Aristotle, *Physics* II, 1, 193a10–11: τὸ πρῶτον ἐνυπάρκον ἑκάστῳ, ἀρρύθμιστον [ὂν] καθ' ἑαυτό.
21. Kant, *Kritik der reinen Vernunft*, AA iv, B xvi.
22. Cf. Paul Valéry, "L'homme et la coquille," in *Oeuvres* 1, 886–907, here 899.
23. Cf. Valéry, "L'homme et la coquille," in *Oeuvres* 1, 897: "Nature, c'est-à-dire: la *Produisante* ou la *Productrice*. C'est à elle que nous donnons à produire tout ce que nous ne savons pas *faire*, et qui, pourtant, nous semble *fait*."
24. Cf. Valéry, "L'homme et la coquille," in *Oeuvres* 1, 894.
25. Cf. Aristotle, *Metaphysics* VII, 7, 1032b1.
26. Valéry, "L'homme et la coquille," in *Oeuvres* 1, 904–905: "Peut-être, ce que nous appelons la *perfection* dans l'art [...], n'est-elle que le sentiment de désirer ou de trouver, dans une oeuvre humaine, cette certitude dans l'exécution, cette nécessité d'origine inté-

rieure, et cette liaison indissoluble et réciproque de la figure avec la matière que le moindre coquillage me fair voir?"

27. Cf. Plato, *Timaeus* 28a.

28. Cf. Plato, *Timaeus* 28c: τὸν μὲν οὖν ποιητὴν καὶ πατέρα τοῦδε τοῦ παντὸς εὑρεῖν τε ἔργον καὶ εὑρόντα εἰς πάντας ἀδύνατον λέγειν.

29. Cf. Benedictus de Spinoza, *Ethica* I, Propositio 29, Scholium: "per naturam naturantem nobis intelligendum est [. . .] Deus, quatenus ut causa libera consideratur." The *Ethics* is cited according to *Opera: Werke,* Lateinisch und Deutsch, vol. 2, ed. Konrad Blumenstock (Darmstadt: Wissenschaftliche Buchgesellschaft, 1967), 84–503, here 132.

30. Cf. Aristotle, *Physics* II, 1, 193a12–17.

31. Cf. Aristotle, *Nicomachean Ethics* I, 1, 1094a9–28.

32. Edgar Kaufmann Jr. *Fallingwater: A Frank Lloyd Wright Country House* (New York: Abbeville Press, 1986), 49.

33. Heidegger, *Vom Wesen und Begriff der* Φύσις, GA 9, 301.

34. Heidegger, *Vom Wesen und Begriff der* Φύσις, GA 9, 300. Here Heidegger translates Heraclitus' statement φύσις κρύπτεσθαι φιλεῖ as "Being loves to conceal itself." Cf. also Martin Heidegger, *Einführung in die Metaphysik*, GA 40, ed. Petra Jaeger (Frankfurt am Main: Klostermann, 1983), 16–17.

35. Heidegger, "Der Ursprung des Kunstwerkes," GA 5, 27.

36. Martin Heidegger, "Vom Ursprung des Kunstwerkes (Erste Ausarbeitung)," in *Heidegger-Lesebuch*, ed. Günter Figal (Frankfurt am Main: Klostermann, 2007), 149–170, here 156.

37. Heidegger, "Der Ursprung des Kunstwerkes," GA 5, 35.

38. Heidegger, "Der Ursprung des Kunstwerkes," GA 5, 32. On the notion that the word, too, belongs to "earth," cf. Martin Heidegger, *Unterwegs zur Sprache*, GA 12, ed. Friedrich-Wilhelm von Herrmann (Pfullingen: Neske, 1959), 208–209.

39. Heidegger, "Der Ursprung des Kunstwerkes," GA 5, 32.

40. Adorno, *Ästhetische Theorie*, GS 7, 91.

41. Cited in Gisela Jahn and Anette Petersen-Brandhorst, *Erde und Feuer: Traditionelle japanische Keramik der Gegenwart* (Munich: Hirmer, 1984), 205.

42. Depicted in Jahn and Brandhorst, *Erde und Feuer*, 42.

43. According to Grimm, *Deutsches Wörterbuch*, 1390–1391, the old Nordic word *gardr*, "fence, grating, wall"; in the Nordic languages, *gard* can mean fenced-in property, just as the English word "yard." The French *jardin* and the Italian *giardino* are loan words that trace back to *gard*. The Latin *hortus* and the Greek χόρτος mean the same thing as this word.

44. Cf. Fondation Beyeler's catalog, *Wolfgang Laib*.

45. On the concept of orientation in general, cf. Werner Stegmaier, *Philosophie der Orientierung* (New York: de Gruyter, 2008).

46. Cf. Heidegger, *Sein und Zeit*, GA 2, 111–119; cf. also Martin Heidegger, *Prolegomena zur Geschichte des Zeitbegriffs*, GA 20, ed. Petra Jaeger (Frankfurt am Main: Klostermann, 1994), 274–278. For an elaboration, cf. Figal, *Martin Heidegger: Phänomenologie der Freiheit*, 93–97.

47. Heidegger, *Sein und Zeit*, GA 2, 217.

48. Husserl, *Ideen* I, Hua III.1, 91.

49. Though it is not necessary here, one could turn to Husserl's analyses of attention for a more exact description of these matters. For an interpretation of these analyses that use hearing as their basis, cf. David Espinet, *Phänomenologie des Hörens* (Tübingen: Mohr Siebeck, 2009), 102–116. Cf. also Anthony Steinbock, "Affektion und Aufmerksamkeit," in *Die erscheinende Welt: Festschrift für Klaus Held*, ed. Heinrich Hüni and Peter Trawny, 241–273 (Berlin: Duncker & Humbolt, 2002); Bernhard Waldenfels, *Phänomenologie der Aufmerksamkeit* (Frankfurt am Main: Suhrkamp, 2004).

50. Peter Handke, *Versuch über die Müdigkeit* (Frankfurt am Main: Suhrkamp, 1989), 52.

51. Handke, *Versuch über die Müdigkeit*, 53.

52. Heidegger, *Sein und Zeit*, GA 2, 247.

53. Cf. Nietzsche, *Die fröhliche Wissenschaft*, 301; KSA 3, 540. On this point, cf. Günter Figal, "Nietzsches Philosophie der Interpretation," in *Nietzsche-Studien* vol. 29 (2000): 1–11.

54. Cf. Günter Figal, "Subjekt und Objekt," in *Verstehensfragen*, 244–257.

55. Handke, *Versuch über die Müdigkeit*, 68.

56. Heidegger, *Sein und Zeit*, GA 2, 180.

57. Ernst Jünger, *Das abenteuerliche Herz*, 2nd ed., in *Sämtliche Werke* (hereinafter cited as SW), volume 9 (Essays III: Das abenteuerliche Herz) (Stuttgart: Klett-Cotta, 1979), 177–330, here 217.

58. Cf. Joachim Gasquet, "Ce qu'il m'a dit," in *Conversations avec Cézanne*, ed. Michael Doran, 106–161 (Paris: Macula, 1978).

59. Cf. Gasquet, "Ce qu'il m'a dit," 109: "réceptacle de sensations."

60. Cf. Gasquet, "Ce qu'il m'a dit," 110: "Le paysage [. . .], s'humanise, se pense en moi."

61. Cf. Gasquet, "Ce qu'il m'a dit," 109: "s'il intervient."

62. The notion that there is an "echo of images," that is, of what is imagistically visible in the world, is accentuated differently in Jünger, *Das abenteuerliche Herz*, 327–328: "With the deep, sensual gaze that we direct toward images, we bring an offering; and we are heard according to our donation."

63. Cf. Gasquet, "Ce qu'il m'a dit," 109: "Toute sa volonté doit être de silence. Il doit faire taire en lui toutes les voix préjugés, oublier, oublier, faire silence, être un echo parfair. Alors, sur sa plaque sensible, tout le paysage s'inscrira. Pour le fixer sur la toile, l'extérioriser, le métier interviendra ensuite, mais le métier respecteux qui, lui aussi, n'est prêt qu'a obéir."

64. Bruno Taut, *Gedanken über Katsura, Mai 34*, facsimile (Tokyo: Iwanami, 2004). Cf. Bruno Taut, *Ich liebe die japanische Kultur*, ed. Manfred Speidel (Berlin: Gebrüder Mann Verlag, 2003), 96, reprinted in Stephen Adiss, *Japan und der Westen: Die erfüllte Leere* (Cologne: DuMont, 2007), 265.

65. Husserl, *Ideen* I, Hua III.1, 48.

66. Edmund Husserl, *Cartesianische Meditationen*, in *Cartesianische Meditationen und Pariser Vorträge*, Hua I, ed. Stephan Strasser (The Hague: Nijhoff, 1963), 124.

67. Husserl, *Cartesianische Meditationen,* Hua I, 127.

68. Maurice Merleau-Ponty, "Le doute de Cézanne," in *Sens et non-sens* (Paris: Gallimard, 1948), 15–44, here 23: "la coupure [. . .] entre l'ordre spontané des choses perçues et l'ordre humain des idées et des sciences."

69. Merleau-Ponty, "Le doute de Cézanne," 23: "c'est le monde primordial que Cézanne a voulu peindre."

70. Merleau-Ponty, "Le doute de Cézanne," 23: "c'est sur le socle de 'nature' que nous construisons des sciences."

71. Merleau-Ponty, "Le doute de Cézanne," 32: "au fonds d'expérience muette et solitaire sur lequel sont bâtis la culture et l'échange des idées."

72. Cf. Merleau-Ponty, "Le doute de Cézanne," 23: "ses tableaux donnent l'impression de la nature à son origine."

73. Husserl, *Cartesianische Meditationen,* Hua I, 137.

74. Slightly later (140), Husserl also speaks of the "primordial sphere."

75. Merleau-Ponty, "Le doute de Cézanne," 28: "C'est un monde sans familiarité où l'on n'est pas bien, qui interdit tout effusion humaine."

76. Cf. 76–92.

77. Cf. Merleau-Ponty, "Le doute de Cézanne," 32: "l'artiste lance son oeuvre comme un homme a lancé la première parole, sans savoir si elle sera autre chose qu'un cri, si elle pourra se détacher du flux de vie individuelle."

78. Merleau-Ponty, "Le doute de Cézanne," 23: "ses tableaux donnent l'impression de la nature à son origine."

79. Husserl, *Cartesianische Meditationen,* Hua I, 128.

80. Cf. Husserl, *Ideen* II, Hua IV, 144–145.

81. Husserl, *Cartesianische Meditationen,* Hua I, 128.

82. Merleau-Ponty, *Le visible et l'invisible,* 175: "chair des choses."

83. Merleau-Ponty, *Le visible et l'invisible,* 172: "l'entrelacs." Husserl, too, already speaks of an interweaving of perceived nature with the body. Cf. Edmund Husserl, *Ideen zu einer reinen Phänomenologie und phänomenologischen Philosophie.* Third volume, Hua V, ed. Marly Biemel (The Hague: Nijhoff, 1952), 124.

84. Merleau-Ponty, *Le visible et l'invisible,* 172: "chiasme."

85. Merleau-Ponty, *Le visible et l'invisible,* 204: "réversibilité."

86. Merleau-Ponty, *Le visible et l'invisible,* 180: "un être à deux feuillets."

87. Gasquet, "Ce qu'il m'a dit," 109: "un réceptacle de sensations," "un appareil enregistreur."

88. Cf. Maurice Merleau-Ponty, *L'Oeuil et l'esprit* (Paris: Gallimard, 1964), 16.

89. Gasquet, "Ce qu'il m'a dit," 113: "Je commence à me séparer du paysage, à le voir."

90. Emerson understands landscapes as nature in this sense: "The charming landscape which I saw this morning, is indubitably made up of some twenty or thirty farms. Miller owns this field, Locke that, and Manning the woodland beyond. But none of them owns the landscape." If the landscape as such is nature, then nature can also be taken as landscape. Then, as for Handke, "everything is together": "the integrity of impression made

by manifold natural objects." Ralph Waldo Emerson, "Nature," in *Essays and Lectures* (New York: Penguin, 1983), 5–49, here 9.

91. Gasquet, "Ce qu'il m'a dit," 109: "traduire inconsciemment."

92. Martin Heidegger, *Parmenides,* GA 54, ed. Manfred Frings (Frankfurt am Main: Klostermann, 1982), 18. Cf. Günter Figal, "Seinserfahrung und Übersetzung: hermeneutische Überlegungen zu Heidegger," in Figal, *Zu Heidegger: Antworten und Fragen* (Frankfurt am Main: Klostermann, 2009), 173–184.

93. Martin Heidegger, "Der Spruch des Anaximander," in *Holzwege,* GA 5, 321–373, here 329.

94. Gasquet, "Ce qu'il m'a dit," 109: "s'inscrira."

95. Gasquet, "Ce qu'il m'a dit," 110: "Le paysage [. . .], s'humanise, se pense en moi."

96. Merleau-Ponty, *L'Oeuil et l'esprit,* 16.

97. Gasquet, "Ce qu'il m'a dit," 109.

98. Gasquet, "Ce qu'il m'a dit," 109: "L'art est une harmonie parallèle à la nature."

99. On this notion, cf. Erich Rothacker, *Das 'Buch der Natur,'* ed. Wilhelm Perpeet (Bonn: Bouvier, 1979); Ernst Robert Curtius, *Europäische Literatur und lateinisches Mittelalter,* 6th ed. (Bern: A. Francke, 1967), 323–329; Hans Blumenberg, *Die Lesbarkeit der Welt* (Frankfurt am Main: Suhrkamp, 1981), 180–198 and 214–299.

100. Cf. Gasquet, "Ce qu'il m'a dit," 109: "il sait bien sa langue, le texte qu'il déchiffre, les deux textes parallèls, la nature vue, la nature sentie, celle qui est là . . . (*il montrait la plaine verte et bleue*) celle qui est ici (*il se frappait le front*)."

101. Cf. Gasquet, "Ce qu'il m'a dit," 109: "Je prends, à droite, à gauche, ici là, partout, ses tons, ses couleurs, ses nuances, je les fixes, je les rapproche. . . . Ils font des lignes, Ils deviennent des objects, des rochers, des arbres, sans que j'y songe. Ils prennent un volume. Ils ont une valeur. Si ces volumes, si ces valeurs correspondent sur ma toile, dans ma sensibilité, aux plans, aux taches que j'ai, qui sont là sous nos yeux, eh bien! ma toile joint les mains."

102. This "all over" of the paint is executed even more decisively in others works of Cézanne's. In the *Montagne Saint-Victoire* located in Basel's Kunstmuseum, the sky's spotty blue is framed by the plain's green and a large tree in the left margin. On this painting and on Cézanne's style in general, cf. Gottfried Boehm, *Paul Cézanne: Montagne Sainte-Victoire* (Frankfurt am Main: Insel, 1988).

103. Gasquet, "Ce qu'il m'a dit," 113: "tout est dense et fluide à la fois."

104. Cf. Aristotle, *De Anima* II, 11, 422b23–27.

105. Rainer Maria Rilke, "Briefe über Cézanne," in *Schriften,* KA 4, ed. Horst Nalewski (Frankfurt am Main: Insel, 1996), 594–638, here 614.

106. Gasquet, "Ce qu'il m'a dit," 113: "Une logique aérienne,colorée, remplace brusquement la sombre, la têtue géométrie. [. . .] Je vois. Par taches. [. . .] Il n'y a plus que des couleurs."

107. Cf. Plato, *Republic* 507d–e; Aristotle, *De Anima* II, 7, 418a26–27.

108. Johann Wolfgang Goethe, *Zur Farbenlehre,* MA 10, ed. Karl Richter (Munich: Hanser, 1989), 20.

109. Hegel, *Vorlesungen über die Ästhetik* III, *Werke* vol. 15, 132.
110. Goethe, *Zur Farbenlehre*, MA 10, 20.
111. Merleau-Ponty, "Le doute de Cézanne," 23: "l'ordre humain des idées et des sciences."
112. Cf. Aristotle, *De Anima* III, 8, 431b28–432a1 and II, 12, 424a17–19.
113. Cf. Günter Figal, "Idee," in *Religion in Geschichte und Gegenwart* (RGG), 4th ed., vol. 4 (I–K) (Tübingen: Mohr Siebeck, 2001), 16–18.
114. Liddell and Scott, *A Greek-English Lexicon* 6, 482: "appearance."
115. Cf. Aristotle, *De Anima* III, 2, 426a27–426b7: εἰ δ' ἡ φωνὴ συμφωνία τίς ἐστιν, ἡ δὲ φωνὴ καὶ ἡ ἀκοὴ ἔστιν ὡς ἕν ἐστι [. . .], λόγος δ' ἡ συμφωνία, ἀνάγκη καὶ τὴν ἀκοὴν λόγον τινὰ εἶναι. καὶ διὰ τοῦτο καὶ φθείρει ἕκαστον ὑπερβάλλον, καὶ τὸ ὀξὺ καὶ τὸ βαρύ, τὴν ἀκοήν. ὁμοίως δὲ καὶ ἐν χυμοῖς τὴν γεῦσιν, καὶ ἐν χρώμασι τὴν ὄψιν τὸ σφόδρα λαμπρὸν ἢ ζοφερόν, καὶ ἐν ὀσφρήσει ἡ ἰσχυρὰ ὀσμή, καὶ γλυκεῖα καὶ πικρά, ὡς λόγου τινὸς ὄντος τῆς αἰσθήσεως.
116. Cf. 127–129.
117. Aristotle, *De Interpretatione* I, 16a4–5.
118. Cf. Aristotle, *De Anima* III, 3, 432a4–5: ἐν τοῖς εἴδεσι τοῖς αἰσθητοῖς τὰ νοητά ἐστι.
119. Cf. Aristotle, *De Anima* III, 3, 432a8.
120. Valéry, "L'homme et la coquille," in *Oeuvres* 1, 905: "liaison indissoluble et réciproque."
121. Cf. 56–57.

5. Space

1. Cf. Klaus Bussmann, ed., *Eduardo Chillida: Hauptwerke* (Mainz: Chorus Verlag, 2003), 92–93.
2. Cf. Figal, *Gegenständlichkeit*, 170–173 and 301–355.
3. In this sense, Picht speaks of the "presentational space" of art as the "presentational space of imagination." Cf. Picht, *Kunst und Mythos*, 224–269.
4. Cf. Niklas Maak, *Der Architekt am Strand: Le Corbusier und das Geheimnis der Seeschnecke* (Munich: Hansa, 2010), 8.
5. Tadao Ando, "Das Museum der Gegenwartskunst auf Naoshima," in Werner Blaser, *Tadao Ando: Architektur der Stille/Architecture of Silence*, 6–11, here 8 (Basel: Birkhäuser, 2001). Cf. also the chapter "The Importance of Sites," in Yann Nussaume, *Tadao Ando* (Basel: Birkhäuser, 2009), 111–114.
6. Martin Heidegger, "Die Kunst und der Raum," in *Aus der Erfahrung des Denkens*, GA 13, ed. Hermann Heidegger (Frankfurt am Main: Klostermann, 1983), 203–210, here 208 and 209.
7. Heidegger, "Die Kunst und der Raum," GA 13, 208.
8. Cf. René Descartes, *Principia philosophiae* I, 53, *Oeuvres de Descartes*, ed. Charles Adam and Paul Tannery, vol. 8.1 (Paris: J. Vrin, 1905), 25: "Extensio in longum, latum et profundum."
9. Heidegger, "Der Kunst und der Raum," GA 13, 206.

10. Cf. 124–127.

11. Cf. Heidegger, *Sein und Zeit*, GA 2, 111–119; Heidegger, *Prolegomena zur Geschichte des Zeitbegriffs*, GA 20. For an elaboration, cf. Figal, *Phänomenologie der Freiheit*, 93–97.

12. Martin Heidegger, "Das Ding (1950)," in *Vorträge und Aufsätze*, GA 7, ed. Friedrich-Wilhelm von Herrmann (Frankfurt am Main: Klostermann, 2000), 165–187, here 178–179.

13. Cf. Heidegger, "Das Ding (1950)," GA 7, 179–182.

14. Martin Heidegger, "Bauen Wohnen Denken," in *Vorträge und Aufsätze*, GA 7 ed. Friedrich-Wilhelm von Herrmann (Frankfurt am Main: Klostermann, 2000), 145–164, here 155.

15. Heidegger, "Die Kunst und der Raum," GA 13, 206. The notion of release already occurs in *Being and Time*, but is not developed there as thoroughly as it is in later works. Cf. Figal, *Phänomenologie der Freiheit*, 84–93 and 143.

16. Grimm elaborates this meaning as *locum cedere*; *Deutsches Wörterbuch*, vol. 3, 246.

17. Heidegger, "Die Kunst und der Raum," GA 13, 207.

18. Heidegger, "Bauen Wohnen Denken," GA 7, 156.

19. Heidegger, "Die Kunst und der Raum," GA 13, 208.

20. Heidegger, "Bauen Wohnen Denken," GA 7, 156.

21. Givenness has become a central theme of phenomenology thanks to Jean-Luc Marion. Cf. Jean-Luc Marion, *Etant donné: Essai d'une phénoménologie de la donation* (Paris: Presses Universitaires de France, 1997). Cf. also Marion, "Die Wiederaufnahme der Gegebenheit durch Husserl und Heidegger," in *Heidegger und Husserl: Neue Perspektiven*, ed. Günter Figal and Hans-Helmuth Gander (Frankfurt am Main: Klostermann, 2009), 25–42. While Marion, following Heidegger, takes givenness to be an event, I am here signaling a spatially oriented conception of givenness that itself needs to be systematically developed. A closer discussion with Marion's conception would be part of this development.

22. In Plato's *Timaeus* (49a), the place (χώρα) is named the reception of all becoming, and compared to a wet nurse: πάσης εἶναι γενέσεως ὑποδοχὴν αὐτὴν οἷον τιθήνην. Shortly thereafter (52b), place is described as that which assures a home to everything that is created: ἕδραν δὲ παρέχον ὅσα ἔχει γένεσιν πᾶσιν. On the Platonic conception of χώρα, cf. John Sallis, *Chorology: On Beginning in Plato's Timaeus* (Bloomington: Indiana University Press, 1999), esp. 91–145.

23. Cf. Aristotle, *Physics* IV, 4, 212a6: τὸ πέρας τοῦ περιέχοντος σώματος.

24. Thus it is not surprising that Heidegger, without expressly indicating it, can make note of the cited Aristotle passage in his discussion of spaces in "Bauen Wohnen Denken." Cf. Heidegger, "Bauen Wohnen Denken," GA 7, 156 note h.

25. Heidegger, "Bauen Wohnen Denken," GA 7, 156.

26. Heidegger, "Die Kunst und der Raum," GA 13, 208.

27. Heidegger, "Der Ursprung des Kunstwerkes," GA 5, 63.

28. Cf. Heidegger, "Bauen Wohnen Denken," GA 7, 151: Here dwelling is defined as "protecting," and the latter is said to occur "when, in advance, we allow something to remain in its essence."

29. Cf. Eliza E. Rathbone, "Der Rothko Room in der Phillips Collection," in *Mark Rothko: A Consummated Experience Between Picture and Onlooker* (Ostfildern-Ruit: Hatje Cantz, 2001), 47–53.

30. Cited by J. E. B. Breslin, *Mark Rothko: A Biography* (Chicago: University of Chicago Press, 1993), 375–376: "It would be good if little places could be set up all over the country, like a little chapel where the traveler, or wanderer could come for an hour to meditate upon a single painting hung in a small room, and by itself." This dream was first realized by Duncan Phillips, then subsequently and most impressively in the Rothko Chapel of Houston, Texas.

31. Gadamer, *Wahrheit und Methode*, GW 1, 116. Cf. 167–168.

32. Johann Wolfgang Goethe, *Italienische Reise*, MA 15, ed. Andreas Beyer (Munich: Hanser, 1992), 42.

33. On the conception of hermeneutic space, cf. Figal, *Gegenständlichkeit*, esp. 153–173.

34. Cf. 91 above.

35. The painting is in the National Gallery of Art in Washington, D.C.

36. The painting is in the Stedelijk Museum in Amsterdam.

37. Cf. John O'Neill, ed., *Barnett Newman: Selected Writings and Interviews* (Berkeley: University of California Press, 1992), 178. Referring to an exhibition in 1951, he states, "There is a tendency to look at large pictures from a distance. The large pictures in this exhibition are intended to be seen from a short distance."

38. Cf. 111–113; 136.

39. On spatial presentations in poetry, cf. Gaston Bachelard, *La poétique de l'espace* (Paris: Presses Universitaires de France, 1957).

40. Cf. Merleau-Ponty, "L'Oeuil et l'esprit," 61: "son effort pour se dégager de l'illusionisme."

41. Merleau-Ponty, "L'Oeuil et l'esprit," 47: "sans cachette."

42. Merleau-Ponty, "L'Oeuil et l'esprit," 65: "La profondeur ainsi comprise est plutôt l'expérience [. . .] d'une 'localité' globale où tout est à la fois, dont hauteur, largeur, et distance sont abstraites, d'une voluminosité qu'on exprime d'un mot en disant qu'une chose est là."

43. Cf. Merleau-Ponty, "L'Oeuil et l'esprit," 64.

44. Cf. Merleau-Ponty, "L'Oeuil et l'esprit," 66: "Il a été droit au solide, à l'espace—et constaté que dans cet espace [. . .] les chose se mettent à bouger couleur contre couleur, à moduler dans l'instabilité. C'est donc ensemble qu'il faut chercher l'espace et le contenu."

45. Mark Rothko, *The Artist's Reality: Philosophies of Art* (New Haven, Conn.: Yale University Press, 2004), 44: "The painter must [. . .] do consciously what we all do unconsciously—construct his third dimension. And he can accomplish his task only as we accomplish ours, by giving tactile values to retinal impressions. His first business, therefore, is to rouse the tactile sense."

46. Cf. Rothko, *The Artist's Reality*, 47: "In painting, plasticity is achieved by a sensation of movement both into the canvas and out from the space anterior to the surface of the canvas."

47. The painting is depicted in the exhibition catalog produced by the Fondation Beyeler, *Mark Rothko: A Consummated Experience Between Picture and Onlooker* (Ostfildern-Ruit: Hatje Cantz, 2001), 106.

48. "Space—as well as motion in a canvas is useless unless you are a raconteur"—so says someone who represents motion and space in an image. "What you mistake for space is breathingness." Cited in Oliver Wick, "'Do they negate each other, modern and classical?': Mark Rothko und die Sehnsucht nach Tradition," in *Mark Rothko: Retrospektive*, ed. Hubertus Gaßner et al. (Munich: Hirmer, 2008), 12–28, here 26 note 16. The notebooks from which the remarks stem are unpublished.

49. On this, cf. Gottfried Boehm, "Das Lebendige: Rothkos Zugänge zum Bild," in *Mark Rothko: Retrospektive*, ed. Hubertus Gaßner et al. (Munich: Hirmer, 2008), 180–184, here 182–183 and 184 note 9.

50. Rothko, *The Artist's Reality*, 47.

51. Heidegger, "Die Kunst und der Raum," GA 13, 209.

52. Heidegger, "Das Ding (1950)," GA 7, 170.

53. [Lao-Tzu. *Tao Te Ching: A New Translation With Commentary*, trans. Ellen Chen (St. Paul, Minnesota: Paragon House, 1989).] Heidegger knew this work and even assisted with a German translation. On this, cf. Otto Pöggeler, "West-East Dialogue: Heidegger and Lao-Tzu"; Paul Shih-Yi Hsiao, "Heidegger and Our Translation of the *Tao Te Ching*," both in *Heidegger and Asian Thought*, ed. Graham Parkes (Honolulu: University of Hawaii Press, 1987), 47–78 and 93–103, respectively. Cf. also Paul Shih-Yi Hsiao, "Wir trafen uns am Holzmarkt," in *Erinnerungen an Martin Heidegger*, ed. Günther Neske (Pfullingen: Neske, 1977), 119–129.

54. Edmund Husserl, *Ding und Raum: Vorlesungen 1907*, Hua XVI, ed. Ulrich Claesges (The Hague: Nijhoff, 1973), 261.

55. Cf. Husserl, *Ding und Raum*, Hua XVI, 63.

56. Husserl, *Ding und Raum*, Hua XVI, 261.

57. Cf. for instance *Blue Nude I* from 1952 (Fondation Beyeler) or *Venus* from the same year (National Gallery of Art, Washington D.C.). Both works are depicted in Pia Müller-Tamm, *Henri Matisse: Figur Farbe Raum* (Ostfildern-Ruit: Hatje Cantz, 2005), 274–275.

58. The image is in the Musée national d'art moderne at the Centre Pompidou in Paris.

59. Bertolt Brecht, "Rudern, Gespräche," in *Werke*, annotated Berlin and Frankfurt edition, ed. Werner Hecht et al., vol. 12 (Gedichte II: Sammlungen 1938–1956) (Berlin: Aufbau Verlag, 1988), 307.

60. Friedrich Hölderlin, "Anmerkungen zum Oedipus," in *Sämtliche Werke und Briefe*, ed. Michael Knaupp, vol. 2, 309–316, here 310 (Munich: Hanser, 1992).

61. The painting is in the Museum of Modern Art in New York.

62. The series *8 Grey Paintings* by Gerhard Richter is located in the Städtisches Museum Abteiberg. Robert Rauschenberg's *White Painting (Three Panel)* is located in the San Francisco Museum of Modern Art.

63. Cf. Democritus, VS 68 B 125, 168.

64. F. W. J. Schelling, *Philosophie der Offenbarung*, SW II, 2, 337.

65. Cf. 38–95.

66. Husserl, *Ding und Raum,* Hua XVI, 124.

67. Walter Benjamin, "Geschichte der Photographie (1931)," in *Gesammelte Schriften* II.1, ed. Rolf Tiedemann and Hermann Schweppenhäuser, 368–385, here 378 (Frankfurt am Main: Suhrkamp, 1977).

68. Benjamin, "Geschichte der Photographie," *Schriften* II.1, 378. Benjamin took over this formulation in a shortened form in his essay on the artwork in the age of mechanical reproduction, the version that is usually cited. Cf. Walter Benjamin, "Das Kunstwerk im Zeitalter seiner technischen Reproduzierbarkeit," 2nd ed., in *Gesammelte Schriften* I.2, ed. Rolf Tiedemann and Hermann Schweppenhäuser (Frankfurt am Main: Suhrkamp, 1974), 471–508, here 479.

69. Walter Benjamin, "Über einige Motive bei Baudelaire," in *Gesammelte Schriften* I.2, ed. Rolf Tiedemann and Hermann Schweppenhäuser (Frankfurt am Main: Suhrkamp, 1974), 605–653, here 646.

70. Cf. Jean-Paul Sartre, *L'être et le néant. Essai d'ontologie phénoménologique* (Paris: Gallimard, 1943), 315.

71. Cf. Sartre, *L'être et le néant,* 323: "Avec le regard d'autrui, la 'situation' m'échappe ou, pour user d'expression banale, mais qui rend bien notre pensée: *je ne suis plus maître de la situation.*"

72. Benjamin, "Das Kunstwerk im Zeitalter seiner technischen Reproduzierbarkeit," *Schriften* I.2, 479. On drawing-closer, cf. Martin Heidegger, "Das Ding (1949)," in *Bremer und Freiburger Vorträge,* GA 79, ed. Petra Jaeger (Frankfurt am Main: Klostermann, 1994), 5–23.

73. Benjamin, "Das Kunstwerk im Zeitalter seiner technischen Reproduzierbarkeit," *Schriften* I.2, 480, n. 7.

74. Valéry, "Degas Danse Dessin," *Oeuvres* 2, 1212: "Les choses nous regardent. Le monde visible est un excitant perpétuel: tout réveille ou nourrit l'instinct de s'approprier la figure ou le modelé de la chose *que construit le regard.*"

75. Cf. Merleau-Ponty, *Le visible et l'invisible,* 183: "la vision qu'il [le voyant] exerce, il la subit aussi de la part des choses, que, comme l'ont dit beaucoup des peintres, je me sens regardé par les choses, que mon activité est identiquement passivité."

76. Cf. 62.

77. Rainer Maria Rilke, "Archaischer Torso Apollos," in *Gedichte: 1895–1910,* KA 1, ed. Manfred Engel (Frankfurt am Main: Insel, 1996), 513.

78. Rainer Maria Rilke, "Auguste Rodin," in *Schriften,* KA 4, ed. Horst Nalewski (Frankfurt am Main: Insel, 1996), 401–513, here 420.

79. Rilke, "Auguste Rodin," KA 4, 421. Cf. also the letter to Clara Rilke from August 2, 1902, mentioned and excerpted in the commentary on the works. Facing Rodin's sculptures, one feels "that everything would be less whole if the individual bodies were complete." "Every one of these chunks is of such an eminent and gripping unity, so singularly possible, not even requiring supplementation," such that one forgets "that they are merely *parts* and *often parts* of *different* bodies" that are put together there. Rainer Maria Rilke, *Briefe in zwei Bänden,* ed. Horst Nalewski (Frankfurt am Main: Insel, 1991), vol. 1, 127–133, here 130.

80. Rilke, "Auguste Rodin," KA 4, 411.

81. Rilke, "Briefe über Cézanne," KA 4, 630.

82. Sartre, *L'être et le néant*, 312: "une pure désintegration des relations que j'appréhendre entre les objets de mon univers."

83. Sartre, *L'être et le néant*, 313: "L'apparition d'autrui dans le monde correspond donc à un glissement figé de tout l'univers, à une décentration du monde qui mine par en dessous la centralisation que j'opère dans le même temps."

84. Sartre, *L'être et le néant*, 313: "c'est un espace tout entier qui se groupe autour d'autrui et cet espace est fait *avec mon espace*."

85. Heidegger, *Sein und Zeit*, GA 2, 141. For a critical discussion of Heidegger's conception of the spatiality of Dasein, cf. Figal, *Gegenständlichkeit*, 159–163.

86. Cf. Figal, *Gegenständlichkeit*, 378–392.

87. Husserl, *Ideen* II, Hua IV, 158.

88. Goethe, "Bedeutende Fördernis," MA 12, 306–307.

89. Cf. 29.

90. The piece is located in the Kunstmuseum in Basel.

91. *Here II* is located in the Fondation Beyeler in Riehen.

92. For a discussion of the various interpretations, cf. Armin Zweite, ed., *Barnett Newman: Bilder—Skulpturen—Graphik* (Ostfildern-Ruit: Hatje Cantz, 1997).

BIBLIOGRAPHY

Adams, William Howard, ed. *Prousts Figuren und ihre Vorbilder.* Frankfurt am Main: Suhrkamp, 1988.
Addiss, Stephen. *Japan und der Westen: Die erfüllte Leere.* Cologne: DuMont, 2007.
Adorno, Theodor Wiesengrund. *Ästhetische Theorie, Gesammelte Schriften,* vol. 7. Edited by Rolf Tiedemann and Gretel Adorno. Frankfurt am Main: Suhrkamp, 1970.
Adriani, Götz, ed. *Gerhard Richter. Bilder aus privaten Sammlungen.* Ostfildern-Ruit: Hatje Cantz, 2008.
Ando, Tadao. "Das Museum der Gegenwartskunst auf Naoshima." In Werner Blaser, *Tadao Ando: Architektur der Stille/Architecture of Silence,* 6–11. Basel: Birkhäuser, 2001.
Aristotle. *De Anima.* Edited by William David Ross. Oxford: Oxford University Press, 1956.
———. *Metaphysics.* Edited by William David Ross. Oxford: Oxford University Press, 1924.
———. *Nicomachean Ethics.* Edited by Ingram Bywater. Oxford: Oxford University Press, 1894.
———. *On Interpretation.* Edited by Lorenzo Minio-Paluello. Oxford: Oxford University Press, 1949.
———. *Physics.* Edited by William David Ross. Oxford: Oxford University Press, 1936.
———. *Poetics.* Edited by Ingram Bywater. Oxford: Oxford University Press, 1897.
Bach, Friedrich Teja. *ArchiSkulptur: Dialoge Zwischen Architektur und Plastik vom 18. Jahrhundert bis heute.* Edited by Markus Brüderlin. Ostfildern-Ruit: Hatje Cantz Verlag, 2004.
Bachelard, Gaston. *La poétique de l'espace.* Paris: Presses Universitaires de France, 1957.
Baeumler, Alfred. *Das Irrationalitätsproblem in der Ästhetik und Logik des 18. Jahrhunderts bis zur Kritik der Urteilskraft,* reprographic reprint of the second revised and expanded edition of 1967. Darmstadt: Wissenschaftliche Buchgesellschaft, 1981.
Baumgarten, Alexander Gottlieb. *Aesthetica,* unaltered reprographic reprint of the Frankfurt edition of 1750. Hildesheim: Olms, 1961.
Baumgartner, Michael, ed. *Paul Klee: Melodie und Rhythmus.* Ostfildern-Ruit: Hatje Cantz, 2006.
Benjamin, Walter. "Das Kunstwerk im Zeitalter seiner technischen Reproduzierbarkeit," 2nd ed. In *Gesammelte Schriften,* vol. I.2, edited by Rolf Tiedemann and Hermann Schweppenhäuser, 471–508. Frankfurt am Main: Suhrkamp, 1974.
———. "Denkbilder." In *Gesammelte Schriften,* vol. IV.1, edited by Tillman Rexroth, 305–438. Frankfurt am Main: Suhrkamp, 1972.

———. "Geschichte der Photographie (1931)." In *Gesammelte Schriften*, vol. II.1, edited by Rolf Tiedemann and Hermann Schweppenhäuser, 368–385. Frankfurt am Main: Suhrkamp, 1977.

———. "Über einige Motive bei Baudelaire." In *Gesammelte Schriften*, vol. I.2, edited by Rolf Tiedemann and Hermann Schweppenhäuser, 605–653. Frankfurt am Main: Suhrkamp, 1974.

Blumenberg, Hans. *Die Lesbarkeit der Welt*. Frankfurt am Main: Suhrkamp, 1981.

Boehm, Gottfried. "Das Lebendige: Rothkos Zugänge zum Bild." In *Mark Rothko: Retrospektive*, edited by Hubertus Gaßner et al., 180–184. Munich: Hirmer, 2008.

———. "Der Stumme Logos." In *Leibhaftige Vernunft: Spuren von Merleau-Pontys Denken*, edited by Alexandre Métraux and Bernhard Waldenfels, 289–304. Munich: Fink, 1986.

———. *Paul Cézanne: Montagne Sainte-Victoire*. Frankfurt am Main: Insel, 1988.

———. *Wie Bilder Sinn erzeugen: Die Macht des Zeigens*. Berlin: Akademie Verlag, 2007.

Bohrer, Karl Heinz. *Plötzlichkeit: Zum Augenblick des ästhetischen Scheins*. Frankfurt am Main: Suhrkamp, 1981.

Brecht, Bertolt. "Rudern, Gespräche." In *Werke*, annotated Berlin and Frankfurt edition, edited by Werner Hecht et al., vol. 12, 307. Berlin: Aufbau Verlag, 1988.

Breslin, J. E. B. *Mark Rothko: A Biography*. Chicago: University of Chicago Press, 1993.

Bubner, Rüdiger. "Ästhetisierung der Lebenswelt." In *Ästhetische Erfahrung*, 143–156. Frankfurt am Main: Suhrkamp, 1989.

Bussman, Klaus, ed. *Eduardo Chillida: Hauptwerke*. Mainz: Chorus Verlag, 2003.

Cooper, Anthony Ashley, Third Earl of Shaftesbury. *Characteristics of Men, Manners, Opinions, Times*. Edited and annotated by John M. Robertson, vol. 1. Indianapolis, Ind.: Bobbs-Merrill, 1964.

Corbier, Christophe. "*Alogia* et eurythmie chez Nietzsche." In *Nietzsche-Studien: Internationales Jahrbuch für die Nietzsche-Forschung* 38 (2009): 1–38.

Cramer, Konrad. "Erlebnis." In *Historisches Wörterbuch der Philosophie*, edited by Joachim Ritter, vol. 2. Darmstadt: Wissenschaftliche Buchgesellschaft, 1972.

Curtius, Ernst Robert. *Europäische Literatur und lateinisches Mittelalter*, 6th ed. Bern: A. Francke, 1967.

Danto, Arthur Coleman. *The Abuse of Beauty: Aesthetics and the Concept of Art*. Peru, Ill.: Carus, 2003.

Davies, Stephen. "John Cage's 4'33": Is it Music?" In *Themes in the Philosophy of Music*, 11–29. Oxford: Oxford University Press, 2003.

DeJean, Joan. *Ancients Against Moderns: Culture Wars and the Making of a Fin de Siècle*. Chicago: University of Chicago Press, 1997.

Derrida, Jacques. *La Verité en Peinture*. Paris: Gallimard, 1978.

Descartes, René. *Principia Philosophiae, Oeuvres de Descartes*. Edited by Charles Adam and Paul Tannery, vol. 8.1. Paris: J. Vrin, 1905.

Dewey, John. *Art as Experience*. New York: Penguin, 1958.

Diels, Hermann, and Walther Kranz, eds. *Die Fragmente der Vorsokratiker*, 7th ed., vols. 1–3. Berlin: Weidmannsche Buchhandlung, 1954.

Dilthey, Wilhelm. "Studien zur Grundlegung der Geisteswissenschaften." In *Gesammelte Schriften*, 2nd ed., vol. 7, 24–69. Göttingen: Vandenhoeck & Ruprecht, 1958.
Emerson, Ralph Waldo. "Nature." In *Essays & Lectures*, 5–49. New York: Penguin, 1983.
Espinet, David. *Phänomenologie des Hörens*. Tübingen: Mohr Siebeck, 2009.
Fehrer, Wolfgang. *Das japanische Teehaus*. Sulgen: Niggli, 2005.
Feuerbach, Ludwig. "Grundsätze der Philosophie der Zukunft (1843)." In *Werke in sechs Bänden*, edited by Erich Thies, vol. 3, 247–322. Frankfurt am Main: Suhrkamp, 1975.
Fiedler, Conrad. "Über den Ursprung der künstlerischen Tätigkeit (1887)." In *Schriften zur Kunst I*. Reprint of the 1913–14 Munich edition with additional texts from the estate, edited by Gottfried Boehm, 183–367. Munich: Fink, 1971.
Figal, Günter. "Die Wahrheit und die schöne Täuschung: Zum Verhältnis von Dichtung und Philosophie im Platonischen Denken." In *Philosophisches Jahrbuch* 107 (2000): 301–315.
———. "Gadamer als Phänomenologe." In *Verstehensfragen: Studien zur phänomenologisch-hermeneutischen Philosophie*, 277–290. Tübingen: Mohr Siebeck, 2009.
———. *Gegenständlichkeit: Das Hermeneutische und die Philosophie*. Tübingen: Mohr Siebeck, 2006. English translation: *Objectivity: The Hermeneutical and Philosophy*. Translated by Theodore D. George. Albany: State University of New York Press, 2010.
———. "Hermeneutik und Phänomenologie." In *Verstehensfragen: Studien zur phänomenologisch-hermeneutischen Philosophie*, 177–188. Tübingen: Mohr Siebeck, 2009.
———. "Idee." In *Religion in Geschichte und Gegenwart*, 4th ed., vol. 4. Tübingen: Mohr Siebeck, 2001.
———. "Kunst als Weltdarstellung." In *Der Sinn des Verstehens: Beiträge zur Hermeneutischen Philosophie*, 45–63. Stuttgart: Reclam, 1996.
———. *Martin Heidegger: Phänomenologie der Freiheit*, 3rd ed. Weinheim: Beltz Athenäum, 2000.
———. *Nietzsche: Eine philosophische Einführung*. Stuttgart: Reclam, 1999.
———. "Nietzsche's Philosophie der Interpretation." In *Nietzsche-Studien* 29 (2000): 1–11.
———. "Seinserfahrung und Übersetzung: Hermeneutische Überlegungen zu Heidegger." In *Zu Heidegger: Antworten und Fragen*, 173–184. Frankfurt am Main: Klostermann, 2009.
———. "Sinn: Zur Bedeutung eines philosophischen Schlüsselbegriffs." In *Verstehensfragen: Studien zur phänomenologisch-hermeneutischen Philosophie*, 148–158. Tübingen: Mohr Siebeck, 2009.
———. "Subjekt und Objekt." In *Verstehensfragen: Studien zur phänomenologisch-hermeneutischen Philosophie*, 244–257. Tübingen: Mohr Siebeck, 2009.
———. *Theodor W. Adorno, Das Naturschöne als spekulative Gedankenfigur: Zur Interpretation der 'Ästhetischen Theorie' im Kontext philosophischer Ästhetik*. Bonn: Bouvier, 1977.

———. "Was ist Wissen? Die Frage des Sokrates." In *Verstehensfragen: Studien zur phänomenologisch-hermeneutischen Philosophie*, 159–166. Tübingen: Mohr Siebeck, 2009.

———. "Zeigen und Sichzeigen." In *Verstehensfragen: Studien zur phänomenologisch-hermeneutischen Philosophie*, 200–210. Tübingen: Mohr Siebeck, 2009.

Fondation Beyeler. *Mark Rothko: A Consummated Experience Between Picture and Onlooker.* Ostfildern-Ruit: Hatje Cantz, 2001.

———. *Wolfgang Laib: Das Vergängliche ist das Ewige.* Ostfildern-Ruit: Hatje Cantz, 2005.

Foucault, Michel. *Les mots et les choses: Une archéologie des sciences humaines.* Paris: Gallimard, 2007.

Gadamer, Hans-Georg. "Bild und Gebärde (1967)." In *Gesammelte Werke*, vol. 8, 323–330. Tübingen: Mohr Siebeck, 1993.

———. "Die Aktualität des Schönen: Kunst als Spiel, Symbol und Fest (1974)." In *Gesammelte Werke*, vol. 8, 94–142. Tübingen: Mohr Siebeck, 1993.

———. *Hermeneutik I. Wahrheit und Methode: Grundzüge einer philosophischen Hermeneutik, Gesammelte Werke*, vol. 1. Tübingen: Mohr Siebeck, 1986.

———. "Lob der Theorie (1980)." In *Gesammelte Werke*, vol. 4, 37–51. Tübingen: Mohr Siebeck, 1987.

———. "Über das Lesen von Bauten und Bildern (1979)." In *Gesammelte Werke*, vol. 8, 331–338. Tübingen: Mohr Siebeck, 1993.

———. "Wort und Bild—'So wahr, so seiend' (1992)." In *Gesammelte Werke*, vol. 8, 373–399. Tübingen: Mohr Siebeck, 1993.

Gasché, Rodolphe. *The Idea of Form: Rethinking Kant's Aesthetics.* Stanford, Calif.: Stanford University Press, 2003.

Gasquet, Joachim. "Ce qu'il m'a dit." In *Conversations avec Cézanne*, edited by Michael Doran, 106–161. Paris: Macula, 1978.

Gass, William H. *Reading Rilke: Reflections on the Problems of Translation.* New York: Basic Books, 2000.

Gaßner, Hubertus, ed. *Das Schwarze Quadrat: Hommage an Malewitsch.* Ostfildern-Ruit: Hatje Cantz, 2007.

Gehlen, Arnold. *Zeit-Bilder: Zur Soziologie und Ästhetik der modernen Malerei*, 2nd rev. ed. Frankfurt am Main: Klostermann, 1965.

Georgiades, Thrasybulos. *Der griechische Rhythmus: Musik, Reigen, Vers und Sprache.* Hamburg: von Schroder, 1949.

Goethe, Johann Wolfgang. "Bedeutende Fördernis durch ein einziges geistreiches Wort." In *Sämtliche Werke nach Epochen seines Schaffens,* Munich edition, vol. 12, edited by Karl Richter, 306–309. Munich: Hanser, 1986.

———. *Briefwechsel zwischen Schiller und Goethe in den Jahren 1794 bis 1805,* Munich edition, vol. 8.1, edited by Manfred Beetz. Munich: Hanser, 1990.

———. *Die Wahlverwandschaften,* Munich edition, vol. 9, edited by Christoph Siegrist et al., 283–529. Munich: Hanser, 1987. English translation: *Elective Affinities.* Translated by David Constantine. New York: Oxford University Press, 1994.

———. *Faust. Der Tragödie zweiter Teil,* Munich edition, vol. 18.1, edited by Gisela Henckmann and Dorothea Hölscher-Lohmeyer. Munich: Hanser, 1997.

———. *Italienische Reise,* Munich edition, vol. 15. Edited by Andreas Beyer. Munich: Hanser, 1992.

———. "Wiederholte Spiegelungen." In *Tag- und Jahres-Hefte als Ergänzung meiner sonstigen Bekenntnisse,* Munich edition, vol. 14, edited by Reiner Wild, 568–569. Munich: Hanser, 1986.

———. *Zur Farbenlehre,* Munich edition, vol. 10, edited by Karl Richter. Munich: Hanser, 1989.

Goodman, Nelson. *Languages of Art.* Indianapolis, Ind.: Hackett, 1976.

Gracián, Baltasar. *El Discreto.* Edited by Miguel Romera-Navarro. Buenos Aires: Academia Argentina de Letras, 1960.

Grimm, Jacob, and Wilhelm Grimm. *Deutsches Wörterbuch.* Leipzig: Hirzel, 1854–1971.

Gumbrecht, Hans Ulrich. *Disseits der Hermeneutik: Die Produktion von Präsenz,* translated by Joachim Schulte. Frankfurt am Main: Suhrkamp, 2004.

Handke, Peter. *Versuch über die Müdigkeit.* Frankfurt am Main: Suhrkamp, 1989.

Haug, Walter, and Rainer Warning, eds. *Das Fest* (Poetik und Hermeneutik XIV). Munich: Fink, 1989.

Hegel, G. W. F. *Vorlesungen über die Ästhetik* I–III, *Theorie-Werkausgabe.* Edited by Eva Moldenhauer and Karl Markus Michel, vols. 13–15. Frankfurt am Main: Suhrkamp, 1970.

Heidegger, Martin. "Bauen Wohnen Denken (1951)." In *Gesamtausgabe,* vol. 7, edited by Friedrich-Wilhelm von Herrmann, 145–164. Frankfurt am Main: Klostermann, 2000.

———. *Beiträge zur Philosophie (Vom Ereignis). Gesamtausgabe,* vol. 65. Edited by Friedrich-Wilhelm von Herrmann. Frankfurt am Main: Klostermann, 1989.

———. "Das Ding (1949)." In *Gesamtausgabe,* vol. 79, edited by Petra Jaeger, 5–23. Frankfurt am Main: Klostermann, 1994.

———. "Das Ding (1950)." In *Gesamtausgabe,* vol. 7, edited by Friedrich-Wilhelm von Herrmann, 165–187. Frankfurt am Main: Klostermann, 2000.

———. *Der Satz vom Grund. Gesamtausgabe,* vol. 10. Edited by Petra Jaeger. Frankfurt am Main: Klostermann, 1997.

———. "Der Spruch des Anaximander (1946)." In *Gesamtausgabe,* vol. 5, edited by Friedrich-Wilhelm von Herrmann, 321–373. Frankfurt am Main: Klostermann, 1977.

———. "Der Ursprung des Kunstwerkes (1935–36)." In *Gesamtausgabe,* vol. 5, edited by Friedrich-Wilhelm von Herrmann, 1–74. Frankfurt am Main: Klostermann, 1977.

———. "Die Idee der Philosophie und das Weltanschauungsproblem (1919)." In *Gesamtausgabe,* vol. 56–57, edited by Bernd Heimbüchel, 1–117. Frankfurt am Main: Klostermann, 1987.

———. "Die Kunst und der Raum (1969)." In *Gesamtausgabe,* vol. 13, edited by Hermann Heidegger, 203–210. Frankfurt am Main: Klostermann, 1983.

———. "Die Zeit des Weltbildes (1938)." In *Gesamtausgabe,* vol. 5, edited by Friedrich-Wilhelm von Herrmann, 75–113. Frankfurt am Main: Klostermann, 1977.

———. *Einführung in die Metaphysik. Gesamtausgabe,* vol. 40. Edited by Petra Jaeger. Frankfurt am Main: Klostermann, 1983.

———. *Erläuterungen zu Hölderlins Dichtung. Gesamtausgabe*, vol. 4. Edited by Friedrich-Wilhelm von Herrmann. Frankfurt am Main: Klostermann, 1981.

———. *Logik: Die Frage nach der Wahrheit. Gesamtausgabe*, vol. 21. Edited by Walter Biemel. Frankfurt am Main: Klostermann, 1976.

———. "Logos (Heraklit, Fragment 50) (1951)." In *Gesamtausgabe*, vol. 7, edited by Friedrich-Wilhelm von Herrmann, 211–234. Frankfurt am Main: Klostermann, 2000.

———. *Nietzsche: Der Wille zur Macht als Kunst. Gesamtausgabe*, vol. 43. Edited by Bernd Heimbüchel. Frankfurt am Main: Klostermann, 1985.

———. *Parmenides. Gesamtausgabe*, vol. 54. Edited by Manfred Frings. Frankfurt am Main: Klostermann, 1982.

———. *Prolegomena zur Geschichte des Zeitbegriffs. Gesamtausgabe*, vol. 20. Edited by Petra Jaeger. Frankfurt am Main: Klostermann, 1994.

———. *Sein und Zeit. Gesamtausgabe*, vol. 2. Edited by Friedrich-Wilhelm von Herrmann. Frankfurt am Main: Klostermann, 1977.

———. *Unterwegs zur Sprache. Gesamtausgabe*, vol. 12. Edited by Friedrich-Wilhelm von Herrmann. Pfullingen: Neske, 1959.

———. "Vom Ursprung des Kunstwerkes (Erste Ausarbeitung)." In *Heidegger-Lesebuch*, edited by Günter Figal, 149–170. Frankfurt am Main: Klostermann, 2007.

———. "Vom Wesen und Begriff der Φυσις. Aristoteles, *Physik* B 1 (1939)." In *Gesamtausgabe*, vol. 9, edited by Friedrich-Wilhelm von Herrmann, 239–301. Frankfurt am Main: Klostermann, 1976.

Hirsch, Rudolf. "Edmund Husserl und Hugo von Hoffmannsthal: Eine Begegnung und ein Brief." In *Beiträge zum Verständnis Hugo von Hoffmannsthals*, 273–280. Frankfurt am Main: Fischer, 1995.

Hölderlin, Friedrich. "Anmerkungen zur Antigonä." In *Sämtliche Werke und Briefe*, edited by Michael Knaupp, vol. 2, 369–376. Munich: Hanser, 1992.

———. "Anmerkungen zum Oedipus." In *Sämtliche Werke und Briefe*, edited by Michael Knaupp, vol. 2, 309–316. Munich: Hanser, 1992.

Holm, Juul Michael, and Paul Erik Tøjner, eds. *Per Kirkeby*. Humlebæk: Louisiana Museum of Modern Art, 2009.

Hsiao, Paul Shih-Yi. "Heidegger and Our Translation of the *Tao Te Ching*." In *Heidegger and Asian Thought*, edited by Graham Parkes, 93–103. Honolulu: University of Hawaii Press, 1987.

———. "Wir trafen uns am Holzmarkt." In *Erinnerungen an Martin Heidegger*, edited by Günther Neske, 119–129. Pfullingen: Neske, 1977.

Husserl, Edmund. "Brief an Hugo von Hoffmannsthal vom 12. 1. 1907." In *Briefwechsel*, edited by Karl Schuhmann, vol. 7, 133–136. Dordrecht: Kluwer, 1994.

———. *Cartesianische Meditationen. Husserliana* I. Edited by Stephan Strasser. The Hague: Nijhoff, 1963.

———. *Die Idee der Phänomenologie: Fünf Vorlesungen. Husserliana* II. Edited by Walter Biemel. The Hague: Nijhoff, 1950.

———. *Die Krisis der europäischen Wissenschaften und die transzendentale Phänomenologie.* Husserliana VI. Edited by Walter Biemel. The Hague: Nijhoff, 1962.

———. *Ding und Raum: Vorlesungen 1907.* Husserliana XVI. Edited by Ulrich Claesges. The Hague: Nijhoff, 1973.

———. *Formale und transzendentale Logik: Versuch einer Kritik der logischen Vernunft.* Husserliana XVII. Edited by Paul Janssen. The Hague: Nijhoff, 1974.

———. *Ideen zu einer reinen Phänomenologie und phänomenologischen Philosophie. Erstes Buch.* Husserliana III.1. Edited by Karl Schuhmann. The Hague: Nijhoff, 1976.

———. *Ideen zu einer reinen Phänomenologie und phänomenologischen Philosophie. Zweites Buch.* Husserliana IV. Edited by Marly Biemel. The Hague: Nijhoff, 1952.

———. *Ideen zu einer reinen Phänomenologie und phänomenologischen Philosophie. Drittes Buch.* Husserliana V. Edited by Marly Biemel. The Hague: Nijhoff, 1952.

———. "Phantasie, Bildbewusstsein, Erinnerung: Zur Phänomenologie der anschaulichen Vergegenwärtigung." In *Husserliana* XXIII, edited by Eduard Marbach. The Hague: Nijhoff, 1980.

———. *Zur Phänomenologie der Intersubjektivität: Texte aus dem Nachlaß. Dritter Teil: 1929–1935.* Husserliana XV. Edited by Iso Kern. The Hague: Nijhoff, 1973.

Ingarden, Roman. *Das literarische Kunstwerk.* Tübingen: Niemeyer, 1960.

Jahn, Gisela, and Anette Petersen-Brandhorst. *Erde und Feuer: Traditionelle japanische Keramik der Gegenwart.* Munich: Hirmer, 1984.

Jauß, Hans Robert, ed. *Die nicht mehr schönen Künste: Grenzphänomene des Ästhetischen* (Poetik und Hermeneutik III). Munich: Fink, 1968.

Jünger, Ernst. *Das abenteuerliche Herz.* 2nd ed. In *Sämtliche Werke,* vol. 9, 177–330. Stuttgart: Klett-Cotta, 1979.

Kant, Immanuel. *Critique of Judgment.* Translated by Werner S. Pluhar. Indianapolis, Ind.: Hackett, 1987.

———. *Critique of Pure Reason.* Translated by Werner S. Pluhar. Indianapolis, Ind.: Hackett, 1996.

———. *Grundlegung zur Metaphysik der Sitten.* In *Kant's gesammelte Schriften,* vol. IV, 385–463. Berlin: Königlich Preußische Akademie der Wissenschaften, 1911.

———. *Kritik der Urteilskraft.* In *Kant's gesammelte Schriften,* vol. V, 166–485. Berlin: Königlich Preußische Akademie der Wissenschaften, 1913.

———. *Kritik der reinen Vernunft.* In *Kant's gesammelte Schriften,* vol. VI. Berlin: Königlich Preußische Akademie der Wissenschaften, 1911.

———. "Logik." In *Kant's gesammelte Schriften,* vol. IX, 3–150. Berlin: Königlich Preußische Akademie der Wissenschaften, 1923.

———. *Logik.* In *Kant's gesammelte Schriften,* vol. XVI. Berlin: Königlich Preußische Akademie der Wissenschaften, 1924.

Kaufmann, Edgar Jr. *Fallingwater: A Frank Lloyd Wright Country House.* New York: Abbeville Press, 1986.

Kierkegaard, Søren. *Der Begriff der Angst.* In *Gesammelte Werke,* translated by Emanuel Hirsch, vol. 11–12, 1–169. Düsseldorf: Diederichs, 1952.

———. *Philosophische Brocken*. In *Gesammelte Werke*, translated by Emanuel Hirsch, vol. 10, 52–107. Düsseldorf: Diederichs, 1952.

Kunsthaus Zurich. *Joseph Beuys*. Paris: Editions du Centre Pompidou, 1994.

Lao-Tzu. *Daodejing: Das Buch vom Weg und seiner Wirkung*. Translated and edited by Rainald Simon. Stuttgart: Reclam, 2009.

———. *Tao Te Ching: A New Translation With Commentary*. Translated by Ellen Chen. St. Paul, Minn.: Paragon House, 1989.

Leeman, Richard. *Cy Twombly: Malen, Zeichnen, Schreiben*. Translated by Matthias Wolf. Munich: Schirmer, 2005.

Liddell, Henry George, and Robert Scott. *A Greek-English Lexicon*. Oxford: Oxford University Press, 1951.

Lukács, Georg. *Die Theorie des Romans: Ein geschichtlicher Versuch über die Formen der großen Epik*. Berlin: Cassirer, 1920.

Lyotard, Jean-Francois. *Die Analytik des Erhabenen*. Translated by Christine Pries. Munich: Fink, 1994.

Lypp, Bernhard. "Spiegel-Bilder." In *Was ist ein Bild?*, edited by Gottfried Boehm, 411–442. Munich: Fink, 1994

Maak, Niklas. *Der Architekt am Strand: Le Corbusier und das Geheimnis der Seeschnecke*. Munich: Hansa, 2010.

Malraux, André. *Le Musée imaginaire de la Sculpture Mondiale*. Paris: Gallimard, 1952–1954.

Marion, Jean-Luc. "Die Wiederaufnahme der Gegenbenheit durch Husserl und Heidegger." In *Heidegger und Husserl: Neue Perspektiven*, edited by Günter Figal and Hans-Helmuth Gander. Frankfurt am Main: Klostermann, 2009.

———. *Étant donné: Essai d'une phénoménologie de la donation*. Paris: Presses Universitaires de France, 1997.

Mark Rothko: Retrospektive. Edited by Hubertus Gaßner et al. Munich: Hirmer, 2008.

Merleau-Ponty, Maurice. "Le doute de Cézanne." In *Sens et non-sens*, 15–44. Paris: Gallimard, 1948.

———. *L'Oeuil et l'esprit*. Paris: Gallimard, 1964.

———. "Le philosophe et son Ombre." In Merleau-Ponty, *Signes*, 259–295. Paris: Gallimard, 2008.

———. *Le visible et l'invisible*. Edited by Claude Lefort. Paris: Gallimard, 1964.

———. *Phénoménologie de la perception*. Paris: Gallimard, 1945.

Mersch, Dieter. *Ereignis und Aura: Untersuchungen zu einer Ästhetik des Performativen*. Frankfurt am Main: Suhrkamp, 2002.

Müller-Tamm, Pia, ed. *Henri Matisse: Figur Farbe Raum*. Ostfildern-Ruit: Hatje Cantz, 2005.

Nietzsche, Friedrich. *Die fröhliche Wissenschaft*. In *Sämtliche Werke*, critical edition, edited by Giorgio Colli and Mazzino Montinari, vol. 3, 343–651. Berlin: de Gruyter, 1980.

———. *Die Geburt der Tragödie*. In *Sämtliche Werke*, critical edition, edited by Giorgio Colli and Mazzino Montinari, vol. 1, 9–156. Berlin: de Gruyter, 1980.

―――. *Menschliches, Allzumenschliches: Ein Buch für freie Geister*, vol. 2. In *Sämtliche Werke*, critical edition, edited by Giorgio Colli and Mazzino Montinari, vol. 2, 367–704. Berlin: de Gruyter, 1980.

―――. *Vom Nutzen und Nachtheil der Historie für das Leben (Unzeitgemäße Betrachtungen II)*. In *Sämtliche Werke*, critical edition, edited by Giorgio Colli and Mazzino Montinari, vol. 1, 243–334. Berlin: de Gruyter, 1980.

Nussaume, Yann. *Tadao Ando*. Basel: Birkhäuser, 2009.

O'Neill, John P. *Barnett Newman: Selected Writings and Interviews*. Berkeley: University of California Press, 1992.

Picht, Georg. "Kunst und Mythos." In *Vorlesungen und Schriften*, edited by Constanze Eisenbart, vol. 2. Stuttgart: Klett-Cotta, 1986.

Pindar. "Zweite Olympische Ode." In Pindar, *Siegeslieder*, Greek/German, edited and translated by Dieter Bremer, 17–25. Munich: Artemis & Winkler, 1992.

―――. "Zweite Pythische Ode." In Pindar, *Siegeslieder*, Greek/German, edited and translated by Dieter Bremer, 120–127. Munich: Artemis & Winkler, 1992.

Plato, *Platonis Opera*. Edited by John Burnet. Oxford: Oxford University Press, 1900–1907.

Pöggeler, Otto. "West-East Dialogue: Heidegger and Lao-Tzu." In *Heidegger and Asian Thought*, edited by Graham Parkes, 47–78. Honolulu: University of Hawaii Press, 1987.

Pseudo-Longinus. *Peri Hypsous: De Sublimitate Libellus*, 3rd ed., edited by Johannes Vahlen. Leipzig: Teubner, 1905.

Rathbone, Eliza E. "Der Rothko Room in der Phillips Collection." In *Mark Rothko: A Consummated Experience Between Picture and Onlooker*, 47–53. Ostfildern-Ruit: Hatje Cantz, 2001.

Recki, Birgit. "Die Dialektik der ästhetischen Urteilskraft und die Methodenlehre des Geschmacks." In *Immanuel Kant: Kritik der Urteilskraft (Klassiker Auslegen 33)*, edited by Otfried Höffe, 189–210. Berlin: Akademie Verlag, 2008.

―――. "'Herabkommen ins Sichtbare': Eine Apologie der Schönheit in pragmatischer Hinsicht." In *Das Leben Denken—Die Kultur Denken*, edited by Ralf Konersmann, 176–196. Freiburg: Alber, 2007.

―――. "Intentionalität ohne Intention: Die Praktizität der Urteilskraft." In *Akten des Siebenten Internationalen Kant-Kongresses*, vol. 2.2, edited by Gerhard Funke, 165–178. Bonn: Bouvier, 1991.

Rilke, Rainer Maria. "Archaischer Torso Apollos." In *Werke*, annotated edition, vol. 1, edited by Manfred Engel, 513. Frankfurt am Main: Insel, 1996.

―――. "August Rodin." In *Werke*, annotated edition, vol. 4, edited by Horst Nalewski, 401–513. Frankfurt am Main: Insel, 1996.

―――. "Brief an Clara Rilke vom 2. 9. 1902." In *Briefe in zwei Bänden*, edited by Horst Nalewski, 127–133. Frankfurt am Main: Insel, 1991.

―――. "Briefe über Cézanne." In *Werke*, annotated edition, vol. 4, edited by Horst Nalewski, 594–638. Frankfurt am Main: Insel, 1996.

———. *Duineser Elegien*. In *Werke,* annotated edition, vol. 2, edited by Manfred Engel and Ulrich Fülleborn, 199–234. Frankfurt am Main: Insel, 1996.

———. *Sonette an Orpheus*. In *Werke,* annotated edition, vol. 2, edited by Manfred Engel and Ulrich Fülleborn, 237–272. Frankfurt am Main: Insel, 1996.

Ritter, Joachim. "Landschaft: Zur Funktion des Ästhetischen in der modernen Gesellschaft." *Schriften der Gesellschaft zur Förderung der Westfälischen Wilhelms-Universität zu Münster,* vol. 54 (1963). Reprinted in Ritter, *Subjektivität: Sechs Aufsätze,* 141–163. Frankfurt am Main: Suhrkamp, 1974.

Rorty, Richard. *Contingency, Irony, and Solidarity.* Cambridge: Cambridge University Press, 1989.

Rothacker, Erich. *Das 'Buch der Natur.'* Edited by Wilhelm Perpeet. Bonn: Bouvier, 1979.

Rothko, Mark. *The Artist's Reality: Philosophies of Art.* New Haven, Conn.: Yale University Press, 2004.

Sallis, John. *Chorology: On Beginning in Plato's Timaeus.* Bloomington: Indiana University Press, 1999.

———. *Transfigurements: On the True Sense of Art.* Chicago: University of Chicago Press, 2008.

Sartre, Jean-Paul. *L'être et le néant: Essai d'ontologie phénoménologique.* Paris: Gallimard, 1943.

———. *L'imaginaire. Psychologie phénoménologique de l'imagination.* Paris: Gallimard, 1940.

Scaramuzza, Gabriele, and Karl Schumann. "Ein Husserlmanuskript über Ästhetik." In *Husserl Studies* 7, no. 3 (1990): 165–177.

Scarry, Elaine. *On Beauty and Being Just.* Princeton, N.J.: Princeton University Press, 1999.

Schelling, F. W. J. *System des Transzendentalen Idealismus. Sämtliche Werke.* Edited by K. F. A. Schelling, div. I, vol. 3, 327–634. Stuttgart: Cotta, 1858.

———. *Philosophie der Offenbarung. Sämtliche Werke.* Edited by K. F. A. Schelling, division II, vol. 2. Stuttgart: Cotta, 1858.

Schiller, Friedrich. *Über das Erhabene.* In *Sämtliche Werke,* edited by Gerhard Fricke and Herbert Georg Göpfert, vol. 5, 792–808. Munich: Hanser, 1959.

———. *Über die Erziehung des Menschen in einer Reihe von Briefen.* In *Sämtliche Werke,* edited by Gerhard Fricke and Herbert Georg Göpfert, vol. 5, 570–669. Munich: Hanser, 1959.

Schlegel, Friedrich. "Lyceums-Fragmente." In *Kritische Friedrich-Schlegel-Ausgabe,* vol. 2, edited by Hans Eichner, 147–163. Darmstadt: Wissenschaftliche Buchgesellschaft, 1967.

Schmidt, Dennis J. *Lyrical and Ethical Subjects: Essays on the Periphery of the Word, Freedom, and History.* Albany: State University of New York Press, 2005.

Schmitz, Hermann. *Was Wollte Kant?* Bonn: Bouvier, 1989.

Schopenhauer, Arthur. *Die Welt als Wille und Vorstellung* I. In *Sämtliche Werke,* edited by Wolfgang Freiherr von Löhneysen, vol. 1. Stuttgart: Cotta-Insel, 1960.

Sedlmayr, Hans. *Verlust der Mitte: Die bildende Kunst des 19. und 20. Jahrhunderts als Symptom und Symbol der Zeit,* 11th ed. Salzburg: Müller, 1998.

Seel, Martin. *Ästhetik des Erscheinens.* Munich: Hanser, 2000.

Sepp, Hans Rainer. "Crisis Imaginis: Sartre zur Lösung des Bildes vom Ding im Kunstwerk." In *Kunst und Wahrheit: Festschrift für Walter Biemel zum 85. Geburtstag,* edited by Madalina Diacanu, 249–268. Bucharest: Humanitas, 2003.

Shapiro, Meyer. "Theory and Philosophy of Art: Style, Artist, and Society." In *Selected Papers,* 135–151. New York: Braziller, 1994.

Spinoza, Benedictus de. *Ethica* I. *Werke,* Latin/German, vol. 2. Edited by Konrad Blumenstock, 84–503. Darmstadt: Wissenschaftliche Buchgesellschaft, 1967.

Stegmaier, Werner. *Philosophie der Orientierung.* New York: de Gruyter, 2008.

Steinbock, Anthony. "Affektion und Aufmerksamkeit." In *Die erscheinende Welt: Festschrift für Klaus Held,* edited by Heinrich Hüni and Peter Trawny, 241–273. Berlin: Duncker & Humbolt, 2002.

Steiner, George. *Real Presences: Is There Anything In What We Say?* Chicago: University of Chicago Press, 1989.

Storr, Robert. *Gerhard Richter: Malerei.* Ostfildern-Ruit: Hatje Cantz, 2002.

Taut, Bruno. *Gedanken über Katsura, Mai 34.* Facsimile. Tokyo: Iwanami, 2004.

———. "Ich liebe die japanische Kultur." In *Kleine Schriften über Japan,* edited by Manfred Speidel. Berlin: Gebrüder Mann Verlag, 2003. Reprinted in Stephen Addiss, *Japan und der Westen: Die erfüllte Leere.* Cologne: DuMont, 2007.

Valéry, Paul. "Degas Danse Dessin." In *Oeuvres,* vol. 2, 1163–1240. Paris: Gallimard, 1960.

———. "L'Homme et la coquille." In *Oeuvres,* vol. 1, 886–907. Paris: Gallimard, 1957.

———. "Philosophie de la danse." In *Oeuvres,* vol. 1, 1390–1403. Paris: Gallimard, 1957.

———. "Propos sur la poésie." In *Oeuvres,* vol. 1, 1361–1378. Paris: Gallimard, 1957.

Wagner, Richard. *Das Kunstwerk der Zukunft.* Leipzig: Wigand, 1850.

———. "Zukunftsmusik." In *Sämtliche Schriften und Dichtungen,* vol. 7, 6th ed., 87–137. Leipzig: Breitkopf & Härtel, 1912.

Waldenfels, Bernhard. *Phänomenologie der Aufmerksamkeit.* Frankfurt am Main: Suhrkamp, 2004.

Webster's New International Dictionary of the English Language. Edited by Philip Babcock Gove. Chicago: Merriam-Webster, 1986.

Whitehead, Alfred North. *Process and Reality: An Essay in Cosmology.* Edited by David Ray Griffin and Donald W. Sherburne. New York: Free Press, 1979.

Wick, Oliver. "'Do they negate each other, modern and classical?': Mark Rothko und die Sehnsucht nach Tradition." In *Mark Rothko: Retrospektive,* edited by Hubertus Gaßner et al., 12–28. Munich: Hirmer, 2008.

Wieland, Wolfgang. *Urteil und Gefühl: Kants Theorie der Urteilskraft.* Göttingen: Vandenhoeck & Ruprecht, 2001.

Wittgenstein, Ludwig. *Philosophische Untersuchungen.* In *Schriften,* vol. I, 279–544. Frankfurt am Main: Suhrkamp, 1969.

Yanagi, Sōetsu. "The Beauty of Irregularity." In *The Unknown Craftsman: A Japanese Insight into Beauty,* 119–125. New York: Kodansha, 1972.
Yilmaz, Levent. *Le temps moderne: Variations sur les Anciens et les Contemporains.* Paris: Gallimard, 2004.
Zahavi, Dan. *Husserl's Phenomenology.* Stanford, Calif.: Stanford University Press, 2003.
Zammito, John H. *The Genesis of Kant's* Critique of Judgment. Chicago: University of Chicago Press, 1992.
Zweite, Armin, ed. *Barnett Newman: Bilder—Skulpturen—Graphik.* Ostfildern-Ruit: Hatje Cantz, 1997.

INDEX OF NAMES

Addiss, Stephen, 19n26, 169n64
Adorno, Theodor W., 2, 22–25, 31, 38, 48, 141–143, 160
Altdorfer, Albrecht, 128
Ando, Tadao, 39, 185, 188, 194
Antiphon, 151
Aristotle, 7, 10, 14, 26, 28, 62, 74–75, 125, 133–134, 144–149, 151–152, 157–158, 171, 176, 178–180, 190–192, 214, 218
Augustine, 114

Bach, Friedrich Teja, 135n96
Bach, Johann Sebastian, 18, 35, 36, 39, 61, 87, 115, 181
Bachelard, Gaston, 199n39
Baeumler, Alfred, 43n2
Baudelaire, Charles, 123
Baumgarten, Alexander Gottlieb, 28, 31, 42
Beethoven, Ludwig van, 115, 163
Benjamin, Walter, 211–213
Benn, Gottfried, 25, 122
Berenson, Bernhard, 200
Berg, Alban, 18, 39
Beuys, Josef, 32, 76
Bissier, Julius, 182
Blaser, Werner, 185n5
Blashfield, Edwin, 200
Blumenberg, Hans, 173n99
Boehm, Gottfried, 86n118, 129n84, 174n102, 201n49
Bohrer, Karl Heinz, 33n71
Bonaparte, Napoleon, 9
Brecht, Bertolt, 206
Breslin, J. E. B., 194n30
Bruckner, Anton, 24, 79
Bubner, Rüdiger, 33

Cage, John, 95, 97, 209
Cellini, Benvenuto, 103

Cézanne, Paul, 35, 92, 149, 168–177, 181–182, 198, 200, 213, 216
Chillida, Eduardo, 183, 185–186, 193, 195
Cooper, Anthony Ashley, Earl of Shaftesbury, 43n1
Corbier, Christophe, 118n45
Cramer, Konrad, 31n61
Curtius, Ernst Robert, 173n99

Dante, 39, 56
Danto, Arthur Coleman, 38n93
Davies, Stephen, 97n1
Debussy, Claude, 87, 108–109, 114
DeJean, Joan, 20n29
Democritus, 210n63
Derrida, Jacques, 35n77
Descartes, René, 186
Dewey, John, 31
Dilthey, Wilhelm, 32
Doderer, Heimito von, 72

Eliot, T. S., 108
Emerson, Ralph Waldo, 171n90
Espinet, David, 165n49

Fehrer, Wolfgang, 120n55
Feuerbach, Ludwig, 22
Fiedler, Conrad, 31
Figal, Günter, 11n10, 12n17, 15n23, 26n45, 36n81, 37n86, 50n22, 58n41, 68n63, 76n89, 84n115, 85n117, 86n118, 88n124, 90n126, 105n11, 114n26, 123n62, 125n71, 126n73, 127n77, 128n80, 158n36, 164n46, 166n53, 166n54, 172n92, 178n13, 183n2, 186n11, 187n15, 189n21, 197n33, 218n85, 218n86
Flaubert, Gustave, 9
Foucault, Michel, 94n131
Friedrich, Caspar David, 94

Gadamer, Hans-Georg, 2, 21–25, 31–38, 54, 64, 86, 116–117, 128, 131–132, 138, 196
Galilei, Galileo, 186
Gasché, Rodolphe, 47n14
Gasquet, Joachim, 168–169
Gehlen, Arnold, 32n67, 38
Georgiades, Thrasybulos, 118n43
Giacometti, Giovanni, 200, 222
Giotto di Bondone, 39, 193–194, 200
Goethe, Johann Wolfgang, 17–18, 35, 75, 87, 91, 94, 106, 123, 136, 176–177, 183, 196–198, 221
Goodman, Nelson, 129n83
Gorgias of Leontinoi, 11n11
Gracián, Balthasar, 43n1
Grimm, Jacob and Wilhelm, 27n47, 115n27, 161n43, 187n16
Gumbrecht, Hans Ulrich, 33n71

Handke, Peter, 25, 165–168, 175
Hecataeus of Miletus, 10
Hegel, G. W. F., 2, 20–21, 30–31, 34–37, 41, 56, 98, 101–105, 108–109, 114, 120, 130, 142, 177
Heidegger, Martin, 2, 15, 31–33, 35–36, 53, 64, 83–85, 113–114, 116, 124–127, 130–134, 146, 157–159, 162, 164–165, 172, 185–188, 190–193, 200, 203–204, 218
Heraclitus, 10, 15, 125, 130, 142
Hesiod, 10
Hirsch, Rudolf, 71n72
Hofmannsthal, Hugo von, 71, 73
Hölderlin, Friedrich, 94, 121, 123, 208
Homer, 10, 12, 94
Hsiao, Paul Shih-Yi, 204n53
Husserl, Edmund, 66–75, 78–80, 83, 87, 93, 114, 164, 169–170, 204–205, 211, 219

Ingarden, Roman, 72n76

Jahn, Gisela, 160n41
James, Henry, 72
Jünger, Ernst, 25, 114, 137, 168

Kafka, Franz, 25
Kandinsky, Wassily, 108, 205, 208–209
Kaneshige, Sozan, 160

Kant, Immanuel, 2–4, 11, 19, 28–31, 39, 42–60, 64–65, 77, 84, 91, 98–101, 104–105, 108–109, 114, 116, 129–130, 133, 137–138, 140–144, 147, 150, 157, 166, 181, 221
Kaufmann, Edgar, Jr., 152n32
Kiefer, Anselm, 17, 112
Kierkegaard, Søren, 21, 23
Kirkeby, Per, 135
Klee, Paul, 17, 19, 38, 61, 108, 110

Laib, Wolfgang, 76, 161–163
Lao-Tzu, 204
Le Corbusier, 185
Leeman, Richard, 120n54
Liddell, Henry George, 64n47, 178n114
Liebermann, Max, 94
Ligeti, György, 114
Long, Robert, 161
Lukács, Georg, 114n25
Lyotard, Jean-Francois, 38n92
Lypp, Bernhard, 94n131

Maak, Niklas, 185n4
Mahler, Gustav, 95, 198
Malevich, Kazimir Severinovich, 79n97
Malraux, André, 32
Mann, Thomas, 25
Maria, Walter de, 97
Marion, Jean-Luc, 198n21
Matisse, Henri, 25, 35, 87, 91, 94, 111, 205, 208–209
Meier, Richard, 195
Merleau-Ponty, Maurice, 79–82, 169–172, 177, 199–200, 214
Messiaen, Olivier, 18
Michelangelo, 103
Milton, John, 56
Mondrian, Piet, 121, 163
Monet, Claude, 47, 92, 94, 198
Monteverdi, Claudio, 196
Mörike, Eduard, 215
Myron, 90, 92

Neutra, Richard Joseph, 18
Newman, Barnett, 25, 35, 38, 199, 221–222
Newton, Isaac, 11, 186
Nietzsche, Friedrich, 2, 7, 11–15, 31, 36, 99, 105–109, 115, 118–122, 130, 166, 215

Nono, Luigi, 196
Nussaume, Yann, 185n5

Petersen-Brandhorst, Anette, 160n41
Phillips, Duncan, 194
Piano, Renzo, 195
Picasso, Pablo, 18, 25, 72, 94
Picht, Georg, 66n55, 184n3
Pindar, 94, 122
Plato, 7, 10–15, 26, 36, 44, 53, 63–64, 86, 89, 117–118, 130, 142, 149, 176, 189, 192, 203, 214
Pöggeler, Otto, 204n53
Pollock, Jackson, 182
Proust, Marcel, 72, 136, 181
Pseudo-Longinus, 39n97
Pythagoras, 10

Rathbone, Eliza E., 194n29
Rauschenberg, Robert, 112, 209
Recki, Birgit, 38n94
Richter, Gerhard, 25, 87, 111, 137, 209
Rihm, Wolfgang, 25
Rilke, Rainer Maria, 38–39, 94, 123–124, 214–217, 221
Ritter, Joachim, 14n21
Rodin, Auguste, 216
Rorty, Richard, 14n20
Rothacker, Erich, 173n99
Rothko, Mark, 25, 35, 38–39, 121, 194–195, 199–202, 210
Rückriem, Ulrich, 140

Sallis, John, 100n4, 189n22
Sartre, Jean-Paul, 212–214, 217–220, 222
Sayers, Dorothy, 72
Scaramuzza, Gabriele, 78n94
Scarry, Elaine, 38n93
Schelling, F. W. J., 2, 31, 37, 41, 210
Schiller, Friedrich, 34, 64–66, 106–108, 115
Schlegel, Friedrich, 23
Schlemmer, Oskar, 77
Schmidt, Dennis J., 54n31
Schmitz, Hermann, 48n17
Schopenhauer, Arthur, 31, 107–108
Schuhmann, Karl, 68n65
Scott, Robert, 64n47, 178n114
Sedlmayr, Hans, 38n89

Seel, Martin, 64n53
Sepp, Hans Rainer, 79n98
Shakespeare, William, 75
Shapiro, Meyer, 35n77
Socrates, 12–13, 63
Sophocles, 121
Spinoza, Baruch (Benedictus de), 150n29
Stegmaier, Werner, 164n45
Steinbock, Anthony, 165n49
Steiner, George, 61n43
Stifter, Adalbert, 114, 137
Storr, Robert, 111n20
Strauss, Botho, 25
Strauss, Richard, 25, 95
Stravinsky, Igor Fyodorovich, 25, 119

Taut, Bruno, 169n64
Titian, 72, 79
Tolstoy, Leo Nikolayevich, 9, 60
Trojahn, Manfred, 25, 108–109
Twombly, Cy, 17, 120–121

Valéry, Paul, 107, 115–117, 121–122, 124, 129, 147–151, 180, 213–214
Van Gogh, Vincent, 35
Velásquez, Diego, 94, 213
Vollmoeller, Mathilde, 176

Wagner, Richard, 22, 95, 118–119
Waldenfels, Bernhard, 129n84
Webern, Anton, 61, 115, 142
West, Franz, 33
Whitehead, Alfred North, 29
Wick, Oliver, 201n48
Wieland, Wolfgang, 28n50
Winckelmann, Johann Joachim, 56
Wittgenstein, Ludwig, 15, 98
Wright, Frank Lloyd, 18, 152–153, 155

Xenophanes, 10

Yanagi, Sōetsu, 56n38
Yilmaz, Levent, 20n29
Yu-Ichi, Inoue, 182

Zahavi, Dan, 67n61
Zammito, John H., 47n14

INDEX OF SUBJECTS

abstraction, 32–33, 121, 177, 200, 202
acting, 7, 84, 166, 206, 218
aestheticization of the lifeworld, 33
Apollonian, the, 105, 107–108
appearance, 3–4, 6, 13, 30, 39, 60–79, 82–83, 85–86, 88–89, 91–92, 99, 101–102, 106–107, 123–124, 126, 130, 134–135, 138, 140–141, 156–162, 164, 166–167, 177–179, 182, 186, 190, 204, 209–217, 220, 222
appearance, form of, 5, 130, 134–135, 137–139, 155, 160, 184
appearance, primordial, 177–178, 180–181
appearance-framework, 75–76
appearing thing, 4, 68, 77, 86, 211
art, experience of, 2, 4–5, 10, 16–17, 19, 26, 33–34, 37, 40, 72, 98, 109, 213, 221
art, modern, 3, 22–23, 25, 37–39
art form, 5, 17, 93–94, 97–105, 107–110, 127, 129–131, 133–135, 137–138, 181, 199
art form, classical, 102–105
art form, romantic, 102–105
art form, symbolic, 102–104
artist, 11–12, 14, 59, 71, 76, 100, 105, 107–108, 112, 132, 134, 138, 140, 149, 160, 168, 170–171, 194, 198, 201, 211
astonishment, 16
attention, 15, 20, 25, 55, 82, 85, 88, 92, 110–111, 151, 164–165, 167, 176, 191, 211, 213
attitude, 2–3, 8, 10, 32–33, 71–73, 83, 92, 114, 164–165, 169, 176
attunement, 9, 101, 106–108, 114–115
aura, 211–213, 215
autonomy, 40, 42, 55, 57, 59–60, 143
avant-garde, 22–23
avant-gardism, 24

basic forms, 95
beauty, 3–4, 27, 31, 34–40, 43–44, 46, 49–51, 53–57, 63–64, 66, 75, 77, 99, 133, 137, 142, 150, 157, 181–182, 192, 210, 215

beginning, 38, 105, 130, 144, 207, 210
being, 3, 21, 29, 33, 35–37, 62, 68, 79, 81, 83–84, 86, 113, 115, 117, 124, 126, 132, 141, 144–145, 151, 153, 157–159, 164–166, 171, 186–187, 193, 203, 218
being-at-work, 171
being-in-itself, 141, 143
body, 64, 79, 163, 170–172, 190, 216, 218–219
book of nature, 173
boundary, 112, 149, 154–156, 161, 171–173, 182, 198–199, 206, 210

cause, 50, 150
classical, the, 20–26, 34, 37, 39
classicism, 3, 20, 23, 56
completeness, 70–71, 177, 215
comprehensibility, 16
comprehension, 15–16, 60, 83, 122, 180, 198, 214
concealment, 84–85, 157–158
concept, 15–16, 18–26, 28–29, 43–45, 49–52, 59, 74, 91
consciousness, aesthetic, 32–35
context, 16, 32, 35, 43, 45, 50–51, 67–68, 74, 88, 114, 117, 123–124, 127, 133, 164, 181, 186, 211, 217
Copernican turn, 147
corporeality, 81–82, 204, 218
correlational a priori, 68–69
critique, 19, 21, 25, 47

decentering, 217
deictic, 4, 82–83, 85–86, 92–93, 98–99, 131, 138, 189, 192, 194, 196, 198
demonstration, 88–89, 125
depiction, 69, 72, 74, 91, 107, 110
depth, 199–201, 209–211, 220
difference, deictic, 82, 86, 93
differentiation, aesthetic, 32–33
Dionysian, the, 105–107, 115–116

disinterestedness, 43
distance, 39, 61, 81, 117, 183, 194, 198–201, 211–213, 215, 218

earth, 150, 158–160, 187
emptiness, 53, 184, 198, 201–210
empty space, 53–54, 204–205, 207–208, 210
essence, 1, 3–4, 7, 13, 18, 20, 23, 26, 50, 54, 57, 64, 66, 75, 78, 83, 93, 98–99, 105, 111, 116, 123–127, 133, 141, 163, 187, 189–191, 199, 203–205, 209
event, 33, 84–85, 158, 189
evidence, 23, 36–37, 64, 75, 177, 222
expanse, 35, 61, 119, 186–187, 191–193, 196, 199, 219
experience [*Erfahrung*], 2–5, 10, 16, 19, 26, 37, 42, 55, 63, 84, 91, 95, 109–110, 115, 140, 170, 201, 205, 212
experience [*Erlebnis*], 31–32
experience, hermeneutic, 16, 34
expression, 5, 13, 31, 79, 81–83, 86–87, 99–101, 103, 105, 119, 123, 142–143, 170, 177, 215, 217, 220
extension, 185–187, 200, 202, 204–205
external, the, 102–103, 154–155, 172–173, 211

family resemblance, 98
fantasy, 113, 212
festival, 37–38
fiction, 70, 72, 78
fixation, 69, 71, 74–76, 127, 183
formation, free, 56, 58, 77, 143, 181
foundation, 15, 17, 66, 155, 166, 170
freedom, 29–30, 44, 48, 55–58, 65, 69, 90, 100, 117, 143

gathering, 34, 125–128, 186–187, 191, 203
gaze, 73, 81, 94, 121, 128, 136, 140, 152–153, 165, 167–169, 172, 176, 187, 193–194, 199, 202, 210–215, 217, 219, 221
genius, 11, 30, 141, 143
givenness [*Gegebenheit*], 12, 49, 62, 64, 66–67, 69, 71–72, 74, 78–79, 83, 85, 87, 91, 93, 98, 133, 164, 186, 211
growth, 140, 142, 144–145, 156, 158

harmony, 29, 46–48, 100, 106, 115, 118–120, 136, 153, 157–158, 173, 194
heteronomy, 55, 142
historical effect, 34, 105
historicism, 20, 34–35

idea, 58, 79, 101–102, 178
idea, aesthetic, 56, 59–60, 100–101, 109
ideal, 30, 34, 43, 56, 79–80, 102, 116
idealism, German, 29, 58
image-form, 113–114
image-object, 78–79, 87
image-thing, 78–79, 93
imagination, 20, 45–46, 49, 56, 62, 65, 69, 76, 113
imagistic, the, 17, 76, 91, 97, 105, 108–112, 114, 122, 128–131, 134–138, 140, 153–155, 167–168, 181–182, 199, 207
inclusion, 150, 154–155, 160, 182, 193, 195
individual, 19, 43–45, 59, 66, 79, 98, 117, 128–129, 197
individuality, 30–31, 137, 160
intelligibility, 4, 179–180, 197, 207
intelligible, the, 180, 208
interplay, 4, 46–47, 157, 160, 169, 186, 201, 220
interpretation, 4, 33–34, 59, 77, 90, 92
interstice, 57, 123, 204–207, 209
intuition, 29, 45, 56–57, 71, 73, 75–76, 84, 98–99, 166
irregularity, 57, 119, 140, 143, 153, 160

judgment, reflective, 45–46
judgment, teleological, 58
judgment of taste, 30, 46–47, 49, 56

knowing, 27–28, 31, 45–46, 64, 84, 133, 145, 166
knowledge, 7, 10–13, 17–18, 28, 42, 45, 64–65, 113, 128, 133, 147, 151, 166, 221

life, 7–9, 12–14, 31–32, 38, 40, 49, 75, 105, 107, 118–119, 129–130, 214, 216–222
life-world, 33–34
living being, 43, 86, 117, 144–145, 157, 159, 171, 180, 213–222

268 Index of Subjects

material, 11, 38, 71, 96, 103, 142, 145–151, 159–160
matter, 15, 66–69, 75, 96, 141–142, 146–147, 180
metaphysics, 14, 107–108, 157
modern, 1–3, 14, 20, 22–25, 37–39, 118, 200
modernism, 1–3, 20, 26
modernity, 14, 18, 22–26, 28, 33, 38–39, 94, 211
movedness, 116–121, 130
movement, 31, 61, 87–90, 92, 95, 106–108, 112, 114–118, 120–121, 129–130, 136, 144–145, 158, 172, 200, 215–216
musée imaginaire, 32
music, 1, 8, 18, 76–77, 87, 93, 95, 97, 100–101, 103–110, 114–122, 127–131, 134–136, 162–163, 183, 195–196, 202, 205, 209
musical, the, 118–122, 129, 131, 134, 137–138, 181, 199
muteness, 38
myth, 10, 12, 150

natura naturans, 150
natura naturata, 150
natural science, 147
naturally beautiful, the, 30, 40, 181
naturalness, 5, 143, 145, 151, 154–157, 160–164, 167, 171, 181
nature, 2, 5, 11, 29–31, 39–40, 48, 51, 57–58, 65, 105, 139, 140–182, 185, 212–213

object, 5, 14, 31, 35, 40, 42–45, 48–50, 52, 55, 59, 64–68, 76, 78–79, 87, 91, 117, 131, 138, 147, 162, 165, 170, 176, 182, 187, 199, 217–218, 221
observation, 7–8, 10, 12–20, 24–27, 40, 49, 66, 73–74, 85–86, 92, 109, 111–114, 128, 131, 136, 189, 196, 198
occurrence, 37, 40, 61, 70, 74, 108, 114, 116, 131, 157–158, 183, 196, 217
open, the, 36, 131, 155, 159, 186
openness, 10, 35–36, 53, 63, 84, 116, 134, 137, 156–157, 159–160, 184, 186, 191–193, 196, 201, 207, 219
order, 16, 31, 51, 53–58, 75–77, 87, 93, 109, 116–122, 127, 129–130, 133–134, 150, 155–156, 160–163, 169, 172, 175, 177, 179, 181, 184, 207, 210, 222
order, beautiful, 56–57, 157
order, decentered, 4–5, 57–58, 60, 75–77, 93, 109, 137, 140, 156, 161–162, 181–182, 184, 189–191, 193, 202, 211

parallel to nature, 173, 181–182, 213
perceivability, 4, 78–80, 95–96, 138–139, 180
perception, 4, 27, 39, 42, 45, 47, 62–66, 69, 78–81, 91, 93, 95, 103, 163–173, 175–180, 190, 198, 213–214
perception, undirected, 167–168
perfection, 3, 56, 149–150
performance, 9, 18, 32–33, 77, 90, 128, 135–136, 177, 183, 195–197, 209
person, 50, 77, 82
phenomena, 4, 66, 68–73, 77, 83–86, 92, 126
philosopher, 12–14, 17
philosophy, 1–2, 7–8, 10, 12–17, 29
philosophy, practical, 29
philosophy, theoretical, 7, 12, 29
philosophy of art, 2, 17–18, 20, 22, 26–27, 30–31, 40, 56, 142
place, 94, 114, 132, 134, 138, 140, 144, 146, 148, 185–198, 203–204, 215–216, 218–219, 222
play, 12, 37–38, 54, 87, 99–100, 116–119, 121, 131–132, 136–138, 140, 155–156, 180–182, 184, 188–191, 193, 197, 200, 209–211, 216
poetic, the, 122, 124, 126–127, 129–131, 134, 136–138, 181, 199
poetizing, 94, 122, 130, 134
poetry, 10–14, 17–20, 56, 70, 74, 76, 94, 99–101, 103–104, 106–110, 114, 121–122, 124–126, 129–130–135, 162, 183, 196, 202, 212–213, 215
possibility, 3, 5–6, 29–30, 32, 46, 51–55, 58–59, 61–63, 65, 67, 73–78, 80, 88–90, 101, 109, 112–113, 123, 136, 138, 146, 148, 155–156, 159–160, 162, 166, 171, 173, 177–178, 182–183, 187, 193–194, 204–205, 209, 218–222

possibility of knowledge, 20
possible, the, 51–54, 65, 74, 77, 138, 182
postmodernism, 1
production, 27, 30, 37, 50–51, 76, 133–134, 144, 146–148, 150–151, 160, 163
proximity, 56, 71, 109, 131, 149–150, 183, 199, 206–207, 213, 218
purpose, 7–8, 14, 50–55, 57–58, 89, 103, 116, 133, 164–165, 167
purposiveness, 50–54, 57–58, 103, 133

querelle des anciens et des modernes, 20, 24, 39

reading, 8, 61, 72, 78, 107, 109, 123–128, 179, 198, 207, 210, 220
reality, 12, 17, 30, 34, 40, 50, 62, 64–66, 72, 74, 77–78, 88–89, 133, 166, 169, 177, 200
reason [*Grund*], 28, 52–53
reflection, 1, 3, 9, 14–17, 20, 26–29, 31, 34, 43–44, 46–49, 55, 57, 59–60, 66, 73, 78, 80, 85, 95, 107
reflection, hermeneutic, 16, 39
reflective taste, 43
region, 186–187, 193
representation, 35, 67, 69, 103, 113, 215
reversibility, 79–81, 171
rhetoric, 122, 129
rhythm, 117–122, 129, 136–138, 140, 153, 155–156, 202, 207
rule, 11, 45, 56, 100–101, 116, 140–141, 143, 151–152

schema, 91–93, 110, 176, 178, 199–200
science, 11–12, 14–15, 19–20, 30, 68, 70, 113, 147
self-deception, structural, 44, 48
self-revealing, 157–158
self-showing, 5, 82–86, 93, 95, 140–141, 156–157, 182, 189–190, 192–193, 196, 198, 201, 209–211, 221
sensation, 8, 30, 43–44, 46–47, 49, 57, 80, 99–101, 103, 121, 124, 168, 171, 177–178, 200
sense, 30, 49, 107, 116, 123–129, 136–138
showing, 5, 29, 82–90, 93, 95–96, 105, 125–126, 131, 138, 152, 156, 160–162, 184, 192–193, 196–197, 209, 211, 222

significance [*Bedeutsamkeit*], 110–111, 138, 164–165, 186
signification [*Bedeutung*], 35, 79
simultaneity, 21, 23, 32, 104, 111–112, 136, 138, 199, 202
simultaneous, 21, 75, 111, 114, 136
situation, 57, 185, 212–213, 217
soul, 39, 118, 121, 133, 148–149, 178, 216
space, hermeneutic, 197–198
space, phenomenal, 192, 195–196, 198–199
spatiality, 5, 95, 182–186, 194–202, 217–219
spatiality, factual, 195
spatiality, phenomenal, 194–195
speechlessness, 38
subjectivity, 31, 68–69, 169
sublime, the, 38–39
symbol, 1, 37, 55, 75, 102–104, 127, 129, 180, 208

taste, 21–22, 24–25, 30, 42–43, 46–47, 49, 55–56, 175, 179
temporal, 21–23, 183
text, 16, 23, 90, 122, 127–130, 136–138, 173, 175, 177–182, 202, 207, 209
texture, 56, 99, 175–184, 198, 200–201, 209–210, 216
textus, 127
thing-in-itself, 141, 165–166
thinking, objective, 17, 221
time, 21–23, 25, 70, 114, 120, 123, 136, 204, 220
timeless, 21–24
totality, 32, 35, 43, 56, 104, 111–112, 114, 125, 136–137, 165, 168, 186–187, 192, 199
transformation into structure, 131–132, 196
translation, 172–173, 197
truth, 2, 34, 36–37, 40, 57, 64, 70, 80–81, 84–85, 102, 131–132, 134, 157–158

unconcealment, 36, 64, 84, 126, 157–158
understanding, 3, 7, 9, 16, 21, 23, 26, 30, 34, 45–46, 49, 76, 80–81, 84, 90, 100, 146–147, 163, 172, 177, 179–180, 197, 218, 222
universality, 17–19, 44, 46, 91, 102
universality, subjective, 44
use object, 2, 40, 162

variation, free, 19, 65–66, 69, 73–74
vitality, 12, 215–216, 218–220

will, 40, 58, 107, 157, 168–169
work, 1–6, 9–11, 17–19, 32, 35, 93, 133, 136, 157, 198, 222

world, 14, 17–18, 29, 35, 65, 67, 72, 105–107, 113–114, 158–160, 165–166, 169–170, 187, 193, 217
world, primordial, 169–170
writing, 17, 77, 106, 125–127, 183, 197

INDEX OF TERMS

αἰσθητικὴ ἐπιστήμη, 28
αἰτία, 150
ἀλήθεια, 64, 84, 158
ἀποφαίνεσθαι τὰ φαινόμενα, 124, 126
ἀριθμός, 125

δημιουργός, 150
δυνατόν, 74

εἶδος, 13, 26, 133–134, 145, 149, 178
εἰκός μῦθος, 150
ἐκφανής, 64
ἐν ἔργῳ, 171
ἐν μουσικῇ τροφή, 118
ἐνέργεια, 133, 171
ἐπιστήμη, 64
ἐποχή, 72–73, 169–170
ἔργον, 133
ἕτερος νόμος, 143
εὐσχημοσύνη, 118

θέσις, 141–142
θεωρία, 14, 113

κόσμος, 54, 150

λέγειν, 124–127
λόγος, 10–11, 64, 125–127, 129–130, 136, 138, 150, 178–180, 186, 202
λόγος ἀποφαντικός, 125–126

μέγιστα γένη, 130
μίμησις, 89
μῦθος, 150

νόμος, 142–143, 151, 159

οὐσία, 151

πλεονεξία, 118
ποίησις, 133

ῥυθμός, 117

σοφία, 11
συμφωνία, 178–179
σχῆμα, 91
σωφροσύνη, 118

τάξις, 54
τέχνη, 133–134, 144–145, 148, 150–152, 154, 159–160, 162, 178
τὸ ἐντὸσ τῆς ψυχῆς, 118
τὸ τί ἦν εἶναι, 178
τόπος, 190

ὕλη, 146
ὑποκείμενον, 166, 178

φαινόμενον, 68, 83
φρόνησις, 64
φύσις, 140, 142, 144–147, 151, 157–159
φυτόν, 158

χώρα, 203

GÜNTER FIGAL is Professor of Philosophy at the University of Freiburg in Breisgau, Germany. He has held many appointments as visiting professor, including at the Kwansei Gakuin University in Nishinomiya (Japan), as the Cardinal Mercier Chair at the Catholic University of Leuven, and as the Gadamer Distinguished Visiting Professor at Boston College, among others. His books and articles have been translated into fifteen different languages. His monographs include *Martin Heidegger: Phänomenologie der Freiheit*, revised edition (Tübingen, 2013); *Kunst: Philosophische Abhandlungen* (Tübingen, 2012); *Verstehensfragen: Studien zur phänomenologisch-hermeneutischen Philosophie* (Tübingen, 2009); *Gegenständlichkeit: Das Hermeneutische und die Philosophie* (Tübingen, 2006; in English: *Objectivity. The Hermeneutical and Philosophy*, Albany N.Y., 2010). He is also editor of *The Heidegger Reader* (Indiana University Press, 2009).

JEROME VEITH holds a PhD in philosophy from Boston College and is currently an instructor of philosophy at Seattle University. He is translator of *The Heidegger Reader* (Indiana University Press, 2009).

www.ingramcontent.com/pod-product-compliance
Lightning Source LLC
Chambersburg PA
CBHW030611230426
43661CB00053B/1939